JON E LE IS is a writer and historian. His many previous books are the best-selling *The Mammoth Book of True War Stories*, *Spitfire: The Autobiography*, and *The Mammoth Book of Cover-Ups*.

D1135770

The Mammoth Book of
COVERT OPS

Edited by JON E. LEWIS

RUNNING PRESS
PHILADELPHIA · LONDON

Constable & Robinson Ltd
55–56 Russell Square
London WC1B 4HP
www.constablerobinson.com

First published in the UK by Robinson,
an imprint of Constable & Robinson Ltd, 2014

A copy of the British Library Cataloguing in Publication
Data is available from the British Library

UK ISBN: 978-1-78033-785-2 (paperback)
UK ISBN: 978-1-78033-786-9 (ebook)

US ISBN: 978-0-7624-4938-5
US Library of Congress Control Number: 2012944620

Running Press Book Publishers
2300 Chestnut Street
Philadelphia, PA 19103-4371

Visit us on the web!
www.runningpress.com

Printed and bound in the UK by CPI Group (UK) Ltd, Croydon, CR0 4YY

CONTENTS

Contents

FOREWORD

If you care to think about it, secret operations in warfare are as old as warfare itself. After all, what was the Trojan Horse but a *ruse de guerre*, a subterfuge, an undercover mission? That said, the great Age of the Covert Operation has been from 1945 onwards; in the Cold War two opposing power blocks faced each other but were unwilling to risk an actual conventional war so pinpricked each other with sabotage and subversion, as well as vicariously battling it out via proxies in the Middle East and Third World. With the decline of the Cold War, there came the War on Terror, where once again standard military methods were inappropriate. Classically, covert operations, by a 1948 definition of the US National Security Committee i (in Directive 10/2), include "sabotage, demolition and evacuation measures, subversion against hostile states, including assistance to underground movements, guerrillas and support of indigenous anti communist elements" and "are so planned and executed that any US Government responsibility for them is not evident to unauthorized persons and that if uncovered the US Government can plausibly disclaim any responsibility for them." That is to say, the sponsor – in this case the USA – can plausibly deny any connection with the hostile activity. The CIA, from Cuba to Vietnam to Afghanistan has been the arch-exponent of such "pure" covert operations.

On the ground, in practice, however, a covert operation is less easily pigeon-holed, less precisely classified. When the US Navy SEALs went into Pakistan to "get" bin Laden, the White House was hardly tempted to deny its sponsorship of the mission. On the other hand, the SEALs themselves are shrouded in secrecy, and many of the preliminaries to the operation – which likely included in situ reconnaissance by CIA and other agents – are obscure. Intentionally. And did the White House really want bin Laden alive? Does the element of plausible deniability lie in what happened to bin Laden – that he was assassinated under the cover of resisting arrest – rather than who did it to bin Laden? In the shadowy world of modern warfare covert, clandestine and special operations endlessly merge and overlap.

For those who commission covert operations, the attraction is increasingly that a small, elite force, such as the US Navy SEALs or Britain's 22 SAS, can be a lever to bring about a strategic outcome. Conventional forces failed to prevent or contain the Iraq insurgency that followed Saddam's fall; among the main responses of the British government was the dispatch of the SAS (in the guise of Task Force Black) to "man-hunt" high-value insurgents in the backstreets of Baghdad, especially of the al-Qaeda variety, with measurable success.

This David versus Goliath aspect of covert operations is as attractive to students of warfare as it is to politicians in plush offices. Tomahawk missiles and Unmanned Aerial Vehicles (drones) are relentlessly efficient in dealing death . . . and yet nothing captures the imagination or stirs the heart like the true stories of small bands of men engaged in secretive enterprises behind enemy lines. Stories like those on the following pages.

NEPTUNE SPEAR

US Navy SEAL Team Six, Pakistan, 2011

Under a moonless Afghan sky, shortly after eleven o'clock on the night of 1 May 2011, two MH-60 Black Hawk helicopters lifted off from Jalalabad Air Field. Inside the aircraft were twenty-three men with hard eyes and long stares from the Red Squadron of Naval Special Warfare Development Group (DEVGRU), better known as SEAL Team Six. A Pakistani-American translator, and a Belgian Malinois dog were also aboard. Radio communications were kept to an absolute minimum.

The SEALs' destination was a concrete house in the small city of Abbottabad, across the border in Pakistan. Abbottabad, situated north of the Pakistani capital, Islamabad, is in the foothills of the Pir Panjal Range. Founded in 1853 by a British major named James Abbott, the city is the home of a prestigious military academy. The cool climate makes it a popular retreat for city dwellers in the baking Indian summer.

According to information gathered by the Central Intelligence Agency, bin Laden was hunkered down in the third floor of a house in a compound just off Kakul Road, a residential street less than a mile from the entrance to the military academy. The plan was simple: the SEALs would drop from the helicopters into the compound, overpower bin Laden's guards, seize or shoot bin Laden – depending on circumstances – and fly the corpse out.

Fifteen minutes after take-off, the choppers ducked down into an alpine valley and slipped into Pakistani airspace. They were undetected. Pakistan's principal air detection systems look towards India.

Even so, the Black Hawk crews, two pilots and a crewman from the 160th Special Operations Aviation Regiment ("The Night Stalkers"), had taken no chances. The Black Hawks were modified "stealth" versions covered with radar-damping "skin".

Flying behind the Black Hawks were two Chinooks, which were to be kept on standby in a deserted area roughly two-thirds of the way to Abbottabad. On board were two additional SEAL teams consisting of approximately twenty-four DEVGRU operators. These were the "Quick Reaction Force" in case anything went wrong on the main raid.

During the ninety-minute flight, sitting in the strangely calm red-lit interior of the aircraft, the SEALs rehearsed the operations in their minds. They were no strangers to action. Since the commencement of the War on Terror in 2001 they had rotated through Afghanistan, Iraq, the Horn of Africa, and the Yemen. DEVGRU had been into Pakistan before too, on at least ten occasions, usually into the tribal badlands of Waziristan, where senior al-Qaeda members liked to hole up.

But the SEALs had never been as far into Pakistan as Abbottabad. The helicopters skirted the north of Peshawar, and continued due east. In this time of waiting, the kit hung heavy and even the desert Digital Camouflage uniform seemed a little too tight. Most of the SEALs had plumped for the Heckler & Koch MP7, a few the short-barrelled silenced M4. Vest pockets held a booklet with photographs and physical descriptions of the people suspected of being inside the compound. One of these is Ahmed al-Kuwaiti, an al-Qaeda courier who unwittingly led the CIA to bin Laden's compound. Or maybe not. There was no *absolute* certainty that bin Laden was in the compound. A CIA analyst called "Jen" had declared herself "100 per cent sure" that America's Most Wanted was there, and it was largely on Jen's call that the twenty-three SEALs were risking their lives that night, in what the Department of Defense has called "Operation Neptune Spear". But other CIA analysts were only 60 per cent certain the al-Qaeda leader was living at Kakul Road.

Whether bin Laden was in the compound or not, the CIA had intimate knowledge of the layout of the compound. In the run-up to the raid one of the SEALs, Matt Bissonnette, asked an intelligence officer about one of the many doors that the commandos would have to breach. The answer came back straight away. The door is metal and opens to the outside.

Pakistan is an ally, of sorts, but not the sort the US wanted to trust on a mission like this. After all, why WAS bin Laden in Pakistan? Was he being hidden and succoured by Islamicists in the government there? A covert operation into the heart of Pakistan carries the possibility of major diplomatic fall-out. The sending of the SEALs into Pakistan had required the approval of President Obama personally. To reassure the president and his advisers, the team had conducted a night-time dress rehearsal of the raid, on a mock-up of bin Laden's house. They were impressed. The President said "Yes".

The helicopters arrived above the compound at around 12.55 a.m. The mission plan dictated that the SEALs from the first helicopter would fast rope to the ground, and enter the house from the ground floor. The second helicopter would fly to the northeast corner of the compound and secure the perimeter.

As the first helicopter hovered over the compound it experienced "vortex ring state", a turbulent air condition, and the heli's tail caught the compound wall. The chopper lunged dangerously on its side, but the pilot managed to bring the nose down which prevented it from tipping over. None of the aircrew or SEALs was seriously injured. The SEALs quickly cleared the chopper and placed explosives against the door of the house.

Meanwhile, the other chopper landed outside the compound, and its SEAL team scaled the 18-foot high walls to get inside. Matt Bissonnette, who was in this second SEAL team, and a colleague deployed to an outbuilding where Ahmed al-Kuwaiti, bin Laden's courier, was thought to be residing. The two SEALs pounded on the door with a sledgehammer. A shot was fired out. Bissonnette and his colleague, an Arabic-speaker, fired back. There was a cry and groan from inside.

Immediately after this exchange of fire, a woman's voice called out from inside the building. The door was unlocked and a woman walked out. Bissonnette:

I could just make out the figure of a woman in the green glow of my night vision goggles. She had something in her arms and my finger slowly started applying pressure to my trigger. I could see our lasers dancing around her head. It would only take a split second to end her life if she was holding a bomb.

As the door continued to open, I saw that the bundle was a baby.

Caught in the exchange of fire, the woman had a shoulder wound from a bullet.

The SEALs had been given rules of engagement, which were precise on the question of unarmed, surrendered women.

Bissonnette and his colleague held fire. Three children trailed the woman into the courtyard. Taking no chances, the SEALs entered the building in textbook fashion, quick and providing cover for each other. Al-Kuwaiti was on the floor. Bissonnette and his colleague "squeezed off several rounds to make sure he was down."

This building cleared, Bissonnette and his colleague joined the first SEAL team, which had now breached the main door of the house. Inside the house, there was total blackness; CIA operatives had disabled the local power station.

Through the green gloom of their night vision goggles, the SEALs spotted al-Kuwaiti's brother, Abrar, as he poked his head into a hallway on the first floor. He was shot and staggered backwards. The SEALs, amid shouting and screaming, followed him into a side room. Abrar was shot again. His wife tried to shield him, and she was shot dead too.

A massive metal door blocked the access to the two top floors. This was blown apart.

As they climbed the main stairs, bin Laden's twenty-three-year-old son, Khalid, rushed towards them. He was killed as he did so. As Bissonnette stepped past the body, he saw an AK-47 assault rifle propped nearby. Later, it transpired there was a round in the chamber. Khalid had been prepared to fight. He just never got the chance.

As they climbed to the last and third floor, the SEAL point man saw someone peeking out from the door on the right of the hallway, and immediately popped off a round through his rifle, which was fitted with a silencer. The man fell backward. The SEALs sprinted into the room, through an unlocked gate on the stairs; in the bedroom the SEALs found bin Laden lying on the floor, with two women standing in front of him trying to protect him. One of them, Amal Ahmed Abdul Fatah, screamed at the SEALs in Arabic and looked as if she was about to charge. She was shot in the leg, and pushed out of the way. Bin Laden's twelve-year-old daughter stood in the darkness, at the back of the room, screaming. She had been named Safia after a contemporary of the Prophet who had killed a Jew, in the hope – bin Laden explained – that she would grow up to do the same.

With the writhing bin Laden on the floor Bissonnette and a colleague applied the *coup de grâce*:

> The point man's shots had entered the right side of [bin Laden's] head. Blood and brains spilled out of the side of his skull. In his death throes, he was still twitching and convulsing. Another assaulter and I trained our lasers on his chest and fired several rounds. The bullets tore into him, slamming his body into the floor until he was motionless.

The SEALs then had to positively identify him. To do this they asked his children. To be doubly sure of the correct ID, they also measured him and took blood samples.

The SEAL team leader then radioed, "For God and country – Geronimo, Geronimo, Geronimo ... Geronimo E.K.I.A." Geronimo was the codename for bin Laden. EKIA is Enemy Killed in Action.

There were two weapons on a shelf next to the door, an AKSU rifle and a Makarov pistol. The raid had taken fifteen minutes to reach bin Laden in his top-floor bedroom. He did not reach for his weapons, either because he was paralysed by fear or because he was hampered by the design of the house and could not understand what was happening. The house was built in segregated compartments with small windows intended to frustrate observation; on that night, it made it difficult for the inhabitants to see what was going on or liaise with each other.

Bin Laden was dead, yet the mission was not over. The SEALs

still had to gather as much intelligence material from the compound as possible and get the body out of Pakistan before local forces were alerted.

After restraining the women and children in the compound with plastic ties and handcuffs, the SEALs began a methodical search. The downed helicopter also had to be destroyed. After smashing the cockpit controls, SEALs packed the helicopter with explosives and blew it up.

Since the SEAL team was reduced to one operational helicopter, one of the two Chinooks held in reserve was dispatched to carry part of the assault team and bin Laden's body out.

Thirty-eight minutes after arriving at the compound the SEALs, together with bin Laden's corpse, were on their way to Afghanistan. They were two minutes under schedule.

No country wanted the body, so it was dumped, after the appropriate Muslim rites, in the Arabian Sea.

And so the long manhunt was over. Bin Laden's last words to his wife were, "Don't turn on the light." He died as he had lived. In darkness.

BLACK HAWK DOWN

Task Force Ranger, Somalia, 1993

No one would accuse Somalia, stuck out on the Horn of Africa, of being kindly treated by fate. Sometimes nature takes a malevolent hand, and droughts cause mass starvation. When nature is not giving Somalia a hard time, humans do; the modern history of Somalia is a story of dictatorship and anarchy. And just sometimes nature and mankind conspire to give Somalia Hell on Earth.

The 1990s were one of those Apocalypses. In January 1991, the Somalian president Mohammed Siad Barre was overthrown by a motley collection of clans; in the Somalian capital, Mogadishu, a city of a million people, the main rebel group was the United Somali Congress, which was anything but united. One armed faction was led by Ali Mahdi Muhammad, who took the presidency; the other faction was led by Mohammed Farrah Aidid. The factions fell to shooting each other and everything, and as if to prove you can't have too much of a bad thing, four (at least) other groups fought for Somalia's soul. Severe fighting caused the deaths of tens of thousands of Somalis; it also destroyed the country's agriculture. Thus yet more Somalis died, this time from starvation; between 1991 and 1992 an estimated 300,000 Somalis perished from lack of food.

Under the aegis of the UN, the international community flew in food. A favourite get-rich-quick tactic of the Somalian warlords was to hijack the aid convoys. While the UN considered that most of Somalia's would-be dictators could be reasoned with and obliged into a ceasefire, Aidid was the recalcitrant, and refused to give up banditry and war. Neither was Aidid too fussed about whom he slew; on 5 June 1993, twenty-four Pakistani UN peace-keepers in Somalia were ambushed and killed by militia loyal to the "warlord" Mohammed Farrah Aidid and his Habr Gidr clan, the mainstay of the so-called Somalia National Alliance. An exasperated UN passed Security Council Resolution 837 ordering that those responsible for the attack on the peacekeepers should be brought to justice. To this end, US Special Operations Command formed a Task Force dedicated to the capture of Aidid: Task Force Ranger.

Two months later Task Force Ranger landed at Mogadishu airport. Task Force Ranger consisted primarily of Special Forces Operational Detachment Delta Operators and US Army Rangers from 3rd Battalion, 75th Ranger Regiment. It worked out of hangars at the airport.

On 3 October 1993, Operation Gothic Serpent was Task Force Ranger's seventh mission; it was an attempt to capture some of Mohammed Farrah Aidid's right-hand men. According to US Air Force Sergeant Dan Schilling, attached to Task Force Ranger:

At approximately 1430 hours on 3 October we received Intel that two targets from our primary hit list were meeting near the Olympic Hotel in the Black Sea district. The Black Sea was adjacent to the Bakara Market, one of the largest arms markets in East Africa, and was saturated with Somali National Alliance (SNA) regulars and sympathizers. The plan was the typical template used on our other raids; helis with Ranger blocking forces and assaulters departed separately for the target followed by our ground reaction force (GRF) convoy as an exfil platform for the "precious cargo" (PC) and all task force personnel. Aside from the challenging target location, right in the middle of town, this raid was mostly indistinguishable from the previous raids we'd conducted.

The GRF on this day was comprised of seven Kevlar armoured High Mobility Multipurpose Wheeled Vehicles [known to everybody from grunt to general as " Humvees"], and three five-ton trucks. The convoy was manned by Rangers, assaulters, SEALs, and me as the combat controller. I was located in my usual spot, the C2 vehicle, third in the order of march. My job, as usual, was to provide mobile command, control, and communications in addition to fire support direction for the convoy or other forces as needed.

The "targets" were Abdi "Qeybid" Hassan Awale, Aidid's putative interior minister and Omar Salad, Aidid's main political adviser. The Bakara Market was, indeed, a "challenging location", as Private First Class Mike Kurth, a Radio Telephone Operator (RTO) with First Platoon, Bravo Company of the Ranger Battalion, on that day describes.

> We had all heard about the Bakara Market before. It was dead in the center of Aidid's territory – which meant that everyone who lived in that area supported Aidid. On all of our previous missions we had dealt with only a few bad guys at a time. We'd gone in and done our jobs in the midst of a lot of curious onlookers. In that sense, we'd just been practising riot control. This was going to be a lot different. We all knew it without talking about it. Everyone in the Bakara Market would either have a weapon or the ability to get a weapon. Watson told us that we could very likely see some action on this one. I don't think anyone knew what to say to that. We knew the drill.

The plan was for the "D-boys" (Delta Force) to go in first and hit the building on Hawlwadig Road, and capture the "precious cargo". Once they were inside, the four Ranger squads ("chalks") from Bravo Company were to fast rope in and set up a defensive perimeter around the target block. The four chalks were to be flown to the target by MH-60 Black Hawk helicopters; the Delta operatives were to be inserted by MH-6 Little Birds. Other helicopters carried back-up, Combat Search and Rescue, and the Command and Control (C2) team; Delta Force's Lieutenant-Colonel Garry Harrell was to oversee the ground op, while Lieutenant-Colonel Tom Matthews co-ordinated the 116 Special Operations Aviation Regiment (SOAR) heli pilots.

At 3.32 p.m. an aerial armada of seventeen choppers lifted off from Mogadishu airport for the three-minute flight to the Bakara Market. On board were the Delta and Ranger assault forces. An Orion navy spy plane circled high overhead. Down on the ground the nine Humvees and three five-ton flatbed trucks of the Ground Reaction Force Convoy, commanded by Ranger Lieutenant-Colonel Danny McKnight, growled their way downtown. The whole raid was projected to take thirty to forty-five minutes tops. As things turned out, it turned out to be the longest night.

As they neared the target, the men in the helicopters could see that the Somalis were burning tyres in the streets. Lighted rubber mixed with animal dung was the Somali militia's standard road-block. Staff Sergeant Matt Eversmann was leader of Chalk Four, responsible for blocking the north-west corner of the building. At the "one minute signal" Eversmann, flying in a Black Hawk given the call sign "Super 67", put on his goggles and Kevlar helmet and moved to his rope. The chopper steadied itself over the inser-tion point, clouds of "brownout" whipped up by the rotor blades. Eversmann heard his pilot say, "I can't see shit".

The four AH-6 Little Birds had already disgorged their D-boys. For what seemed like ten minutes but can only have been seconds, Eversmann's Black Hawk hung in the swirling dirty air; then the Rangers were told to throw out their ropes. The rest of Eversmann's chalk consisted of Staff Sergeant Jeff McLaughlin, Forward Observer or Fire Support Officer (FO); Specialist Jason Moore, the Radio Telephone Operator; Specialist Kevin Snodgrass, machine gunner; Private First Class Todd Blackburn, ammo bearer; First Sergeant Glenn Harris and Sergeant Scott Galentine, riflemen; Specialists Adalberto Rodriguez and Dave Diemer, Squad Automatic Weapon gunners; and Privates First Class Anton Berendsen and Marc Good, 40mm grenadiers.

As he swung onto the rope 70 feet above the ground, Eversmann was told the bad news that Super 67 was two or three blocks from the assigned position:

As I started my descent I was looking up toward the belly of the helicopter. I wanted to make sure I knew the direction of flight and therefore the target. I remember the air was so cloudy and thick with dust, and without the benefit of eye protection it was hard for me to see. The seventeen other aircraft also stirred up debris, so it was no wonder we couldn't see anything. Bless those pilots for holding our Black Hawk steady while we were on the way down. Despite my leather gloves, the nylon of the rope made my hands burn, so I looked down to see how much farther it was to the ground. It seemed like I was on the rope forever.

When I saw the ground, my heart sank. At the bottom of the rope was a crumpled tan-clad body. My God, someone's been shot? Who is it? And is he dead? Were the first thoughts through my head. That was my first real feeling of fear, a feeling of helplessness, as if I couldn't defend myself. I had always thought that making a combat parachute jump must be as scary as hell since you are floating down into harm's way, watching a firefight in a hot drop zone all the while. This was as close as I got to what the situation must feel like, except I couldn't see or hear any shots. Thank the Lord, I finally got my feet on the ground, literally straddling the body. The medics were already working on him. It was Todd Blackburn. As I made a quick check for the rest of the men it dawned on me that we were under fire.

We were in the middle of a four-way intersection and were taking fire from the north, the east and the west. The fire wasn't that accurate at first but, unlike during previous missions, the Somalis were not just spraying their weapons at us with reckless abandon; this time they were aiming. The objective was only a few blocks to our south, but ... we wouldn't be making the movement to the objective as quickly as we had planned.

Private Good was busy giving first aid to Blackburn. I couldn't believe that Blackburn was even close to being alive. He was bleeding out of his mouth, nose and ears, and his body was horribly contorted. It was one of those surreal moments – there would be many more that day – and one that never in my wildest imagination would I have thought I would witness. Good and another medic had opened Blackburn's airway and were stabilizing his neck when the fire started to get heavier. As I checked the intersection to see where the men were, I realised that we had definitely landed right in the middle of the worst part of town, and the Somalis seemed none too pleased with our intrusion. As I checked the men I asked my RTO to call the commander, Captain Steele, to give him a sit rep and request an immediate extraction. All Specialist Moore got was nothing – no response, no acknowledgement. We had no communications with headquarters.

My first thirty seconds as the leader of Chalk Four sucked, plain and simple. We were in the wrong spot, had no commo, had an urgent casualty, and were being shot at from three directions. Things were going south in a hurry. The good news was that the Rangers from Chalk Four were performing phenomenally. I had no combat experience other than the previous missions, but watching them fight was a thing of beauty. They hit the ground running and were doing their job. We were dealt a bad hand of cards, but what really amazed me was just how fast the Somalis started to fight. It seemed that we were on the ground for a few seconds and then *bam* – the heavens opened up with small-arms fire. It really was like the movies, with the dust kicking up in the road as a hail of bullets ripped open the dirt. It was actually kind of wild to watch.

Contrary to what Eversmann initially assumed, Blackburn hadn't been hit by incoming; he'd missed the rope and fallen 70 feet. Eversmann ordered Blackburn to be moved to the east of the intersection, where he set up a command post. With the RTO's radio still "fucked" (a wire had broken during the rope-descent), Eversmann tried his own hand-held radio. By shouting, Eversmann got through to nearby Delta medics, who came running over, ducking bullets. They looked at Blackburn and told Eversmann that the wounded man needed to be extracted "right now or he's gonna die".

Eversmann ordered Sergeant Casey Joyce to arrange an aid and litter team to carry Blackburn to the target building, where he could be picked up by the ground convoy. All the while, the Somalis laid down withering fire. They seemed to be without number. When one was neutralized, another popped up to take his place. To Eversmann's incredulity, the Somalis came on to the perimeter; they would not stay back unless forced by weight and accuracy of fire.

Then Berendsen took a round to the arm; as Eversmann bandaged him up, Berendsen continued to fire his M203 grenade launcher, manipulating the weapon with just one hand.

Scott Galentine was hit in the hand, and rushed across the street to Eversmann who hurriedly applied a field dressing, and told him to keep it above his heart. Ten seconds later Kevin Snodgrass was hit. Fire was coming from everywhere, as crowds of people rampaged around, the gunmen mingled in with pedestrians, sometimes using them as shields.

By now the RTO had established comms. About the first thing he heard on the command net was that Black Hawk Super 61 was down.

Super 61 was piloted by Chief Warrant Officer Cliff Wolcott. He was flying the bird low over the target area at speeds down to fifty knots to allow the Delta snipers and the two crew chiefs, Dowdy and Warren, to select targets. Big and slow, the bird made a plump target for a Somali militiaman called Little Ears with his RPG launcher. The grenade hit Super 61, causing a massive jolt; for a brief welcome second all seemed okay. Then the helicopter began to shudder violently. Wolcott made a last radio transmission with a cool laconicism that became legendary, "61 going down".

The helicopter skittered down the sky, clipped the side of a house, tipped forward and crashed head first into an alley a few blocks from the target house on Hawlwadig Road. Nobody on the ground could believe it. Nobody could believe that a Black Hawk could be shot down. The big birds were the great protector in the sky.

Chief Warrant Officer Keith Jones was about the first to recover his wits, immediately screaming his MH-6 Little Bird, call sign Star 41, down low over the teeming alleyways to search for the downed Black Hawk. He located it within minutes, daringly landing his Little Bird in the same street. As he landed, a Delta operator from the wrecked Black Hawk ran up, an arm hanging limply by his side. "I need help," he said. Jones scrambled out, a pistol in his hand, and followed him to the wreck, popping off the gun as they went. The other surviving Delta sniper was badly wounded. They pulled him to the side of the street. All around bullets were pinging.

Almost in the same instant that Jones reached the crash site the first Delta operators and Rangers, led by Chalk One's Lieutenant DiTomosso, arrived. Like Jones, DiTomosso had determined on a personal mercy mission to aid the stricken Black Hawk. Having fought his way along two blocks from the target building to the crash site, DiTomosso narrowly missed being shot by CWO Karl Maier, the co-pilot of the Little Bird Star 41, who was firing off at anything moving with a hand gun. Now there were boots on the ground, the air commander in the C2 helicopter ordered Little Bird 41 to evacuate the wounded Delta operators.

Jones and Maier evacuated SSG Busch and SGT Smith, though SSG Busch later died of his injuries.

No sooner had CWO Jones got his Little Bird airborne than the CSAR helicopter, Super 68, came whomp-whomp-whomp above the crash site, then hovered 30 feet above the ground. The medics roped-down like their pants were on fire. In the adrenaline excitement almost all forgot their kit bags; there was a delay as the kit bags were heaved out. As the last men started their descent, Super 68's pilot, Dan Jollata, felt the aircraft stagger. An RPG round hit plum on the left side.

The accompanying Little Birds confirmed on the radio: "You have been hit. Behind your engines. Be advised you are smoking".

Some of the CSAR team were still on their ropes. Somehow Jollata kept the Black Hawk hovering in position until they reached the ground. As soon as the last man hit the ground, Super 68 roared away, Jollata radioing: "All systems are normal right now, just a little whine in the rotor system. I think I can make it back to the field."

On a rotor and a prayer, Jollata nursed the helicopter low across the city, its progress marked by a thin tail of grey smoke. As he cleared the boundary fence of the airport, Jollata radioed for emergency crews. Then he put the helicopter hard down on the floor.

There was a kind of mayhem now at the target and crash site. Told to break his holding pattern north of Mogadishu, and provide air cover for men in the Bakara Market, Chief Warrant Officer Mike Durrant, pilot of Black Hawk Super 64, could see Rangers hunkered down and Somalis running everywhere along the main streets and intersecting alleyways as they tried to get at the US forces.

Only minutes after taking up orbit over the Bakara Market, Durrant's Black Hawk was hit in the tail by an RPG round. Chunks of metal and a mist of oil spewed out. Despite the damage the Black Hawk seemed to handle normally. Then Durrant felt tremors as the engine ran dry. An almighty bang signalled the end of the crankshaft. The Black Hawk began to spin. Durrant succeeded in shutting down one engine, and throttling the other to half power, and the rate of spin slowed sufficiently for him to bring the nose up before impact. "Going in hard! Going in hard!" Durrant shouted into his radio.

Super 64 crashed upright on top of a hut in the Wadigley shanty town, about a mile from the target building. Durrant and his co-pilot blacked out. The time was 4.40 p.m.

Flying just behind Super 64 was Mike Goffena's Super 62 Black Hawk. Making a low pass over the crashed bird, Goffena saw movement in its cockpit. There were survivors; that was the good news. The bad news was the crowds of Somalis converging on the crashed Black Hawk. Goffena radioed for permission to insert two of the Delta snipers he had aboard down on the ground, but he was told by Harrell in the C2 to wait. To keep the Somalis at bay, Goffena and two accompanying Little Birds made repeated, urgent gun runs. But they could not stop the tide of people. One of the Little Bird pilots reported:

We've got to get some ground folks down here or we're not going to be able to keep them off. There are not enough people left on board the aircraft to be able to do it.

From the C2 Harrell decided to put in the Delta snipers aboard Goffena's helicopter. When the two Delta-boys reached the cockpit of Super 64, they found Durrant and his co-pilot each with a broken leg. The Delta operatives helped Durrant out of the cockpit and sat him down on the right-hand side of the helicopter, where he squeezed off rounds from a 9mm MP-5K machine-pistol every time a Somali appeared. To the US forces in Somalia the locals were "Skinnies"; and an MP-5K was a "Skinny-Popper". There were a lot of "Skinnies" clamouring to get at the downed Black Hawk, and not all the popping from Durrant's machine-pistol or the rest of the small arms carried by the survivors could keep them back.

Super 62 and the two Little Birds kept making passes firing wildly into the crowd. Almost every time the three helicopters swung down, an RPG round snaked up. On one pass over the crash site, Goffena saw one of the Delta operators shot. He radioed to Harrell in the C2 that the crash site had "no security right now".

As Goffena was making a banking turn, there was a bang. A bang louder than a Goffena could ever believe could be made. All the Black Hawk's screens went blank. Goffena himself was momentarily deafened by the RPG blast. As his hearing returned, Goffena could hear the screams of the emergency alarms going off, telling him that the engine was dead.

He looked across at his co-pilot, who was slumped forward in his seat. "This is it," thought Gofenna, "we're going down". Suddenly, his co-pilot sat up and started shouting grid co-ordinates. They were just 20 feet above a row of electricity poles. Goffena pulled back on the control stick. To his delight, the Black Hawk responded and the aircraft lumbered forward. He could see a Humvee driving towards him, and touched the helicopter down with barely a bump.

By now the Somalis were almost on top of Durrant's Black Hawk. On the left-hand side of the downed chopper the surviving Delta commando was trying to hold off the Somalis. At length Durrant, on the other side of the wreck, heard a splatter of heavy incoming fire. There was a moan of pain, then silence from the operative. This left Durrant as the sole survivor.

Durrant ran out of ammunition. Some Somalis cautiously came along the side of the craft; Durrant lay his exhausted pistol on his chest and prepared to die. When they saw he was defenceless, the Somalis ran wildly forward and started stripping him, beating and kicking him all the while. Salvation came in the unlikely form of a local militia leader, Mo'Alim, who realized that Durrant was worth more alive than dead.

While the Black Hawks had been going down, the Ground Reaction Force had been making its way to the target building on Hawlwadig Road. At 4.02 p.m, shortly after arrival, a trio of Humvees containing Rangers, SEALs and Delta-boys had been detailed off to take Todd Blackburn back to base. They made it, after a running fight all the way that took the life of Sergeant Pilla, killed by a round to the head. Meanwhile, the rest of the GRF loaded up the twenty-four Somali prisoners, as well as the Ranger and Delta wounded from the assault force. And then everything started to go wrong. Harrell, the Delta colonel in the command helicopter, instructed the convoy, instead of returning to base, to go through Mogadishu's maze of narrow streets to rescue Wolcott and the crew of Super 61. They soon got lost, and came under withering fire. A babel of directions from the helicopters above confused the ground convoy drivers.

Uniform 64, this is Romeo 64. Next right. Next right! Alleyway!
Alleyway!
They just missed their turn.
Take the next available right, Uniform.
Be advised they are coming under heavy fire.
Goddamn it, stop! Goddamn it, stop!
Right turn! Right turn! You're taking fire! Hurry up!

To make a bad thing worse, the drivers' inexperience led them to stop at each intersection for the vehicles behind to catch up. All that actually happened was that the following vehicles got "bottle-necked" and caught in crossfire. In the C2 Humvee, US Air Force Sergeant Dan Schilling grumbled to himself: "We're going to keep driving around until we're all fucking dead".

Having travelled around in a circle, the convoy then lumbered to the block where Matt Eversmann's chalk was pinned down. Eversmann was delighted to see them. He made sure Blackburn, the rest of the wounded and all men were aboard the Humvees then clambered in himself. Losing his balance, he fell flat on his back and lay there like an inverted turtle unable to right himself. He had to wait until the vehicle stopped at a four-way intersection before he could scramble up and get off. Then, recalled Eversmann:

The next thing I knew, I was kneeling behind a Humvee with a wounded Ranger on the ground, his head resting on my knees. One of my team leaders, Sergeant Casey Joyce, had been shot. He had been with Telscher across the street from me and was engaging the enemy down the road to the right when he was hit. Unfortunately, as Casey had been engaging the enemy to the right of the vehicles, he had been hit by a bullet from the unprotected side. Despite the Kevlar vest he was wearing, the round entered his body right under his arm where it was not covered by the vest. This was the first life-threatening gunshot wound I had ever seen. The wound was small, almost the size of my pinky nail. So small, in fact, that I almost overlooked it as we tried to assess its severity. Jim and I followed the first aid procedures just as we had been taught. It's going to be okay; it's going to be fine, I told myself. Casey did not seem to be in any pain, and he did not move or make any sound; he just looked up at me. As I tried to reassure him, Jim and I frantically worked on the wound to his chest. I had no idea what was happening around us until the senior medic bent over and checked Casey's vital signs. He already knew. He checked the vital signs and told us to put the litter on the vehicle. I don't think it registered with me that one of my men had just been killed. Nothing in my training had prepared me for that. There is nothing that can replicate that feeling of loss. But the reality of the events all around me kicked back in.

Checking that no one was left on the street, Eversmann boarded another Humvee. Someone screamed at him; it was Sergeant Chris Schlief, the Humvee's machine gunner. Eversmann had landed on his ankle as he jumped in. Looking down, Eversmann saw also that he was partly lying on a dead Ranger. Then they came under attack, yet again. Eversmann recalled:

The sound of metal being torn apart was deafening. Much like the sound of a burst from miniguns, you know that something real bad had just happened when you hear it. We had just driven through an ambush and some vehicles were hit by small-arms fire and rocket-propelled grenades (RPGs). It was so loud that it hurt. I saw a Humvee behind us swerve and pass us on the right as we came to a screeching halt just past an intersection. There were soldiers wounded and lying in the street. One of our Humvees had been hit by a rocket, and the men riding in the back had been literally blown out of the vehicle. Several of us immediately jumped from the convoy to help the wounded. As I started to climb out from the back of my Humvee, I watched as a Somali pipe grenade landed between one of our wounded Rangers and my vehicle. It looked like one of those old World War II potato mashers that the Germans used. Regardless of who made it, it was going to hurt. There was no place to go. The vehicle was stopped, and there was this grenade right in front of me. I tucked in my head and waited behind the tailgate. A couple of seconds later there was a puff of white smoke, and that was it. It was a dud. What a lucky bastard.

We began to take care of the wounded, but the bad news was that we were still pretty much in the kill zone. All we could do was move the wounded to a good vehicle, police all our equipment, and get ready to move again. Most of the men in the vehicles were engaging the enemy, while those on the ground attended to the wounded. We began to take heavy gunfire from down a street. In one of those vivid moments, I watched Sergeant Aaron Weaver appear out of nowhere and toss a grenade with the grace and accuracy of a Nolan Ryan fast ball. It was awesome. Like Berendsen's one-handed M-2013 shot back at the blocking position, Weaver threw that grenade with all the confidence of a major leaguer, and the grenade sailed right in the direction of the firing. The grenade detonated after a few seconds, buying us some time to load our casualties onto the remaining vehicles.

How many Rangers were wounded? I had no idea. All I knew was that we were taking fire from every direction and were in a fight for our lives. We had lost a vehicle or two in the ambush. In concert, all the Rangers on the ground were taking care of business. Watching men like Weaver jump into the mix was so reassuring to us all. We were reacting to the events all around us and doing, like the old Shaker adage, "the next thing". In this case the next thing was taking care of our casualties, policing all our men and equipment, and fighting the enemy with all our might, though not always in that order.

It wasn't too long after we began moving again that we ran into yet another ambush. Again, the wretched sound of metal crashing through metal slapped me back to the moment. We stopped and had to begin another round of fighting, aiding the wounded, and policing the battlefield.

Eversmann recalled that the Somali battle tactics were crude, yet effective:

They would race down both sides of the street, turn toward the center, and start pulling the trigger, waiting for us to drive through the wall of bullets. *Macabre* would be the adjective that best describes this tactic. There was no way of telling how many of their own people they killed. I could only focus on the right side of the street, and I knew that the Rangers on the other side of the vehicle were doing the same. The only person that I remember being in the vehicle with me was Sergeant Marc Luhman. He was sitting in the front passenger seat, riding shotgun. As we raced down the street, we were following an unwritten rule: pull the trigger faster than the bad guy. With the window down, I had to contort my body in order to get a good shot. Because I wanted to engage the enemy to the front, I decided that I would open the door and lean out. That way I was not restricted by the door frame and would have more room to traverse my barrel. Plus, being a right-handed shooter, it would give me more room. Good initiative, bad judgement.

The Somali militiamen had plenty of time for their scattershot tactic; the convoy was going slower than the Somalis could run along.

With the convoy hopelessly lost and unable to get through to the first crash site, Lieutenant-Colonel Danny McKnight, the Ranger battalion commander, radioed Harrell: "We've got a lot of casualties that are almost impossible to move. Quite a few casualties. Getting to the crash site will be awful tough. Are pinned down."

Lieutenant-Colonel Harrell insisted McKnight continue to the crash site. But McKnight called back: "Gotta get these casualties out of here ASAP."

As the Lost Convoy began making its way back to base, an emergency convoy, the "Quick Reaction Force", was dispatched to rescue the crew of Durant's Black Hawk. Raleigh Cash, twenty-two-year-old sergeant from Bravo Company, had scrambled "as much ammo as possible" on to his Humvee: two crates of 5.56, two more of .50 calibre and about 150 rounds for the Squad Automatic Weapon. As well as his CAR-15-2-3, he carried as his personal armoury a Remington 870 sawn-off shotgun and two hand grenades.

Going out into the city, the convoy soon encountered road-blocks of burning tyres. As 3rd Platoon's Forward Observer, Cash had access to the heli common, the helicopter common net, and was trying to get the Little Birds to give them directions. However:

> When I did get directions from the helicopter, I would tell Lieutenant Moores, who would tell Sergeant Struecker, who was up in the lead vehicle; but by the time it got to him, it was too late – we had missed the turn. We'd get turned around and have to drive right back through the area we'd just received fire from. I'd yell to take the left, and the lead vehicle would miss it. I can't tell you how many times we did this. It seemed like a hundred.

To try and even the odds, the driver of Cash's Humvee drove along with his right hand on the wheel and his left hand out of the window firing off shots. After constant missed turns, they joined up with McKnight's ground convoy, which was on its way back to the base, on the National Road. Cash:

That's when a Somali jumped out from behind one of the stone walls and shot an RPG at the vehicle in front of us. Milliman slammed into the back of the stopped Humvee. All of us got smashed up inside, bouncing our heads off things. I remember looking at my strangely oriented pinky and thinking it might be broken. I grabbed some electrical tape off my web gear and taped it up in case it started swelling. I then went back to pulling security on the vehicle.

The RPG blew a lot of sand into our vehicle, and it was hazy for a second. I couldn't tell if we were being fired at or not. I couldn't really hear anything – my ears were ringing. Then it cleared up and we started moving again. We had to drive some crazy crisscross pattern back toward the hangar – turn left here, turn right here – to avoid the burning roadblocks and piles of debris. We started receiving fire again, and this time they were shooting from the windows, from the alleyways, the doors, everywhere. I could hear the alleyways erupting like crazy as we were going past them. We were picking off onesies and twosies as best we could, discriminating among those who had a weapon and those who didn't. We were still following the rules of engagement as written. But as we were driving farther it was getting crazier; more and more people were coming out. I was seeing more and more weapons and fewer and fewer civilians until it seemed we were engaging everybody. There were so many of them. I recall hitting another roadblock and having to back up to go around it. Finally, as we got closer to the airfield, the fire began letting up a little bit. The vehicles in front of us were still firing sporadically, engaging targets as best they could. I think at this point the very front of the convoy was getting hit hard, but by the time we got to their position, it was only sporadic fire.

I remember pulling back into the airfield and it was like we had crossed an imaginary line to safety. As soon as we crossed that line everything stopped and it was quiet. It went from crazy noise and shooting and RPGs blowing up all around us and people yelling out directions and orders to – nothing. You could hear some chatter on the radio but it was only background noise.

The time was 5.45 p.m. The convoy unloaded the wounded, and repaired the vehicles as best as they could. Out in the city there were some ninety Rangers and Delta-boys utterly stranded, and all falling back on the first crash site for mutual protection. RTO Mike Kurth was one of the Rangers who had to fight his way block-by-block to the wreck of Wolcott's craft. Kurth's chalk moved in single file on either side of the street, constantly scanning for hostiles. As well as operating the radio, Kurth was pulling security. Private First Class Neathery was Chalk Three's M60 machine gunner. To the Rangers an M60 was "the Pig", because of the grunting noise it made when firing. Kurth:

I squeezed off a couple of bursts. I heard Neathery fire a burst, so I got up and ran back to him and covered his rear. I had just turned around to cover Neathery when he fired, his muzzle right next to my left ear. The last thing sergeant Watson wanted was a radio telephone operator who couldn't hear.

Our chalk was pretty much intact. The only casualty was Sergeant Boren, and he was walking wounded. I looked ahead at the next corner, and the battle going on there was incredibly fierce. I looked to our rear and saw a small road – more like an alley than anything else. If we had continued on the major road, we would have gone straight into the alley, but instead, in order to get closer to the crash site, we'd taken a left. I noticed that the road we were on had a slight elevation to it, which gave us a slight advantage, but at the same time it was crowned, so it was hard to get a really clear field of vision all the way across the street.

Our chalk and part of the CO's chalk were all within about a block of each other. We were in a kind of U-shaped court-yard. To our rear was a house with a small patio, and to our front was a pretty large intersection. The fiercest part of the battle was taking place there. The volume of fire had grown so intense that it had been a little while since anyone had crossed the street. In our immediate area the major threat was coming from a small road that veered away from the crash site – somehow the enemy had managed to backtrack away from us and had found small alleys to make their way down the road that led to our chalk. We were between them and the crash site, but we didn't know exactly how close our position was to it.

Moving cautiously along the street, Chalk Three reached an intersection. Here one of the Delta operators took a round to the head. Kurth saw his head snap back, and blood spray onto the wall behind. Another Delta operator pulled him to safety. Someone screamed into the radio for an aerial medevac. This was refused. The streets around the Bakara Market were now deemed too dangerous for a helicopter to land in.

Kurth was crouching beside Neathery when the machine-gunner was hit. Errico took over the M60, then he, too, was hit. Someone had a bead on the machine gun. The chalk fired off a light anti-tank weapon. The respite it brought lasted barely minutes.

Moving over to help their medic, Doc Strauss, Kurth noticed a trail of smoke out of the corner of his eye. It was an old-fashioned "pineapple grenade". He yelled a warning and they all dived to the ground. Kurth felt the earth hit in the chest. He staggered to his knees, coughing up dirt. Miraculously, only one of the chalk had been hurt, taking shrapnel to the leg. Kurth concluded that the grenades had been so close that the main blast had risen above their prone bodies.

By now it was getting dark, and they were almost at the crash site. Sergeant Watson decided to take over a house on the street, where the medics set up a Casualty Clearing Point (CCP). By coincidence, members of Chalk One had also taken up position in the house. Occasionally, Kurth heard Little Birds making gun runs; on one occasion the Little Birds "neutralized" a party of thirty Somalis carrying an RPG approaching Kurth's position.

When the sun went down, another mission to rescue the stranded men was set up. To the relief of the Americans, the Malaysian and Pakistani components of the UN peacekeeping force agreed to help. Both had armour; the Pakistanis had four American M-28 tanks and the Malaysians had thirty-eight Russian BTR Armoured Personnel carriers. What the Malaysians and Pakistanis did not have was uniform comms, so it was decided that the Malaysians would provide the drivers and gunners for their APCs but that the infantry carried would be Americans, from the 10th Mountain Division, and each vehicle would have a US Army radio set. Meanwhile, the Pakistanis were reluctant to use their M-28s to smash the burning-tyre roadblocks; they would only agree to clear the obstacles immediately outside the base, then they would fall back behind the column leaders.

Several hours later, at 11.23 p.m. the new convoy left for the Mogadishu badlands. According to Sergeant Raleigh Cash there were roadblocks at every intersection, and "it was a moving fire-fight, pretty much a non-stop engagement, all night long". Cash's Humvee lost radio and visual contact with the vehicle behind. Then drove past the smoking, flaming hull of one of the Malaysian APCs.

Among the vehicles caught in a Somali RPG ambush was the APC carrying Lieutenant AB Hollis, a platoon commander 2nd Battalion, 14th Infantry, 10th Mountain Division. Hollis and his men were going to have one very long, dark night indeed, as Hollis recalled:

My vehicle was struck a moment later in the engine compartment (the front right-hand side of the vehicle). The blast felt like someone had lifted the vehicle up and was trying to balance it on a pedestal. The vehicle teetered back and forth a bit, I heard a high-pitched ring, and the smell of an explosion filled the compartment.

The 1st Squad leader called from the lead vehicle, saying his vehicle was hit and requesting guidance. I instructed him to get out of the vehicle and establish security. I was going to do the same. When I opened the door and got out, I realised we were on our own. Looking back the direction we had traveled, I saw a long upward sloping hill with no one behind us. Green tracers and RPG rounds were hitting all around us.

At this point, I turned back to my RTO, and we moved to a building east of the vehicle and occupied some low ground on the south side. I still did not want to believe we were alone. I made contact with the squad leader and told him to stay in his security position. I told him that my group was going to move north, back up the hill, and try to reestablish contact with the rest of the company. Low ground and the buildings were blocking all radio transmissions.

I led my platoon headquarters group with the engineer team north past two buildings, attempting to gain sight of the company. Small arms fire began to intensify from the direction of travel farther up the hill. The M60 gunner engaged targets from the corner of what appeared to be some sort of garage. All he was actually doing, however, was drawing fire; every time he engaged someone, the RPG fires into our location intensified. I instructed the gunner to engage only identified targets to limit the RPG fires and not to suppress the area. He said that he *was* only engaging identifiable targets and that there were a lot of people up the road.

With the enemy fires getting even worse as we pulled away from the squad leader in the security position, and with the fear of the enemy coming in between my divided forces, I decided to return to the original location. Before moving out, I heard the clearing of a weapon on the other side of the wall. I pulled out a grenade, pulled the pin, flipped the thumb clip, and threw the grenade. There was no explosion. I pulled out another grenade, repeated the arming process, released pressure from the spoon, and the spoon did not fly off. The tape we used to silence the grenade rings had left small strands that kept the grenade from arming. I then pulled the spoon off and threw the grenade, and a huge explosion followed. The weapon noise stopped.

Throughout the entire movement, the RTO kept trying unsuccessfully to initiate radio contact. About fifteen minutes from the time of the ambush, I led the element back to the original security position and reestablished a secure perimeter. An M60 assistant gunner, in his haste to leave the vehicle, had left behind his gear and additional ammunition, and I sent him back to recover it.

When he returned, the Malaysians in the vehicle apparently decided they were going to exit the vehicles as well and join our perimeter. When they came running from the vehicles, the M60 gunner, catching their movement out of the corner of his eye, spun with the M60 and engaged. Luckily for the Malaysians, this spinning movement caused the M60 to double feed, and they were not shot.

One previously injured Malaysian dived right on top of me. I pushed him off me and over to my RTO, telling the RTO to bandage him up. At this point, my unit was still under heavy fire, and I decided we had to get inside a building to survive. I asked the engineer squad leader if he could make a hole in a wall (pointing to the wall), and he assured me he could. I then contacted the squad leader, telling him my plan was to blow a hole in the compound he was backed up against and establish security positions inside. He was to make sure he had no personnel beyond the corner of the wall.

Once I received confirmation that all his personnel were out of the direct blast radius, the charge was set. It had a forty-two-second time fuse, which seemed to burn forever, and I in my haste looked up just as the blast went off, receiving a chunk of concrete in my face. The PVS-7As I was wearing took the brunt of the blast. The device's optics tube bent sideways, and I had only a small cut above my right eyebrow.

Everything on the battlefield seemed to go quiet after the blast, as if it had surprised the Somali gunmen. The blast was so large that it not only made a hole in the wall but knocked down the wall and a small building on the other side. The squad leader reported that part of the wall on his side had come down on his soldiers as well. (Next time, I will specify how large a hole I want.)

In the quiet after the blast, I figured someone would have to make the initial entry, and all my soldiers were pulling security. So I jumped up, sprinted across the street, and entered the compound, firing at the house I was entering. No fire was returned. I then called the squad into the compound to establish a more defensible perimeter.

We formed two mutually supporting battle positions. The squad was oriented south, west and east. The engineers and an M60 team were oriented north, west and east.

The RTO and the Malaysians also entered the compound. The RTO continued to work to establish voice communications. He put up the long whip antenna and tried different nets. The Malaysians were placed in the hallway toward the rear of the building. The squad's combat lifesaver began working on the injured Malaysians while I checked security.

Two adults and several children who were in the house positioned themselves in the back room, and we left them alone. I figured we had done enough, blowing up their home and occupying it as a defensive position.

Then screams of pain were reported, coming from the lead APC, apparently from a wounded Malaysian who had been left behind. I told a team leader to go out there and get the man. Without concern for his own life, he ran back into the kill zone and retrieved the mortally wounded soldier and attended to his wounds. (This act earned him a Bronze Star with Valor device.)

Returning to the RTO, I found that he still had not been able to contact anyone on any net. In my frustration, I pulled the PRC-77 radio out of the rucksack, took off all secure devices, and transmitted in the red. The battalion commander's voice was the first I heard, and this was the most calming influence I had that night. He said, "Keep doing what you're doing. You're alive, and I will work on getting you out."

The battalion commander then told me to drop down to the Company C net and make contact with the commander. I did so, and the captain and I conducted recognition procedures. I shot a red star cluster so he could see how far away I was, and he shot a green one. We agreed that we were about one kilometer apart. He then informed me that he would work on getting his company down toward our location once he had completed the search of the crash site, and that we should stay put.

While I was speaking to him, an AH-1 Cobra helicopter flew over us. The battalion commander must have talked to someone and sent some fire support to our location. The Cobra flew east and started engaging targets a block or two away. This prompted me to place my M203 gunners on the roof of the building, and they engaged targets toward the east throughout the night.

During that time, Somalis continued to conduct sporadic attacks. Their favourite action was to stand off and lob RPGs at the compound. I counted no fewer than ten impacts in a one-minute period, and this kept up throughout the night.

Hollis and his men were not picked up until about 5 a.m. on 4 October.

While Hollis was holed up, the main rescue convoy had halted for nearly two hours midway between the two crash sites, pulling security on the alleyways and streets that fanned out from the main road. When they moved off, again the convoy split so as to cover both downed Black Hawks. The incoming became more and more intense. Cash used tracer rounds to locate targets for the machine gunners. A Pakistani tank accompanying them fired its main gun; it was the loudest noise the Tenth Mountain boys had ever heard. Reports started to come in from the Combat Search and Rescue teams that they were having problems cutting the body of CWO Cliff "Elvis" Wolcott out of the first downed Black Hawk.

At about 1.55 in the morning of 4 October the rescue convoy finally reached the trapped Ranger force around the crash site. In a thankful lull in fire from the Somalis, which reduced to pot shots and the odd burst from an AK-47, the bodies were finally cut out of the Black Hawk and the exfil organized.

Dawn brought fresh cares. As light filtered over the city, the firing regained momentum. But the convoy was now ready to roll home. Sergeant Raleigh Cash:

I told Specialist Milliman to back up our vehicle to get close to some of the guys who were running from their positions [towards the convoy]. We filled up the back of our Humvee. There must have been four or five guys in the back, maybe six. They jumped in, and grabbed some of the Kevlar that we had lying back there for added protection in case we hit a mine. While we stopped and the guys were hopping in, I started organizing who would shoot where – who had what.

Everybody seemed to be working well together. As the ranking NCO, I was in charge of my vehicle.

I looked around and began to see the damage to the vehicles around us, to the city, the streets themselves, the buildings, and the bodies of the dead – the casualties taken by our opposition. There were quite a few on the ground in various positions around the vehicles. We found out that many Somalis had been a lot closer to us than we would have liked to believe. All night we'd been engaging targets that we could only guess at how close they were. Now, during the day, we could *see* them. Some bodies were as close as four or five metres away. In the night we'd fired at muzzle flashes or outlines of bodies; now we were seeing the result. The utter destruction to the city and the sheer number of Somalis that had been taken out by our fire-power was mind-numbing. As we pulled forward, it seemed like the city erupted on us again. Maybe they knew that we were leaving. The vehicles in front of us were shooting down alleyways, shooting everything that posed a threat.

RTO Mike Kurth, Ranger Chalk Three, was among those who had been stranded near the crash site. Exhausted, he'd fallen asleep in a sequestered house. On being woken up, he was told by Sergeant Watson:

All the APCs are filled with casualties, and some of the chalks, including the rest of us, are going to walk out beside the APCs and use them as cover. We're going back the way we came. About four-fifths of a mile past the Olympic Hotel there is a secure intersection with more vehicles, and we will load up there.

The walk to the rally point on National Road went down in history as "the Mogadishu Mile". Mike Kurth:

We were going out with guns blazing! If they *were* still hanging around by this time, you knew they were up to no good. There were about twenty-five of us out there fighting for our lives. I turned the corner and started laying down some heat. I got about six rounds off and my M-16 jammed. I yelled "Jam!" as loud as I could about three times and pulled back from the corner. I completely forgot I had traded my M-16 with Kent at some point in the night, and I didn't know he had fired it so much. The carbon build-up had caused a double feed, a real nasty one. I couldn't get the rounds out to save my life. I was slamming the butt of my weapon on the ground, trying to force the round out, but no luck. Finally the last guy told me to go, so I hauled ass across the street. I made it about halfway down the block before I stopped to try to unjam my weapon again. Nothing was working; those two rounds were so wedged in that I couldn't pry them out. I needed to find someone carrying two weapons and fast. I couldn't believe how badly this was going. It's daylight, there's no room on the APCs, we have to walk out, the APCs leave us, and now I'm running out of this thing naked with no weapon!

Crossing an intersection, Doc Strauss got hit, disappearing in an eruption of smoke. His ammo pouch had been hit and a flash bang grenade detonated. When the smoke cleared, Kurth saw Strauss get to his feet. Catching up with Sergeant Elliot, Kurth saw he had a spare M-16. Elliot gave him the spare, and Kurth immediately located a target and began to fire.

At one intersection they were held up by a sniper. Not for long, though; one of the Pakistani tanks fired off its main gun and the sniper was silent.

They reached the designated link-up position, where they were picked up by APCs and Humvees. Kurth kept the back door of the vehicle open with his foot looking for targets. But the people on the street barely looked at them. There were out of the battle zone. Ten minutes later, at 6.30 a.m., they pulled into the Pakistani Stadium.

The day of the Black Hawks Down was over. In all, eighteen US soldiers had been killed and seventy-three wounded. Somali dead were approximately five hundred, with more than a thousand injured.

Aidid bought Mike Durant from his original captors. After eleven days of negotiations, he was delivered to the Red Cross. He was the only member of Super 64 to come back alive.

Another casualty that day was American desire for military interventions abroad. TV footage of dead American troops being dragged through the streets of Mogadishu by the mobs was too much for the public to bear. Six months later, the US had withdrawn from Somalia. Among those celebrating the humbling of Uncle Sam was al-Qaeda.

The Islamist group had helped train Aidid's militia.

MALAYAN EMERGENCY

Malayan Scouts/22 SAS, Malaya, 1952–6

Officially, the wartime SAS founded by David Stirling in 1941 ceased to exist on 8 October 1945; in actuality, it remained alive. Just. A team of SAS men, including L Detachment Original Bob Bennett, was attached to the Military Reparations Committee in Greece, where they proudly sported their winged-dagger badge. Brian Franks, still pained and outraged by the murder of SAS soldiers during *Loyton* and other operations, organized a team to investigate the crimes and bring those responsible to justice. This became the SAS War Crimes Team, which operated for four years and successfully identified several Nazi perpetrators. Beyond these two small SAS remnants, the Regiment's veterans kept in personal contact. Johnny Cooper was invited by David Stirling, long since released from Colditz, to lunch at White's in London. Stirling, thought Cooper, "looked none the worse" for his stay at Hitler's pleasure. Also in attendance were George Jellicoe, Fitzroy Maclean and Randolph Churchill. Such social occasions were pleasant chances to air memories. They were also opportunities for ex-SAS men to plan the Regiment's rise anew.

Eventually, lobbying of the War Office by SAS veterans, chiefly Mike Calvert and Brian Franks, brought its reward, and in 1947 an SAS unit was formed within the Territorial Army. It was attached to a former officers' training unit, the Artists' Rifles, to become 21 (Artists) TA, based at Duke's Road, Euston. The commanding officer was Lieutenant-Colonel Brian Franks, 2 SAS's sometime commander during World War II, and a post-war hotel manager. Wartime SAS soldiers flocked to the new TA

SAS, so many indeed that Johnny Cooper found the first training camp "a splendid reunion". This TA SAS unit, which still exists and is complemented by another TA SAS unit, 23 SAS, provided many of the volunteers for a long-range patrol Franks raised for Korea, where the first major war since 1945 was being fought between the Communist North and the UN-backed South. Before Franks' jeep patrol could be sent to Korea, though, the UN commander, General McArthur, decided he had no use for it. What was McArthur's loss was Britain's gain. A communist insurrection – known as "the Emergency" for insurance-claim purposes – had broken out in the British dominion of Malaya.

From hide-outs in the jungle, communist terrorists ("CTs"), led by Chin Peng of the Malayan Races Liberation Army (MRLA), were murdering British rubber-plantation owners and their families. The Commander-in-Chief Far East, Sir John Harding, summoned Mike Calvert to Malaya and asked him to find ways of dealing with the CT campaign. Before becoming commanding officer of the SAS Brigade during World War II, Calvert had commanded 77 Chindit Brigade. Mad Mike, along with Freddie Spencer Chapman, soldier and author of the memoir *The Jungle is Neutral*, was as close to an expert jungle-fighter as the British possessed.

Looking at the situation in Malaya, Calvert realized that the Emergency required the British to have a special force that would "live, move, and have its heart in the jungle" just as the enemy did. His proposal for a new unit, the Malayan Scouts (SAS), was accepted. For personnel for the unit, Calvert milked three sources: A Squadron was formed from 100 volunteers in the British Army already in the Far East; B Squadron was comprised of soldiers from 1 SAS, primarily those who had put up their hands for the Korean job; and C Squadron was made up of Rhodesian volunteers.

Unfortunately, while B Squadron – thoroughly marinated in SAS philosophy, discipline and training either by war service or Brian Franks' Duke's Road regime – was the right SAS stuff, the Rhodesians were keen but undertrained. But the real headache was A Squadron, who, save for a few good apples, were poseurs and party-animals. It did not help that Calvert himself was keen on wild drinking parties. So notorious was A Squadron's indiscipline that the Malayan Scouts were almost disbanded. Instead, Calvert was sent home from Malaya with a convenient (and fictitious) kidney illness, and Lieutenant-Colonel John Sloane was brought in as commanding officer. A straight-backed, by-the-book officer from the Argyll and Sutherland Highlanders, "Tod" Sloane unsentimentally returned misfits to their units and implemented proper admin. He was ably assisted in his makeover of the Malayan Scouts by John Woodhouse and Dare Newell, men who were both to become legendary figures in SAS history. To make the regiment more attractive to volunteers, its name was changed from Malayan Scouts – which, after all, suggested members would only serve in Malaya – to the 22nd Special Air Service regiment (22 SAS). And yet, for all Calvert's waywardness, he was, more than Sloane, Woodhouse and Newell, the architect of the modern SAS.

Quite aside from creating a unit to bear the appellation "Special Air Service", Calvert proposed that the SAS should work in three- or four-man patrols, the SAS should win over local tribes by kindness (what later became known as "hearts and minds"), notably by setting up medical clinics, and that the SAS should establish long-term counter-guerrilla bases deep in the jungle. All three of these principles still shape the modern SAS.

The men of the 22 SAS Regiment underwent an experience in Malaya that their successors down the decades would come to know and empathize with too: fighting in appalling conditions. Johnny Cooper, who had transferred to 22 SAS as 8 Troop's commander (thus becoming, by his reckoning, the oldest lieutenant in the Army, at twenty-nine years of age), was dismayed by the rain. "If there was no great downpour after three or four days, it was reckoned a drought." There were also other unpleasantnesses in the jungle. After communist terrorists, Cooper wrote, leeches were the main adversary: They would fall off the leaves and latch on to one's softest area, around the neck, behind the ears, under the armpits, and on a long patrol they would even find their way to one's private parts. You couldn't feel them, but as they slowly sucked blood they enlarged into horrible black swollen lumps. Sores festered, clothes and boots rotted in the damp, and fevers such as Weil's Disease abounded. Lying in an observation post or in an ambush could be particularly trying, as Trooper Geordie Doran, a recent recruit, found:

> The duty was set in pairs for four-hour stags, or watches, during which time all SAS soldiers involved had to lie perfectly still, watching and listening, rifles loaded and at the ready. Conversations were in whispers. If a man wanted to relieve himself, he would first indicate to the others what he intended, then slither slowly and silently to the rear. Washing and shaving in the jungle, especially on ambush duty, was sometimes banned. The CT, with their sharpened sense, could pick up the odour of soap from quite a distance. Also, soap suds in rivers could be seen a long way downstream before they dispersed. Lying in ambush I was again conscious that the jungle is never quiet, nor still. Among other sounds, a troop of gibbons entertained us with their hooting most days. There was also the constant falling of leaves and debris from trees, and nearby a regiment of ants went about their business. Leeches gathered expectantly, and pig flies fed on the backs of my legs. Luckily we hadn't disturbed any red tree ants when getting into position. They are vicious little buggers and have a pair of pliers for a mouth. We had to take all the bites and stings in silence, as a slap or curse could have alerted an approaching enemy and been fatal.

By the end of a patrol, a soldier would have lost on average ten pounds. Despite the hardships, however, patrols stayed out in the jungle for longer and longer periods, as the Regiment's jungle education grew. Johnny Cooper once led a 122-day patrol in the jungle to establish a military fort in the region of Sungei Brok. Cooper recalled:

> The first job was to clear a small area and then we radioed for confirmation that we were on the correct site. An Auster aircraft came over and we were informed that we were at least in the right place. To secure the place from the attentions of CTs, I placed three screens out on the most dangerous approaches to our clearing. Then the heavy work began,

blowing down the huge jungle trees, clearing the area of bamboo and building a wooden bridge over the river which was at that point about thirty feet wide. In the latter job, our local Iban trackers were of great help with their skill in splicing creepers to tie the bridge together. The structure lasted for many months, although only two men could cross at any one time, and one had to get used to the swaying motion in midstream over the raging torrent.

By the middle of November we had cleared the site for the building of the fort and also constructed a helicopter landing ground as there was not enough room for a proper airstrip. This gave us the opportunity for more active patrolling into the aboriginal areas. Bruce Murray had a great success when he sorted out a complete CT gang, killing some and dispersing the others from our immediate area. To the west, however, we suffered a tragedy when another patrol under the command of Corporal Digger Bancroft ran into an ambush. Digger, who was in the lead, was killed and Trooper Willis behind him was also shot. Fortunately the rest of the patrol reacted promptly, engaged the enemy and drove them off. I received the news by runner, immediately informed our headquarters of the casualties and requested a helicopter to bring out the bodies. Volunteers stepped forward to carry out the dead men; one of them was Bill Speakerman, the Korean War VC who was doing his jungle training with C Squadron. This party disappeared off to Bancroft's old base and I ordered others to search for further traces of the enemy.

In the dark and the tangle of the Malayan jungle, contacts with the enemy were fleeting. On his epic patrol Cooper lost just two of eighty men to enemy action; nearly forty, meanwhile, had to be helicoptered out because of illness. Cooper's Sungei Brok patrol also advanced the "hearts and minds" programme by establishing "diplomatic relations" with a tribe previously under the spell of the communist terrorists, by befriending the aboriginals and giving them medical and food aid.

Perhaps fortunately, Cooper's Sungei Brok patrol went into the jungle on foot; during the Malayan campaign the SAS experimented with parachuting into the jungle. A successful jump by fifty-four troopers of B Squadron ("Big Time Bravo", as it was known by envious troopers in the other squadrons) in the Belum Valley in 1952, persuaded senior officers that "tree-jumping" was viable, even desirable. Numerous personnel were thereafter injured, among them Johnny Cooper, whose arm was broken when it became entangled with a fellow parachutist's static line. Disabled, Cooper crashed into the treetops; due to his broken arm he was unable to tie his scaling rope to a branch and climb down its 150-foot length to the ground. Thanks to clever thinking and climbing by the medical officer, Freddie Brunton, Cooper's scaling rope was attached to a piton in a tree; Cooper then cut himself free from his parachute and fell 60 feet before the rope pulled him up. He was lowered the remainder of the way. The wrenching action of the fall, however, added nerve damage to his list of injuries. Cooper was far from being the only casualty of tree-jumping. Another high-profile victim was Lieutenant-Colonel Oliver Brooke, who took over from Sloane as 22 SAS's commanding officer; Brooke broke his ankle.

By 1956, the Regiment was up to a strength of 560 men and was making a real contribution towards containing the Emergency; its tally of communist terrorists killed was eighty-nine. Captured communist terrorists confessed that the SAS patrols, even when failing to make contact with the enemy, were so disruptive as to render guerrilla warfare all but impossible. Four years later, the Emergency was over. The leaders of the MRLA had fled to Thailand, and the murders of civilians had almost ceased. After its eight years in Malaya, the Regiment had, despite an inauspicious start, become a highly professional unit. In 1957, in recognition, 22 SAS was placed in the order of battle of the British Army, and as a result was able to readopt both the beige beret and the winged-dagger badge. For all this, the future of the Regiment was far from assured: the whispers from Whitehall were that 22 SAS would be disbanded when it was finally pulled out of Malaya.

History, however, was on the side of the SAS. In the death agony of Empire there came other small wars.

DOCUMENT: J. M. Calvert:
"Future of SAS Troops", 1945

Subject: Future of SAS Troops
HQ SAS Tps/80/17/G
Lt Col W. Stirling
Lt Col D. Stirling, DSO
Lt Col R. B. Mayne, DSO
Lt Col B. M. F. Franks, DSO MC
Lt Col I. G. Collins
Lt Col E. C. Baring
Lt Col The Earl Jellicoe
Lt Col D. Sutherland
Lt Col D. Lloyd Owen, MC
Major J. Verney, MC
Major R. Farran, DSO, MC

The Director of Tactical Investigation, Maj Gen Rowell, has been ordered by the Chief of Imperial General Staff that his directorate should investigate all the operations of the Special Air Service with a view to giving recommendations for the future of the SAS in the next war and its composition in the peacetime army. The actual terms of reference were: "An investigation of SAS technique tactics and organization without prejudice to a later examination of all organizations of a similar nature which were formed and operated in various theatres of this last war".

Brigadier Churchill is Deputy Director of Tactical Investigation and lives at Flat 110, 4 Whitehall Court, London, SW1 (Whitehall 9400 Ext 1632), just behind the War Office. The officer immediately concerned is Lt Col C. A. Wigham. Lt Col Wigham has in his possession all the reports on SAS operations in western Europe. The reports on SAS operations in Italy and in the Mediterranean theatre are also being obtained and forwarded. I have given Lt Col Wigham your names so that he may either have a talk with you to obtain your views and to find out about incidents which are not clear in the reports, or to ask you to write your views to him.

We all have the future of the SAS at heart, not merely because we wish to see its particular survival as a unit, but because we have believed in the principles of its method of operations. Many of the above-named officers have had command of forces which have had a similar role to that of the SAS, as well as being in the SAS at one time. The object of this investigation is to decide whether the principles of operating in the SAS manner are correct. If they are correct, what types of units should undertake operations of this nature, and how best to train and maintain such units in peace, ready for war. I will not start now by writing about the principles of the SAS, which have been an intrinsic part of your life for the past few years, but I will mention what I think are some of the most important points which need bringing out. The best way to do this is to consider the usual criticisms of the SAS type of force.

1. *"The Private Army"*
From what I have seen in different parts of the world, forces of this nature tend to be so-called "Private Armies" because there have been no normal formations in existence to fulfil this function – a role which has been found by all commanders to be a most vital adjunct to their plans. It has only been due to the drive and initiative of certain individuals backed up by senior commanders that these forces have been formed and have carried out their role.

2. *"The taking up of Commanders' valuable time"*
This has often been necessary because it has very often only been the Comds of armies who have realized the importance of operations of this nature, and to what an extent they can help their plans. The difficulty has been that more junior staff officers have not understood the object or principles of such forces. They have either given us every help as they have thought us something rather wonderful, or they have thought we were "a bloody nuisance". I feel that the best way to overcome this is that once the principle of the importance of Special Raiding Forces operating behind the vital points of the enemy's lines is agreed to, it should become an integral part of

the training of the army at the Staff College, military colleges, and during maneuvers, etc. Students should be asked not only what orders or directives or requests they have to give to the artillery, engineers, air, etc., but also what directives they would give to their raiding forces. There should be a recognized staff officer on the staffs of senior formations whose job it is to deal with these forces, i.e. the equivalent of a CRE or CRA. This should also be included in the text books FRS, etc.

3. *"These forces, like airborne forces, are only required when we pass to the offensive, which – judging by all previous wars – is when the regular army has been nearly wiped out in rearguard actions whilst the citizen army forms, i.e. about 3 years after the beginning of the war."*

The answer here, I feel, is that it is just when we are weak everywhere that forces of this nature are the most useful, and can play a most vital part in keeping the enemy all over the world occupied. Also there is little difference between the roles of SAS and "Auxiliary Forces" who duck when the enemy's offensive rolls over them and then operate against the enemy's L or C from previously constructed bases. An SAS formation, by its organization and training, is ideally suited to operate in this defensive role.

4. *"Overlapping with SOE and other clandestine organizations"*
My experience is that SOE and SAS are complementary to each other. SAS cannot successfully operate without good intelligence, guides, etc. SOE can only do a certain amount before requiring, when their operations become overt, highly trained, armed bodies in uniform to operate and set an example to the local resistance. SOE are the "white hunters" and produce the ground organization on which SAS operates. All senior officers of SOE with whom I have discussed this point agree to this principle.

5. *"SAS is not adaptable to all countries."*
This has already been proved wrong. SAS is probably more adaptable to changes of theatres than any regular formation.

Also, as I have said in 4 above, SAS work on the ground organization of SOE. It is for SOE to be a world-wide organization with an organization in every likely country. Then when necessary, SAS can operate on this organization using their guides and intelligence knowledge, etc.

6. *"Volunteer units skim the regular units of their best officers and men."*

Volunteer units such as SAS attract officers and men who have initiative, resourcefulness, independence of spirit, and confidence in themselves. In a regular unit there are far fewer opportunities to make use of these assets and, in fact, in many formations they are a liability, as this individualistic attitude upsets the smooth working of a team. This is especially true in European warfare where the individual must subordinate his natural initiative so that he fits into a part of the machine. Volunteer units such as the Commandos and Chindits (only a small proportion of the Chindits were volunteers although the spirit was there) have shown the rest of the army how to fight at a time when it was in low morale due to constant defeat.

A few "gladiators" raises the standard of all. Analogies are racing (car, aeroplane, horse, etc.), and test teams.

7. *"Expense per man is greater than any other formation and is not worthwhile."*

Men in units of this nature probably fight 3 or 4 times more often than regular units. They are always eager for a fight and therefore usually get it. If expense per man days *actually in contact with the enemy* was taken into account, there would be no doubt which was the more expensive type of formation. I have found, as you will have done, the "old familiar faces" on every front where we have seen trouble. I consider the expense is definitely worth it without even taking into account the extra results. One SAS raid in North Africa destroyed more aeroplanes in one day than the balloon barrage did during 6 years of war.

8. *"Any normal battalion could do the same job."*

My experience shows that they definitely cannot. In Norway in 1940, a platoon of marines under a sergeant ran away when left on its own, although they had orders to stay, when a few German lorries appeared. Mainly owing to the bad leadership of this parade-ground sergeant, they were all jittery and useless because they were "out of touch". A force consisting of two Gurkha Coys and a few British troops, of which I was one, was left behind in 1942 in Burma to attack the enemy in the rear if they appeared. The Commander, a good Gurkha officer with a good record, when confronted with a perfect opportunity (Japs landing in boats onto a wide sandy beach completely unaware of our presence), avoided action in order to get back to his Brigade because he was "out of touch" and could not receive orders. By avoiding action, the unit went into a waterless area and more perished this way and later by drowning than if he had attacked.

My experience with regular battalions under my command in Burma was that there were only 3 or 4 officers in any battalion who could be relied on to take positive action if they were on their own, and had no detailed orders. This "I'll 'ave to ask me Dad" attitude of the British Army is its worst feature in my opinion. I found the RAF and dominion officers far better in this respect. I have not had experience with the cavalry. They should also be better. Perhaps cavalry could take on the SAS role successfully? I admit that with training both in Burma and North Africa there were definite improvements amongst the infantry, but in my opinion, no normal battalion I have seen could carry out an SAS role without 80 per cent reorganization. I have written frankly and have laid myself open to obvious criticism, but I consider this such a vital point I do not mind how strongly I express myself. I have repeated this for 5 years and I have nowhere seen anything to change my views, least of all in Europe.

I have mentioned some points above. You may not agree with my ideas but I write them down as these criticisms are the most normal ones I know. Other points in which the DTI wants to obtain information are:

1. *Obtaining of recruits.* Has anybody got the original brochure setting out the terms and standards required?

2. *Obtaining of stores and equipment.* Here again, I imagine SOE has been the main source of special stores. My own HQ is producing a paper on this when in England.

3. *Signal communication.* This is of course one of the most important parts of such an organization and it has, as in other formations, limited the scope of our operation.

4. *Foreign recruits and attached civilians.*

5. *Liaison with RAF and Navy.*

6. *Command.* How is an organization of this sort best commanded and under whom should they be?

7. Suggestions re survival in peacetime including auxiliary formation, command, technical development, etc.

You may expect a communication from Lt Col Wigham. Please give your views quite candidly. They certainly need not agree with those I have written down. I am sending Lt Col Wigham a copy of this letter so that it may give you something to refer to if necessary.

I hope, from the army point of view, and for all that you have worked for and believed in during the last few years, that you will do everything you can to help Lt Col Wigham to obtain all the information that he requires. We can no longer say that people do not understand if we do not take this chance to get our views put before an impartial tribunal whose task it is to review them in the light of general policy, and then make recommendations to the CIGS. Send along any reports or documents you have got. Lt Col Wigham is thirsting for information.

[Mike Calvert]
Brigadier,
Commander,
SAS Troops
Sloe House,
Halstead, Essex.
12 Oct 45.
JMC/LGM.

THE KOEMBA JOB

22 SAS, Borneo, 1965

Between 1963 and 1966 the mountainous jungle island of Borneo became the theatre for war between the former British colony of Malaya and an expansionist Indonesia under President Sukarno. To counter the latter's infiltration of guerrilla insurgents from Indonesian Borneo (Kalimintan) into northern Malaysian Borneo, the British organized a border guard of Malaysian, British and Commonwealth troops. A main constituent of this guard was 22 SAS, which eventually proved so successful that Indonesia abandoned its confrontationist policy.

For the most part, SAS effort in Borneo took the form of insertion of four-man patrols into the jungle, where they "lived off the land", often for weeks at a time. The main task of these patrols was to gather intelligence about hostile forces and carry out a "hearts and minds" programme to secure the friendship of the natives. (Numerous SAS troopers, having taken part in the Malayan Emergency of 1948–1960, spoke Malay, the lingua franca of the Borneo tribes.) The standard patrol always included a signaller and a medic, while movement through the jungle followed a set procedure: the patrol would be led by a scout, with the commander, medic and signaller following behind at set intervals. The last man usually carried a Bren or 7.62 GPMG, the others SLRs, M16 rifles or, the choice of many, the American Armalite AR-16.

As the war in Borneo wore on, the role of the SAS began to be modified, not least because Indonesia began committing properly organized units of its army to the frontier war. By early 1964 the SAS was not only detecting Indonesian incursions but guiding "killer groups" of infantry across the border into Kalimintan to attack insurgents on their home soil. And, increasingly, the Regiment's own recces ended in engagement with the enemy. These offensive forays, codenamed "Claret" operations, were ultra secret because any trace of British presence on Indonesian soil would have been intensely embarrassing to the British government, and would have led to international accusations that Britain was escalating the Borneo conflict.

The codename Claret was apposite; much red liquid was spilled in these ops. Like Malaya, the jungle-fighting in Borneo was split-second and close-up. A report in *Mars and Minerva* gave a flavour of the combat:

On a recent February morning [1965] a small SAS patrol was moving down from a ridge on a jungle track towards an old Indonesian Border Terrorist camp. This camp had been found the day before and appeared as though it had not been used for some six months. As the leading scout, Trooper Thompson ducked under some bamboo across the track – there was a lot of it in the area – a movement attracted his attention. He looked up and saw an Indonesian soldier six yards away to his right, just as the latter fired a burst at him. Several other enemy opened fire simultaneously. Thompson was hit in the left thigh, the bone being shattered, and was knocked off the track to the left. He landed in a clump of bamboo two yards away from another Indonesian soldier lying concealed there. As the latter fumbled for his rifle, Thompson picked up his own, which he had dropped as he fell, and shot him. The second man in the patrol, the commander, Sergeant Lillico, was also hit by the initial bursts and had collapsed on the track, unable to use his legs. He was still able to use his rifle, however, and this he did, returning the fire. The remainder of the patrol had meanwhile taken cover.

Thompson, unable to walk, hopped back to where Sergeant Lillico was sitting and joined in the firefight. As he had seen Thompson on his feet, Sergeant Lillico was under the misapprehension that he could walk and therefore sent him back up the track to bring the rest of the patrol forward and continued to fire at sounds of enemy movement.

As Thompson was unable to get to his feet he dragged himself along by his hands and, on arriving at the top of the ridge, fired several bursts in the direction of the IBT camp. Whether the enemy thought that this fire came from reinforcements moving into the area is not known, but about this time, some ten minutes after the initial contact, they apparently withdrew. During the remainder of the day Thompson continued to drag himself towards where he expected to find the rest of the patrol. He had applied a tourniquet to his thigh, which he released from time to time, taken morphia, and bandaged his wound as best he could with a shell dressing.

After sounds of enemy movement had died down, Sergeant Lillico pulled himself into the cover of a clump of bamboo, took morphia, bandaged his wound, and passed out until mid-afternoon. He awoke to hear the sound of a helicopter overhead. Realizing that it would never find him amongst the bamboo, he decided, in the morning, to drag himself to the top of the ridge which was covered in low scrub. The balance of the patrol had decided that the best course of action was to move to the nearest infantry post, close by, and lead back a stronger party to search the area. This they did, starting back towards the scene of the contact late that same day.

The following morning Thompson continued on his way and by evening had covered 1,000 yards, about half the total distance he had to cover. However, soon after he had stopped for the night, a short while before last light, he heard the search party and was found about 1800 hours. An attempt was made to winch him out by helicopter but this failed due to the height of the trees. The next day, therefore, he was carried to a larger clearing nearby and was successfully evacuated at 0930, 48 hours after the contact. Meanwhile, Sergeant Lillico had dragged himself to the ridge as he had planned – a distance of 400 yards – and on arriving there at 1500 hours, had fired some signal shots to attract the attention of the search party which he expected to be looking for him. These were immediately answered by three bursts of automatic fire some few hundred yards distant.

Not by the search party, however, which at that time was too far away to have heard him firing. He therefore hid in the scrub as best he could and was able both to hear and see the enemy looking for him. One man climbed a tree about forty yards away and remained there for about half an hour in full view as he looked around and about.

While this was going on, he heard a helicopter close by, but because of the enemy's nearness and obvious risk to the aircraft, he decided to make no use of the means at his disposal to attract it towards him. Not until the observer climbed down from his tree was he able to drag himself further away from the enemy and out into the scrub. The helicopter, continuing its search operation, returned in the early evening. This time he signalled to it and without delay it flew over, lowered the winch and lifted him out. In all, a rescue operation reflecting great credit on both RAF and Infantry, but most of all on Sergeant Lillico and Trooper Thompson for their courage and determination not to give in.

For this action Lillico was awarded the Military Medal and Thompson a Mention in Dispatches.

Britain was certainly tightening the vice on the Indonesian guerrillas. In early 1965 the new Commander of British Forces in Borneo, Major General George Lea, decided that the Claret ops should be stepped up. One objective chosen was the Koemba River, which was believed to be one of the enemy's major supply routes. There had been no fewer than six previous attempts by SAS patrols to reach the Koemba, but all had failed to penetrate the dense natural swamps which lay along the river. Nonetheless, a four-man patrol from D Squadron, led by Sergeant Don "Lofty" Large, was ordered to investigate traffic on the Koemba near the town of Poeri. The betting in the "the Haunted House" (SAS squadron HQ) was that Large's patrol, like the others, would become bogged down and fail; Large, however, after poring over all the maps and aerial photos he could find, found what seemed to be a spur of high ground running south from the border. With luck the spur would run all the way to the Koemba. The primary task of the patrol was to "river watch", gather information on riparian traffic. After a suitable interval it was to disrupt the traffic.

Despite Large's optimism, the patrol's departure on 10 May was marred by what seemed a bad omen. Following the advice of the informal Regimental motto "check, then check again", the patrol members had spent many hours working on their weapons before handing them over to the armoury for safe-keeping on the night before leaving for the missions. The next day, on the way to the airfield from which they were to fly to Lundu, one of the patrol, Trooper Pete Scholey, realized that he had been given the wrong SLR rifle. As his life might depend on his weapon, he was bitterly unhappy. Even a thorough strip down and check of the weapon by the rest of the patrol failed to convince him that it was working perfectly.

After arriving at Lundu, the patrol was whisked to a waiting chopper and dropped that same afternoon at a "hot" landing position just on the border, from where they set off on a bearing west of their intended course to confuse any "Indos" who might discover their tracks. On the second day out the patrol ran into trouble. Large, hearing a faint noise, scouted ahead and found an Indonesian unit of around platoon strength directly in their path. The SAS patrol was forced to take a detour through thick jungle, without making a noise or leaving a track, an exercise that tested their skills in jungle movement to the limit.

Things went from bad to worse. On the third day, after successfully crossing trails used by the Indonesians to intercept Claret operations, the patrol made for the spur Large hoped would lead to the bank of the river. To the team's dismay all they encountered was dense swamp, tangled with roots and screened with walls of hanging moss and vines. A particular hazard was a carpet of huge leaves on the surface of the water, which crackled loudly when stepped on. Each time the patrol probed for the ridge they found themselves deeper in the jungle quagmire. Progress was exhausting, the men losing body weight by the hour. Failure seemed certain. And yet there was one small note of encouragement; they could hear the sound of boat engines, so the river must be near. After breakfast on a piece of dry ground, the team decided to carry on, taking a route through the swamp parallel to the Koemba in the hope of finding a causeway through to the river. At first they made little headway – but then, to their amazement, they found Large's spur, rising fully 30 feet above the swamp. They negotiated the spur, which had a light covering of jungle, before coming to a rubber plantation. Cautiously skirting round the plantation they saw before them the muddy, fast-moving water of the Koemba. They had made it.

Without wasting a moment, Large set up an observation post (OP), choosing a place on the river bank bounded by a ditch and which provided cover in the form of a tree and some bushes. He also hoped that this would be the spot the enemy would least expect an ambush from and that Indonesian patrols would concentrate on the jungle nearby. To celebrate their arrival, the team disregarded all normal operational procedures, cooked curries, brewed tea, and smoked cigarettes. Large wanted their morale to be sky high when action came.

The days passed, with a steady amount of boat traffic – some of it military, as HQ had suspected – passing the patrol's OP, all of it reported back to base on the radio. When Large considered that the patrol had done enough observation, he sent off a signal requesting permission to carry out their secondary task, an ambush of a boat carrying troops or war cargo. The code he used was "Request 007 Licence". Unfortunately, the officer in charge of the operations centre was the only person in Britain not to have seen a James Bond film, and sent back a signal "Message not understood". Cursing the Ops Centre officer, Large sent another – and longer – coded message requesting permission, with the danger that this extended signal would be intercepted by the enemy and give a fix on the patrol's position. The patrol duly received permission, and fortunately the morse radio traffic was not spotted by the Indonesian army.

For the ambush, Large decided he would wait until a military boat had passed the bend in the river and then have troopers Pete Scholey, Paddy Milliken and Kevin Walsh rake it with fire from the rear, which should ignite the fuel tanks. Large himself would direct the fire and keep a watch out for enemy retaliation.

The team settled down to wait for a suitable target. Boats went past but Large ruled boat after boat as unsuitable, being too small, going in the wrong direction, or non-military. "What's he waiting for," thought Peter Scholey to himself, "the fucking Ark Royal?"

It started to rain. A lovely white barge appeared, which looked highly promising as a target – until they noticed there was a woman on the bridge. So it too sailed past unharmed.

Time was moving on. Then a large boat appeared. With soldiers in the stern. This was the one. Peter Scholey recalled what happened next:

> Lofty took out the two soldiers on the stern, the only ones visible because the drapes were down along the sides of the boat. The boat got arse-end and I opened up. Bang, bang, bang, click. Stoppage. I clicked it double click and then it fired again. It was the weapon I'd been honking about on the way in. It was lucky all four of us were lined up, firing at once, and that we hadn't been caught short in a head-on contact.
>
> The boat took sixty-nine rounds in only a few seconds. The odd nine came from me. Next moment there was a great flash, then a jet of flame and smoke and the boat began to list.
>
> Time to bug out.

Grabbing their packs, the patrol made a hasty getaway towards the spur. As they reached the top of a slope, they found their passage blocked by a snake. Large recalled:

> I immediately brought up my rifle sight, and it reared up four or five feet so that with the slope, we were eye to eye. It was a king cobra, ready to strike. I aimed at the centre of its hood but I didn't dare shoot. The Indos might have been just ahead.

The "Mexican stand-off" continued for several long seconds, before the snake dropped down and slithered off. Hurrying on, they reached a deployment track, crossing as one, not in single file, since the latter manoeuvre allows an ambusher to sight those following the leader. The patrol spent the night among some felled trees, the jungle silence disturbed by the sound of mortar fire but far down river. The Indos had obviously been fooled by an eastern loop the patrol had put in their route out.

The next day, as the patrol made for the landing zone (LZ) into which they had been inserted, Milliken began to suffer from fever. The LZ was proving too difficult to find in the featureless jungle terrain, so Large made a snap decision to call in a helicopter to hover over the LZ so they could get a definite fix on it. As the patrol neared the area of the LZ a helicopter arrived, but instead of remaining above the LZ it began to circle around it as though looking for the patrol. Large then switched on his SABRE (search and rescue beacon) and the chopper soon found them. A winch cable was lowered and the patrol was hoisted up and flown back to base. Sergeant Large's patrol had been a resounding success. To guard their now demonstrably vulnerable supply route, the Indonesians had to redeploy 700 front-line troops. Indeed, so many troops had to be diverted that the Indos never mounted a major attack across the border thereafter. The Indonesian generals began to lose faith in President Sukharno, and in March 1966 he was overthrown in a coup. Five months later Indonesia made peace with Malaya.

DOCUMENT: David Stirling: "The Philosophy of the SAS"

To understand the SAS role it is important first to grasp the essential difference between the function of Airborne Forces and Commandos on the one hand and that of the wartime Special Operations Executive on the other. Airborne Forces and Commandos provided advance elements in achieving tactical objectives and undertook tactically scaled raids, while the SOE was a *para*-military formation operating mainly out of uniform.

In contrast, the SAS has always been a strictly military unit, has always operated in uniform (except occasionally when seeking special information) and has functioned exclusively in the *strategic* field of operations. Such operations consisted mainly of: firstly, raids in depth behind the enemy lines, attacking HQ nerve centres, landing grounds, supply lines and so on; and, secondly, the mounting of sustained strategic offensive activity from secret bases within hostile territory and, if the opportunity existed, recruiting, training, arming and coordinating local guerrilla elements.

The SAS had to be capable of arriving in the target area by air and, therefore, by parachute; by sea, often by submarine and foldboat; or by land, by foot or jeep-borne penetration through or around the enemy lines. To ensure surprise the SAS usually arrived in the target area at night and this required a high degree of proficiency, in all the arrival methods adopted for any particular operation.

Strategic operations demand, for the achievement of success, a total exploitation of surprise and of guile – accordingly, a bedrock principle of the Regiment was its organization into modules or sub-units of four men. Each of the four men was trained to a high level of proficiency in the whole range of the SAS capability and, additionally, each man was trained to have at least one special expertise according to his particular aptitude. In carrying out an operation – often in the pitch-dark – each SAS man in each module was exercising his own individual perception and judgement at full strength. The SAS four-man module could be viable as an operational entity on its own, or be combined with as many other modules as an operation might require.

In the early days of the SAS, Middle East HQ sometimes tended to regard us as a baby Commando capable of "teasing" the enemy deep behind the lines during the quieter periods but available, in the circumstances of a major defensive or offensive confrontation, to undertake essentially tactical tasks immediately behind or on the flank of an aroused enemy. It took some further successful raids to persuade HQ to acknowledge that our role should remain an exclusively strategic one.

In today's SAS the importance of good security is thoroughly instilled into every man. Certain delicate operational roles require the Secret Service to invest in the SAS Command highly classified intelligence necessary for the effective planning of these operations and, just as importantly, for special training. For such intelligence to be entrusted to the SAS, its security disciplines have to be beyond reproach.

As the SAS was operating at a distance of up to 1,000 miles from Army HQ, an exceptionally efficient wireless communication was essential. Frequently we would require interpretation of air photographs of target areas, taken while an SAS unit was already deep in the desert on its way to attack them. An effective communication system became even more important to the SAS in Europe. (Their own dedicated and special communications are still an essential feature of SAS operations.)

Recruitment was a problem, as we had to depend on volunteer recruitment from existing Army units. Not unnaturally, Commanding Officers were reluctant to see their most enterprising individuals transfer to the SAS, but eventually Middle East HQ gave us firm backing and we were usually able to recruit a few volunteers from each of the formations which had undergone general military and desert training. We always aimed to give each new recruit a very testing preliminary course before he was finally accepted for the SAS. Today the SAS is even more ruthless in its recruitment procedures.

Once selected, our training programme for a man was an exhaustive one and was designed to give him thorough self-confidence and, just as importantly, equal confidence in his fellow soldiers' capacity to outclass and outwit the enemy by use of SAS operational techniques.

We kept a careful track record of each man and capitalized whenever possible on the special aptitude he might display in various skills such as advanced sabotage technique, mechanics, enemy weaponry, night-time navigation and medical knowledge, etc. This register of each man's special skills was vital to make sure that each of our modules of four men was a well-balanced entity. Historical precedents, demonstrating how vital this concept could be to the winning of wars, were ignored and we, therefore, had to start again nearly from scratch. Luckily, the British, for one, now acknowledge the validity of the strategic raid, hence the continuing existence of the SAS regiment. The SAS today fully recognizes its obligation to exploit new ideas and new developments in equipment and, generally, to keep a wide open mind to innovation and invention.

From the start the SAS regiment has had some firmly held tenets from which we must never depart. They are:

1. The unrelenting pursuit of excellence;

2. Maintaining the highest standards of discipline in all aspects of the daily life of the SAS soldier, from the occasional precision drilling on the parade ground even to his personal turnout on leave. We always reckoned that a high standard of self-discipline in each soldier was the only effective foundation for Regimental discipline. Commitment to the SAS pursuit of excellence becomes a sham if any *single one* of the disciplinary standards is allowed to slip;

3. The SAS brooks no sense of class and, particularly, not among the wives. This might sound a bit portentous but it epitomizes the SAS philosophy. The traditional idea of a crack regiment was one officered by the aristocracy and, indeed, these regiments deservedly won great renown for their dependability and their gallantry in wartime and for their parade-ground panache in peacetime. In the SAS we share with the Brigade of Guards a deep respect for quality, but we have an entirely different outlook. We believe, as did the ancient Greeks who originated the word "aristocracy", that every man with the right attitude and talents, regardless of birth and riches, has a capacity in his own lifetime of reaching that status in its true sense; in fact in our SAS context an individual soldier might prefer to go on serving as an NCO rather than have to leave the Regiment in order to obtain an officer's commission. All ranks in the SAS are of "one company" in which a sense of class is both alien and ludicrous. A visit to the sergeants' mess at SAS HQ in Hereford vividly conveys what I mean;

4. Humility and humour: both these virtues are indispensable in the everyday life of officers and men – particularly so in the case of the SAS which is often regarded as an elite regiment. Without frequent recourse to humour and humility, our special status could cause resentment in other units of the British Army and an unbecoming conceit and big-headedness in our own soldiers.

RED DAWN

Task Force 20/Task Force 121, Iraq, 2003

"Ladies and gentlemen, we got him!" So announced L. Paul Bremer III, head of the Coalition Provisional Authority in Iraq, that Saddam Hussein, the nation's erstwhile dictator, had been captured by US forces. The dictator who had once enjoyed opulence and omnipotence was found scared and skulking in a spider hole near a farmhouse in Ad-Dawr at approximately 8.30 p.m. on 13 December 2003.

But Bremer's use of "we" was generous, if not actually a blind. The unit that found and arrested Saddam was the highly secretive Task Force 20, whose existence Washington rarely even confirmed. For anyone possessed of the belief that special forces operations are all macho daring do, the work of Task Force 20 is a surprise. The unit was as reliant on the PC as it was on the HK416.

The events that ended with Saddam's capture outside of Tikrit – his home town – began 19 March 2003, when the US led a "coalition of the willing" offensive against Saddam's Ba'athist regime. Among the bomb targets on that day was Saddam's palace in Baghdad. From then onwards Saddam was not seen for 254 days.

When Coalition forces entered Baghdad some days later, they began the systematic dismantling of Saddam's regime. Chief among the Coalition goals was the capture of leading members of the Ba'ath regime, who became the Coalition's most Highly Valued Targets (HVTs). Saddam himself was Number One. His sons Uday and Qusay were HVTs Numbers Two and Three. The "most wanted targets" were depicted on a deck of playing cards, with Saddam Hussein the Ace of Spades. So important was the capture of Saddam and his sons that the United States Department of Defense set up a special operations group to hunt for them: Task Force 20. Based at Baghdad International Airport, Task Force 20 comprised elements from Delta Force, US Navy DEVGRU, US Navy SEAL Team Three, and the 75th Ranger Regiment. The Force was approximately 1,500 strong.

At the end of June, an Iraqi building contractor told the 101st Airborne Division in Mosul that Saddam's sons Uday and Qusay were holed up in one of his houses in the city's Falah district. With a $15 million bounty on the heads of HVTs One, Two and Three, such "tip-offs" were running at a dozen a day. So for three weeks Uday and Qusay remained in the house untroubled, with their feet up.

Finally the information was relayed to Task Force (TF) 20, who investigated and decided that the intel was "hot". On 22 July a TF 20 assault team was assembled and a cordon placed around the building by the 2nd Brigade of the 101st. An interpreter with a bullhorn shouted out to the two men to surrender. Their reply was a barrage of machine-gun fire. Using C-4 explosives, TF 20 operators stormed through the iron front gate into the walled compound. From there, some operators began clearing the first floor, while others climbed the back stairs. As TF 20's assault team began working its way into the building it came under fire from positions behind reinforced concrete on the first and second floors. They retired outside into the street where grenades were dropped on them, injuring three special forces operators and one of the paratroopers.

An almighty firefight started up, with the 2nd Brigade pouring in covering fire from vehicle-mounted fifty-calibre machine guns as TF 20 again tried to penetrate the building. However, return fire from the building kept them at bay. The TF operators discovered that the defenders had a strong position at the head of the stairs, making any internal assault calamitous.

Colonel Joe Anderson, the CO of 2nd Brigade, decided that heavy weapons were called for, and ordered a strike on the building by Kiowa Warrior helicopters, which fired four 2.75 inch rockets at the target. While these missed, the bullets from the choppers' belt-fed .50 cal machine guns did not and shot up the building.

Again, TF 20 attempted to assault the building, and again it was repelled by small arms fire. At this, Colonel Anderson decided on his own mini-me version of "shock and awe", and ordered that Tube-launched Optically-tracked Wire-guided (TOW) missiles be fired at the house. Eighteen of them. Colonel Anderson later declared that his goal was "a combination of shocking them if they were still alive and damaging the building structurally so that it was unfeasible to fight in".

On finally entering the building, the operators from TF 20 found four bodies – three men and a fourteen-year-old boy. Two of the men were identified by their DNA and dental records as Uday and Qusay. The boy was Qusay's son.

While the killing of Uday and Qusay Hussein demonstrated America's resolve in Iraq and removed two key figures around which insurgents might rally, it also destroyed a crucial lead to Number One HVT. The dead bodies of Uday and Qusay could hardly be interrogated as to their father's whereabouts.

The trail seemed to go cold. In the back rooms of Intelligence units, however, people were starting to have bright ideas. Hitherto, the main mindset was fixed on searching for Saddam and the other leading Ba'athists around the capital, Baghdad. Yet the Ba'ath regime had been a modern "Arab Socialist" crust on an old tribal society. Therefore the best way of getting to Saddam was to piece together the network of tribal loyalties in the Tikrit area.

Saddam's birthplace was in the village of Owja near the town of Tikrit, beside the Tigris, north-west of Baghdad. The area around Tikrit was where Saddam had his extended family, and where his tribe was based. Such was the Tikriti domination of Iraq that Saddam abolished the use of surnames to conceal the fact that so many of his key supporters bore the same surname – al-Tikriti – as did Saddam himself. He had hidden around Tikrit once before, in 1959, when on the run. Perhaps he had gone to ground there again? In which case, the focus of the piecing together of the tribal network should be Tikrit.

The US 4th Infantry Division, commanded by Colonel Hickey, took over the area around Tikrit, and almost immediately the Intelligence officer (S-2) of the 1st Brigade's Combat Team, Major Stan Murphy, begin developing an extended link diagram of the network of tribal figures who held any kind of position under Saddam, especially the men and boys who were his "enablers" – the yes men and the errand boys. Major Murphy's intel was fed to Task Force 20, which was renamed in July Task Force 121. "Hits" on suspected insurgents gradually brought more and more vital information. A raid on the farm of one of Saddam's bodyguards near Tikrit turned up jewellery worth $2 million belonging to Saddam's wife, Sajida Khairallah Telfah, and $8 million in US currency secreted away in two fireproof bank boxes. Better still, First Lieutenant Chris Morris's 1-22 platoon found the Saddam family photograph album.

Captain Mark Stouffer's A Company 1-22 captured one of Saddam's bodyguards. A joint Task Force 121–1st Brigade raid on 16 June captured Abid Hamid al-Tikriti (HVT Four). Between July and December 2003 Task Force 121 made twelve unsuccessful raids to capture Saddam, together with 600 other operations against targets on the linked diagram. More than 300 interrogations were conducted. Again and again, the intel led to five extended families based in Tikrit.

An important break came on 1 December, when a former driver divulged the name of Muhamed Ibrahim Omar al-Musslit. Ibrahim was Saddam's right-hand man, known to Task Force 121 as "the Source" or "the Fatman". Ibrahim was a regular face in the Saddam family photo album. Over the next two weeks nearly forty members of Ibrahim's family were interrogated in an attempt to track him down.

The turning point moment came on 12 December 2003. During a raid on a house in Baghdad that functioned as an insurgency HQ, the Fatman was picked up and interrogated by Staff Sergeant Eric Maddox. By now it was 5 a.m. on 13 December, and Maddox was scheduled to leave Iraq at 8 a.m. on a C-17 for Doha. Just when Maddox was about to abandon hope, Ibrahim grudgingly gave up a location where Saddam *might* be found. On this intel, a 600-strong raiding force was assembled from 1st Brigade, Fourth Infantry Division. The raiding force, led by

Colonel James Hickey, would isolate and secure the area. After this, Task Force 121 would go in and get Saddam.

At precisely 8 p.m. on 13 December two sites, "Wolverine 1" and "Wolverine 2", outside the town of Ad-Dawr, were searched and cleared within minutes. There was no trace of Saddam. The searchers from Task Force 121 then moved in on a mud hut in a palm grove just to the north of Wolverine 1. Lieutenant-Colonel Steve Russell was the Commanding Officer of the 1st Battalion, 22nd Infantry of the 1st Brigade. He takes up the story:

> Through their night-vision goggles and thermal sights, soldiers of the 4th ID could see Special Operators moving soundlessly through the dark night to the target. Occasionally, the red beams of laser-aiming lights would reflect off trees and leaves, but it was deathly silent, save for the distant hum of OH-58 Little Birds and other Special Operations aircraft waiting for extraction, reinforcement, or attack. From his position, Saffeels could hear noises in the darkness. He and his fellow soldiers grew "a little jumpy", waiting for Saddam's forces. For Bocanegra the scene and all the activity became more intense. The assault force started clearing through the palm groves and came upon a little mud-hut structure with a courtyard. In that courtyard they heard a noise.

At 2010, with Hickey's troops sealing off the area, Special Operations forces burst into the hut, a simple construction behind a fence of dried palm leaves. It had been an orange picker's hut with one room and an open kitchen. They immediately seized one man trying to escape and another man in the hut. As it turned out, one was Saddam's cook; the other was the cook's brother and owner of the property.

Inside, they found that the hut consisted of one room with two beds and a refrigerator containing a can of lemonade, a packet of hot dogs, a can of "Happy Brand" tuna, an opened box of Belgian chocolates, and a tube of ointment. A poster of Noah's Ark hung on the mud-brick wall. There were also two AK-47 assault rifles, various packages of new clothes, and a green footlocker containing $750,000 in American hundred-dollar bills. More telling: an orange-and-white

Toyota Corolla taxi was parked outside. Rumors that Saddam had hidden in taxis and even masqueraded as a taxi driver appeared to be true.

Saddam was nowhere to be seen. It looked like yet another dry hole when, suddenly, one of the detainees broke away from the Special Operators and ran, telling them Saddam was hiding elsewhere and he would lead them to him. His sudden desire to cooperate and zeal to get them out of there further convinced the operators they were close.

At the command vehicle, CW2 Gray stood next to Colonel Hickey, listening to the radio reports from the Special Operation forces. Those two individuals were exactly who the source stated would be at the farm. Things were going well.

Reports continued to come in that Special Operations forces were still searching the area but had not found the tunnels that the source had said Saddam would be hiding in. Hickey calmly told them to take their time. Task Force Raider owned that portion of Iraq. He'd hold the cordon all night if necessary.

Another ten minutes went by. Still nothing.

Outside the hut, the two dozen or so Special Operators were preparing to move off and expand their search. Something caught an operator's attention in the darkness of the moonless night, through the unearthly glow of his night vision goggles. The ground just didn't look quite right. The sensation of an odd landscape was nothing unusual under the glow of a night vision device, but it just didn't feel right, either.

The closer the operator looked, the more it appeared to be out of place. The bricks and dirt were spread about too uniformly, as if someone were trying to conceal something. A thread of fabric protruded just slightly under the dirt.

Strange.

At 2030 hours, the operators brushed away the debris, revealing a Styrofoam plug. True to his training, one of the Special Operators pulled the pin on a hand grenade while his colleagues prepared to remove the plug so he could drop it in. The remaining twenty or so soldiers prepared to fire their weapons, if engaged. The plug revealed a hole; the hole revealed a ratty-looking bearded man. The man raised his hands and announced: "I am Saddam Hussein. I am the President of Iraq, and I am willing to negotiate."

The Task Force 121 commando covering the hole calmly replied: "President Bush sends his regards."

Hickey's radio broke the silence as the Special Operator reported simply, "Sir, we may have the jackpot."

Hickey waited breathlessly.

Back on the objective, several Special Operators yanked the dishevelled, disoriented man to the surface, unavoidably scratching his head in the tight confines of the hole.

The operators quickly removed the 9mm pistol from his belt and checked him for the markings and other features that would preliminarily confirm they had their man. They began to prepare him for transportation with the standard, empty sandbag over his head and flex-cuffs on his hands. As they attempted to secure him, Saddam resisted – trying to shrug off the operators, acting belligerent, and even spitting in one soldier's face. In return, he was treated "just like any other prisoner", and forcefully subdued to the ground, where several operators held him down while others trussed him up.

At Hickey's command vehicle, everyone waited in painful silence. The word finally came. Although it was only minutes behind the first call, it had seemed like weeks. "Sir, we've got him. Jackpot." Hickey replied simply and unemotionally, "That's great."

Within minutes Saddam was strapped into a Special Operations Little Bird and spirited out of the immediate area. There was a quick stop at FOB Iron Horse for a transload onto a larger Black Hawk helicopter for the flight to the Baghdad Airport prison that once boasted his name. As he moved through FOB Iron Horse, Saddam passed through a cordon of Special Operations forces. It was the only time they would see their prize, and the only recognition of their accomplishment these shadow warriors would ever receive. Hickey was not so lucky. It happened so fast that by the time Hickey's command vehicle arrived, Saddam was gone.

In the Raider TOC (Tactical Operations Center), Murphy had heard the objectives were clear with only two detainees and felt the letdown of failure. As he'd feared, they'd waited too long and came away empty-handed once again. He got up and was about to head over to the phone bank to call home when a single codeword broke the building silence: "Jackpot."

Following his capture Saddam was taken to the American base Camp Cropper near Baghdad. On 30 June 2004 Saddam was handed over to the interim Iraqi government to stand trial for crimes against humanity. The trial found Saddam Hussein guilty, and he was sentenced to death. Although the verdict and sentencing were both appealed, they were affirmed by Iraq's Supreme Court of Appeals. On 30 December 2006, Saddam was hanged.

WRATH OF GOD

Sayeret Matkal, Lebanon, 1973

Beirut, Lebanon, the night of 9 April 1973. A few miles off the coast, on a mill-pond sea, the men in the Zodiac rubber dinghies make their way to the brightly lit shore. The city has not yet fallen to anarchy, and is a sophisticated resort of grand hotels, elegant boulevards and bikini-wearing women.

Some of the men in the boats have taken advantage of Beirut's Western liberalism; they are disguised as girls, who will accompany their "lovers" in an arm-in-arm promenade. Their mission is anything but romantic. The men in the boats are Israeli commandos, some of them from the country's ultra-secret special-ops outfit, Sayeret Matkal, the "General Staff Reconnaissance Unit". The men from the Unit have come to kill.

On reaching the beach, the soldiers ditch their dinghies and cross to where agents from Mossad, the Israeli intelligence service, are waiting for them in rented Mercedes cars. The commandos split up into three groups; aside from the Sayeret Matkal, there are commandos from Shayetet 13 and Sayeret Tzanhanim who are to take on secondary targets, the HQ of Palestinian skyjacker-in-chief, George Habash, and a PLO arms factory.

The Sayeret Matkal leader, thirty-one-year-old Ehud Barak, dressed in a brunette wig and red lipstick, watches out of the window as his Mossad driver steers the Mercedes through the maze of streets. Like the other commandos, Barak, a future prime minister of Israel, knows the route off by heart. They are getting closer to the target, a building on the outskirts, home of two of the leaders of Black September, the splinter group of the PLO that, a few months earlier at the 1972 Olympic Games in Munich, had kidnapped and murdered eleven members of the Israeli Olympic team.

The terrorists are convinced that the Israelis cannot bear the spilling of their own blood, and will succumb to Palestinian demands rather than fight. The PLO leader Yasser Arafat says that the Israelis "show no courage. They are too afraid of dying." Arafat is badly, badly mistaken. Golda Meir, Israel's Babushka-like prime minister, is a woman of the Old Testament. An eye for an eye (and then some more body parts) is Meir's philosophy. In the aftermath of Munich, she orders the military to hunt down the Black September terrorists in the Operation Wrath of God.

Sayeret Matkal gets the plum role. Formed in 1957, the Unit consists of around 200 commandos, and is free of the dead hand of accountants and bureaucrats. It believes in leadership, yet vaunts debate, with missions picked over and planned to the nth. Muki Betser, a legendary Unit commando, explains:

> The hierarchy in The Unit is very different from anywhere else in the army. It's friendlier, more intimate and thus more candid and open, and this unique atmosphere is best seen during the planning phase of an operation. Rank doesn't count in planning a mission. All that matters is inventiveness and originality. Everyone throws out ideas, in a round-table brainstorming session. Nothing is rejected out of hand, as the best ideas are set aside while more are raised. Eventually, the best idea stands out.

Sayeret Matkal believes in unyielding resistance, yet practises the striking cunning of a cobra. Since Grandma Golda ordered God's Wrath to be brought down on the heads of Black September, the Unit has been involved in the blowing up of fourteen Lebanese planes on the runway at the international airport in Beirut; in Tunisia it took a hand in the death of Abu Jihad, a PLO military leader; in southern Lebanon, it helped capture a bunch of Syrian officers who were then traded for Israeli pilots held in Damascus.

Then the Unit was given intelligence that three Black September terrorists had been tracked by Mossad, the spy service, to Beirut. Mossad had also come up with blueprints of the buildings in the fashionable neighbourhood of Verdun, West Beirut, where the men lived. The targets were Muhammad Youssef Al-Najjar (Abu Youssef), Kamal Adwan and Kamal Nass. For days, the commandos of Sayeret Matkal practised for the operation in apartment buildings in North Tel Aviv, similar in construction to those they would be assaulting in Beirut. They also practised walking around in disguise as lovers. Shortly before the operation, Muki Betser, who was a Unit leader on the mission, told his team:

> "We're going on a very unusual operation . . . A civilian target in the heart of a city. The targets will have guards. They also might be armed, themselves. Civilians live all around them and we have to be extremely careful not to harm them. We have a lot of good intelligence. But the best intelligence we have is that these are people with blood on their hands." I paused to let my words sink in. "We are taking a relatively great risk. But we are convinced," I said, knowing that I spoke for all the officers who planned the raid, "that the level of risk is logical and reasonable. If we do it right, we can get away without any harm. But anything can happen. That's true. If it does, we need to stay cool, take heart and remain confident that we know how to manage." I looked around at them. Only a couple of years younger than myself, I felt confident in all of them, and told them so. "And because I have that confidence, I am convinced we will succeed."

At the last moment, Yoni Netanyahu, the brother of future Prime Minister Benjamin Netanyahu (and himself a sometime Sayeret Matkal command), joined Muki Betser's team. Netanyahu would continue to be involved in secret operations until he was killed during the Israeli raid and rescue of Jewish hostages at Entebbe in 1975.

The hit on the Black September leaders in Beirut was code-named "Operation Spring of Youth".

On nearing the target apartment blocks, the Mossad drivers drop the assassination teams off, so they walk the last couple of hundred metres disguised as lovers as planned. They walk past a

Lebanese policeman, who gives them not a second glance. On reaching the buildings the Sayeret Matkal commandos split into three teams; Ehud Barak and Amiram Levine (dressed as a blonde) stand on guard on the street, two girls waiting for their boyfriends. Meanwhile, the kill teams climb the stairs at a half-run and place explosives in the front of each apartment door.

A pause. And then on the signal, each team sets off its charge. The blasts echo around the apartments. The teams are inside the target apartments while the smoke is still swirling. Muki Betser, the rangy dark-haired team leader, runs into his target apartment, knowing exactly where to go thanks to his close study of the blue-prints. He, like the others, is armed with a mini-Uzi.

I burst in with Tzvika, instinctively taking the left-hand turn into the main corridor of the apartment, running down the hall I knew so well from my drills. Four strides and I reached my target's office. Half a dozen empty chairs faced the desk. Behind it, filing cabinets reminded me that military intelligence wanted any piece of paper we found. To my right, said the architectural plans I memorized, was the master bedroom door. I swung in that direction, just as the door flew open. The face I knew from three weeks of carrying his picture in my shirt pocket looked at me as I raised my gun. He slammed the door. Bursts from my Uzi and Tzvika's stitched the bedroom door. I rushed forward and kicked through the remains of the door.

The man inside was dead.

The other two assassination teams are similarly effective. Hearing shooting outside, Betser and Tzvika sprint back down the echoey apartment block stairs. Muki Betser:

Out the front door, I ducked into the shadow of a tree, scanning the intersection just as a burning Lebanese police Land Rover rolled through the intersection. Straight ahead, Amiram Levine in a blonde wig looked like a crazed dancer in the middle of the intersection, his tiny powerful body swinging his Uzi back and forth from target to target. To my right,

Ehud (Barak) stood in the middle of the intersection, doing the same. I added my own fire at the Land Rover, giving Amiram cover for him to run toward me. The Land Rover crashed to a halt against a building. But a second vehicle, a jeep full of reinforcements, came screeching into the box of fire we created at the intersection.

They take out this Land Rover too. There are explosions in the distance, which they assume are Amnon Shahak's paratrooper unit attacking the HQ of George Habash, the PLO's mastermind of skyjacking. The assassinations by Sayeret Matkal are just a facet of Israeli's wrath this night. Grandma Meir will have an eye, a tooth – a whole head – in revenge for Munich.

The Mossad cars come screeching to a halt outside the buildings. The Sayeret Matkal units, mission completed, jump into the cars – only two minutes have passed since they hit their targets. Barak checks with the other Sayeret Matkal units; no one is dead, although one commando is wounded. Then according to Betser:

Ehud cut off radio contact and we rushed in a crazy race down the hills of Beirut. The Mossad drivers knew the city and they knew the big American cars well enough to make them slip and slide around the corners as we raced through the city. No whooping and shouting broke out inside the getaway car. Each man sat alone with his thoughts, alert for enemy forces taking chase.

Once outside of the danger zone, the Mossad drivers slow down. They do not want to draw attention to themselves. As they are about to turn onto the beach road, they see a Lebanese Army troop carrier patrolling the shoreline. It fails to spot the beached Zodiacs.

Pushing the boats out to sea, Barak checks the luminous dial on his watch. The operation has taken a little longer than expected – thirty minutes instead of the anticipated twenty.

The sea is calm. Behind them in Beirut, three senior PLO terrorists are dead, and Habash's six-storey HQ is a pile of rubble. The arms manufactory has also been blown apart. Israeli losses are small, two men from the IDF killed in the attack on Habash's HQ which turned in a firefight that lit up the darkness. As many as 100 Palestinian militants have perished in all. The wrath of Israel has been terrible.

The next morning, a Beirut newspaper reported an attack by "beautiful she-devils, a blonde and a brunette, who fought off the police and the army like dervishes with machine guns."

BAY OF PIGS

CIA/Brigada 2506, Cuba, 1961

When the men of Brigada 2506 left the coast of Florida on the night of 16 April 1961, they believed they were sailing to liberate their homeland from the grip of Castro's Communism. Instead, they sailed into history as the men who committed the most ignominious covert operation of all time. The Bay of Pigs Landings.

Three years before, the US-backed Cuban dictator Fulgencio Batista y Zaldivar had failed to keep power when a guerrilla army led by former New York Yankee's pitching hopeful turned revolutionary, Fidel Castro, moved out of the Sierra Maestra mountains into Havana.

Once in power, Castro, under the prompting of his left-hand-man, Ernesto "Che" Guevara, turned the Cuban Revolution redder and redder. By 17 March 1960 the CIA had a plan prepared entitled, "A Program of Covert Action Against the Castro Regime". President Eisenhower gave it his stamp of approval.

The plan originally called for a daylight assault on the southern coastal city of Trinidad, near the Escambray Mountains. When President John F Kennedy entered the White House, the plan changed. Kennedy needed "plausible deniability" for America's role in the invasion, so the landing place was changed to Playa Girón. At night.

Playa Girón was also known as the Bay of Pigs. As the plan had it, after the Bay of Pigs had been seized, a provisional Cuban government under José Miró Cardona would be landed there. This provisional and thoroughly "stooge" government would request recognition and military support from the United States – meaning a full-scale invasion.

The initial invasion force was to be recruited and trained by the CIA from Cuban exiles in the US. Recruitment centres were openly established in Miami, and prospective volunteers could simply walk in off the street and join the CIA-funded unit, first known as "the Cuban Brigade". What was easy for exiles to join, was easy for Castro to monitor. From the outset, Castro spies followed the Brigade's activities.

Training was conducted at various facilities in Florida, Panama and Guatemala, where Camp JM Trax in the Sierre Madre was the Brigade's main infantry-training base. The country was both geographically close to Cuba and its government sympathetic to the CIA; it could hardly be otherwise, since it had been placed in power by the Agency in 1954. Not everyone in Guatemala, however, was so pro-Langley (CIA HQ); an army officer's revolt against the presence of the CIA/Cuban Brigade on Guatemalan soil had to be put down by the Brigade itself.

Slowly, the Cuban Brigade, whose numbers reached 2,500, came to resemble something like a military outfit. Under the eyes of advisers from the Green Berets as well as the CIA the insurgents trained in small arms weapons, communications and demolitions. Progress was helped by the presence of a significant number of former soldiers in the Brigade's ranks; equally, training was hampered by language difficulties. Few of the CIA advisers spoke Spanish. The Brigade's aircrew were trained by the Alabama National Guard detailed to Guatemala.

During a training exercise in the Guatemalan jungle, a Brigade soldier, Rodriguez Santana, fell to his death attempting to climb a ledge. In his honour his comrades re-named the Brigade "Brigada 2506", this being Santana's Brigade number.

The luckless invasion, known to the CIA as Operation Zapata, began with an air attack on 15 April 1961. Eight bombers left Nicaragua to bomb Cuban airfields; they missed most of their targets and left most of Castro's air force intact. Although the CIA had painted the obsolete B-26 bombers to look like Cuban aircraft, no one was fooled, and photographs of the planes on the world's media pointed the finger of suspicion directly at Washington, DC. Kennedy cancelled a second airstrike.

Just after midnight on 17 April 1961, the invasion began with two CIA Landing Craft Infantry, the *Blagar* and *Barbara J*, approaching the mosquito-infested beaches along the Bay of Pigs. Under their direction the five infantry battalions of the invasion force were landed at two beaches around 20 miles apart, beach "Blue" and beach "Red". The Brigade's 177-strong parachute battalion dropped at 7.30 a.m.; although some sticks lost all their kit on the descent, about 100 men took up positions on the road at San Blas which they would hold on to for two days.

A diversionary landing 30 miles east of Guantanamo by a group of 160 men failed to take place, leaving the Castro forces able to concentrate on one area of action.

On the beaches, the Brigade initially only encountered token resistance. However, Castro's airforce, the FAR, far from being destroyed, flew sortie after sortie over the Bay, strafing the troops and sinking the two escort ships. Realizing the seriousness of the situation, Castro took charge of the Cuban defence personally. Over the next twenty-four hours the Cuban dictator ordered 20,000 troops to advance towards the beaches. The FAR gained air superiority over the Brigade's limited air force. With the situation becoming increasingly grim, Kennedy allowed an "air-umbrella", consisting of six unmarked US Skyhawk fighter jets flying off USS *Essex* early on the morning of 19 April. These were to defend the Brigade's B-26 bombers; in the final Brigade air attack four of the five B-26s were flown by either members of the Alabama National Guard or aviators contracted by the CIA. Two of the bombers were shot down by FAR Sea Furies and T33s, the B-26s having arrived an hour after the air umbrella had departed.

After holding out for nearly two days, with no chance of resupply, the Brigade surrendered to the pro-Castro forces. Some 114 Brigade members had died in the action. The remainder managed to get away by sea due to overt action by US Navy ships, submarines and flying boats. Cuban armed forces suffered 176 killed.

The Brigade prisoners remained in captivity for 20 months, while the US negotiated a deal with Havana. Castro eventually settled for $53 million worth of medicines and baby food in return for the prisoners.

On Saturday, 29 December 1961, surviving Brigade members gathered for a ceremony in Miami's Orange Bowl, where the Brigade flag was handed over to President Kennedy. He replied, "I can assure you that this flag will be returned to this brigade in a free Havana."

Beneath the smiles and goodwill of that day lay a resentment amongst a minority of Brigade members towards Kennedy for calling off the air support over the landings. To add a note of conspiracy to the invasion saga, Bernard de Torres, the Brigade's intelligence chief, often crops up as suspected of involvement in JFK's assassination.

DOCUMENT: The Cuba Study Group: "The Taylor Report", 1961

On 22 April 1961, President Kennedy asked General Maxwell D. Taylor, Attorney General Robert F. Kennedy, Admiral Arleigh Burke and CIA Director Allen Dulles to form the Cuba Study Group, to report on the lessons to be learned from the abortive invasion. Two months later the Cuba Study Group reported to the President. The Group's "Eyes Only. Secret" report is now de-classified.

230. Letter From the Chairman of the Cuba Study Group (Taylor) to President Kennedy
Washington, June 13, 1961. SECRET

Dear Mr. President: By your letter of April 22, 1961, you charged me in association with Attorney General Robert Kennedy, Admiral Arleigh Burke and Director of Central Intelligence Allen Dulles to study our governmental practices and programs in the areas of military and paramilitary, guerrilla and anti-guerrilla activity which fell short of outright war with a view to strengthening our work in this area. You directed special attention to the lessons which can be learned from the recent events in Cuba.

We are now prepared to make our final report to you orally, supported by the following memoranda:

Memorandum No. 1 "Narrative of the Anti-Castro Operation Zapata"

Memorandum No. 2 "Immediate Causes of Failure of the Operation Zapata"

Memorandum No. 3 "Conclusions of the Cuban Study Group"

Memorandum No. 4 "Recommendations of the Cuban Study Group"

In your letter of April 22, you invited me to submit an individual report subject to the review and comment of my associates. As we have found no difficulty in reaching a unanimous view on all essential points under consideration, we are submitting this view as a jointly agreed study.

In closing, may I express our view of the great importance of a prompt implementation of our first recommendation to establish a Strategic Resources Group supported by a Cold War Indications Center which will allow our government readily to focus its resources on the objectives which you set in the so-called Cold War. We feel that we are losing today on many fronts and that the trend can be reversed only by a whole-hearted union of effort by all Executive departments and agencies of the Government under your guidance.

Sincerely yours,

Maxwell D. Taylor

231. Memorandum No. 1 From the Cuba Study Group to President Kennedy

Washington, June 13, 1961.

NARRATIVE OF THE ANTI-CASTRO
CUBAN OPERATION ZAPATA

[. . .]

6. At dawn on 15 April, the D−2 air strike took place against three Cuban air fields, a total of eight B-26s being employed for the purpose. Initial pilot reports indicated that 50% of Castro's offensive air was destroyed at Campo Libertad, 75%–80% aircraft destruction at San Antonio de Los Banos,

and that the destruction at Santiago included two B-26s, one DC-3, one Lodestar and one T-33 or Sea Fury. Subsequent photographic studies and interpretation have assessed a greatly reduced estimate of the damage, amounting to five aircraft definitely destroyed and an indeterminable number of other planes suffering some damage. The attacking force lost one aircraft and crew to antiaircraft fire.

[. . .]

37. At about mid-day on D–1, 16 April, the President formally approved the landing plan and the word was passed to all commanders and officials involved in the operation. The frame of mind at that moment of the senior officials responsible for the approval of this operation seems to have been about as follows. It offered what appeared to be a last chance to overthrow Castro by Cubans before the weapons and technicians acquired from the Communists and repressive internal measures would make the task too hard without overt U.S. intervention. It was recognized as marginal and risky, but the Cuban Brigade, if not used quickly, would become a political liability, whereas used in a landing it might achieve important success before Castro became too strong. Even if unable to hold the beachhead, something would have been accomplished as the Brigade could turn guerrilla and provide a strong reinforcement to the resistance movement in the island.

38. CIA authorities had developed an elaborate propaganda program (See Annex 19) to support the military action against Castro. This was based on the use of the clandestine radio SWAN, the programs of 11 CIA-controlled radio stations and extensive leaflet drops. The program was executed as planned, except for the D-day leaflet drops for which no means of delivery was available. The plan had been to drop the leaflets from B-26s and other aircraft involved in the support of the landing, but the military situation did not permit the diversion of effort. The content of the propaganda program was developed and approved within CIA.

39. There is no evidence of any effort at any higher level to guide and coordinate the over-all propaganda effort. In

particular, the United States Information Agency was left in the dark with regard to the operational plans. On 5 April, Mr. Edward R. Murrow, Director of the United States Information Agency, heard from a *New York Times* reporter that operations were under way for a landing in Cuba, backed and planned by the CIA. The reporter indicated that the *Times* had a very full story on the operation which, however, they did not intend to print but he did hope to persuade USIA to authorize briefings of the press in Miami following the landing.

40. Armed with this information, Mr. Murrow called on the Director of Central Intelligence who informed him that preparations were indeed under way, but did not give him details of the magnitude or the time of the landing which, indeed, had not been determined at that time. Under the terms of the interdepartmental coordination paper referred to in paragraph 31 above, the Department of State undertook to provide policy guidance beginning D−3 to the USIA in support of the plan, but this guidance was apparently not given. Hence, word of the landing received over the wire services on D-Day caught the USIA unprepared and without guidance.

41. In parallel with its propaganda program, the CIA had continued and accentuated activities directed at stimulating political unrest in Cuba and harassing the Castro government. These actions included such things as clandestine broadcasts in Havana utilizing dormant TV channels, the infiltration of small provocateur groups equipped with printing presses and radios, the development of additional agent and guerrilla assets within the island, and the penetration of pro-Castro organizations. [*3 lines of source text not declassified*]

42. With regard to agent, guerrilla, and dissident assets, the pre-invasion reports differed somewhat but suggested considerable strength. It had been estimated by the CIA that from 2500 to 3000 persons supported by 20,000 sympathizers were actively engaged in resistance in Cuba, and that some 25 per cent of the Cuban populace would actively support a well-organized, well-armed force which was

successful in establishing a stronghold on the island. At a CIA briefing on April 3, the view was expressed that the percentage of the Cuban population opposed to Castro at that time was much higher than the foregoing estimate, but that many would probably remain neutral until there was a strong indication of which side was winning.

43. At about 9:30 P.M. on 16 April, Mr. McGeorge Bundy, Special Assistant to the President, telephoned General C.P. Cabell of CIA to inform him that the dawn air strikes the following morning should not be launched until they could be conducted from a strip within the beachhead. Mr. Bundy indicated that any further consultation with regard to this matter should be with the Secretary of State.

44. General Cabell, accompanied by Mr. Bissell, went at once to Secretary Rusk's office, arriving there about 10:15 P.M. There they received a telephone call from Colonel Jack Hawkins who, having learned of the cancellation of the D-Day strikes, called to present his view of the gravity of the decision. General Cabell and Mr. Bissell then tried to persuade the Secretary of State to permit the dawn D-Day strikes. The Secretary indicated that there were policy considerations against air strikes before the beachhead airfield was in the hands of the landing force and completely operational, capable of supporting the raids. The two CIA representatives pointed out the risk of loss to the shipping if the Castro Air Force were not neutralized by the dawn strikes. They also stressed the difficulty which the B-26 airplanes would have in isolating the battlefield after the landing, as well as the heavier scale of air attack to which the disembarked forces would be exposed. The Secretary of State indicated subsequently that their presentation led him to feel that while the air strikes were indeed important, they were not vital. However, he offered them the privilege of telephoning the President in order to present their views to him. They saw no point in speaking personally to the President and so informed the Secretary of State. The order cancelling the D-Day strikes was dispatched to the departure field in Nicaragua, arriving when the pilots were in their cockpits ready for take-off. The

Joint Chiefs of Staff learned of the cancellation at varying
hours the following morning.

45. Realizing the seriousness of this cancellation, the CIA officials set about to try to offset the damage. The invasion force
was informed, warned of likely air attacks and the ships told to
expedite unloading and to withdraw from the beach by dawn. A
continuous cover of 2 B-26s over the beach was laid on. General
Cabell arranged with the JCS to alert the fleet to a possible
requirement for air cover and Early Warning destroyers. At
0430, he called on the Secretary of State at his home, reiterated
the need to protect the shipping and by telephone made the
request to the President. The request for air cover was disap-
proved but the Early Warning destroyers were authorized,
provided they remained at least 30 miles from Cuban territory.

II. The Battle for the Beachhead, D-Day to D+2
D-Day
Blue Beach

46. The ships in which the Cuban Expeditionary Force was
embarked reached the objective area generally on time in the
night of D−1 and the morning of D-Day. At Blue Beach the
Brigade Commander, José Perez San Roman, went ashore at
0115 and immediately commenced the unloading of troops
and supplies. The landing was discovered at once by local
militia, some firing occurred, and the alarm was transmitted
to troop and air headquarters throughout the island. In view
of the situation, it was decided to give up the planned trans-
shipment of the force earmarked to Green Beach and to put
this force ashore at Blue Beach.

47. Castro's forces, though tactically surprised, reacted with
speed and vigor. At dawn they began air attacks against the
shipping and the beaches. In spite of these attacks, all vehicles
and tanks at Blue Beach were unloaded from the LCUs by
0730, and all troops were ashore by 0825.

48. At 0930 an enemy Sea Fury hit and sank the freighter *Rio
Escondido*, which carried in it 10 days' supply of ammunition
for the Brigade and other valuable supplies. All crew members
were rescued and transferred to the *Blagar*.

49. In the face of continuous air attacks, at 10 o'clock [*less than 1 line of source text not declassified*] the contract skipper in charge of the shipping radioed CIA Headquarters that if jet air support were not immediately available, the ships would put out to sea. By this time, not only had the *Rio* been sunk at Blue Beach, but the *Houston* had been hit at Red Beach. CIA Headquarters approved the movement of the vessels to the south which began at once. The freighters *Atlantico* and *Caribe* preceded the two LCIs and three LCUs which followed the cargo ships at a slower speed imposed by the presence of the LCUs.

50. After landing, the troops ashore pushed out from the beach as planned. Parachutists of the First Battalion dropped at 0730, seized the important road center of San Blas 10 miles northeast of Blue Beach, and established outposts to the north and east to cover the routes of ingress into the beachhead. They were quickly reinforced by the Third Battalion and a heavy weapons (4.2 mortars) detachment. They made contact with Castro forces in the afternoon which pushed back their outpost situated to the east. Starting at about 1700 and intermittently thereafter, San Blas was under attack from forces coming down the road from the north.

51. Radio communications within Blue Beach were non-existent during the entire operation. In going ashore, the troops had been obliged to wade through fairly deep water with the result that most of the portable radios got wet and never functioned thereafter.

Red Beach

52. The Second Battalion at Red Beach ran into militia units almost immediately upon landing, but cleared them from the beach area. The landing of the Battalion was slowed down by motor trouble with the aluminum ships' boats which were the only landing craft available. Out of nine, only two boats were usable for the 20-minute run from the *Houston* to the beach. The Fifth Battalion which was to follow the Second never did get ashore, partly because of the boat troubles, partly because of lack of initiative on the part of the Battalion Commander.

Very few supplies were got ashore, other than those carried by the Second Battalion while debarking.

53. At daybreak, Red Beach was attacked by enemy aircraft, and at about 0630 the *Houston* was hit. Somewhat later, the ship went aground on the west shore of the Bahia de Cochinos about five miles from the landing beach. At that time it still had on board about 180 men of the Fifth Battalion who landed but never got into the fight at Red Beach. Later, many worked their way south to be picked up on the swampy keys by the U.S. Navy after the operation. In this air attack, the LCI *Barbara J* was also damaged by machine-gun fire which disabled two of its engines, and a near miss, which caused it to take water. The damage to the *Barbara J* was not reported to CIA Headquarters until the next day at about 1700.

54. After cleaning up the beach area, the troops of the Second Battalion pushed north about four miles but soon encountered militia forces which prevented them from reaching the southern exit of the road across the swamp which they were to block. Fighting went on astride the road throughout the day, enemy tanks appearing in mid-afternoon and enemy artillery becoming active at about 1800.

Air Action

55. The parachute drops made by 5 C-46s and one C-54 took place at 0730 on D-Day. Indications are that the drops were reasonably accurate but considerable ammunition was lost near San Blas. The parachutists north of Red Beach apparently landed in the presence of the enemy and were not heard from thereafter. A total of 172 parachutists took part in the drops.

56. B-26 aircraft rotated over the beachhead through D-Day, sank one gunboat, and made effective strikes against enemy ground troops at Red Beach, inflicting several hundred casualties, according to report. In all, a total of 13 combat sorties were flown on D-Day, in the course of which 4 B-26s were lost to enemy T-33 action. In the same period, the Castro air force lost 2 Sea Furies and 2 B-26s to anti-aircraft fire.

57. Impressed by the ease with which the T-33 aircraft could destroy the obsolete B-26 type aircraft, the CIA leaders decided to attempt, by a bombing attack, to destroy the remaining Castro aircraft at night on the ground. Six aircraft were scheduled to strike San Antonio de los Banos, believed to be the main base of operations, in two waves of three each during the night of 17–18 April. The mission was flown but was unsuccessful because of heavy haze and low clouds over the target.

58. Because of the developing shortage of ammunition in the beachhead at the end of D-Day, an air supply drop was arranged consisting of four C-54s and two C-46s. Of these drops, five were successful, but in one case most of the supplies drifted into the water from which only a part could be salvaged.

D+1

59. During the night of D-Day–D+1, the invasion shipping departing from the landing area for the south proceeded to a point about 50 miles off the Cuban coast. Here the two LCIs and three LCUs rendezvoused as directed, but the two freighters, the *Atlantico* and the *Caribe*, continued south without pausing. They did not turn back until intercepted and encouraged to return by the United States Navy, the *Atlantico* some 110 miles to the south, and the *Caribe* 218 miles south of the Cuban coast. Thus, the *Caribe* was never available for resupply operations while the fight on the beach lasted and the *Atlantico* did not get back to the rendezvous point until 1645 on D+1, 18 April.

Red Beach

60. The troops north of Red Beach came under heavy attack during the early hours of D+1. At 0300 enemy tanks were reported approaching from the north and by 0730 the situation was so difficult that the decision was made to move the force to Blue Beach. This movement began at 0900 and was completed about 1030. By that time, ammunition was low in the Red Beach force, but casualties, about 20, were comparatively light.

61. After reaching Blue Beach, the retreating force was allowed about two hours of rest, after which they were given additional ammunition and ordered back toward Red Beach in order to block the coast road to the movement of the force with which they had been engaged in the Red Beach area. They encountered this force somewhere west of Blue Beach and heavy fighting ensued. Exactly what occurred is not known, but it is assumed that the invaders eventually succumbed to the superior numbers of Castro forces moving down from the north.

Blue Beach

62. Enemy artillery fire began falling on the troops in the San Blas area at 0400 and continued most of the day. In the absence of radio communication, it was necessary to send officer couriers from the San Blas area to Blue Beach in order to communicate with the Brigade Commander who had set up his command post on the beach. At 0730 Roberto San Roman, brother of the Brigade Commander, went back to the beach for this purpose, reporting the situation around San Blas and seeking information. The Brigade Commander at that time indicated that the situation at Red Beach was critical. In order to cover Blue Beach, he had stationed some of his reserve forces to the east blocking the coast road coming from that direction and others to the northwest to cover the approaches from that quarter.

63. During the day artillery fire and enemy pressure on the San Blas forces compelled a gradual contraction of their position around the town. They attempted a counterattack to the north in the afternoon, but it soon bogged down in the face of superior forces.

64. By the end of the day, ammunition was very low throughout the beachhead. Only M-1 ammunition seems to have been reasonably plentiful, although the commander of the Heavy Weapons Company indicates that he was never out of 4.2 mortar ammunition. He indicates, however, that it was necessary to ration it carefully. In spite of the heavy fighting,

there appeared to have been surprisingly few casualties among the invaders.

65. In the evening, the Brigade Commander was asked by CIA Headquarters via the *Blagar* whether he wished evacuation. He replied, "I will not be evacuated. We will fight to the end here if we have to."

Air Action

66. On D+1 it became necessary to utilize some American civilian contract pilots to protect the beachhead area because some of the Cuban pilots either were too tired to fly or refused to do so. Six sorties were flown during the afternoon of D+1, attacking a long column of tanks and vehicles approaching Blue Beach along the coast road from the north. The attack was reported to have been very successful with an estimated 1800 casualties inflicted on the enemy and the destruction of 7 tanks. Napalm was used in these attacks, as well as bombs and rockets.

D+2

67. As events turned out, the night of D+1/D+2 offered the last opportunity to get ammunition to the beach. The *Atlantico* had returned from its trek to the south, rendezvousing with the other ships about 50 miles off the coast at 1645 on D+1. It began discharging cargo at once into the LCUs, completing the transfer at 2200, at which time [*less than 1 line of source text not declassified*] reported to CIA Headquarters that the LCI *Blagar* would escort the LCUs to Blue Beach unless otherwise advised. He indicated that his estimated time of arrival on the beach would be 0630, that is to say, dawn on D+2.

68. The *Blagar* began to move northward with the three LCUs, reporting to CIA Headquarters, however, that if low jet cover were not furnished by first light, the Captain believed that he would lose all the ships. Prior to this time he had requested the escort of a U.S. Navy destroyer. At 2145 CIA Headquarters wired the *Blagar* that a destroyer escort was not possible, to which message the Captain replied that if he

could not get destroyer escort in and out of Blue Beach, his Cuban crew would mutiny. At CIA Headquarters in Washington these messages were discussed and the critical decision was taken to stop the northern movement of the ammunition ships and direct them to rendezvous some 60 miles south of the Cuban coast.

69. The reasons for this decision appear to have been as follows. The CIA leaders in Washington were aware of the liberal amount of ammunition (3 days' supply) which had been taken ashore on D-Day and also of the air drops on the night of D+1. (See Annex 27) Further, they had ordered additional drops on the night of D+1/D+2. Considering the climate in which this operation had been planned in Washington, the CIA leaders apparently felt that it was hopeless to ask for either destroyer escort or jet cover for the ammunition convoy. Without this overt U.S. support, it was felt that the loss of the ships would be inevitable if they tried to run in in daylight—if, indeed, they could get the Cuban crews to make the attempt. Under these circumstances, they felt justified in calling off the sea resupply effort and made no further attempt beyond an arrangement for another air drop to get in ammunition before the final surrender. Except for one C-46 which landed on the Blue Beach airstrip, the attempt to resupply by air was unsuccessful because of enemy control of the air over the beachhead.

70. Although permission was not sought for jet escort for the ammunition ships, Mr. Bissell of CIA sought and received Presidential authority to have the Navy to fly CAP (Combat Air Patrol) over the beachhead from 0630 to 0730 on the morning of D+2. The purpose of this mission was to allow the B-26s to provide close support to the troops in the beachhead and cover for air resupply. This CAP was flown but, as indicated below, was of no avail.

71. Within the beachhead, the troops in the San Blas area began a general retreat in the morning of D+2. The last message received from the Brigade Commander by the *Blagar* at 1432 read: "Am destroying all equipment and

communications. I have nothing left to fight with. Am taking to the woods. I can't wait for you." Units and individuals arriving at Blue Beach shortly thereafter found the Brigade Command Post gone and heavy artillery fire falling in the vicinity. Pressure on the beachhead was coming from the north and the northwest. The last known report on the situation indicates that at 1700 Blue Beach was still clear of the enemy. It appears that fighting ceased shortly thereafter and by nightfall resistance in the beachhead had ended.

Air Action

72. On the morning of D+2 American pilots were again used for the protection of the beachhead. The morning sorties were directed to arrive over the beachhead in the period 6:30 to 7:30 A.M. to take advantage of the one-hour period of Navy cover. For an undetermined reason, they came in almost an hour early with the result that two B-26s were destroyed by the T-33s. A total of 7 sorties were flown on this occasion with undetermined results.

73. As indicated above, three cargo aircraft tried to fly in ammunition on the morning of D+2 but were turned back by the presence of enemy air. A fourth C-46, succeeding in landing on the Blue Beach airstrip in the hours of darkness, unloaded ammunition and picked up a B-26 pilot who had been shot down, departing at daylight. (See Annex 28)

74. These sorties ended the action of the invasion force which began stand-down activities thereafter with a total of 21 aircraft still in commission. It is difficult to be sure of the losses suffered by the Castro Air Force. The D-2 air strikes positively destroyed 5 Castro aircraft, with undetermined damage to others, and 4 other combat aircraft were destroyed in the beachhead area.

It may be asked how near the landing ever came to success. Had the ammunition shortage been surmounted, which is to say, had the Castro air been neutralized, would the landing force have accomplished its mission?

Considering their lack of experience, the Cubans ashore fought well and inflicted considerable losses on the Castro militia while they had ammunition. Contrary to the view held prior to the landing that with control of the air the C[uban] E[xpeditionary] F[orce] could have maintained themselves for some time, with the rapid appearance of the vastly superior Castro forces on the scene, the ultimate success of such a small landing force became very unlikely. The limited number of B-26 crews, if forced to continue to operate from Nicaragua, would have been strained to provide continuous daylight air support to the beachhead. An attempt by the landing force to exercise the guerrilla option and take to the hills would have been virtually impossible because of the presence of the encircling Castro forces and of the instructions which the Cuban invasion units had received to fall back on the beaches in case of a penetration of the beachhead. Under the conditions which developed we are inclined to believe that the beachhead could not have survived long without substantial help from the Cuban population or without overt U.S. assistance. Although under these conditions the guerrilla alternative did not exist, with control of the air the CEF might have been able to withdraw wholly or in part by sea.

Admiral Burke and Mr. Dulles consider that there is insufficient evidence to support the conjectures in this paragraph. The well-motivated, aggressive CEF fought extremely well without air cover and with a shortage of ammunition. They inflicted very severe losses on the less well-trained Cuban Militia. Consequently, it is reasonable to believe that if the CEF had had ammunition and air cover, they could have held the beachhead for a much longer time, destroyed much of the enemy artillery and tanks on the roads before they reached the beachhead, prevented observation of the fire of the artillery that might have been placed in position and destroyed many more of the local Militia en route to the area. A local success by the landing party, coupled with CEF aircraft overflying Cuba with visible control of the air, could well have caused a chain reaction of success throughout Cuba with resultant defection of some of the Militia, increasing support from the populace and eventual success of the operation.

III. Involvement of the U.S. Navy

83. Upon the request of CIA and with the approval of the President after a conference at the White House, the JCS at 0334R, 19 April directed CINCLANT to furnish air cover of 6 unmarked aircraft over CEF forces during the period 0630 to 0730 local time 19 April to defend the CEF against air attack from Castro planes. He was directed to not seek air combat but to defend CEF forces from air attack. Further to not attack ground targets. (Note: The purpose of this CAP was to provide cover to CEF transport and B-26 type aircraft which were due at the beachhead during this period.) In this same message CINCLANT was directed to be prepared to conduct evacuation from Blue Beach using unmarked amphibious craft with crews in dungarees, and that if the evacuation by U.S. ships were ordered he was to furnish air cover to protect landing craft.

84. At 1157R the JCS confirmed a telephone call to CINCLANT made by Admiral Burke at 1020R upon orders from the White House directing CINCLANT to send two destroyers to a position off Blue Beach to determine possibilities for evacuation. CINCLANT was also directed to fly reconnaissance over the beach to determine the situation. No ground attacks were authorized but active air-to-air combat was authorized.

85. On 19 April at 1312R, based upon a call from Admiral Burke from the White House, the JCS directed CINCLANT to have destroyers take CEF personnel off the beach and from the water to the limit of their capability; use CEF boats and craft as practicable; provide air cover; if destroyers fired on they are authorized to return the fire to protect themselves while on this humanitarian mission. (Note the reason that amphibious force craft were not used was that Phibron 2 had not yet arrived off the objective area.)

232. Memorandum No. 2 From the Cuba Study Group to President Kennedy

Washington, June 13, 1961.

SECRET. EYES ONLY. ULTRASENSITIVE.

IMMEDIATE CAUSES OF FAILURE OF THE OPERATION ZAPATA

Summary

1. The proximate cause of the failure of the Zapata Operation was shortage of ammunition which developed from the first day of the landing, April 17th, and became increasingly critical until it resulted in the surrender of the landing force about 1400 on April 19th.

2. There were three primary reasons for this shortage of ammunition. The logistical plan for the landing made ample provision for ammunition with the men and in floating reserve. However, upon landing there is evidence that the Cubans wasted their ammunition in excessive firing, displaying the poor ammunition discipline which is common to troops in their first combat.

3. Far more serious was the loss of the freighters *Rio Escondido* and *Houston* through air attack at about 0930 on the morning of April 17th. The *Rio* was a particular loss as it had ten days of reserve ammunition on board, as well as other important supplies. The *Houston* should have been able to land most of its supplies before being hit, but the unloading was delayed by trouble with the outboard motors of the ship's boats as well as by the apparent lethargy of the Fifth Battalion charged with the unloading.

4. The air attack which sank these ships caused all others in the landing area to put out to sea, as the only available protection in the absence of control of the air, with the order to rendezvous 50 miles off the coast. The freighters *Atlantico* and *Caribe* headed south and never stopped until intercepted by the U.S. Navy at points 110 miles and 218 miles, respectively, south of Cuba.

5. The *Caribe* was so far away that its cargo, principally aviation supplies, was never available for movement to Blue

Beach while the fight lasted. The *Atlantico*, which had considerable ammunition on board, did rejoin the other ships of the expedition at 1816, April 18th, at a point about 50 miles south of the beach and transferred her supplies to the waiting two LCIs and three LCUs for a night run to the beach.

6. By the time the supplies were transferred and the convoy had started north it was too late to hope to resupply the beach under cover of darkness. The convoy commander asked CIA Operational Headquarters, Washington, for destroyer escort and U.S. Navy jet cover without which he believed that he would lose his ships to air attack the next morning. He added that without U.S. Navy support the Cuban crew would mutiny if sent back to the beach.

7. As a result of these messages, CIA Headquarters, feeling that it would be futile to order these ammunition craft to attempt a daylight unloading, called off the mission and the attempt to get ammunition to the beach by sea ended. The President was not requested for specific authority to extend the air cover to protect the ammunition convoy.

8. These causes for the ammunition shortage rested in turn on others which lay deeper in the plans and organization of this operation and the attitude toward it on the part of Government officials. The effectiveness of the Castro Air Force over the beach resulted from a failure to destroy the airplanes on the ground (particularly the T-33s whose importance was not fully appreciated in advance) before or concurrently with the landing. This failure was a consequence of the restraints put on the anti-Castro Air Force in planning and executing its strikes, primarily for the purpose of protecting the covert character of the operation. These restraints included: the decision to use only the B-26 as a combat aircraft because it had been distributed widely to foreign countries; the limitation of pre-landing strikes to those which could be flown from non-U.S. controlled airfields under the guise of coming from Cuban strips, thus eliminating the possibility of using jet fighters or even T-33 trainers; the inability to use any non-Cuban base within short turn-around distance from the target area (about nine hours were required

to turn around a B-26 for a second mission over the target from Nicaragua); prohibition of use of American contract pilots for tactical air operations; restriction on munitions, notably napalm; and the cancellation of the strikes planned at dawn on D-Day. The last mentioned was probably the most serious as it eliminated the last favorable opportunity to destroy the Castro Air Force on the ground. The cancellation seems to have resulted partly from the failure to make the air strike plan entirely clear in advance to the President and the Secretary of State, but, more importantly, by misgivings as to the effect of the air strikes on the position of the United States in the current UN debate on Cuba. Finally, there was the failure to carry the issue to the President when the opportunity was presented and explain to him with proper force the probable military consequences of a last-minute cancellation.

9. The flight of the *Caribe* and *Atlantico* might have been prevented had more attention been paid in advance to the control of the ships to include the placing of some Americans aboard. The CIA officer responsible for all the ships involved was a [*less than 1 line of source text not declassified*] who was aboard the LCI *Blagar* with no means to control the freighters, or, indeed, to locate them after they disappeared. Only the initiative of the U.S. Navy in the vicinity brought them back to the scene of action. The absence of Americans on board these vessels was an application of the general order to keep Americans out of the combat area. This order had been violated in a few cases, but it was apparently not considered important to do so in the case of the freighters.

10. The lack of full appreciation of the ammunition situation at the end of D+1 in the CIA Operational Headquarters was largely the result of the difficulty of keeping abreast of the situation on the beach, and the location and movement of the ships at sea from the distance of Washington. Also, there was a confidence in the supply of the beach by air which turned out to be unjustified. Had there been a command ship in the sea area with an advance CIA command post on board, a more effective control would have been possible.

11. The Executive branch of the Government was not organizationally prepared to cope with this kind of paramilitary operation. There was no single authority short of the President capable of coordinating the actions of CIA, State, Defense, and USIA. Top level direction was given through ad hoc meetings of senior officials without consideration of operational plans in writing and with no arrangement for recording conclusions and decisions reached.

HEART OF DARKNESS: OPERATION BARRAS

22 SAS/1 PARA, Sierra Leone, 2000

On 25 August 2000, in war-torn Sierra Leone, a UN patrol was passing through the village of Magbeni when it encountered a group of fighters from a local militia known to themselves as the "West Side Niggers". The UN patrol, which was in heavily armed WMIK Land Rovers, was manned by eleven men from the 1st Battalion Royal Irish Regiment of the British Army.

Initially the twenty-five men and women from the "West Side Niggers" appeared friendly, and asked the CO of the patrol, Major Alan Marshall, to meet their leader, Foday Kallay. Twenty-four years old, Kallay had been a sergeant in the Sierra Leone Army; in the West Side Niggers he had promoted himself to brigadier.

Kallay arrived, incensed that the British patrol was on his turf without permission. The mood around the Land Rovers changed. On the road to the south of the village a West Side Niggers Bedford truck, mounted with a twin ZPU 214.5mm heavy machine gun, appeared. Hemmed in by the crowd, there was little the RIR soldiers could do. Major Marshall tried to reason with the West Side Niggers, but they grabbed his SA 80 5.56 rifle. The crowd then attacked the Sierra Leone liaison officer with the patrol. Within minutes the British soldiers had been stripped down to their underwear, their watches and wedding rings torn off them, and were being herded down to a ferry point to be taken across the Rokel Creek to the militia's HQ at Gberi Bana.

The rebels contacted the British authorities, and a face-to-face meeting took place between the West Side Niggers and the RIR's CO, Lieutenant-Colonel Simon Fordham, on the track to the village of Magbeni. Fordham had already been prepped by two police negotiators from the Metropolitan Police's Hostage and Crisis Negotiation Unit who had been hurriedly flown out. The West Side Niggers gave a list of demands, which included the release of a rebel leader, plus medicine and food. While the negotiations were going on, the Ranger's RSM observed a seventeen-year-old girl from the militia adjust the sights on her RPG-7 to cover their vehicles. Fordham had his own demands. He wanted proof that the hostages were still alive.

On 29 August, Foday Kallay met Fordham again, this time at the UN camp at Masiaka. Kallay brought with him Major Marshall and the Regimental Signals Officer, Captain Flaherty. The RSO, before he was taken back to the camp, managed to hand over to Fordham – via a handshake – a map of the rebel camp.

Two days later, five of the Rangers were released in exchange for medical supplies. The British also pressed on Fallay a satellite phone, ostensibly to make negotiations easier. The phone was a trick. Electronic warfare specialists from the Royal Corps of Signals were able to use it to track the exact location of the West Side Niggers.

Negotiations began to break down and the rebels began to threaten the lives of their hostages. Six were marched to a swamp, tied to wooden posts, and put through a mock execution. The decapitated heads of children were paraded before them. The West Side Niggers were highly unstable due to copious cannabis and cocaine use. Their demands increased daily and exponentially. On one occasion they announced they wanted safe passage to Britain to take up university courses in politics. Understanding that the term "Niggers" did not sit well with international politicking, the rebels more and more called themselves the "West Side Boys".

MI6 intelligence had determined that the seven hostages were being held in mud and cement buildings at Gberi Bana, a small camp on the banks of the Rokel Creek. Across the creek, about

400 metres away, was a rebel base at Magbeni, which was where the stolen WMIK Land Rovers were being kept.

D Squadron 22 SAS, augmented by a number of Special Boat Service (SBS) operators, was clandestinely flown into the country to prepare for a hostage rescue mission. When it was determined that there may be hundreds of troops stationed at Magbeni, A Company from the 1st Battalion Parachute Regiment was brought in to take out the main base. A Company was selected because it had recently undergone jungle training. The combat group would consist of a Company HQ and three Rifle platoons.

Using inflatable raiding craft, Boat Troop from D Squadron, together with SBS operators, inserted observation teams upriver of Gberi Bana. The obs teams sneaked through the tropical jungle to conceal themselves near the camp. Their hides were less than 250 metres from the village. Once concealed, they began monitoring the camps, relaying back intel about the strength and disposition of the enemy forces. Parabolic microphones allowed the obs teams to listen in on the rebels' conversations. The obs teams reported back that the West Side Boys were also holding Sierra Leonian hostages.

The decision to launch a rescue operation was taken on 9 September. Intel from the SAS/SBS troopers in the hides suggested that the hostages were being subjected to sexual attacks. The chances of the West Side Boys releasing the hostages alive seemed slim. Sandbanks on the river and the density of the jungle foliage around the camp ruled out both an amphibious and overland rescue. The only way in was an aerial assault. Officially codenamed "Operation Barras", the participants called it "Operation Certain Death". The total number of West Side Boys was gauged to be about 1,000.

At first light on the morning of 10 September 2000, the helicopter assault force went into action. The assault force consisted of: one Mil-24 Hind gunship manned by pro-British crew from Sierra Leone; two Lynx Mk7 attack helicopters from 657 Squadron AAC; and three Chinook HC2 helis from RAF Special Forces 7 Squadron carrying 70 men in integrated SAS/SBS fire teams (which "fast roped" down from the back of the Chinooks into the camp) and the paras of A Company, 1st Battalion, Parachute Regiment.

Early morning was selected as the time for the raid, as it was hoped most of the West Side Boys would be asleep. Mohammed Kamara was a West Side Boy woken in the half light of dawn by the rotors of the approaching helicopters. The Lynxs came in first. Kamara said, "The helicopters were almost on the water. They fired and fired again . . ."

Kamara ran off into the swamps. The Lynx air assault, plus the sight of heavily armed SAS/SBS teams dropping from the sky into the camp, worked. Many of the West Side Boys were too befuddled to do anything. Their confusion was only exacerbated by the downdraught from the Chinooks destroying their shanty huts, and the emergence of the SAS/SBS obs teams from the jungle. They went straight to the huts where the hostages were held to hold off "interference".

Under the cover of all this shock and awe the SAS hostage rescue team were able to secure the seven British hostages. Meanwhile, the rest of the SAS/SBS assault teams cleared buildings and set up defensive positions. Finding their liaison officer, Bangura, proved more difficult; eventually he was found in an open pit used as a lavatory. Less than twenty minutes after the arrival of the SAS/SBS, the RIR hostages and Bangura had been evacuated. Shortly afterwards twenty-five Sierra Leone captives, among them young boys and sex slaves, were lifted to freedom.

Across the creek, at Magbeni, the paras of A Company had landed. To the surprise of the first men down the ramp the "grass" turned out to be reeds, meaning the 100-metre sprint to the treeline became a chest-high slog through swamp. The paras pushed on to the tree line, where they came under fire from the now very wide awake West Side Boys. This was partially suppressed by all guns blazing passes from the Lynx helicopters and mortars from the paras themselves. A returning Chinook brought in the second wave of paras. Now at full strength, the company shook out and began to move through the village west to east.

The West Side Boys – many of whom were actually women – may have worn shower caps and fluorescent wigs and received next-to-no military training, but they were fearless. Voodoo made them believe they were invulnerable. And any courage voodoo failed to provide, drugs did. A hard core of West Side Boys stood their ground, and as the Company HQ was moving forward to join 2 Platoon an RPG round hit the ground in front of them. Seven soldiers were injured. Para Private Julian Sheard recalled: "There was a loud explosion and we could hear these agonizing screams." Among the injured was the CO, Major Lowe. He called up Captain Danny Matthews and told him to take over. An unwounded signaller transmitted a casualty evacuation request.

Still A Company pressed on with its attack, with the GPMG gunners standing up so they could see over the vegetation, firing their weapons from their shoulders. By 7.00 a.m. the West Side Boys withdrew, and 3 Platoon took up a blocking position on the village track against a counter-attack. With the village secure, the paras methodically proceeded through the village destroying the Bedford with the ZPU-2, the ammunition dump, and three "technicals" (pick-ups mounted with machine guns). The paras also discovered the RIR's three Land Rovers. Spare keys were brought in by Chinook and they were underslung and lifted out.

Fighting at Gberi Bana also raged for hours as the SAS/SBS fire teams searched through the buildings engaging "hostiles". The official British figure for West Side Boys dead was later given as around twenty-five; more probably the total was nearer 200. At Gberi Bana and Magbeni the West Side Boys were finished off as fighting force.

By about 11.00 a.m. the last helicopters lifted the last men from the battleground. Aboard were a number of prisoners; they included Foday Kallay. Survivors from the West Side Boys came out of the jungle. Sixteen-year-old Unisa Sesay was a member of the West Side Boys youth unit. He described the scene:

> There were many corpses and wounded people lying on the ground. One commander was standing and his friend was trying to remove a fragment from his shoulder. The rest of the people were on the ground.

One British soldier died in the action. This was Trooper Brad Tinnion, 22 SAS, who had been hit by a 7.62mm round which passed through his body and exited via a shoulder. It had been his first time in action with the Regiment.

The tragedy of Trooper Tinnion's death aside, Operation Barras was a resounding success, with all British hostages safely rescued. For the first time SAS and SBS fire teams had been integrated, and for the first time the paras had been deployed alongside United Kingdom Special Forces. The mix worked so well it would be invoked again.

DOCUMENT: Gilbert Sadi-Kirschen: Belgian SAS, Operation Benson, 1944

Numerically tiny, with about 300 personnel at its greatest strength, the Belgian SAS Regiment (also known as 5th SAS Regiment) of World War II was commanded by Captain E. Blondeel. It tended to be used for intelligence-gathering operations; in late August 1944, Lieutenant Gilbert Sadi-Kirschen, accompanied by five troopers, dropped near Compiègne to report on enemy dispositions in the area. By now the Allies had broken out of their Normandy beachhead, and northern France became an increasingly important area of SAS activity.

Below is Sadi-Kirschen's diary of the operation, which was code-named *Benson*.

London, 26 August 1944
It was the first day of my leave and I had to go back to Fairford Camp that evening. I didn't like the idea of a long journey by train and truck. Then I thought of ringing up Special Air Service Brigade Headquarters at Moor Park. They were sure to have a jeep doing a shuttle service between London and Fairford.

Captain Blondeel answered the telephone. "Certainly, my boy. I'm going back to Fairford this evening. Be here by four o'clock."

Blondeel had hardly set eyes on me when he said: "Ah, there you are. How would you like to go off on an operation tomorrow evening?"

"Certainly. Where to? Belgium?"

"No, I'm sorry; north of Paris. It's another intelligence mission. SHAEF need to know every movement in that area. You'd have to send reports daily or even twice a day on the volume of traffic on the roads running from Paris to Compiègne, and Paris to Soissons. You may say they ought to be able to find that out with aerial reconnaissance, but the countryside is stiff with anti-aircraft batteries. You're also asked to pinpoint these Ack-Ack batteries, so that the RAF can either avoid them or beat them up, depending on how they feel.

"This time you'll be met on arrival by a reception committee provided by the local resistance, and of course that'll save you a lot of time – Oh, and I forgot to say that the name of your operation is *Benson*."

"Who's *Benson*?"

"No idea. Look him up in the *Encyclopaedia Britannica*. There'll be six of you altogether – two WTs of course. Who would you like?"

"Moyse and Pietquin – I was very pleased with them last time."

"Good. As second-in-command I thought Lieutenant Franck might be good. He's a Frenchman, and before the war he had a factory in the area where you're to operate."

"Excellent. I came across Franck during training last year and we get on well together. For the two others, let's see, what about Flips and Bouillon who were with me in Normandy? They're real toughs. They used to be in the Foreign Legion."

We were driving fast through the English countryside. It was a wonderful summer evening, and I felt far less nervous than the day before my first operation. Blondeel also was much less strung up. The squadron hadn't had many casualties up to the present in these French operations, and the results had been satisfactory.

"We're in Belgium at last," he said. "The office was against parachuting men into Belgium, and I had to drop Paul Renkin's group into the French Ardennes, but they were attacked and crossed over into the Belgian Ardennes, where they were received with open arms by the local Maquis, and I'm hoping to send them some reinforcements very soon."

He was humming to himself at the wheel, and to my surprise, he suggested stopping and having a drink in a pub on the banks of the Thames.

"You're a lucky devil, Kirschen," he sighed suddenly, as we raised our glasses. "When I think that in a day or two you'll be overrun by the Americans and you'll be able to go and enjoy yourself in Paris."

27 August

Fairford Camp was a foretaste of the Apocalypse: every uniform of the United Nations was to be seen, every language spoken. Scotsmen tested their weapons by firing over your head. Frenchmen checked over their WT sets or tried on their parachute harness. Norwegians, lying flat on their stomachs, studied their maps. There were some on their way to France and others who'd just come back, and who were telling stories of their experiences. And there were a few emaciated airmen who had just been fished out of the Channel after days in the water.

Lorries picked their way carefully between the tents looking for men who were due to leave for somewhere behind the German lines. "Who's pinched my helmet? Anyone seen my parachute?"

There was a crowd round a jeep which was armed with a machine gun, a bazooka, one or two Brens and fitted with several reserve petrol tanks. Evidently this jeep was to be dropped by parachute. We wondered what sort of state it would be in after landing.

In all this confusion I managed with great difficulty to find Freddy, who was in great spirits. He had just been told that he was to speak daily on the radio in the five o'clock broadcast to the Belgian SAS. The thought of this greatly amused him.

"The broadcast will be preceded by the first notes of 'Sur le Pont d'Avignon'," he explained. "No one could fail to recognize it, even if they were as unmusical as you are. Messages for you will begin with the words, 'Hello, Loulou Two'."

"That's charming. And what sort of stories will you tell us?"

"I'll give you the latest news of the various SAS groups, and also what schemes are being hatched in high places. As soon as your mission is over, I'll tell you if you have to come back direct or if you can stop in Paris and come back by easy stages."

Everyone talked about Paris to me as if I were already there. For this departure I felt as though I were going through an old routine. The number of people who saw me off this time was much less impressive than for my first operation.

Freddy was the only one at the take-off, and he gave me a great wink as the door of the plane closed on us. The operation was to be a short one and I was to be met on landing. I felt that things were going very well.

28 August

Things went far from well.

First, of course, the kitbag went wrong. I remembered to unhitch it as I jumped, but I didn't manage to hold on to it tightly enough as it fell. I tried to slow its fall, but all I did was to rip the skin off my fingers. That damned kitbag. I always knew it would give me trouble before I finished.

Then I saw Moyse limping up to me. He had made a good landing, but had managed to sprain his ankle walking into a rut in a cart track.

And Flips had winded himself by falling on to his kitbag and getting the barrel of his carbine stuck into the small of his back.

Franck had injured his foot pretty badly.

Otherwise everyone was all right.

There was a storm somewhere in the distance, and we found each other by the light of lightning flashes. But what was so comforting was that there wasn't the slightest trace of the famous reception committee who were supposed to meet us. We peered vainly into the darkness.

There was no movement, no shouting.

It had hardly been worthwhile the pilot of the Stirling who had dropped us making me spend the last twenty minutes before jumping crouched beside the hole we were to jump through ... His idea was not to let us drop without being absolutely certain of having found the right ground, and recognizing the signal letter.

"My instructions are quite clear," he had said, "if I'm not dead certain of the ground, I take you back to England." He was a conscientious man, this Australian pilot, and his conscience was surely quite clear, having persuaded himself that he had seen the lights of the reception committee. And then he came back over the ground. He must have uttered a sigh of relief as he dropped the twenty-four containers to his imaginary reception committee. We heard the aircraft disappearing towards England, the sound of the engines getting softer and softer.

Franck came up and whispered. "King, what are we going to do with these containers? Where are we? Has anyone found the case with the WT equipment in it?"

"I know no more than you do. It's so dark we'll never find the wretched containers or the cage. Besides, with four out of the six of us injured, how could we carry them? Forget the containers. Let's get out of here double-quick. As soon as it gets light the Germans will realize that parachutists have been dropped. Just a minute. Do you see that red light winking over there? Maybe that's where the reception committee is waiting for us, because the pilot did say he saw lights."

In the blinding rain we walked as far as the red light. It wasn't the reception committee – it was a light on an abandoned train. Luckily there were no sentries, no Germans.

Perhaps we were somewhere in liberated territory. History repeated itself. As in Normandy, I looked for a signpost and then I studied my map and discovered we were ten kilometres further away from those delights of Paris which I had been promised so consistently. We set off walking eastwards, and after five kilometres of difficult going, we went through a village, Valescourt. An hour before dawn all we had found in the way of shelter was a miserable clump of about a dozen stunted trees. Otherwise there was nothing but bare plateau and cornfields which had already been cut. Oh, for the deep forests of Normandy.

We woke up from a short sleep, soaked to the skin. Without moving from our clump of trees we looked about us. It was a dull, grey day. We could see German cars moving along the main road about 500 yards away and in the other direction we could hear tanks and carriers clanking along cart tracks.

This place was not too healthy for us. There was no farm to be seen. It wasn't like Normandy – here all the farmers and labourers lived in the villages. Just as Franck and I were wondering how we were going to make contact with the local inhabitants we noticed a peasant on his way to work in a nearby field.

I decided to disregard all the accepted rules. I knew one should not show oneself during the day, especially when wearing uniform. I knew one should not reveal one's hideout to local people. But our wretched little wood gave us such uncertain cover that some relaxation of the rules was justified. I went out and accosted the peasant. We were lucky. He was the son of a Belgian farmer and he offered to give us all the help he could.

"You've come to the right place," he said. "There are Germans in every village and thousands of them pass through here, because the main roads cross at Saint-Just-en-Chaussée, a few kilometres away. Personally, I'm not in the Resistance, but I can get Monsieur Lucien to come along later. He's one of the chiefs, I think. Won't you take my sandwiches? You must be hungry and cold under those trees . . ."

In our first message to London I gave our position and asked to be allowed to remain where we were, so as to observe the Paris–Beauvais and Amiens–Montdidier roads. I explained that with things as they were, it would be difficult as well as a waste of time to shift our position.

In the afternoon, Monsieur Lucien of the Resistance came to see us. He was a local farmer, short and thick-set, with bright eyes.

"The first thing to tell you," he said, "is that one of my chaps has found all the stuff that was parachuted last night.

He and the others made a real good job of it and everything was unpacked and hidden away before the Jerries got up this morning."

"You didn't by any chance find my cigarettes, did you?" said Moyse.

"No, I don't think so," said Monsieur Lucien, looking slightly embarrassed. "I'll bring you some bread and smoked sausage this evening. Is this where you sleep, under the trees? It doesn't look very comfortable."

"Do you know anywhere else we could go?"

"Why not try Folly Cellar?"

"Did you say Folly?"

"The Folly's what we call the barn over there, the other side of the hill. It's a very good barn. Loving couples used to use it at one time. The entrance to the cellar is hidden by bushes. I could take you there this evening if you like."

At five that afternoon we got a message confirming that we could operate in this area. We sent them the position of an anti-aircraft battery Lucien had told us about. I wondered what Blondeel had thought when he heard we had not been met. He'd been so proud of having that reception committee arranged for us.

At nightfall we settled ourselves in the cellar of Folly Barn. The name was ominous and so was the atmosphere of the place. "The local couples can't have been hard to please," sighed Franck. We lay on the damp stone floor of the cellar and thought regretfully of the warm sleeping bags we had purposely left in England, to give us less weight to carry about. But at least it wasn't raining directly on us.

29 August

We lay in the cellar till Lucien came and brought us some food and a detailed summary of last night's traffic on the roads.

"I asked Dr Caillard to come and see you," he said. "He's a good doctor and a good man. He'll attend to the sprained ankle and to your hand, Captain. He should be here in a minute or two."

While waiting for the doctor to come, we went into the barn, about twenty yards away from our cellar, to try and get a message through to London.

The doctor, seeing this bunch of crocks, would hardly be impressed by us as professional parachutists, so we would try and put on a clandestine radio exhibition for his benefit. The doctor arrived on a motorbike and introduced himself. I've seldom seen a man so calm and methodical as he was. He dealt with Moyse's ankle and Franck's foot and while he was bandaging my hand he suddenly began to talk.

"Maybe this will interest you, Captain. Yesterday, at the crossroads at St-Just-en-Chaussée, there was a German major directing the traffic. He stopped each vehicle to examine the driver's papers and pointed out which road he should take. I was rather intrigued by all this so I stopped and watched him for a few minutes. And suddenly the major wiped his forehead and went off to the café to have a drink. I followed him and noticed he put his map on the table. While he wasn't watching I made a copy of the map." At this point he carefully unfolded a piece of paper. "There's my rough sketch. That's the Channel coast and that line there's the Somme."

"But it's incredible, Doctor. It shows every German division on the Somme. All the division numbers, the ones up in the line, and those in reserve. It even shows the position of Army Headquarters." We looked at one another astounded.

"I'm very pleased to have been of service to you," said the doctor quietly. "Goodbye, and good luck," and off he went.

We had an hour before our next period of transmission. Franck went into the cellar to shave. The five of us in the barn were sitting bunched up together while the rain rattled on the roof and swept in through the door which wouldn't shut. I began to dictate. Never had a message been composed with such fervour or coded with such care.

"Following enemy divisions on Somme. Between Abbeville-Amiens . . . Between Amiens-Peronne . . . south of Doullens . . ."

"Can you hear that noise?" whispered Pietquin.

We listened. Yes. There was a strange noise – it sounded like a carrier clanking along a muddy lane. The noise got nearer. We grabbed our arms. The noise ceased and three yards in front of us a German self-propelled gun came to a standstill. The five or six soldiers riding on the gun carriage stared at us stupefied.

Flips and Bouillon opened fire at once. The Germans replied, firing incendiary bullets. The firing quickly became intense and then one side of the barn caught fire. Suddenly the gun carriage went into reverse and took up a position on the other side of the barn. Flips and Bouillon seized their chance, rushed outside and disappeared.

The firing started up again.

"Destroy the set, Moyse, quick." But Moyse preferred to take it to pieces. He was very expert and he only took thirty seconds to do it. Moyse was very attached to his wireless set.

I stuffed the doctor's plan into my pocket. The smoke was getting very thick and at any moment the straw would catch fire. We ran out, screened by the smoke. We threw the parts of the set into a bush and ran towards the only thing which offered any cover at all – a row of trees.

We threw ourselves down in the wet grass under the trees.

"I don't think they've seen us," said Pietquin.

For a minute or two there was silence, then the firing started up again more violently than ever. We saw two men running towards us, bullets whistling round them. Flips arrived first and threw himself down. He was followed by Franck who still had his face covered in shaving soap. He murmured: "They've got me in the arm, but it's nothing much."

"Where's Bouillon?"

"No idea."

For a moment there was a lull. The Jerries had probably gone off to get some reinforcements, so we decided the best thing to do was to get away. But there was no cover, nothing but a field of stubble.

"We could hide under the cornstacks," Flips suggested.

"They're damned small but it's better than nothing at all."

Each of us crept under one of those miserable cornstacks. The straw had gone brown with all the rain there'd been. Franck kept a bit apart from the rest of us. I went over and gave him some sulphonamide tablets. "Don't worry about me," he said, "I can manage all right."

We waited all through that long afternoon. Between the sheaves I could see Folly Barn burning. A wave of depression swept over me. There I was, soaked to the skin, bent double, wretched, not able to move one yard and knowing that in my pocket was a document of the most vital importance which was quite valueless if I didn't succeed in getting away.

I was hungry.

And what had happened to Bouillon? I'd been so proud of coming back from Normandy with all my men. And this was the operation which was to have gone so well, so smoothly and was to take me, after a few days, to Paris. And now it was raining torrents and I had cramp. Here and there I could see cornstacks moving a little and I guessed my men were as impatient as I was. But there was no question of leaving our hiding places before it got dark.

By nightfall we were all ravenously hungry, all of us that is except Franck who had gone off on his own with a peasant.

"We may find something to eat in a village," said Moyse.

"Perhaps the Germans have left by now."

He was indulging in a little wishful thinking. We tried approaching several villages but we heard nothing but shouts and orders in German. We would have to last out until the following day.

Luckily we found a few bales of straw and made ourselves a kind of roofless hut. Compared with our cornstacks of the afternoon, it was wonderfully comfortable.

We hardly slept that night and everyone woke up about four, in a very bad temper.

"Of course it's raining," groaned Flips.

"And no smokes," added Moyse.

I had one idea only and that was to transmit the message at all costs. I had to go back to the barn. We moved off in single file and arrived safely at the row of trees where we had hidden the previous day. I told the men to wait there, and taking my carbine, I set off towards the barn. I crawled slowly forwards stopping every two or three yards to look around me in the half light of dawn. I saw no Germans near, only a column of smoke from the barn rising slowly into the air.

I went back to the trees to fetch Moyse. I wanted him to collect the parts of his set from the bush where he had hidden them.

I decided to go down to the cellar in the hope of rescuing some chocolate I had left in my haversack. As I entered, I heard a strangled voice say in French: "Who goes there?" It was Bouillon's voice. "Oh, it's you, sir. That's wonderful. I thought you were all roasted alive in the barn. I've been hiding here since yesterday. How are all the others?"

A few minutes later we were all five of us together behind the line of trees which had become our new base. But I'd learnt my lesson and I got Flips and Bouillon to keep a look-out, while Moyse and Pietquin fixed up the radio. Making contact wasn't easy. London could hardly hear us. Pietquin put all he'd got into turning that generator handle while Moyse, swearing and groaning, adjusted the dials and knobs on the set. At last they could start sending. We held our breath.

Q.S.P. (I have an important message for you). Q.S.P. It was a long message: 125 words, each word repeated for safety and several times London stopped to ask for extra repeats. Pietquin and fat old Flips took turns at the handle, smiling and sweating. Five hundred yards away we could see German cars going along the road. I wondered if we'd ever come to the end of the message.

We had been on the air for more than an hour when Moyse said: "At last. They've received all of it, and I'd give a lot to see their faces when they start decoding that."

We all relaxed. Our one problem now was food. We waited for Lucien as if he had been the Messiah. Late in the afternoon he appeared. He had expected to find our remains in the smouldering ruins of Folly Barn, and he was quite surprised to find us full of life and very hungry. He went off at once in search of provisions.

While we were eating, a German battery came and took up its position between our line of trees and the barn. We felt they might have had the decency to choose somewhere else. Luckily it was very dark and yet another thunderstorm came and broke over our heads. We retired discreetly from the tactless battery and slept in our shelter of the night before. We woke to a sunny day at last. We dried our uniforms and watched the German convoys go past, thinking each one would be the last one. We went on sending reports of enemy traffic.

At midday, London had a message for us. As Moyse decoded it, he beamed all over. "A personal message from the General, sir," he said, trying to seem unconcerned.

It was Brigadier McLeod who sent us his personal congratulations and thanked us for the information transmitted, which was of the greatest value.

"Very good of him," said Flips, "but we were damned nearly roasted."

We listened at five o'clock. Freddy's voice was jubilant.

"Good work, Kiki. You should have seen the excitement here when your message arrived. Everyone rushed to telephone SHAEF. You never heard such a noise."

"You might almost think that message had given them more trouble than it gave us," said Flips, taking a large bite at a sausage.

For the last few minutes an artillery duel had been raging just over our heads. From our observation post we could see the road clearly and we followed the battle with great interest, but without understanding very much about it.

More German cars came along the road. We counted them almost mechanically. Then they got fewer and fewer. We talked in whispers, watching the road. A Jerry motorcyclist scorched past, and as the noise of his engine died away, a silence seemed to settle down on the whole countryside. The sun began to set. And then, as we were sitting there, a little surprised at this strange lack of noise, suddenly all the bells of St Just pealed out together.

1 September
Liberation was followed by a kind of explosion of joy. We were invited everywhere, fêted, gorged, kissed. We went to St Just to fetch Franck, who had been put up by the mayor and whose wound in the arm was recovering.

Toasts, ceremonies, speeches. I managed to repeat the talk I had given at Longny a fortnight before, which still suited the occasion.

In a German truck and with American patrol, we bowled along towards Paris.

2 September
At Paris.

3 September
"Hello, Loulou two. Hello, Loulou two." Freddy's voice was calm and cheerful as ever. His first message was for Eddy. He promised him some food in the near future. Eddy? So Eddy Blondeel had gone into action. I wondered where he was. Probably in the Ardennes; that was always his great ambition.

Then there were a number of short messages for Paul, Jean, John, Jean-Claude Pilou. Each name made me jump – all my friends were "in the field".

At last he got to me. "Hurry up and come home, my boy, I'm off myself this evening. So long."

We set off once more. We crossed Normandy, going via Longny to collect Regner, who had spent a pleasant conva-lescence at Monsieur Bignon's house. As for good old Bignon, he'd progressed a long way since we'd last seen him. He talked about jeeps and MPs and doughnuts as if he'd lived for years on the banks of the Missouri.

6 September
Our arrival in England marked the happy ending of Operation *Benson*. And to this day I don't know who Benson was.

The Belgian SAS was one of the few special forces to survive the end of World War II. After control of the regiment was passed to the Belgian government the unit was renamed the 1st Regiment of Parachutists, then in 1952 it joined the Commando Regiment to become the 1st battalion of the Paracommando Regiment. The most storied post-War exploit of the Belgian SAS came in 1978, when the unit evacuated hostages from the Zairean town of Kolwezi.

LIGHTNING STRIKE

Sayeret Matkal, Uganda, 1976

Just after midday on 27 June 1976, Air France Flight 139 was hijacked en route to Paris by members of the German Baader-Meinhof terrorist gang (aka the Red Army Faction) and the Popular Front for the Liberation of Palestine. Fifteen hours later the skyjacked Airbus which had 258, mostly Israeli, passengers aboard landed at Entebbe airport in Uganda. There the four hijackers were joined by other Baader-Meinhof and PFLP members. The terrorists were personally welcomed by Uganda's crazed dictator, His Excellency Field Marshal Doctor Idi Amin. For all of his fine titles, Amin was a former NCO in the British Army.

On the following day, Wilfred Boese, the terrorists' leader, announced their demands to the waiting world: fifty-three of their comrades held in prisons in Israel, Kenya, West Germany and Switzerland must be released. They also required $5 million in cash. If this failed to happen, they would start shooting the Israeli hostages, now segregated from the remainder of the passengers in a separate room in the airport's old terminal. Apparently Boese, a German, at least had the decency to look uncomfortable when dividing the Jews from the Gentiles; some of the Israeli passengers were actually Holocaust survivors.

The hostage situation left the Israeli cabinet of Yitzak Rabin with an agonizing dilemma, as the minutes of their meetings demonstrate: Should Israel capitulate to the hijackers' demands or mount a rescue bid? And what rescue bid could possibly succeed over such a long distance in a country that, while not exactly hostile, was not neutral. Entebbe was no less than 2,500 miles from Sharm el-Sheik, the southern-most airfield in Israel. Much of that 2,500 miles was over the airspace of Arab countries, all of which had the capability of attacking Israeli aircraft.

29.6. 1976: Cabinet meeting, Jerusalem.

Israeli Defence Staff Chief of Staff Lt. Gen. Mordechai "Motta" Gur: "The IDF has prepared a mission."

Prime Minister Yitzhak Rabin: "I suggest we don't discuss it here."

Defence Minister Shimon Peres: "We need to rally up the editors' committee [an informal forum comprised of the editors and owners of the main Israeli media] so they don't begin to speculate. They have already cooperated and not published the passengers' list. We are in a tough situation, but not the toughest thing that can happen to us."

Rabin: "I think it is the toughest."

30.6: Prior to a Cabinet meeting Rabin and Peres meet with IDF officials at 12.20 p.m.

Gur: "We put together a team to look into all the military options, and Ehud Brog [aka Ehud Barak, then assistant to the head of the Military Intelligence Directorate] is working with the Air Force and Navy."

Rabin: "An article about 'Heartburn' [military operation executed by the Mossad and Shin Bet during which Palestinian and German terrorists planning to bomb an El-Al airplane were captured in Nairobi] told almost the entire story, written by a military correspondent in one of the news-papers, but it was disqualified. Everything was mentioned inside. The fact that we can't take a military correspondent, put him in jail and question him how he got this information – this is a catastrophe."

Gur: "I think we have to do it, no later than today."

1.7, 7 a.m.: Cabinet meeting
[Peres reads aloud from text of the conversation between Amin and Baruch Bar Lev, a former head of Israel's mission that trained Ugandan soldiers in the early 1970s, in which Bar Lev tried to convince Amin to free the hostages]

Yaacobi: "Last night around 11 p.m., I met with the passengers' families. To their credit I must say that the mood was very calm and responsible. Most of them claimed that due to the special circumstances, an Israeli military operation is impossible so the only thing they demand is to begin negotiations."

Peres: "The problem isn't simply the families' claims. It should be made clear that negotiations and surrendering open the door to future terror attacks."

Rabin: "Who says?"

Peres: "I do."

Rabin: "I ask you to clarify yourself and tell us why."

Peres: "Until now, the Americans haven't surrendered because Israelis were a world-class standard. If we surrender, there won't be any country in the world that will stand it. It will cause more and more pressure."

Rabin: "This is the situation at the moment: Without making a decision, that is a decision, including everything that comes with that, with all the question marks. We must remember that we'll be the first government to show willingness to enter into negotiations regarding exchanges."

Allon: "I am opposed to accepting the terror organization's terms, and I know this is a strong statement, because we truly are putting people's lives at risk, and they have proven before that in certain cases when the ultimatum wasn't answered – they carried out (their threat)."

Rabin: "I wish to clarify: We don't have time for evasions. The question is – are we fundamentally willing to enter negotiations or no? I ask the government members to not avoid answering this question."

Education Minister Aharon Yadlin: "Since anyone who saves an Israeli life is actually saving the entire world, and for pikuach nefesh (the preservation of human life) of those Israelis caught in this situation, I support any effort to save them, including negotiations."

Rabin: "They aren't willing to return them under these conditions, there is no point in announcing negotiations. If we do – what would we negotiate? Their non-return? Let's not run away from the issue."

Minister without Portfolio Yisrael Galili: "I suggest the government begin negotiations immediately in order to save the hostages, while showing readiness to free detainees. I don't suggest we elaborate which ones."

Rabin: "I second Galili's suggestion simply because of this: I'm not willing to explain to the public why we have traded 130 terrorists for corpses till this day, eight of which were part of hostile destructive activity including murder. And based on this, I don't wish to explain to the Israeli public or to anyone else why we can return corpses but not live people."

Peres: "Precedents aren't the problem. The problem is the future, the people's future and the future of Israeli airplanes and aviation. We should be concerned with the fate of the people here, of what will happen to the country and her status regarding hijacking, terror and so on, in addition to the fate of those taken hostage. For now, all of the terror organizations, aside from Wadie Haddad, have disagreed with hijacking, mostly because of Israel's strict and persistent stance."

Rabin: "This was a political decision made by the Fatah [the largest faction within the PLO, Palestinian Liberation Organization] to cease their operations abroad, had nothing to do with Israel's strict stance."

Peres: "If Israel had surrendered every time, the Fatah would have made the decision to continue its terror operations."

Rabin: "I wish to know whether anyone is opposed. I don't want any misunderstandings on this issue. I don't propose we discuss negotiations, but that the government authorizes the team to continue our attempts to release the hostages, including exchange of prisoners in Israel. We'll say 'prisoners', and that doesn't mean accepting the terrorists' terms. No numbers and no names. Those in favor of this offer raise your hands? It's unanimous."

1.7: Briefing by Gur to Rabin and Peres.
[Gur proposes conquering Entebbe with an option of landing at the nearby Lake Victoria and beginning a widespread operation]

Peres: "If we surrender, Israel will look so wounded and ridiculed. And if we execute an imaginative military operation it could be huge all around. I have no doubt that the IDF can do it, but then we run the risk of people being killed."

Gur: "It's an operation that's nearly impossible to plan in two days."

Peres: "We can wait one more day."

Rabin: "I feel it might end up being a lot like the 'Bay of Pigs', the biggest operation we've done so far. When I examine three different operation options – chances aren't great."

Gur: "We can't deny: The IDF isn't really built for operations in Entebbe."

Rabin: "I'm not complaining, I think we don't have military capabilities over there."

(Security forum convenes at 5 p.m.)

Peres: "We must ask ourselves whether we are willing to return all terrorists, without any exceptions."

Rabin: "What does that have to do with the mission?"

Peres: "It has a lot to do with it, since you're going to have to explain to the public why you were willing to kill them for X but not kill them for [Y]."

Rabin: "If I believe we had a chance to rescue them, I would support it regardless of the price."

Peres: "If there is a military operation, it's preferable. Until now, I admit that there's no concrete proposal, only ideas and imagination. The second proposal is complete and utter surrender. If we want to negotiate, we should send someone to Kampala [Uganda's capital]."

2.7, 12.15 p.m.: Cabinet Meeting with Gur in attendance.
[Gur proposes a practical military plan for the first time.]

Allon: "It's a flight without aerial defence."
    Rabin: "Without. The problem is interception."
    Peres: "The advantage is the element of surprise."
    Rabin: "I am still uncertain about this operation. We have never had so many hostages. The military information we have is the most limited we've ever had. This is going to be the riskiest operation I have ever known."

(Cabinet convenes at 2 p.m.)

Rabin: "Begin suggested that the government not get entangled in these reservations that we won't commit to the number of prisoners or their names, so we don't face yet another humiliating fold. I admit to accepting his proposal. We should know that from the moment they separate the hostages, it becomes Israel's problem. No one will stand with us. The decisions will be ours. The world couldn't care less. Best case, they'll be sympathetic, or not. We have no one to turn to but ourselves, and the decision isn't going to be made by anyone else but by Israeli government. We are conducting negotiations regarding the release of prisoners, but I don't recommend they start arguing about the numbers, 40 or 50. We didn't say – 'blood avenger', no. I wouldn't want to see this whole thing fail."

    Peres: "Starting tomorrow we only have half a day left, and I recommend that all ministers be prepared to stay here for a while. Tomorrow is going to be a dramatic day."

3.7, 1 p.m.: Cabinet meeting
Rabin: "New information has come into play and as of today we have a military option."

Peres: "The heart-wrenching question is whether we should risk the lives of innocent unarmed civilians, and save the future of this country, or not. If we surrender, the respect for terrorism will grow, and encourage more operations like this, seeing as how it pays off. In the eyes of the world, Israel's honor will deteriorate, and so will her deterring capabilities. Countries around the world might understand our ways, but mock us in their hearts."

Gur [presenting the military plan]: "To summarize: The operation risk is, as I see it, very calculated and can be taken. There is a possibility of injuries, just like in any other operation we've ever done to rescue civilians, but over all I think the circumstances are reasonable and a military operation can be done."

Industry and Trade Minister Haim Bar-Lev: "If they fail to refuel, how long is the flight?"

Gur: "They won't be able to return home."

Bar-Lev: "What about weather issues over there?"

Gur: "It's risky."

Minister Yosef Burg: "What if we find out they moved the hostages' location overnight?"

Rabin: "The mission will be a complete and utter failure."

Peres: "It's an IDF operation like never before. This is the first Israeli military mission in history executed outside of Middle Eastern borders."

Rabin: "I admit that after receiving the data regarding the landing I calmed down a bit, relatively of course, because I'm not saying there aren't any risks."

Allon: "I support this mission. Questions have already been raised in this country, why did we act quickly in the Ma'alot attack when there were children from a certain ethnicity involved, whereas we were willing to settle when it came to people belonging to a different ethnic group."

Bar-Lev: "If we fail, we'll have about 300 Israelis in Uganda, including soldiers, and we have to know that. But even if we don't succeed, we've done all that we can."

Rabin: "We're going to execute a complex mission with expected injuries. Nonetheless, I recommend the government approve it, though not with a light heart."

The mission was approved unanimously.

The mission the Israeli cabinet had consented to involved flying four C130 Hercules transports from Israel to Entebbe non-stop. Aboard would be a composite fifty-strong force of Sayeret Matkal ("the Unit") and the Israeli paras. On landing at Entebbe, the first "Hippo" aircraft would disgorge a Sayeret Matkal "break-in crew", which would try to reach the airport terminal before their purpose was discovered. To this end the Unit decided to use subterfuge, and commandeered a white Mercedes from a civilian parking lot in Tel Aviv and repainted it black. As Lieutenant Moshe "Muki" Betser from the Unit explained to the planners:

I know the Ugandan soldiers. I trained them. We don't need hundreds of soldiers. Instead we use a Mercedes. Every battalion commander in Uganda rides around in one. A soldier spots a Mercedes, he snaps a salute. They'll see us in the Mercedes with a couple of Land Rovers carrying soldiers and they'll assume a general's about to drive by. They aren't going to stop to shoot us.

For good measure, the twenty-nine men from the break-in crew would wear leopard-spot fatigues like those worn by Ugandan paratroopers. The break-in crew would drive off the Hippo in the Mercedes and Land Rovers to the old terminal building, less than two kilometres away, with their lights on, which would take five minutes. After arriving at the terminal they would free the hostages and secure the building. Lieutenant-Colonel Yonatan Netanyahu was placed in charge of the Unit's break-in crew. A former paratrooper, Netanyahu had been decorated for valour during the Six Day War. Somehow he managed to combine soldiering with studying philosophy at Harvard. He was also an ardent patriot, prepared to give his life for his country. At seventeen he had written:

Death does not frighten me, it arouses my curiosity. I do not fear it because I attribute little value to a life without a purpose. And if it is necessary for me to lay down my life in the attainment of the goal I set for it, I will do so willingly.

While Netanyahu was driving to the old terminal, the second Hercules, carrying another Unit team and two Armoured Personnel Carriers, would land and secure the perimeter around the old terminal.

Unit troops, paratroopers and air-force technicians aboard a third Hercules would seize the new terminal and the refuelling station. (The air-force technicians were to be responsible for refuelling the planes for the long haul home.) An APC would also speed to the adjoining military airfield where eleven MiG fighters were stationed and shoot them up.

A final and fourth Hercules would carry medical crews.

While the Cabinet had been deliberating, the Unit had built at high speed a full-size mock-up of the old terminal building; in this they were helped by civilians from the Solel Boneh construction company, who had happened to have built the terminal where the hostages were held. Strips of two-by-four wood made doors and canvas the walls for the facsimile building. All night the Unit's men practised their roles. Then the air-force technicians and paratroopers arrived and they too had a dress rehearsal. A Hercules was landed so everyone could practise their disembarkation and embarkation duties.

Meanwhile, the terrorists at Entebbe had released all the hostages who were not Israeli or aircrew as a gesture of "good will". One of the released hostages was a retired French army officer who was able to give Mossad, the Israeli intelligence agency, critical information about the hostage situation. The hostages were kept under twenty-four-hour guard in one room, and the Ugandans were definitely aiding the terrorists. Indeed, the Ugandans were acting as extra guards over the hostages. The key moment of opportunity for the rescuers seemed to be just after midnight when the hostages were ordered to lie down and go to sleep. Not only would prone hostages be out of the line of fire, the guard over them would be at its minimum, with the majority of the hijackers in the adjoining room. The French army officer was also able to give a complete run-down of the terrorists' armoury.

At 3.30 p.m. on the afternoon of 3 July, the rescue mission took off from Sharm el-Sheikh on the Red Sea. The task force's route took the international flight path over the Red Sea, mostly flying at a height of no more than 30 metres to avoid radar detection by Egyptian forces. While the rescue mission was in the air it received the absolutely definitive go ahead from Rabin. Accompanying the Hippos were Phantom jets, who would provide an escort for part of the journey, and two Boeing 707s. The first Boeing contained additional medical facilities, and would land at Nairobi airport in Kenya, the only East African country vaguely sympathetic to Israel. The other Boeing would act as a command and control centre and circle Entebbe during the raid. Near the southern outlet of the Red Sea the C-130s turned and passed south of Djibouti, and thence to Kenya, finally approaching Entebbe from the direction of Lake Victoria.

As the lead C-130 approached Entebbe after the eight-hour flight, Yonni Netanyahu, Betser and seven others climbed into the Merc, and the rest of the assault squad clambered into the Land Rovers.

When the Hercules came to a stop, the flight crews released the blocks holding the vehicles, and the rear door was lowered. Netanyahu shouted "Go!". Muki Betser was second in command:

The car lunged forward and memories poured into me as we came out of the Hercules and into the fresh night air of Africa right after rain. I felt calm, almost serene, looking out into the darkness as Amitzur drove slowly and steadily, like any convoy of VIPs in the Ugandan army, not too fast to attract attention, not too slow as to cause suspicion. The silence of the night was absolute. Far ahead, the old terminal was but a glow in the dark.

I turned to look over my shoulder. Right behind us, the Land Rovers did indeed look like Ugandan troop carriers – though the soldiers' faces were white, not black. Nonetheless, everything felt right.

I broke the radio silence between the three vehicles with the code word to my break-in crews to prepare their weapons. The ratcheting sounds of seven assault rifles clicking their first round into the chamber filled the car. I used the code to order the break-in crews to set their weapons to single-shot mode for selective shooting.

The distant halo of the old terminal's lights sharpened into detail as we rolled closer. I could see the canopied entrances to the building, just as we expected, and began the countdown in my mind to the moment when the car would stop in front of the building. And we'd rush out into action.

Out of the corner of my eye, I noticed two Ugandan soldiers. One of them was walking away from his comrade, disappearing into the dark. But I concentrated on the building ahead. We could ignore the Ugandan guards – that's why we were in the Mercedes.

The lone Ugandan sentry noticed our arrival and, in the standard operating procedure of a Ugandan soldier, raised his rifle and called out, "Advance".

It was nothing to get excited about. Just routine. I used to see it all the time in Uganda. We could drive right by him. That's why we were in the Mercedes. "Eighty, seventy, sixty," I was saying to myself under my breath, concentrating on the first canopied entrance, where I would push through the doors and enter the hall where the terrorists held the hostages. When I reached zero, the action would begin.

"Amitzur," Yonni suddenly said, breaking the silence in the car, and my concentration. "Cut to the right and we'll finish him off." The car swerved to the right.

"Leave it, Yonni," I said quietly but emphatically. "It's just his drill."

There was a moment of silence. Then Yonni repeated his order. Like me, he and Giora were carrying silenced .22 caliber Berettas, useful for very close quarters shooting. Giora Zussman cocked his Beretta, and aimed it out his window to the Ugandan. The car continued veering toward the Ugandan, away from the terminal.

"Giora, let's take care of him," Yonni said, cocking his own gun.

"No," I tried again. The entire effort of the last week was to deliver us to the front doors of the terminal in peace and quiet. The memory of Ma'alot raced through my mind. We were making a mistake, even before we reached the terminal. "Forget it, Yonni," I tried again. But I was too late.

Yonni and Giora both fired from the moving car from 10 meters away, using the silenced .22s. They were the only guns at the time that could carry silencers. I knew them well from my El Al air marshal work. It was a shot I wouldn't have tried to make. But it was too late. The silencers turned the crack of the small handguns into bare whispers. The Ugandan fell.

I sighed with relief. We could still get there and get our job done before he caused us any trouble. I tried to resume my focus on the terminal building. Amitzur continued driving toward the old terminal, now barely 50 meters away. The Land Rovers kept to the path behind us.

Suddenly, from behind us, came a terrifying sound – the long burst of a Kalashnikov. I jerked my head around, just in time to see the Ugandan, back on his feet and aiming his rifle at us, cut down by a burst of fire from the Land Rover.

The order was clear and simple. No shooting until the operation starts, but then heavy fire to keep the Ugandans away. Someone in the Land Rover behind us saw the Ugandan soldier get up, and take aim at us. Instinctively, he wanted to protect us. But now all of us were in danger, as shooting erupted all around us.

Fifty meters from the target, I was seeing the entire element of surprise evaporate in front of my eyes. The rattling gunfire certainly alerted the terrorists. At any moment the terminal building might turn into a fireball of explosions as the terrorists followed through with their threats to blow up the hostages.

From the very start of the planning, I recited the lessons of Ma'alot. "We failed there because of our own mistakes," I warned. And now it was happening again.

"Drive!" Yonni shouted at Amitzur, who braked instinctively with the first burst of Kalashnikov fire from the Land Rover behind us. "Fast!" Amitzur sped ahead another 10 meters. Fire came at us from the darkness around the tarmac.

Crammed together in the car, we became sitting ducks for the Ugandans. Yonni realized it, too. We shouted at the same time, "Stop!" Amitzur braked hard. The car slid to a stop, the Land Rovers behind us screeching to a halt.

I flung open the door and began running toward the building, still at least 50 meters away, instead of the 5 meters we planned for. I flanked left to avoid the pool of light on the tarmac directly in front of the terminal, hearing the thumping of the fighters' boots behind me. Long bursts of fire shattered the night air. But I continued running, still focused on the canopied entrance to the terminal building, my target, aware that I was pulling the fighters behind me in the same direction.

Some Ugandan fire blasted toward us from my right, screaming lead past my head. Still running, I flicked the Kalashnikov to automatic, and aimed a long burst at the source. I needed to create cover for all of us – myself and everyone in the column behind me. It was just like this in El Hiam, I thought for a second, as I raced ahead at the front of the column, creating as much fire as possible. The African flew backwards and I ran on, followed by all the fighters.

Finally I reached the building, directly below the control tower, barely a dozen meters away from the entrances to the building. The rattle and crack of rifle and submachine-gun fire shook the air, kicking up bits of asphalt at our feet. And behind me, thirty-three Sayeret Matkal soldiers bunched up, instead of heading to the assigned entrances. It was a complete contradiction of the battle plan, indeed of any combat formation.

But then I realized that no explosions yet rocked the building. We still could prevent another Ma'alot. I was first in line, and the only way to proceed was forward. I took a deep breath and resumed the race to my assigned entrance, knowing that my example would spur the fighters behind me to follow suit.

Half a dozen strides into my run, a terrorist came out of the building from the second canopied entrance. I knew I had used up most of the magazine creating the cover fire in order to reach the control tower. But I also knew that once inside I only needed a few bullets to do the job.

Now, surprised by the terrorist, I aimed and fired. Only a couple of bullets spat out of the barrel. And I missed. He ducked back into the terminal building.

Racing forward, I pulled out the empty ammo magazine, and flipped it over, reloading on the run, all the while keeping my eyes on my target – the canopied entrance to the building a few meters away. Still, no explosion racked the building. The plan could still succeed.

Instead, a second disaster struck.

No glass doorway opened at the end of the canopied path into the hall. I found myself facing a blank wall. We planned according to Solel Boneh's original architectural plans, and they clearly showed an entrance. Somehow, we lost one of the most crucial pieces of information the Frenchman gave Amiram.

Withering machine-gun fire poured down at us from the control tower. Yonni's back-up fighters were supposed to take out the machine-gun nest up there. But obviously, the fighters were still confused by the bad start. The 50-meter run from the cars, instead of the few meters we practised, threw everything off. At any second, I feared, the terrorists would ignite the explosives they planted in the hallway. I had no choice but to get inside, to prevent that from happening.

With my pre-assigned entrance blocked, I began running to the second entrance, where I saw the terrorist duck inside. Amir, a fighter from my second break-in, suddenly ran past me, followed by his team leader, Amnon. Later, Amir said that in the confusion he lost his crew and thought they already made it inside. Meanwhile, he became the first of us to get into the building.

He immediately spotted a terrorist and cut him down with a burst. Just then, Amnon ran in, and saw the German male and female terrorists kneeling side by side, aiming guns at

Amir's back. Amnon fired at the two Germans, sending them flying, just as I came in through the door, with Amos Goren on my heels.

I immediately added my own shots to the two German terrorists, to make sure they were out of the action.

For a second, silence fell over the room. Then suddenly, shooting erupted again from the outside, and screaming began inside the hall. I stood in the doorway, Amnon to my left and Amos and Amir on my extreme right, totally focused on the fully lit hall, searching for more terrorists.

People were lying all over the floor on mattresses. Some froze with fear, others screamed and shouted. People covered their heads with blankets as if to protect themselves from the bullets.

To my left, about 15 meters away, a man came out from behind a column, bringing a rifle up to firing position. Amos and I fired simultaneously, the terrorist dropping. Again we scanned the hall. A dark-haired young man jumped up from amidst the hostages. Bullets from all four Kalashnikovs cut him down.

The shooting continued outside. Suddenly, Amir remembered the megaphone he carried. "Lie down, we're the IDF. Don't get up!" He shouted the instructions in Hebrew and English. We stood that way in the room for a long moment, ready to fire again.

Hesitantly, one of the hostages raised his hand. "You got them all," he said. "All of them. But that one," he added sadly, pointing at the body of the young man we just shot, "he was one of us. A hostage."

The radio clasped to my web-belt gave me no time to respond. "Muki, Muki," it squawked.

"Muki here."

"Giora here. Mission accomplished."

He took the VIP room, which the terrorists made into their dormitory. "Two terrorists down. No casualties on our side."

The assault team then began loading the hostages on to the waiting Hippos. As they did so, they came under fire from the airport control tower. During this brief firefight Netanyahu was shot in the chest, possibly by a Ugandan sniper. The wound was mortal. At this Betser took over command of the rescue force and directed light machine-gun and RPG fire at the control tower until it was suppressed. Meanwhile, one of the APCs riddled the Ugandan MiG jets with bullets and RPG rounds, while accompanying paratroopers attached explosives to the aircraft for good destructive measure; when the Israeli force came under fire from the control tower, Betser ordered the other APC to take it out.

Fifty-three minutes after the first Hippo had touched down on Ugandan soil, all the hostages and IDF men were airborne and on the way home. Since they had been unable to refuel as planned due to the firefight around the control tower, the Israelis refuelled the Hippos by permission in Kenya.

Yonni Netanyahu was the only member of the raiding party to die. All seven of the terrorists were killed. Three hostages died at the airport during the rescue attempt; one was killed because he was close to an armed terrorist, and the second died in the terrorists' return fire; the third dead hostage was the young man who had jumped up, and the Unit men, thinking he was a terrorist, had shot him four times. Around fifty Ugandan soldiers also died.

The last victims of Entebbe were those who felt Amin's desire for revenge. Dora Bloch, a 75-year-old hostage who, after choking on food, had been taken by the Ugandans to a nearby hospital, was dragged from her bed and murdered by two of Amin's officers. When the dictator heard that the Kenyans had aided the Entebbe rescue, he rounded up hundreds of Kenyans living in Uganda and had them shot.

UN Secretary General Kurt Waldheim described the raid as "a serious violation of the national sovereignty of a United Nations member state", meaning Uganda. In his address to the Council of the UN, Israeli ambassador Chaim Herzog said:

> We come with a simple message to the Council: we are proud of what we have done because we have demonstrated to the world that in a small country, in Israel's circumstances, with which the members of this Council are by now all too familiar, the dignity of man, human life and human freedom

constitute the highest values. We are proud not only because we have saved the lives of over a hundred innocent people – men, women and children – but because of the significance of our act for the cause of human freedom.

Whatever the politics, the Entebbe operation set the military gold standard in post-War hostage rescues.

The Merc commandeered by the Unit was returned to its owner in Tel Aviv. He insisted that the IDF paint it white again.

CONTACT!

RT Vermont, MACV-SOG, Vietnam, 1970

Military Assistance Command, Vietnam – Studies and Observations Group (MACV-SOG) was a highly secret multi-service unit created in January 1964 as a result of the decision of the Kennedy administration to take the Vietnam War to the North – but covertly. Ostensibly MACV-SOG analysed combat so that lessons learned could be fed into the US Army training system. The principal task of MACV-SOG was strategic reconnaissance, but it also undertook sabotage, rescue missions, running agents into North Vietnam, and black psy-ops, by such ruses as setting up false North Vietnamese Army (NVA) radio stations.

MACV-SOG comprised around 20,000 US soldiers – almost all of them special forces – along with South Vietnamese troops from the Special Commandos and 2,700 Army, Navy, Marine and Air Force personnel.

In 1967 MACV-SOG reorganized its recon teams (RTs) into three field commands: Command and Control North (CCN); Command and Control South (CCS) and Command and Control Central (CCC).

While the teams operated across the theatre, their main hunting ground was the mountain jungle along the tri-border land where Cambodia, Laos and Vietnam met. Typically an RT was comprised of three Americans, one of whom was Team Leader ("One-Zero"), another was second-in-command ("One-One"), and the third a radio operator ("One-Three"). The rest of the team, which was typically eight to ten strong, was comprised of Montagnards, mountain people from the tribes of the Hmnong,

Nung, Sedang and Bru. In SOG speak the Montagnards were "Yards". To a man and woman they loathed the Vietnamese, who had historically deprived them of their lands.

Unusually for US units, RTs were given a high degree of independence and the leader was not the ranking soldier, but the soldier with the most experience. It was common for the leader to be an NCO and the number two an officer.

"Over the fence" or cross-border missions were code-named in the interests of secrecy. Missions into Cambodia were known as "Daniel Boone" (later "Salem House") and missions into Laos were known as "Shining Brass" (later "Prairie Fire"). Once across the border and deep into enemy territory, the RTs had no hope of fire support, and extraction by helicopter could be a long time coming. Some dozen RT teams disappeared entirely, never to be heard of again after infiltration.

Staff Sergeant Franklin D Miller, leader of RT Vermont (the 30 or so CCC RTs were named after US states), was one of MACV-SOG's legendary figures. He joined the SOG from the 1st Cavalry in 1968. On 5 January Miller's RT was tasked with a mission to locate an enemy base in the tri-border area. On their way to the target they were to try and find an intelligence-gathering helicopter that had crashed the previous day. Miller's RT consisted of three Americans: Miller himself, Hobart (RTO) and Green (medic); and four "Yards": Prep (number-two), Gai (interpreter), Yube (tail gunner) and Hyuk (point man).

After insertion by "slicks" (UH-1D Hueys), RT Vermont cautiously approached the crash site. About halfway across a grass clearing, they could see the wreck of the helicopter. Inside the cockpit the dead pilot was clearly visible.

Also clearly visible were about forty enemy troops around the helicopter. Miller fixed the chopper's position and called in a "sit rep". Withdrawing from the crash area, the team began to make their way through dense brush towards the suspected enemy base, with Hyuk and Miller out front. Suddenly there was a massive explosion. Looking around, Miller saw Prep staggering, with severe wounding to his lower jaw. A booby trap had been set off. Pushing Hyuk towards Prep and telling him to take care of the injured Yard, Miller caught movement in his peripheral vision

– an enemy platoon was coming out of the trees. Miller and Hyuk opened fire with such volume and accuracy that, although they were in the open, the enemy faltered. Miller:

> Our initial bursts hit several NVA. I'm not sure how many, maybe six or seven. When you hit a large element out in the open, especially from the flank as we did, you can mess them up badly, even with just a few guys doing the shooting.
>
> Not all of the people we hit were killed; some were wounded and fell out of our sight in the vegetation. But the key thing was that we were hitting people. We tried to concentrate on small groups of people as they ran down the slope. Every now and then I'd see one of my tracer rounds impact on someone, knocking him flat. I always loaded my magazines with two tracers near the bottom and two more rounds under them. That way I knew I was near the end of the rounds in that magazine when the tracer rounds flew.
>
> It took a few moments for them to realize we were there. When they did discover our presence, they turned and tried to fire on us. However, they quickly realized that they were shooting through their own people. When they figured out that their position was very awkward, they performed a mass withdrawal.
>
> There was still a slight haze in the air when the enemy disengaged. As Hyuk and I quickly headed down into the kill zone to inspect the damage, I saw people lying everywhere.
>
> It looked like the bodies had been put through a meat grinder. Dead enemy troops were mixed in with the prone members of my team.
>
> Prep, who staggered up the slope after the blast, still clung to life by a bare thread. Yube, the one who'd discovered the booby trap, was – unbelievably – still alive. He'd taken the brunt of the blast and had hundreds of holes over his entire body. Amazingly enough, not only was he still alive, but he was the least critically injured of the five who were caught in the explosion.
>
> Hobart, Gai and Green were all very seriously injured and not capable of moving under their own power. I turned to

Hyuk and as calmly as I could said, "Let's get the fuck out of this area. We'll move everyone across the stream and get it between us and them. That way, if they come for us, we'll have some kind of barrier and open ground to help us deal with them."

Less than a minute had elapsed since the enemy withdrew. They wouldn't stay away very long; of that I was positive. I was sure that any second they'd regroup and come slamming into us. Fighting down panic, I threw Gai's arm around my neck, grabbed Hobart by his web gear, and literally dragged them across the rocky stream bed and through the water to the other side. Hyuk gathered up Yube and placed Green over his shoulder.

They moved the injured men up on the bank behind the stream, down behind some vegetation.

Miller radioed back that he had a Tactical Emergency; a Quick Reaction Force at Dak To, the centre for the mission, was put on standby.

No sooner had Miller made his radio call, than Prep died. And then he could hear the sounds of a large group of enemy soldiers shouting, "We hit them! We got some of them!" The NVA had seen the blood at the ambush site.

Moments later, the NVA platoon appeared, with the sergeant in command ordering two soldiers out on a flanking manoeuvre. He also set up a machine gun.

As one of the flanking soldiers swept wide, he saw the little huddled group of RT Vermont – and opened fire:

It startled me when he started shooting. By now half of my attention was focused on the machine gun by the stream. That was the big hammer, and I was trying to decide how I was going to deal with it when – I knew it would be when and not if – we were discovered.

There was no more time to think.

Instincts took over.

Seconds after the enemy troop started firing I leaned back, raised myself up slightly to get a clear shot, and cranked off a single round. It caught him square in the shoulder and slammed him to the ground like a rag doll.

The soldier lying near the stream bed saw me rise up and immediately took me under fire. As he was shooting at me, I was already pivoting in the direction of the machine gun. My primary hope was to somehow luck out and damage the weapon with a burst of rounds. However, it would be tough enough just to hit around it under the circumstances.

But when I turned I found the assistant gunner standing straight up, wondering what was going on. His mental lapse proved costly. I cut loose with a controlled automatic burst in his direction and managed to drop him. The gunner quickly shifted his sights and put some major smoke on me. I hit the ground in a hurry.

After the machine gun opened up, everyone on the hillside followed suit. Since I was the lone target they concentrated their fire on me. They threw rounds at me the likes of which I'd never experienced before. I was concealed in bushes and tall grass only; I didn't have any type of cover available – such as a tree or rock – to stop the rounds. They ripped through the vegetation all around my prone form, miraculously missing their mark.

Chucking CS and White Phosphorus grenades caused the enemy to halt their attack. Under cover of the smoke, Miller and Hyuk carried and escorted the wounded parallel to the stream. After 100 metres they paused to rest from the effort. Almost immediately there was a heavy burst of fire from bushes twenty metres to their left. Hyuk returned fire, then was killed by a round to the neck. Miller desperately threw a fragmentation grenade. This neutralized the attack.

RT Vermont needed a better defensive position. Looking around, Miller saw some rocks and fallen timber, which provided protection and also fair lines of fire, and made towards it.

Seconds later, five or six enemy stepped out of the trees, walking casually. They had the machine gun with them. They had misjudged Miller's position.

For once, Miller had the advantage of surprise. He opened fire, taking out the machine gunner first. Their return of fire ricocheted harmlessly off the rocks. A grenade was not so harm-less. The explosion blew his weapon from his hands, and nearly caused him to black out. Just as he came round he saw two NVA scouting the rocks for him. Snatching his weapon from the ground, he shot both.

Calling in a situation report, the Forward Air Controller in the area, who had been monitoring Miller's comms, told him that there was a bomb crater 150 metres to the east, and this was the closest possible extraction site. Miller went to recce it. On finding the crater clear of NVA, he signalled the FOAC by flashing a mirror, then started back to the team.

Then he was on the ground, vomiting, blood running out of his nose. Looking at his front, he could see froth. There was a horrible wheezing sound. A bullet had entered his chest and exited his back. Half dazed, he spent agonizing fumbling minutes dressing his wound.

He was dimly aware of some men approaching him. They thought he was dead. He was not and fired his weapon, which was slung around his waist. The three men went down.

Getting to his feet, Miller stumbled back to the team. Hobart took one look at him and said: "man are we fucked now".

He had a point. Despite having a bullet hole through his chest, Miller was the "most physically fit guy there".

And all he had to do was carry his men the 150 metres to the crater. Franklin D Miller:

I can hardly begin to describe the genuine effort it took for me to carry, push and drag everyone to that giant hole in the jungle. The entire episode remains blurred in my mind to this day; I really don't remember too many details. I do recall feel-ing incredibly tired – I wanted to go to sleep so badly. I remember concentrating on putting one foot in front of the other as one of the Yards hung limp at my side. Once I was on my hands and knees as I pulled someone along by his web gear. Crawl forward a few feet, pull hard, fight the pain. Crawl, pull. Crawl, pull.

In time I somehow managed to assist or flat-out transport each member of RT Vermont to the extraction point. Once we were all in the crater, I established some semblance of security. Hobart and Yube were capable of firing their weapons if push came to shove, so I positioned them where they could provide the most help in our defense.

We waited.

Shortly after taking up residence in the crater, we were assaulted by a sizeable force. Rounds began to fly back and forth. Just as the battle was beginning to heat up, a new and unexpected variable entered the equation.

Dramatically, a Huey materialized out of thin air! It simply came out of nowhere and dropped down to within five meters or so of the crater's rim, where it hovered unsteadily. I looked skyward and spotted the door gunner shifting around behind the M60, scanning the area. I didn't have a clue as to who was in the chopper or what operation they were running. All I knew was it didn't belong to my organization. But man, it was the first sign of friendlies I'd seen all day, and my emotions ran wild.

Too bad I didn't have any time to enjoy the moment.

Mere seconds after the Huey dropped in from out of the blue, the jungle surrounding the crater came alive in a frightening display of firepower. 7.62mm, mortar and anti-tank rounds burst out of the light vegetation. All the destructive force was focused on one target: the chopper.

I didn't attempt to return any fire. It would have been useless and a waste of ammo. We were in a whirlwind of devastation, and the best course of action was to hug the ground and ride out the storm. I watched in awe as the drama unfolded.

The noise was deafening. Shit was flying everywhere. Scores of tracers ripped up through the trees, and rockets spewing smoke crisscrossed every which way. If even one of the anti-tank rounds had hit the chopper it would have been all over; as it was, none found the mark. However, the 7.62mm rounds found their target often. The Huey was being eaten up by the rifle and machine-gun fire. The door gunner was hit and hung limp over the M60. The chopper's skin was pockmarked from hundreds of rounds. There must have been fifty or more enemy troops assaulting the Huey with but a single thought – bring that son of a bitch down!

All this activity occurred within ten to twenty seconds. How the chopper stayed in the air I'll never know. By all rights it should have been shot down. But stay aloft it did and, badly scarred from the effort, it beat a hasty – if somewhat erratic – retreat. Its departure sent a chill down my spine.

Now the enemy would focus his attention on us.

A lull ensued after the chopper left. No more 7.62mm, mortar or anti-tank rounds were fired. There was movement all around us, but no hostilities were directed our way. I couldn't understand why they didn't attack immediately. They knew we were in the crater, surely they could have overwhelmed us with sheer numbers or simply lobbed a few mortars or frags on top of us. As strange as it may seem, I was irritated and concerned as to the reasons for the delay. I knew the asskick was coming. Finally, I concluded that they were toying with us.

Ten minutes later they mounted an assault, although it wasn't quite as strong as I had expected. They laid into us with a heavy barrage of fire as we met the challenge. Hobart, Yube and I gave as good as we got, and we forced them to back off after a few minutes of frenzied action.

With the slick gone, Miller decided to go on the offensive. RT Vermont had been in action for over four hours. It would be dark in two or three. They were running short on ammo.

Telling Hobart and Yube to remain where they were, he crawled to the edge of the jungle and hid down. And waited.

About an hour before dark, he heard the enemy coming on. Not expecting a firefight in advance of the crater, his opening rounds dropped two or three. They responded with an anti-tank rocket which hit the rock he was hiding behind. Miller then threw his last fragmentation grenade just as the NVA was running towards his position. With a burst of fire at the survivors, Miller then threw his last two CS grenades and crawled and ran back to the crater.

Just as he cleared the crater, the NVA came on through the gas cloud. Miller, Yube and Hobart all returned fire. The NVA charge was stopped ten metres from the crater rim.

Now the NVA sniped at the survivors. Miller was hit in the arm. Yube was hit again. Hobart was hit again.

The NVA riflemen edged themselves into better and better shooting positions. It was 7 p.m. and almost dark.

Miller looked at Hobart. They both had tears running down their faces. The end had surely come.

Miller looked out of the crater. And thought he was "seeing things". There was a Yard approaching, the point man of a "Hatchet Force" platoon-strength relief unit. The American lieutenant commanding the unit reached the edge of the crater, looked at the bloody and bleeding survivors of RT Vermont and the NVA bodies sprawled around and said: "Motherfucker, this looks like Custer's Last Stand".

After a secure perimeter was established, RT Vermont was extracted by helicopter. Miller was the last to go, as he was still the least wounded.

Gai and Green died during surgery. Miller, Yube and Hobart were the only survivors.

Staff Sergeant Franklin D. Miller was awarded the Medal of Honour for his actions that day. The citation read:

For conspicuous gallantry and intrepidity in action at the risk of his life above and beyond the call of duty. S/Sgt. Miller, 5th Special Forces Group, distinguished himself while serving as team leader of an American-Vietnamese long-range reconnaissance patrol operating deep within enemy-controlled territory. Leaving the helicopter insertion point, the patrol moved forward on its mission. Suddenly, 1 of the team members tripped a hostile booby trap which wounded 4 soldiers. S/Sgt. Miller, knowing that the explosion would alert the enemy, quickly administered first aid to the wounded and directed the team into positions across a small stream bed at the base of a steep hill. Within a few minutes, S/Sgt. Miller saw the lead element of what he estimated to be a platoon-size enemy force moving toward his location. Concerned for the safety of his men, he directed the small team to move up the hill to a more secure position. He remained alone, separated from the patrol, to meet the attack. S/Sgt. Miller single-handedly repulsed 2 determined attacks by the numerically superior enemy force and caused them to withdraw in disorder. He rejoined his team, established contact with a forward air controller and arranged the evacuation of his patrol. However, the only suitable extraction location in the heavy jungle was a bomb crater some 150 meters from the team location. S/Sgt. Miller reconnoitered the route to the crater and led his men through the enemy-controlled jungle to the extraction site. As the evacuation helicopter hovered over the crater to pick up the patrol, the enemy launched a savage automatic weapon and rocket-propelled grenade attack against the beleaguered team, driving off the rescue helicopter. S/Sgt. Miller led the team in a valiant defense which drove back the enemy in its attempt to overrun the small patrol. Although seriously wounded and with every man in his patrol a casualty, S/Sgt. Miller moved forward to again single-handedly meet the hostile attackers. From his forward exposed position, S/Sgt. Miller gallantly repelled 2 attacks by the enemy before a friendly relief force reached the patrol location. S/Sgt. Miller's gallantry, intrepidity in action, and selfless devotion to the welfare of his comrades are in keeping with the highest traditions of the military service and reflect great credit on him, his unit, and the U.S. Army.

Of all special forces in Vietnam, MACV-SOG RT teams took the highest percentage of casualties, making up just 10 per cent of special forces but 50 per cent of the KIA. In recognition of MACV-SOG's bravery and efficiency the whole unit was given the Medal of Honour by President George Bush. The citation read:

By virtue of the authority vested in me as President of the United States and as Commander in Chief of the Armed Forces of the United States, I have today awarded THE PRESIDENTIAL UNIT CITATION (ARMY) FOR

EXTRAORDINARY HEROISM TO THE STUDIES AND OBSERVATIONS GROUP, MILITARY ASSISTANCE COMMAND, VIETNAM SOG-MACV 11:00 AM April 4th, 2001 at Ft. Bragg, NC

The *Studies and Observations Group* is cited for extraordinary heroism, great combat achievement and unwavering fidelity while executing unheralded top secret missions deep behind enemy lines across Southeast Asia. Incorporating volunteers from all branches of the Armed Forces, and especially, U.S. Army Special Forces, SOG's ground, air and sea units fought officially denied actions which contributed immeasurably to the American war effort in Vietnam.

MACV-SOG reconnaissance teams composed of special forces soldiers and indigenous personnel penetrated the enemy's most dangerous redoubts in the jungled Laotian wilderness and the sanctuaries of eastern Cambodia. Pursued by human trackers and even bloodhounds, these small teams outmaneuvered, outfought and outran their numerically superior foe, to uncover key enemy facilities, rescue downed pilots, plant wiretaps, mines and electronic sensors, capture valuable enemy prisoners, ambush convoys, discover and assess targets for B-52 strikes, and inflict casualties all out of proportion to their own losses. When enemy counter-measures became dangerously effective, SOG operators innovated their own counters, from high altitude parachuting and unusual explosive devices, to tactics as old as the French and Indian War. Fighting alongside their Montagnard, Chinese Nung, Cambodian and Vietnamese allies, special forces-led Hatchet Force companies and platoons staged daring raids against key enemy facilities in Laos and Cambodia, overran major munitions and supply stockpiles, and blocked enemy highways to choke off the flow of supplies to South Vietnam.

SOG's cross-border operations proved an effective economy-of-force, compelling the North Vietnamese Army to divert 50,000 soldiers to rear area security duties, far from the battlefields of South Vietnam. Supporting these hazardous missions were SOG's own U.S. and South Vietnamese

Air Force transport and helicopter squadrons, along with USAF Forward Air Controllers and helicopter units of the U.S. Army and U.S. Marine Corps. These courageous aviators often flew through heavy fire to extract SOG operators from seemingly hopeless situations, saving lives by selflessly risking their own. SOG's Vietnamese naval surface forces – instructed and advised by U.S. Navy SEALs – boldly raided North Vietnam's coast and won surface victories against the North Vietnamese Navy, while indigenous agent teams penetrated the very heartland of North Vietnam.

Despite casualties that sometimes became universal, SOG's operators never wavered, but fought throughout the war with the same flair, fidelity and intrepidity that distinguished SOG from its beginning. The Studies and Observations Group's combat prowess, martial skills and unacknowledged sacrifices saved many American lives, and provide a paragon for America's future special operations forces.

President of the United States   George Walker Bush

DOCUMENT: Mike Force After Action Reports

Mobile Strike Force Command or "Mike Force" was a unit-controlled MACV-SOG. Like the RT teams, Mike Force teams comprised indigenous soldiers led by US Special Forces, and sometimes the Australian SAS. Mike Force was primarily a quick reaction and combat reconnaissance unit:

AFTER ACTION REPORT: ATTLEBORO,
1–7 NOVEMBER 1966
SUBJECT: After Action Report MIKE Force/"Attleboro" 1–7 Nov 66 General:
a. Third Corps MIKE Force had moved to Loc Ninh on 30 October 1966 in support of moving to new camp site, and was on an operation in Loc Ninh area. b. Third Corps MIKE Force was alerted 2 November 1966 to move from Loc Ninh to Suoi Da. The move was completed at 1430 2 November 1966.
[. . .]

3. Task Organization

a. 530 Nungs in three (3) companies. b. Seven USASF EM. c. One USASF Officer.

4. Mission: Combat Reconnaissance.

5. Sequence of Events:

1 Nov

2210 China Boy alerted for movement from Loc Ninh to Suoi Da.

2 Nov

08001st MIKE force company extracted from LZ. 0900 Company closed Loc Ninh. 10452nd Company extraction began. 1215Completed extraction 2nd Company. 1030C-123 aircraft began arriving Loc Ninh. Direct support helicopter company moved from Loc Ninh to Tay Ninh East to lift MF from Tay Ninh East; and to lift MF from Tay Ninh West to Suoi Da. 1352Tay Ninh. 1530Movement of MF from Tay Ninh to Suoi Da completed.

2 Nov

1630 China Boy Company 3 deployed.

3 Nov

0830 China Boy Company 1 deployed. 1220China Boy Company 3 engaged est VC Co vic XT486687, VC broke contact 1245, fled north. SSG Monaghan wounded right arm and fingers (GSW): 1815China Boy Company 1 made contact vic XT458587 with est VC platoon. VC broke contact 1830. SSG Garza WIA (GSW).

4 Nov

0730 China Boy Company 1 hit mined area vic XT561588. One MF KIA, two MF WIA. Medevac chopper downed by SF fire vic XT485622, while enroute to China Boy Company 1's location. One US KIA (Crew Member), chopper was recovered. 1445 China Boy Company 3 made contact vic XT416670 with est VC Bn or Regt. China Boy Company 3 withdrew south and called in airstrike. On initial contact chain saws, generators, and trucks could be heard. VC counterfired with 81mm and 60mm mortar, AW and SA fire, then tried to close with China Boy Company 3 elements. 1800 Received resupply of ammunition and food vic

XT435668. 2200China Boy Company 3 indicated that he was receiving heavy casualties and VC were encircling him. 2300 China Boy Company 3 indicated light contact.

5 Nov

0230 China Boy Company 3 indicates contact with VC has ceased. 0730China Boy Company 3 receiving heavy volume of fire. Requested reinforcements. 0745Radio contact with China Boy Company 3 broken. 0800China Boy Companies I and 2 proceeding to China Boy Company 3's location. 0845China Boy Company 2 hit VC bunkers. Negative contact. 094028 MF personnel picked up by CIDG CO from Suoi Da. 0935China Boy Company 3 having casualties evacuated vic XT388634. 1200Three USSF MIA. 55 MF from China Boy Company 3 made linkup with China Boy Companies 1 and 2. Of those 15 to 25 WIA.

5 Nov

1330 One MF drowned while crossing river with China Boy Company 1.

6 Nov

1040 Est VC platoon with mortars attacked Suoi Da airfield, 4 CIDF KIA, 2 WIA. 1700 9 MF personnel closed in to Suoi Da.

7 Nov

1430 MF begins move to Loc Ninh. 1600MF completes move to Loc Ninh. 1645One US body found. 1830MF bodies returned to Bien Hoa by CV-2 aircraft.

6. (C) On 30 October, all 3 companies of the Mike Force deployed to Loc Ninh, A-331 Binh Long Province, to conduct operations in response to intelligence reports that the camp was a possible target for a major VC attack prior to 11 November 1966. However, hard intelligence reports received on 1 November indicated that a VC regiment had moved into the operational area of Camp Suoi Da, A-322, Tay Ninh Province. A decision was made to move the Mike Force into that area, and this was accomplished on 2 November. On 031220 November, the 3rd Mike Force Company made contact with an estimated VC company. The VC immediately broke contact and an airstrike was

called in on their route of withdrawal. At 031845, contact was again established with an estimated VC platoon which resulted in 10 VC KIA and two USASF WIA. At 040730, the 1st Mike Force Company hit a mined area and suffered one KIA and two W1A. A Med Evac chopper in the same general vicinity was shot down by small arms fire and resulted in one US KIA. At 041445, the 3rd Mike Force Company made contact with an estimated battalion or regimental sized VC force. This contact resulted in 15 VC KIA and two Mike Force WIA. The Mike Force Company was still in contact at 041540 and attempted to withdraw to the south. At 042000 the Mike Force Commander reported that he was surrounded and had suffered 35 casualties (KIA). The remaining two CIDG companies departed Camp Suoi Da to reinforce the operation. At 042305 the 3rd Mike Force Company Commander reported that he was still in contact. Enemy casualties reported at this time were 50 VC KIA. Contact with the VC was broken at 050330. At 050900 the 3rd Mike Force Company again reported that they were receiving a heavy volume of fire. They were instructed to secure an LZ so that an attempt could be made to extract them from the area. This was accomplished at 051200. All Mike Force elements were extracted at 051830.

Interview with SFC Heaps, 7 Nov 66 At 021630 Nov China Boy 3 landed at LZ vicinity XT491644, and began moving north (see attached overlay). At 031220 Nov vic XT473683 China Boy 3 discovered tunnel complex and fortifications. While destroying complex, VC fired on China Boy 3 wounding SSG Monaghan. China Boy 3 withdrew east to LZ, vic XT487686. Med Evac arrived, casualties were loaded, but because chopper was overloaded it could not take off. SSG Hunt, who came in with the Med Evac, elected to remain with China Boy 3 so that casualties could be evacuated. Again China Boy 3 moved west to tunnel complex, but could not take it because of intense fire. China Boy 3 broke contact and moved to vicinity XT465692 (see overlay). Here they heard several motors that sounded like generators and trucks, plus several chain saws. Heavy contact was made. China Boy 3 received heavy automatic weapons fire and mortar fire. Mortar sounded like 60mm. China Boy 3 broke contact and moved to LZ vicinity XT435667 (see overlay). All during the time they were moving to LZ they were receiving sporadic small arms fire. Also when they crossed road vic XT453667, they received mortar fire.

At LZ vic XT435667 China Boy 3 received resupply of food and ammunition. From resupply LZ the unit moved to vicinity XT444672, went into defensive perimeter and began breaking down ammo. While they were breaking down ammo, the VC attacked from the east in a "U" shaped formation. It was beginning to get dark and the VC withdrew to approximately 100 meters east of China Boy 3's position and maintained contact all night. At approximately 0645–0700 the following morning the VC made another assault on China Boy 3's position and overran them. SFC Heaps and SSG Hunt were wounded during this assault. SFC Heaps said he was knocked unconscious and when he came to SSG Hunt was giving him first aid. Heaps and Hunt decided to get to the LZ vic XT424680. They had two Mike Force with them, one was wounded. They couldn't move very fast or very far without resting, and Heaps and Hunt would pass out periodically. Finally Hunt said he could go no further so Heaps left one Mike Force with Hunt and continued to the LZ. After this Heaps didn't remember anything.

Interview of SFC E7 Heaps on 7 Nov 66, 3rd Field Hospital. REFERENCE: LOC NINH Map Sheet 6245 II 465691 to 473681, first contact;

Area of Operations: Major contact overrun at 440669

Weather: Excellent, high clouds, temperature.

Terrain: Jungle (thick) close to water supply, within 500 meters of road on high ground.

Fortifications: Tunnel and bunker complexes for one, two or squad size positions. All with overhead cover and pre-arranged fields of fire. Positions were hardened against direct fire.

Weapons, uniforms and equipment: Automatic weapons were in abundance; of the two weapons captured they were AKs. They had a lot of machine guns, sounded like 30 cal, heavy. Uniforms were mixed, personnel KIA had on black shoes. All of the soldiers encountered had complete sets of web gear.

Significant weapons: Grenade launcher which looked like our "IAW", light in weight, approximately 3 feet long, markings appeared to be Chinese, possible identification: Chinese anti-tank grenade launcher type 56, P. 155 DA pamphlet 381-10. Indirect fire was provided by 60mm mortars, identification by rounds.

Tactics: Fire discipline was excellent. Upon making contact, VC fired in mass; upon breaking contact VC ceased fire without sporadic firing. The VC maintained contact while the unit was trying to break contact.

They mortared and sniped at them in the retreat. After fixing the new location of the 3rd Company they (VC) attacked using squad fire and maneuver up to grenade range and then reverted to individual action. By this time, it was almost dark, so the VC withdrew approximately 100 meters and maintained contact all night. At 0645–0700 the next morning they assaulted using the same tactics with a heavy volume of fire suppressing the 3rd Company's position.

Movement was forward by flanks and frontal assault forces.

Other: The VC troopers were young and aggressive.

At grid 465691 Generators and chain saws were heard.

[. . .]

US units committed to Operations. US 173d Abn Bde2 Bns ARVN Ranger Bns (Attached)2 US 1st Div8 Bns US 25th Div3 Bns 196th Bde1 Bn

AFTER ACTION REPORT: OPERATION BLACKJACK 33

1. SIZE AND COMPOSITION OF OPERATION: Reconnaissance Company with company headquarters; Nine Roadrunner Teams composed of four Vietnamese Nations (VNN) each; Seven Reconnaissance teams

composed of two USASF and four VNN each; Three Mike Force Companies composed of 11 USASF and 428 VNN; Detachment A-303/Mobile Guerrilla Force 957 composed of 13 USASF and one Mobile Guerrilla Company, 174 VNN.

2. MISSION: To conduct extended reconnaissance and Mobile Guerrilla Force operations in AO Blackjack as directed by CG, 1st Infantry Division.

3. TIME OF DEPARTURE/RETURN: Operation Blackjack 33 was conducted from a Forward Operations Base (FOB) located at Phuoc Vinh, RVN inside the perimeter of 1st Bde, 1st Inf Div. during the period 24 Apr–24 May 67. Project SIGMA advance party began movement by C-130 from Bien Hoa Airbase to FOB 240800 Apr and completed movement 241700 Apr 67. FOB activated 241730 Apr. The main body was moved by C-123 transport from Bien Hoa Airbase with the first element arriving 261000 Apr and the last element closing at 261630 Apr 67. The operation terminated 240700 May and the Detachment command element (-) was returned to Base Camp by helicopter closing 240800 May. The main body began movement 240820 May by C-130 transport to Bien Hoa Airbase. Project SIGMA elements closed at Base Camp 241548 May 67.

4. CONDUCT OF OPERATIONS: Operation Blackjack 33 began with the issuance of a verbal OPORD on 191300 Apr 67. CO, Det B-56 issued a fragmentary order for movement of an advance party to Phuoc Vinh, RVN, on 24 Apr 67. On 20 Apr 67 the units airlift requirements were submitted by the S3 to II FFV. An advance coordination party departed for Phuoc Vinh to select a unit location. The S2 visited II FFV, CICV, and G2, 1st Inf. Div and obtained current intelligence and requirements concerning the assigned AO. A message was received placing Project SIGMA in direct support of the 1st Inf Div effective 25 Apr 67 for period of 60 days. On 21 Apr. CO, Det B-56, CO, Recon Company, S2, Det B-56 and

CO, MGF 957 made a coordination visit to Hq, 1st Bde, 1st Inf Div. Det S3 published a unit movement order for Operation Blackjack 33. OPORD 8-67 (Operation Blackjack 33) was published 242300 Apr 67. On 271400 Apr an aerial reconnaissance of the entire AO was conducted. Helicopter support, provided by 162d Assault Helicopter Company, was composed of four transport and two armed helicopters. Two O1E radio relay were provided by 184th Avn CO. CO, Det B-56 ordered three Roadrunner Teams to begin preparation for infiltration on 27 Apr. On 281055 Apr. CO MGF 957 arrived at the FOB and briefed the CO, Det 3-56. On 281345 Apr. CO, Det B-56 and CO, MGF 957 briefed the CO, 1st Inf Div and on 290800, S3, Det B-56 briefed CO, 1st Bde and staff. On 021907 May MGF 957 (-) was lifted by helicopter into AO vicinity Chi Linh. On 022020, CO Det B-56, DCO and S3 returned from visit with MGF 957 at Trang Sup and Chi Linh. MGF 957 was extracted from AO with KIA and MIA and closed FOB 032030 May. On 040830 May, CO, 5th SFGA and DCO, Spec Opns, arrived FOB for briefing on MGF 957 engagement. On 041145 May MGF 957 was moved to Trang Sup by 2 CH-47 helicopters. On 071500, CO, MGF 957 presented mission briefback at FOB for DCO Spec Opns, 5th SFGA and party. MGF 957 closed at Dong Xoai 091700 May and entered AO on foot at 092400 May 67.

a. Reconnaissance Team Operations:

(1) Recon Msn 1: Team received order 290930 Apr and presented mission briefback 29200 Apr. Team infiltrated 300626 Apr vic XT971400 without incident. At 301025 Apr team sighted approx 5–10 VC vic XT971679 and requested artillery at 301049 Apr. Results of artillery fire are unknown. Team was extracted by sling under fire vic XT988682 at 011810 May.

(2) Recon Msn 2: Team received mission order 291000 Apr and presented mission briefback 292030 Apr. Team attempted infiltration vic XT975397 at 300759 Apr. Team

leader suffered a broken leg exiting the helicopter and the mission was aborted.

(3) Recon Msn 3: Team received mission order 302000 Apr. conducted aerial recon of RZ 010900 May and presented mission briefback 012030 May. While attempting infiltration vic XT9l8571 at 020620 May, the helicopter crashed, not as a result of enemy action. Four USASF personnel were slightly injured, but all returned to duty. Gunner of helicopter crew was medevaced. All personnel, radio and weapons were immediately evacuated. A reaction platoon was airlanded at 020710 May and secured the downed helicopter until evacuated.

(4) Recon Msn 4: Team received mission order 011400 May, conducted aerial recon of RZ 020900 May and presented mission briefback at 021300 May. Team was infiltrated vic YT012814 at 030650 May. At 030715 May 2 VC were sighted and a hasty ambush was set up in an attempt to capture a PW. The two VC sighted returned in approx 20 minutes with estimated 25 men and team heard signals from three sides. Team requested exfiltration and moved to a LZ vic YT008813 and were extracted by sling at 030850 May under fire.

(5) Recon Msn #5: Team received mission order 042000 May, conducted aerial recon at 051400 May and presented mission briefback 051900 May. Team infiltrated vic XT994563 at 061159 May without incident, and exfiltrated vic XT980568 at 071205 May when two VNN team members became too ill to continue. No significant sightings.

(6) Recon Msn 6: Team received mission order at 052000 May, conducted aerial recon of RZ at 061000 May and presented mission briefback 061900 May. Team infiltrated vic YT022582 at 070952 May without incident, and was exfiltrated vic YT010613 at 080740 May due to faulty radios. Team was re-infiltrated in vic YT036633 at 081339 May without incident after securing a new radio at the FOB. Team moved to a well used trail vic YT036638, turned west on trail for 100 meters then observed and killed one VC (BC). Team called for exfiltration and was extracted by sling vic YT039639 at 081445 May.

(7) Recon Msn 7: Team received mission order 062000 May, conducted aerial recon of RZ 071000 May and presented mission briefback at 071600 May. Team infiltrated vic YT061372 at 080730 May and moved crosscountry until 081550 May at which time they observed a VC jump from a tree vic YT051700. Team assumed position was compromised and requested exfiltration which was completed from vic YT052200 at 081605 May without incident.

(8) Recon Msn 8: Team received mission order 071000 May, conducted aerial recon of RZ 071500 May and presented mission briefback at 082030 May. Team infiltrated vic YT030440 at 090655 May. Team observed an estimated 200 VC moving southwest. Airstrikes were called in and a ground assessment by two platoons of 1st Company reported 43 VC KBA (BC), 9 VC KIA (BC) and 2 VC CIA and a large amount of medical supplies recovered. Two team members became separated due to a misunderstanding and were exfiltrated vic YT055414 at 111130 May. Remainder of team was exfiltrated from LZ at 111145 May.

(9) Recon Msn 9: Team received mission order 082000 May, conducted aerial recon of RZ at 091300 and presented mission briefback at 091700 May. Team infiltrated vic XT 946404 at 100705, moved only 100 meters and found themselves surrounded by an estimated two platoons of VC. At 100750 May team was receiving fire from three directions. Gunships suppressed the area with fire and the team was extracted at 100815 May. Artillery fire was placed in area with unknown results.

(10) Recon Msn 10: Team received mission order 091600 May, conducted aerial recon of RZ 100800 May and presented mission briefback at 101230 May. Team infiltrated vic YT023711 at 101558 May without incident. Team moved immediately into an ambush position with the mission of capturing a POW. Team remained in ambush position with negative contact and was exfiltrated from vic YT023705 at 111732 May. Team was exfiltrated because one VNM team member was believed to have appendicitis.

(11) Recon Msn 11: Team received mission order 110800 May and conducted aerial recon of RZ 111500 May and presented mission briefback at 120800 May. Team infiltrated vic YT036634 at 121340 May with the mission of capturing a PW. Team set up ambush on a trail vic YT039639 and at 121510 May ambushed one VC, wounding him. Team then called for extraction but POW DOW before they were extracted from infiltration LZ at 121530 May without incident.

(12) Recon Msn 12: Team received mission order 131000 May and conducted aerial recon of RZ 131500 May and presented mission briefback 141700 May. Team had planned infiltration for RZ HOTEL, but team leader was medevaced with a perforated eardrum. A new team leader was assigned and team infiltrated RZ GOLF vic XT945348 on 141458 May. Team captured one VC (female) nurse in close proximity to infiltration LZ and was exfiltrated from that location at 141528 without incident. PW was turned over to 1st Inf Div for interrogation.

(13) Recon Msn 13: Team received mission order 141000 May, conducted aerial recon of RZ 141500 May and presented mission briefback 142000 May. Team infiltrated vic XT981651 at 151245 May. Team encountered a VC force of 7 men at 151500 May and opened fire, killing 2 VC (BC). Team, was extracted under fire at 151545 May from infiltration LZ.

(14) Recon Msn 14: Team received mission order 151000 May, conducted aerial recon of RZ 161430 May and presented a mission briefback at 161910 May. Team infiltrated vic YT045645 at 170655 May and moved to a well used trail to observe and capture a PW. Team observed an estimated VC Battalion using the trail, artillery fired with unknown results and team was extracted vic YT036644 at 181510 May without incident.

b. Roadrunner Team Operations.

(1) RR Msn 1: Team was infiltrated vic XT687572 at 271617 Apr without incident. Team made contact with 3 VC vic

XT684568 at 271630 Apr. Team was fired on vic XT678527 during movement to LZ. One man WIA, left arm (DOW) and team extracted under fire at 281710 Apr vic XT665509. (2) RR Msn 2: Team was infiltrated vic XT614525 at 271655 Apr without incident. Observed 4 VC at XT625546 with machettes.

Team fired on from church vic XT658579. Team threw grenade into the church with unknown results. Team suffered negative casualties, and was exfiltrated 281707 Apr vic XT084590 without incident.

(3) RR Msn 3: Team was infiltrated via XT615630 at 271640 Apr. Team moved approx 200 meters off the LZ and were observed by 6 VC. Fire was exchanged with unknown results. Team threw emergency smoke and were extracted under fire at 271700 Apr vic of the Infiltration LZ. Negative friendly casualties.

(4) RR Msn 4: Team was infiltrated 281902 Apr vic XT688444 without incident. Team observed a VC platoon (40 men) at 282130 Apr vic XT833521 moving south on road. Team contacted 8 VC at 290910 Apr vic XT844479 and were followed and fired on with negative casualties. Team was extracted at 291647 Apr vic XT837473.

(5) RR Msn 5: Team was infiltrated at 281855 Apr vic XT840525. Team sighted one VC Platoon moving south on road vic XT641489 at 291400 Apr. VC fired at team at 291415 Apr and wounded team leader and one other team member. Team returned fire and killed 4 VC. Team evaded and were extracted at 291657 Apr vic XT632487

(6) RR Msn 6: Team infiltrated 291808 Apr vic XT944633 without incident. Team made contact with approx one VC Platoon at 300745 Apr vic XT896748. VC were in foxholes and fired at the team, team didn't return fire and were exfiltrated at 301705 Apr vic XT917735 without incident.

(7) RR Msn 7: Team was infiltrated at 291759 Apr vic XT944633 without incident. One man became lost from team upon infiltration and other three members became lost during movement. Team of three was fired on vic XT949631. Team returned fire with unknown results. Team

encountered one VC at 0292300 Apr vic XT954630 in a hut and estimated a VC Platoon later tried to locate them with flashlights. Entire team joined up and were extracted by sling at 300705 Apr vic XT957768 without incident.

(8) RR Msn 9: Team infiltrated at 301840 Apr vic XT889608 without incident. No contact or significant observations were made and team was exfiltrated at 011709 May vic XT916511 without incident.

(9) Msn 10: Team infiltrated at 301845 Apr vic XT924345 without incident. Team contacted an unknown number of VC vic XT933356, who fired approx 15 rounds with an automatic weapon. After team retreated, VC fired single shots and signaled during the night, firing two shots every hour. Team was exfiltrated at 011658 May vic XT931356 without incident.

(10) RR Msn 8: The scheduled infiltration of RR Msn 8 at 301830 Apr was aborted due to weather and was later infiltrated at 010739 May vic XT978625 without incident. Team had negative contact and was exfiltrated at 011719 May vic XT939564.

(11) RR Msn 11: Team infiltrated at 011734 May vic YT101824, moved to a trail where 3 VC were observed at 011740 May vic YT073825. VC signaled with two shots, the team answered with one shot and the VC moved away. AT 011830 May vic YT056815 the team observed a Vietnamese dispensary with 3 VC guards, who fired on the team. Team withdrew to a CIDG OP vic YT078765 at 011950 May, then moved to Dong Xoai. Team was exfiltrated at 021040 May vic YT088757 without incident.

(12) RR Msn 12: Team infiltrated at 011739 May vic YT056854 without incident. 4 VC fired on team vic YT073912. Team returned fire with unknown results. Team moved to the USASF Camp Dong Xoai and were exfiltrated at 021600 May.

(13) RR Msn 13: Team infiltrated 021600 May vic YT1081759 without incident. Team sighted 5 VC YT149843 without being detected. Team was exfiltrated at 031915 May vic YT136068.

(14) RR Msn 14: Team infiltrated at 050802 May vic YT023554 without incident after infiltration of 03 May was cancelled due to increased activity of MGF 957 and aborted on 04 May due to weather. Team made no contact or significant sightings. Team was extracted by vehicle at 051150 May vic XT995522, after contacting a friendly PF post.

(15) RR Msn 15: Team infiltrated at 050808 May vic YT074417 after being delayed for the same reasons as RR Msn 14. Team returned to FOB by truck 051400 May.

(16) RR Msn 16: Team infiltrated at 051403 May vic XT930535. Helicopter received approx 10 rounds all fire departing the LZ after infiltration. Team was exfiltrated 061008 May vic XT914573 without incident.

(17) RR Msn 17: Team was infiltrated 051402 May vic XT960530 and exfiltrated 061012 May vic XT983573 without incident.

(18) RR Msn 18: Team infiltrated 061202 May vic YT027529 and VC immediately fired three warning shots and began signaling one another. Team retreated south for 300 meters, then captured a VC suspect vic YT013533 at 061330 May. Team with suspect were extracted vic XT993519 at 061415 May.

(19) RR Msn 19: Team infiltrated vic XT956594 at 071414 May. Immediately on leaving the helicopter and moving north into the tree line they observed 20 VC to their front in foxholes with overhead cover. The VC opened fire and told them to throw down their weapons. Team returned fire killing two VC (BC) and one team member slightly WIA. Gunships suppressed the VC and team was exfiltrated from the same LZ at 071426 May.

(20) RR Msn 20: Team infiltrated vic YT062719 at 101136 May and was extracted vic YT028629 at 101605 May. Team encountered 9 VC vic YT033638 at 101555 May.

(21) RR Msn 21: Team infiltrated vic YT062342 at 120851 May. At 121200 vic YT019346, team sighted 4 VC who fired two rounds, but team did not return fire. At 130830 May team observed 2 VC vic YT012282. Team was exfiltrated vic YT011284 at 13100 May.

(22) RR Msn 22: Team infiltrated vic XTD38346 at 140807 May and was extracted by rope ladder vic XT973389 at 151000 May.

(23) RR Msn 23: Team infiltrated vic XT941622 at 150837 May. Team observed 30 man VC Platoon vic XT956637. At 151430 May, team was observed by estimated 2 VC Platoons vic XT963363. VC fired a rifle grenade near the team then began advancing without firing. One team member threw a M-26 grenade when the VC were about 15 meters away, and killed 5 VC (BC). Team then took cover in two old foxholes and killed 4 additional VC (BC). Gunships suppressed fire and team was extracted under fire vic XT963636 at 151525 May.

(24) RR Msn 24: Team was infiltrated vic YT015262 at 160934 May. Team fired upon by estimated 14 VC at 161000 May vic YT024264. Team exfiltrated vic YT034266 at 161512 May.

(25) RR Msn 25: (8 man team): Team infiltrated vic XT972623 at 190903 May. Team made contact with 3 VC vic XT966651 killing one VC (BC) and capturing one home-made weapon. Team then moved towards the LZ and were fired upon by VC with 3 rifle grenades. Team made contact with interpreter in the radio relay aircraft at 191155 May and requested immediate extraction from vic XT962638. During the recovery of this team two helicopters were downed by enemy fire. Two USASF WIA, 1 US pilot WIA, 1 interpreter WIA and 1 Roadrunner WIA. Downed aircraft were secured by 1st Company and MGF 957 and later recovered.

(26) RR Msn 26: Team infiltrated vic XT845449 at 210820 May and moved a short distance when they discovered 7 VC following. Team fired, killing 2 VC (BC) and requested extraction. Team extracted vic XT848451 at 210840 May with negative friendly casualties.

(27) RR Msn 27: Team infiltrated vic XT823498 at 211312 May. Team made contact with 4 VC vic XT829497 at 211420 May. They exchanged fire and VC disappeared. Team was extracted under fire at point of enemy contact at 211428 May. Team suffered two cases of heat exhaustion.

(28) RR Msn 28: Teams infiltration was cancelled enroute to LZ due to supporting Aviation unit being returned to control of 1st Bde, 1st Inf Div for another mission.

c. Mike Force Company Operations:

(1) 2d Mike Force Company: The company was alerted on 1 May to move to Dong Xoai with the mission of acting as a reaction force at that location. Unit closed Dong Xoai 020847 May. On 050500 the unit departed Dong Xoai on a reconnaissance in force mission. The patrol apprehended 2 VCs vic YT074834. At 070800 May an estimated VC platoon was observed vic YT073843 moving east. Company fired on VC and they fled east without returning fire. The Company received AW fire 070805 May from vic YT074826 by unknown number VC. Company had 4 WIA and requested a medevac. Company covered approx 40 KM on patrol and closed at Dong Xoai 071445 May. VCs were turned over to LLDB for interrogation. Company was moved from Dong Xoai to FOB by CV-2 aircraft and closed FOB 072145 May.

(2) 3d Mike Force Company: Received mission on 061400 May from S3, Det B-56, gave briefback for 3 day mission in RZ CHARLIE at 071900 May. At 080800 May company departed from vic YT045490 on foot. Unit moved east for 7000 meters and set up a patrol base vic YT030490 and conducted local patrols with negative results. At 081800 May 5 shots were fixed about 300 meters west of the base along the route company had moved in on. A patrol was sent to the vicinity of the shots with negative contact however. On 090700 May company moved from patrol base and at 090800 May 1 shot was fired from area of the patrol base. Again a patrol was sent out to the area, but with negative contact. Company moved on for 500 meters and found 2 graves vic YT038470. Graves contained 2 bodies in body bags, approx 2 months old. Unit moved south at 091150 May and vic YT041450 set up second patrol base. Ambushes were set along Song Be River with

negative contact. Company moved from night location 100700 May. At 100900 May another body was found vic YT034456, similar to first two. Company closed FOB at 101500 May.

(3) 1st Mike Force Company: Company was infiltrated into RZ ECHO by helicopter at 121100 May vic XT876578. After company plus recon element landed and was formed, recon element, took point and moved from LZ on 120 deg AZ. Unit came upon main trail vic XT887565. Unit moved for approx 600 meters and stopped for noon meal. At this time fire was heard from vic XT8755 at 1430 hrs. Fire was directed at FAC aircraft. At 1700 hrs unit stopped for night at XT887538. Unit moved out 130645 May continuing west along trail. At trail junction vic XT870537, unit stopped while numerous trail complexes were reconned. Upon rejoining unit, recon element took point and unit moved SE. At 131730 unit stopped for night vic XT903487. Unit moved south at 140700 May and was resupplied at XT925447 at 141330 May. After re-supply unit continued south. At approx 1600 hours unit began moving due east stopping for night vic XT963437. Unit moved SW at 150700 May and at 171245 May FOB was notified that unit needed water trailer to meet them at 1600 hrs vic YT938457. Unit returned to FOB from water re-supply point. (See tab N for further operations by 1st Mike Force Company).

(4) 3d Mike Force Company: The company received the mission of conducting a recon in force to determine a possible VC buildup in RZ DELTA. Unit was moved by truck at 161020 May to vic XT993525. At 161315 May vic XT999542, 4-6 VC were observed wearing black uniforms. No weapons were observed due to distance. At 161340 May two more VC were observed vic YT004547 wearing mixed uniforms, no weapons observed. Unit went into defensive position at 161800 May vic YT008568 and manned an ambush position along LTL 1A. Negative sightings along route. Company was picked up by truck vic XT994521 at 171600 May and returned to FOB.

5. ENEMY INFORMATION:

a. On 3 May 67 MGF 957 contacted a multi-battalion sized force vic XT951669. This unit was equipped with AK-47s, RPG-2 rocket launchers, 2–3 heavy MGs, unknown type mortars and recoilless rifies. There were many ethnic Chinese fighting with this unit. The ethnic Chinese were all wearing khaki uniforms. One other group of VC were wearing black uniforms with camouflage soft hats. Some VC were wearing blue uniforms. This unit was well trained. They employed both fire and maneuver (well executed) and human wave attacks were attempted after many of the MGF were casualties. This unit is believed to have been 271 VC Main Force Regiment AKAQ761 – subordinate to the 9th VC Division. This is based on reports placing 271 MF Regt in the immediate vic, and on a report that the 271 employs many ethnic Chinese mercenaries. On 11 May vic YT039408 recon mission 8 observed a total of 200–250 VC moving south from 0355H to 0515H. The VC were using flashlights and traveling in 4 different groups (approx company size). At 0734H the SIGMA FAC located 50–75 of the VC in an open area vic YT023378 and at 0802H TAC air was put in on the VC. Reaction by 2 platoons of 1st Company resulted in capturing 2 PW's and numerous documents that identified the units as 2d Company, 2d Bn, 273 VC Regt, AKAQ763, subordinate to VC 9th Div. Also, C-23, Medical Detachment, subordinate to 273 VC regt. Uniforms were mixed cloths of black, blue, and green. On 17 May MGF 957 located a large concentration of VC vic YT143578 (center of mass). There were many well used trails running coast-west throughout the area. Commo wire was run along some of the trails. All VC in the area were equipped with new CHICOM series of weapons (1956). Uniforms were well cared for and troops appeared well groomed and healthy. This is believed to have been part of 9th Div HQ Security. SPAR reports indicated that 9th VC Div is located northeast of center of mass coordinates given.

b. The 9th VC div is apparently massing its subordinate regiments in War Zone "D". This could be a temporary move for attacks on targets near War Zone "D" but more probably the 9th VC Div has moved into War Zone "D" on a permanent basis. Presently, the only two 9th Div Regiments believed to be in War Zone "D" are the 271 and 273 VC Regts. Both located and identified by Operation Blackjack 33.

KEENI MEENI

22 SAS, Aden, 1964–7

With the unerring instinct for seizing strategically important real estate that gave it control of the world in the nineteenth century, Britain grabbed the land of Aden in 1839. Positioned next to the entrance to the Red Sea, Aden guarded the route to India. Aside from its geographical position, Aden had nothing save sand, and the region's impoverished inhabitants proved easy to control through the old imperial tactic of divide and rule. For a hundred years, the factionalized inhabitants of Aden were far too busy arguing among themselves to challenge British rule.

Everything changed in the 1960s, when Britain, in the long retreat from Empire, decided to abandon Aden. Understanding that withdrawal was likely to take the top off the powder keg and throw a match in, the British responsibly proposed a political settlement for the protectorate: a "federation" of the land's various tribes. On paper this was a wonderful idea; in practice, years of factionalizing made it a pipe dream. More, tribal differences in Aden were also being stoked by politics, with the Soviet Union backing the "National Liberation Front" and Egypt's Pan-Arabist regime actively seeking destabilization of Aden via its client state, North Yemen.

By 1963 Aden was in a state of simmering multi-faceted civil war. With the situation deteriorating by the minute, the British decided to support the protectorate's Federal Republic Army with a Joint Reaction Force ("Radforce") comprised of elements of the Royal Marines, the FRA, the East Anglian Regiment, 3 Para and the Royal Horse Artillery, with RAF support.

In 1964 the British government decided to send out the SAS, and D Squadron, which had anyway been due to go to the region for desert warfare training, was duly deployed. On arrival in Aden the main body of D Squadron moved up to the town of Thumier, about 35 miles from the border with North Yemen. The intention was that D Squadron should "road watch" the supply routes used by the rebels, and call in air attacks when appropriate.

No one expected the inhabitants of the Radfan Mountains to hang out bunting for more British soldiers; what Intelligence failed to realize was just how numerous and combative were the "hostiles" locally. A patrol under the command of Captain Robin Edwards from D Squadron's 3 Troop was pinned down in a cave for more than twenty-four hours by villagers, who killed two of the patrol (Trooper Warburton and Edwards himself) by sniping and full-frontal attacks that bordered on the suicidal. Neither did RAF bullet-and-bomb sorties do much to dampen rebel ardour. In the end the SAS survivors had to fight their way out at night, mounting snap ambushes on rebels following them. Eventually, the patrol reached the Dhala road, where a passing armoured car picked up their wounded and ferried them to hospital.

To clear the Radfan Mountains took Radforce a month of operations.

But the insurgency was not confined to the outback. The port of Aden, with its myriad narrow alleys, was becoming a battle-ground between the pro-Soviet NLF and the Egyptian-backed Front for the Liberation of South Yemen (FLOSY), with British soldiers a target for both sides. Even the school children of British soldiers and administrators were attacked. A favourite tactic of the terrorists was the hand grenade attack. Attacks by such Cairo Grenadiers, as they were known, caused appalling casualties. Between 1964 and the beginning of 1967, thirteen British soldiers were killed and more than 320 were injured.

Increasingly D Squadron was tasked with counter-terrorist work in the Crater and Sheik Othman districts of the port. Twenty troopers were selected for this highly sensitive work, which required the men to pass themselves off as Arabs. They subse-quently gathered intelligence and killed terrorists, work which became known as "Keeni Meeni" jobs – "keeni meeni" being the Swahili for moving unseen like a snake in the grass. Indeed, the idea of undercover infiltration in this manner had first been employed by Major Frank Kitson in Kenya during the Mau Mau uprising and further developed in Cyprus and Palestine. The team's HQ was a block of flats, Ballycastle House, in the Kormaksar military district of the port.

The SAS had better success in infiltrating themselves into the bazaars and alleys as Arabs than many in Radforce allowed. This was partly because many of the SAS undercover team were bearded, desert-tanned troopers who spoke Arabic, and partly because a Fijian contingent was naturally dark-skinned.

One favourite tactic in the bazaars was to use a white SAS trooper as bait. He would pretend to be an aimless tourist, and if he attracted hostiles these would be tracked by disguised troopers.

Definitely identified terrorists were assassinated by the "double tap" or Grant-Taylor method, with a triangular stance taken by the shooter who fires two shots in rapid succession from a range of not more than 15 feet, before disappearing into the crowd. The usual weapon for this "neutralization" work in Aden was the 9mm Browning pistol.

Unfortunately, the SAS were not the only British units undertaking covert ops in the port. When an SAS team opened fire on a group of Arabs in Sheikh Othman, they seriously wounded two members of the Royal Anglican Regiment's newly formed undercover Special Branch Squad.

No one had informed the SAS that there was another undercover unit in the field.

It was in Aden that the Regiment's CQB (Close Quarters Battle) expertise was refined, with the CQB course that John Slim had set up in Kenya developed further at the Cemetery Vale range in Aden. After the Regiment left Aden as part of the definitive British withdrawal in 1967, CQB and counter-terrorist (CT) work became staples of 22 SAS activities. In the early 1970s the Regiment became desperately short of work, so much so that training the bodyguards of foreign VIPs became a major strand of regimental activity. In the same period, the camp of 22 SAS, now based after a period of itinerancy at Bradbury Lines (later christened Stirling Lines), saw the construction of a special house to train marksmen in the skills of shooting gunmen in the confines of a room without hitting VIPs or hostages. Properly called the Close-Quarter Battle House, the building was more usually known as the "Killing House". One significant spur to the development of CT work came in September 1972, when Palestinian terrorists from the "Black September" group seized the dormitory occupied by Israeli athletes at the Munich Olympic Games. The West German government allowed the gunmen and hostages safe passage out of the country, but as the group moved through Munich airport the German security forces opened fire. In the wild gun battle that followed they mistakenly killed all the hostages. Alarmed by their incapacity to deal with terrorism, European governments began developing elite anti-terrorist units. The British government was no exception.

Following a direct request from the Director of Military Operations in September 1972, the new commanding officer of 22 SAS, Lieutenant-Colonel Peter de la Billière, reorganized the CRW (Counter-Revolutionary Warfare) cell into "Op Pagoda". In charge of Pagoda was Captain Andrew Massey, who selected twenty troopers from all sabre squadrons for special CT training.

The Pagoda team was put on constant standby. Later, the Pagoda role became rotated through the squadrons – so every trooper in the Regiment had a turn – and the team was issued with black overalls and Ingram sub-machine guns. However, following their observation of the successful German GSG9 storming of a hijacked aircraft at Mogadishu airport in 1977, SAS Major Alistair Morrison and Sergeant Barry Davies recommended adopting the GSG9's main firearm, Heckler & Koch MP5A2. Tests confirmed its superiority over the American Ingram sub-machine gun, and the 650-rpm, 2kg Hockler was adopted by the Pagoda troop.

The Pagoda team's first major call to action came in 1975, when an IRA active-service unit machine-gunned a Mayfair restaurant and then took hostages in a flat in Balcombe Street, London. On hearing on the radio that an SAS team was preparing to storm the flat, the IRA gunmen surrendered without a fight. The Balcombe Street siege ended without bloodshed, but it ignited a bloodbath of violence in Northern Ireland, starting with the "Kingsmill Massacre" in which IRA terrorists pulled Protestant line-workers from a bus and mowed them down.

The techniques the SAS had learned in Aden would be called on again when the Regiment was deployed to Northern Ireland.

EAGLE CLAW

Delta Force, Iran, 1979

The flames from the burning petrol tanker made a convenient, if unintentional, beacon for the pilot of the Sea Stallion helicopter. Even through a windscreen blasted by sand, he could easily see where to land in the vast Persian desert. That was the good news; the bad news was that he was running almost an hour behind schedule due to a dust storm. Two of the helis that had lifted off from the nuclear-powered USS *Nimitz* at 7.30 p.m. had turned back. Now they were down to six. The omens were not looking good for Operation "Eagle Claw" – the attempted rescue of American hostages being held in Tehran by followers of the Ayatollah Khomeini.

On 4 November 1979 a group of Iranian students and militants had rushed into the American Embassy in the Iranian capital and taken sixty-four occupants hostage; another three Americans were held in the Foreign Ministry. (Fourteen of the hostages were subsequently released by the Iranian militants.) The public of America was shocked and angered. Diplomatic attempts to secure the release of the hostages stuttered and flagged. As the days went on, US President Jimmy Carter became increasingly concerned about the hostages' safety.

From the get go, a rescue operation was a distinct possibility, and contingency plans were worked up. Inevitably, Colonel Charles Beckwith's Delta Force was assigned the lead role. The men of Delta Force were, after all, the US Army's "door-busters".

The rescue plan that Beckwith and Delta Force developed was highly complicated; it could not be anything else. Fifty-six

Americans were held in the middle of a hostile capital in a hostile land far from the US of A. In phase one of the operation, the assault force was to fly to Masirah airfield in Oman in Lockheed C-141 Starlifters of the USAF. At Masirah they were to tranship to three MC-130E Hercules flown by USAF Special Operations Squadron crew, which would take them below radar level across the Gulf of Oman and land them at a remote spot in the Dasht-Kavir salt desert in southern Iran. This landing site, codenamed "Desert One", was located some 300 miles south-east of Tehran.

Thirty minutes after the Hercules landed at Desert One, the eight Sea Stallions were to land at the site. The Sea Stallions were minesweeping versions of the HH-53, selected because of their range and carrying capacity. The Sea Stallions were to be flown by USMC crews from the *Nimitz* in the Indian Ocean to Desert One, where they would refuel from EC-130E Hercules on the makeshift landing strip.

Major-General James Vaught, located at Wadi Kena airfield in Egypt, was in overall command of the rescue mission; Colonel Beckwith was commander of the rescue forces on the ground. Since Desert One was near a road, a twelve-man road watch team, comprised of Delta men and Rangers, was included in the main party. In addition to the road watch team, this comprised a thirteen-man Green Beret "A" Team tasked to assault the Foreign Ministry, and three Delta "elements": Blue Element (40 men) was to secure the eastern sector of the Embassy compound; Red Element (40 men) the western end; and White Element (13 men) Roosevelt Avenue.

After refuelling at Desert One, the eight Sea Stallions were to fly the assault force to a forward landing zone, where the men would be dropped off; the Sea Stallions would then hide in a wadi 14 miles to the north. Four Department of Defense agents, already infiltrated into Tehran, would meet the assault force's drivers and collect six Mercedes Benz trucks, which would be used to ferry the assault force to their destinations.

At 8.30 p.m. the assault team would board the Merc trucks and drive into Tehran. The rescue was timed to start at 11 p.m. After "negotiating" the Embassy guards, the Delta elements were to release the hostages and, if possible, clear the poles the students had erected as anti-landing devices so the helicopters could come in. If this was not possible, the Delta-boys were to take the hostages to a nearby football stadium, where the helicopters would pick them up. Simultaneous with the Delta assault, the Green Beret "A" Team was to storm the Foreign Ministry, grab the three hostages, and take them to a nearby car park for "exfil" (extraction). Meanwhile, a Ranger company was to capture Manzarieh airfield 34 miles south of Tehran, where C-141s would fly in and collect the assault force and hostages, who had all been flown there from central Tehran by the indispensable Sea Stallions.

Such was the plan. And for a few tantalizing moments it worked beautifully. At 10 p.m., right on schedule, the first MC-130 landed at Desert One. The road watch team unloaded and deployed – Colonel Beckwith deplaned with them, and enjoyed some breaths of cool night air after the fug in the interior of the Starlifter.

Moments later a bus came rolling along the highway, right into the perimeter of Desert One. After shooting the bus's tyres, the road watch team herded the forty-five frightened passengers off and put them under guard. Only moments later, to the dismay of the road watch team, more vehicle lights appeared through the darkness on what was meant to be a quiet desert track. This time it was a petrol tanker. The road watch team launched an M72 Light Antitank Weapon, which set the tanker alight. The driver leaped out, jumped into the cab of a pickup behind, and went off into the night. The flames from the tanker reached 300 feet into the air.

In this eerie hellish glare the assault force waited for the Sea Stallions. And waited, and waited. Although the eight Sea Stallions took off at 7.30 p.m. local time, as scheduled from *Nimitz*, two hours into the 600-mile flight Number 6 had had to land due to "catastrophic blade failure". The crew burned any sensitive documents, and were picked up by heli Number 8. Nearly an hour later the lead RH-53Ds flew into a sandstorm, with the pilots having to fly on instruments. Emerging from the whirling storm of dust, the pilots breathed a sigh of relief to see stars in a clear sky. The respite was brief; the Sea Stallions then flew into another, more violent, dust storm, within the hour. Helicopter 5 then had a catastrophic electrical failure, lost use of its navigation and flight instruments, and was forced to return to the *Nimitz*. This left just six helicopters flying, the absolute minimum needed for the main phase of the rescue missions.

Helicopter Number 3 was the first to clear the sandstorms, arriving at Desert One fifty minutes late. On getting out of the heli, the pilot, Major James Schaefer, told the waiting Beckwith, "It's been one hell of a trip". Over the next thirty minutes, the remaining helicopters straggled in, their pilots to a man exhausted from battling the elements.

The schedule was now eighty-five minutes over time. As the helicopters refuelled from the EC-130Es, Beckwith directed the emplaning of the assault force. Despite being behind time and down to six helicopters, the mission was still viable. Just.

Then came the mortal blow; it was discovered that helicopter Number 2 had hydraulic problems and needed to be counted out.

The mission now had fewer than the minimum necessary number of helicopters. Colonel Beckwith was left with Hobson's choice: abort, and accept failure; or try for success at impossible odds. The overall mission commander, General Vaught, was asked for his opinion over the sat comm. Vaught asked Beckwith "to consider going on with five".

For agonizing minutes Beckwith tussled over whether to go ahead, or go back. Then he announced, "Delta's going home". By radio link the President of the US, Jimmy Carter, concurred in the decision that the mission could not continue, and preparations began for withdrawal of the five operational helicopters, the C-130s, and the rescue force.

Wearily the assault force got out of the choppers, and began loading onto the C-130s. It was nearly 2.40 a.m.

Something had to be done about the helicopters. Major Seiffert, the commander of the helicopter force, decided they would try to fly back to the *Nimitz*. Helicopter Number 4, however, had to refuel, since it had been on the ground longest, with engines idling. This meant that one of the Sea Stallions, *Bluebeard 3*, had to be moved from directly behind the required EC-130 to clear a space. *Bluebeard 3* took off and banked to the left; due to the dust churned up by the rotor, the pilot was unable to see properly and struck the EC-130's vertical stabilizer with its main rotor, causing it to crash into the tanker aircraft. Both planes exploded, blasting debris in all directions. Ordnance on board the helicopter started popping, and Redeye missiles began "pinwheeling through the night like it was the Fourth of July".

Eight members of the mission died in the explosion and subsequent fire. Five USAF aircrew in the EC-130 (Major Richard L. Bakke, Navigator; Major Harold L Lewis Jr., Pilot & Aircraft Commander; TSgt Joel C. Mayo, Flight Engineer; Major Lyn D. McIntosh, Co-Pilot; and Captain Charles T. McMillan, Navigator) and three USMC in the Sea Stallion (TSgt John D. Harvey, Cpl George N. Holmes Jr. and SSgt Dewey L. Johnson). Somehow, the sixty-four Delta men in the C-130 managed to get out of the burning aircraft, rescuing its loadmaster in the process.

With the heat from the burning C-130 and *Bluebeard 3* about to set a chopper nearby alight, it was decided to abandon the Sea Stallions, others of which had been struck by shrapnel from the explosion or burning ammunition. The Marine helicopter pilots scrambled aboard the C-130s. In the haste to emplane, not all the helicopters were "sanitized", leaving the Iranians a gift of a cache of classified information, plus two working choppers. What began as a special forces mission first became a tragedy then became a farce. At almost 3 a.m., after being on the ground for four hours and fifty-six minutes, Delta left Desert One.

Flying back to Masirah, Beckwith, a man whose Magnetic North was duty to his country, entered the slough of despond:

> Oh, shit. I felt let down. And I cried. That's when I really sat down and said, Jesus Christ you know, what a fucking mess. We've just embarrassed our great country.

The White House announced the failed rescue operation at 1 a.m. the following day. Planning began for a second rescue operation, Project Honey Badger, but Eagle Claw's failure because it was too "lightweight" caused an over-reaction in the opposite direction; Honey Badger envisaged the use of fifty aircraft and a battalion of troops. This was not a rescue force, this was an invasion army.

President Carter continued to press for a diplomatic resolution to the hostage crisis. Despite extensive last-minute negotiations, Carter did not succeed. On 20 January 1981, minutes after Carter's term ended and Ronald Reagan assumed the Presidency, the fifty-two US captives held in Iran were released. They had been held hostage for 444 days.

Meanwhile, retired Chief of Naval Operations Admiral James Holloway III led the official investigation into the causes of Eagle Claw's failure. The subsequent "Holloway Report", though clearing "the able and brave men who planned and executed" the operation, found deficiencies in planning, command, communications, availability of suitably trained personnel, and inter-service co-operation. As a result of the Holloway Report, more properly the Department of Defense's "Rescue Mission Report", special forces were reorganized in the US, and the report played a role in the streamlining of the Department of Defense ordered by the Goldwater-Nichols Act of 1986.

DOCUMENT: Department of Defense. Rescue Mission Report. Washington, August 23, 1980. Includes Statement of ADM. J. L. Holloway III, USN (Ret) Chairman, Special Operations Review Group.

The selection of extracts below highlights some of the issues that Holloway and his team found most troubling about the covert op Eagle Claw, together with their recommendations for improvement in the US's special forces capability.

When the hostage seizure incident occurred in Iran on 4 November 1979, a small planning cell, working in the Organization of the Joint Chiefs of Staff (OJCS) area, and augmented by two officers from the ground rescue force, began to formulate concepts for military options as directed by the CJCS (Chairman of the Joint Chiefs of Staff). The planning group received intelligence support within a week, although the full array of intelligence capabilities were not integrated for over a month.

During this early period, the organizational and planning framework of an existing JCS CONPLAN was not adopted, although some of its provisions were incorporated. These included utilization of intelligence assets and selection of the ground rescue force. Other major areas of endeavor, such as task organization planning, integration of concurrent planning by subordinate units, and determination of support and requirements, were compartmentalized and reliant upon *ad hoc* arrangements.

When COMJTF received his tasking on 12 November 1979, the rescue planning cell became the nucleus JTF staff. A CINCREDCOM (Commander-in-Chief, Readiness Command) joint table of distribution was the basis for JTF headquarters manpower requirements. A USAF general officer was appointed special consultant to COMJTF because of experience and knowledge gained during a recent tour of duty in Iran.

Training began immediately. Concurrently, conceptual plans were developed by the JTF staff and reviewed by the CJCS. On 19 November 1979, COMJTF recommended a helicopter option as having the greatest potential for success.

The helicopter detachment (pilots and aircrew) was initially formed from Navy and Marine resources. As operational requirements increased, additional pilots and crewmen were provided from other locations. Special mission training was moved to the western United States for a more realistic desert environment. On 9 December 1979, a new helicopter detachment commander was assigned and a vigorous training program was instituted to attain the special mission capabilities required. No overall naval component commander or provisional squadron command/staff capability was provided.

The senior Marine officer involved in the operation was assigned to the Office of the CJCS and, while not officially designated a member of the JTF staff, became involved in mission planning and execution. At the direction of the Director for Operations, Joint Staff, he reviewed the early November helicopter planning, examined the aircrew selection against special mission requirements, arranged for the assignment of more experienced pilots, assessed the helicopter force training effort, and planned the movement of the unit to the western United States desert training site. During this period, it was implied that this officer was in charge of the helicopter force during the preparation phase, and he believed this to be so. However, COMJTF may have thought differently, and it was evident throughout the first two months of training that much (if not all) of the COMJTF direction of effort concerning helicopter preparation and special mission capability training was done through the general officer who was thought to be the consultant on Iran. In mid-January 1980, the role of the senior Marine had evolved into that of overall helicopter force leader, since no other designation had been made, and, at his request, he began to attend the COMJTF planning meetings.

Early in the planning, a senior USAF officer with special operations experience was assigned as Deputy COMJTF/Air Component Commander. His role evolved into the task of supervising and coordinating the C-130 training. Just prior to mission execution, he was assigned as "on scene" commander at Desert One, responsible for supervising the refueling operations.

The decision process during planning and the command and control organization during execution of the Iran hostage rescue mission afforded clear lines of authority from the President to the appropriate echelon. From COMJTF downward, command channels were less well defined in some areas and only implied in others.

During the training phase, command channels provided for dissemination of guidance to individual elements of the force from COMJTF. Each element was provided only those portions of the plan considered essential for its particular purpose. Because of the stringent OPSEC requirements, compartmentalization was considered necessary. The rigid compartmentalization during the early stages is considered to have been a deterrent to training and readiness progress. Clearly, during the final stages of preparation, all element leaders should have been thoroughly familiar with the overall plan. This could have enhanced greater integration of all elements of the force.

Informally, the senior Marine was advisor to COMJTF regarding helicopter operations. Additionally, he supervised helicopter training, although not formally in the chain of command. The helicopter flight leader/detachment commander was made responsible for unit flight proficiency to achieve a special mission capability requiring flight regimes never achieved by any helicopter force in the world (and to do it as soon as possible). Further, as detachment commander, he was responsible for the total performance and welfare of his men, but not provided adequate staff or administrative support.

Early on, the designated Deputy COMJTF/Air Force Component Commander role involved the task of supervising and coordinating the C-130 training. The C-130 elements were directly under individual squadron commanders. Just prior to execution, he was designated "on scene" commander Desert One, implying a command, control and communications (C^3) capability to exercise command. This capability was not fully provided. A general officer served primarily as a consultant on Iran from late November 1979 to mid-February 1980. He spent considerable time during this period at the western United States training site and monitored helicopter and other air training. On 12 April 1980, he was designated the Deputy COMJTF.

The ground force chain of command was simplified in that the Army elements reported directly to COMJTF, who was also the Ground Component Commander.

JTF Rationale. OPSEC was the overriding consideration in every aspect of mission planning, training, deployment, and execution because of the absolute requirement to reach the Embassy compound undetected. OPSEC, coupled with the dynamic planning process and development of special mission capabilities, drove COMJTF to the techniques adopted for this organization, planning, and preparation by the JTF.

Alternative. The requirements for stringent OPSEC are clearly recognized. Nevertheless, it is considered essential that there be a balance between rigid compartmentalization, to include secrecy through informal or *ad hoc* arrangements, on the one hand and sound organization, planning, and preparation efforts on the other.

The JCS Crisis Action System (CAS) provides guidance for the conduct of planning for the use of military forces during emergency or time-sensitive situations. When the hostage seizure occurred in Iran, the group would have implemented existing JCS procedures intended to provide the Joint Chiefs of Staff, Services, commanders of unified and specified commands, and other agencies information with which to develop recommendations to the NCA pertaining to military courses of action.

An existing JCS CONPLAN provides the NCA with a wide range of options for utilizing military forces for rapid emergency actions to counter terrorism directed against US interests, citizens, and/or property in other nations. The plan does not abrogate those responsibilities found in plans or tasking currently in effect, but rather provides the conceptual basis for an additional capability. Supporting plans have been prepared by the commanders of unified commands.

The group's alternative for organization, command, and control would have used the stable, existing framework of the relevant JCS CONPLAN to organize, plan, train, and execute the mission, as well as to provide the mandatory OPSEC.

Prolonged *ad hoc* arrangements often result in tasking from different sources and can cause confusion at the operating level. These situational arrangements may hinder preparation and can impact adversely on overall cohesion of effort. The review group's alternative would strive for a better balance between more appropriate disclosure policy, particularly at the Service Chief/CINC level, to enhance the organizing, equipping, and training of forces.

Further, basic JCS CONPLAN methodologies and/or existing unified/specified command procedures make full provisions for compartmentalization. OPSEC can be, and has been, preserved when appropriate steps are taken. Thus, the entire preparation phase could have been accelerated and overall readiness enhanced.

Implications. On the positive side, the group's alternative would have led to a "quicker start" in the preparation phase. Additionally, task organization and force planning would have been enhanced and command relationships clarified. These in turn would have led to more effective command and control at all levels. On the negative side, the group alternative would have increased the number of people involved and, therefore, increased the OPSEC risk.

Evaluation. The potential for increased capability and readiness must be weighed against possible OPSEC risk. Although it is not possible to measure the outcome of the proposed alternative in terms of mission success, it is believed that application of an existing JCS CONPLAN and JCS/Service doctrinal precepts could have improved the organization, planning, and preparation of the force through unity of command and cohesion of effort. That, in turn, would have led to more effective command and control and enhanced overall JTF readiness.

Issue 6: Overall coordination of joint training
Event. The overall joint training supervision function was retained at JTF level in the Pentagon. At the western US site, coordination and supervision were performed in part by two officers who were advisers to COMJTF yet retained responsibilities related to their primary office of assignment outside the JTF. Neither was responsible for the overall management of joint training activities. Tasking for joint training was accomplished by messages issued by the JTF J-3 from the JTF headquarters in the Pentagon. Principals from the JTF staff proceeded to the western US training site to observe and supervise the directed events. Onsite support was handled individually by force elements in many instances or arranged by the JTF staff. It was related by force participants that C-130 and helicopter crews did not brief or critique jointly prior to and after every joint training exercise. Briefings and

critiques were generally conducted at the respective locations of force elements. Critique results were provided to JTF headquarters by secure telephone, by teletype, or in some instances by personal contact. An example is the C-130 participation, where in some cases the crews did not land at the western US training site for joint face-to-face critiques, but flew back to their home base and submitted critique items. There was limited opportunity for face-to-face exchange of views and problem solving that would have enhanced accomplishment of training objectives, e.g., more training on communications equipment and procedures to ensure effective force integration. COMJTF conducted post-exercise conferences for the commander and staff a few days following training exercises. These proved very beneficial in determining procedural and equipment problems and areas needing training emphasis.

JTF Rationale. The dynamic nature of the mission concept resulting from new intelligence inputs, availability of support bases for the actual mission, testing of various helicopter refuel procedures, and JTF assessment of unit readiness militated against shifting joint training responsibility to the field. Training exercises were observed personally by COMJTF or his representative. Creating an additional staff element was not considered necessary.

Alternative. Recognizing that COMJTF had the overall responsibility for training, the myriad other important activities related to concept development, planning, and extensive coordination would indicate the need for assignment of an officer and small staff to be in charge of the very important function of joint training at the western US training site. The group would have designated the Deputy Commander of the JTF and made him responsible for coordinating joint training activities, including but not limited to training schedules, operational and administrative support, and outside support. He would have made arrangements for joint mission briefings and critiques. He would have submitted progress reports to COMJTF periodically, as appropriate. He could have taken prompt actions to correct deficiencies to the extent possible as they arose. Coordination of training site support would have assured equitable allocation of available assets and contributed positively to morale and overall training progress. Participant interviews indicated a need for better supply and administrative support and more responsive tactical and intelligence briefings. The review group recognizes that joint doctrine assigns the Service component commanders unit training and support responsibilities; however, for this mission, forces were so interdependent that complete force integration was essential.

Implications. The group would have relieved COMJTF of the burden of day-to-day supervision of training. It would have provided a central point of contact at the training site for each element of the force, as well as for COMJTF and members of the JTF staff. It is believed that the achievement of the training objectives would have been enhanced by an individual responsible for early identification of deficiencies followed by prompt corrective actions. Additional personnel would have been required, but perhaps not more than three or four.

Evaluation. It cannot be stated categorically that adoption of the review group's alternative would have made the difference between mission success or failure. However, centralization of overall joint training responsibility and coordination would have enhanced force readiness and is recommended for future JTF operations involving joint training at a site geographically separated from the JTF headquarters.

Issue 11: Helicopter force size
Event. Approximately two weeks after US Embassy personnel in Iran were taken hostage, six RH-53D Sea Stallion helicopters were delivered to the carrier *Kitty Hawk*, and eventually transferred to the carrier *Nimitz* when she arrived on station. These six, augmented by two more brought in on *Nimitz*, launched on 24 April in support of the rescue operation. The mission was aborted on the morning of 25 April because the number of RH-53D helicopters available to proceed was less than required.

JTF Rationale. As planning for the rescue progressed, the number of helicopters perceived necessary to execute the mission grew from four, to six, to seven, and eventually to eight. These incremental increases were the result of unforeseen growth in the force believed necessary to achieve an acceptable probability of success in assaulting the Embassy and freeing the hostages. In addition, more helicopters were required to compensate for the lift capability lost because of seasonal temperature increases in the objective areas.

The JTF decision on helicopter requirements was based on the collective professional judgment of highly experienced helicopter pilots participating in rescue mission planning. A risk analysis based on fleet-wide RH-53D statistical data for an 18-month period from 1 July 1978 to 31 December 1979 seemed to support the planners' conclusion that eight RH-53D helicopters aboard *Nimitz* provided an acceptable degree of risk. Moreover, the always-primary OPSEC concern apparently influenced the planners' rationale, driving them to seek minimum practical force levels. In hindsight, it is clear that the eight helicopters put aboard *Nimitz* provided adequate redundancy to airlift the initial assault force. However, as personnel and equipment grew in response to evolving intelligence, the minimum airlift requirement at Desert One increased.

Alternative. The review group concluded that additional helicopters and crews would have reduced the risk of abort due to mechanical failure, were operationally feasible, and could have been made available until quite late in the planning evolution. An unconstrained planner would more than likely have initially required at least 10 helicopters under JTF combat rules, 11 under the most likely case, and up to 12 using peacetime historical data. *Nimitz* was capable of onloading a few more helicopters with little or no impact on other missions. Aircrew availability did not limit the force. By reducing the contingency margin, fuel available at Desert One was sufficient to accommodate at least 10 helicopters. In sum, aside from OPSEC, no operational or logistic factor prohibited launching 11 from *Nimitz* and continuing beyond the halfway point to Desert One with 10 helicopters.

Implications. The negative implications of this alternative include abandoning more helicopters in Iran, an increased threat to OPSEC generated by additional aircraft, and a reduction in contingency fuel at Desert One. On the positive side, the group's alternative would have decreased the probability that the number of mission-capable helicopters would fall below the required minimum.

Evaluation. The number of mission-capable helicopters available at Desert One was critical to allowing the mission to proceed. It is too simplistic to suggest that adding more helicopters would have reduced the likelihood of the mission aborting due to mechanical failure. The problematic advantages of an increased helicopter force must be balanced against the increased threat posed to OPSEC throughout the continuum of training, deployment, and execution and the reduced contingency fuel reserve at Desert One. In retrospect, it appears that on balance an increase in the helicopter force was warranted; however, such an increase could not itself guarantee success.

Issue 12: Alternate helicopter pilots
Event. At the outset, with the fate of the hostages unknown and unpredictable, an immediate capability to mount a possible rescue attempt was mandatory. Although a residue of similar capability from the Vietnam conflict existed, it was not intact; therefore, it was expedient to select an integral unit proficient in the RH-53D and carrier operations. To bolster the unit's night assault capability, Navy pilots were paired with Marine Corps pilots versed in assault missions. In this crew configuration, training progress was viewed as unsatisfactory by COMJTF. As a result, pilots progressing slowly were released in late December 1979, and USN/USMC pilots known to have demonstrated capabilities more akin to the mission were recruited. Training in preparation for the rescue progressed more rapidly with the revised crews, and no further wholesale aircrew changes were made or contemplated.

JTF Rationale. The need to be ready at any moment precluded a smooth program designed to achieve a specific capability by 24 April 1980. The requirement to be ready when windows of opportunity opened resulted not in one five-month training program, but several discrete two- or three-week programs—shingled, one overlapping the other.

Alternative. During this period, USAF pilot resources included 114 qualified H-53 pilots, instructors, and flight examiners. Of these, 96 were current in long-range flight and aerial refueling. In addition, there were another 86 former H-53 qualified pilots identified, most of whom had fairly recent Special Operations Forces (SOF) or rescue experience. These USAF pilots, more experienced in the mission profiles envisioned for the rescue operation, would have probably progressed more rapidly than pilots proficient in the basic weapons systems but trained in a markedly different role. USAF pilots, as well as those from other Services, with training and operational experience closely related to the rescue mission profile could have been identified and made available. The real question to be addressed is: is transition to a new and highly complex mission in the same aircraft more or less difficult for an experienced pilot to master than transition to an aircraft variant in the same mission? Mastering a new, difficult, and complex mission requires a pilot to acquire and hone new skills and, more importantly, a new mind-set. Transitioning from an HH- or CH-53 to an RH-53 requires only learning a few new flight parameters and slightly altering already established procedures, something every experienced pilot has done several times. This point is not new. Experience gained in Project "Jungle Jim" (circa 1961) illustrated that learning new and vastly different complex mission skills is far more difficult than transitioning to an aircraft of similar design and performance characteristics.

Implications. Teaming carefully selected pilots of all Services, with a heavy weight on USAF SOF/rescue and USMC assault experience, would most likely have produced the most competent crews at an earlier date. However, introduction of large numbers of USAF pilots would have complicated the OPSEC problem in training and aboard the carrier.

Evaluation. Should a rescue mission have been attempted in the early days after the Embassy seizure, it is probable that a complement of selected pilots with extensive or current assault and rescue experience would have been more effective. However, there is nothing to suggest that any other combination of aircrews could or would have performed the mission better than those who flew it on 24 April 1980. While this issue was not crucial to the mission, it does indicate the importance of designating an operational helicopter unit responsible for maintaining mission capability in this area.

Issue 13: Established helicopter unit

Event. Selection of the RH-53D helicopter for the rescue mission naturally led to selection of an RH-53D squadron as the unit to perform the mission.

JTF Rationale. The JTF selected a minesweeping helicopter squadron as the most expedient solution when it became evident the RH-53D was the helicopter to use.

Alternative. The group would marry up the appropriate helicopters and their maintenance capability with an operational unit compatible with mission requirements. When it was clear that RH-53D helicopters were required, selection of a USMC assault squadron would have facilitated training and in constructing a credible OPSEC cover story. If necessary, highly qualified pilots from other Services could have augmented the Marine squadron to bolster its capability. The main point is that the squadron's institutional structure would be preserved; e.g., training, tactics, and standardization. Personnel performing and experienced in these functions would greatly enhance the unit's ability to smoothly transition into its new role. Perhaps one of the key squadron staff functions referenced above would have perceived the Blade Inspection Method (BIM)-associated abort experienced during training as a major potential cause of abort during the mission and pursued the facts as the review group did. (See Issue 17.) Armed with knowledge of the circumstances surrounding BIM failures, the pilots of Helicopter #6 could have reached a more informed decision on the risk associated with continuing.

Evaluation. It is believed the preservation of an established squadron's inherent unit cohesion could have facilitated training, enhanced information flow, and increased aircrew knowledge, all of which could lead to a more integrated unit operation. It cannot be demonstrated nor is it suggested that these factors would have altered the outcome. However, they would have enhanced training and more likely increased the chance of success.

Issue 14: Handling the dust phenomenon
Event. There was serious and justifiable concern with the ability to accurately forecast weather along planned low-level routes to Desert One. Therefore, the JTF had to develop a catalog of weather phenomena that could likely occur in Iran and the ability to accurately and reliably forecast their occurrence. Difficulty of accurate weather prediction was compounded by the need to accurately forecast Iranian weather that could meet required minimums for a 40-hour period to accommodate the planned two-night operation. Diplomatic initiative, moon phase, and other "windows" exacerbated the problem. The JTF weather team researched and identified hazardous weather that aircrews could encounter in Iran. Among these was the phenomenon of suspended dust actually encountered along a 200-nm stretch of the helicopter route. Information extracted from the National Intelligence Survey (NIS 33, 34-Iran and Afghanistan) July 1970 was available to the JTF in December 1979 and was eventually included in the OPLAN weather annex. A table in this annex indicated, by location and month, the frequency of suspended-dust occurrences. Helicopter pilots, however, were surprised when they encountered the dust, were unprepared to accurately assess its impact on their flight, and stated that they were not advised of the phenomenon. C-130 pilots were also unaware of the possibility of encountering suspended dust.

JTF Rationale. The AWS team was assigned to the JTF J-2 section and did not have direct contact with the helicopter and C-130 aircrews. Weather information was passed through an intelligence officer to the pilots on regular visits to the training sites. However, pilots with extensive C-130 and H-53 experience on the JTF J-5 section had direct access to AWS personnel. Information flow to the mission pilots was filtered as a result of organizational structure. The traditional relationship between pilots and weather forecasters was severed. This was done to enhance OPSEC.

Alternative. The question to be addressed is not where the fault lay for the lack of aircrew knowledge but, more importantly, what should be done in future situations where there exists a paucity of weather information and the price of failure is high. Air Weather Service meteorologists can be denied information in several ways: (1) a closed society does not release information, (2) the phenomenon is so infrequent that it had never before been observed in recorded history (e.g., Mount St. Helen's ash), or (3) the area of interest is so sparsely populated that although the phenomenon occurs frequently, and perhaps predictably, it is not observed by "civilized" inhabitants and therefore not recorded. The suspended dust encountered along the helicopter route falls more appropriately into the third category. If they were fully aware of the high degree of uncertainty associated with limited data and the attendant risk, mission planners should have more aggressively pursued options that reduced this uncertainty to a manageable and acceptable degree. One cannot build a data base overnight; it takes years of observations to accurately and reliably predict weather patterns. Therefore, active measures could have been pursued. Of equal importance, the interplay of meteorologist and operator is the process that most often surfaces the questions that need to be answered—the uncertainties that size risk. In this regard, the AWS team had little or no direct interface with the mission pilots—they were both exclusively compartmented. By and large, an intelligence officer passed weather information to the pilots. Operators were placed in a receive only mode—forecasters and weather researchers received no direct feedback. The group would have required direct interface between mission pilots and their supporting weather team.

Implications. The negative aspects of the review group's alternative impact on OPSEC and administrative procedures. The AWS officer would have had to make frequent trips to the training sites for direct interface, or a second weather officer could have been temporarily assigned to the western United States training site with the aircrews. It is unlikely that either of these alternatives would have compromised OPSEC. On the other hand, there is no assurance that face-to-face interaction would have surfaced the dust phenomenon or made pilots more aware. However, the group believes that direct interface between mission pilots and air weather officers would have increased the likelihood of foreknowledge of the suspended dust phenomenon, that informed planners would have more aggressively pursued alternative approaches to reduce and manage this uncertainty, and that pilots encountering the suspended dust would have been better prepared.

Evaluation. The potential for increased awareness of weather phenomena through better interface with the AWS team on the planning staff must be weighed against the possible OPSEC risk. While it is unlikely that direct interface between AWS personnel and mission pilots could have altered the outcome on the night of 24 April, it is possible that helicopter pilots would have gained insight into the dust phenomenon and might well have made a better informed decision when they encountered it. For example, a decision to abort would have preserved the option to launch the mission at a later time. The larger issue for future consideration is the need for planners to be more sensitive to areas of great uncertainty that could impact significantly on the planned operation and, where possible, to reduce these uncertainties. Yet weather was an uncertain factor, which would lead to the conclusion that the chances for successful helicopter ingress would have been enhanced by any and all means which would have improved the helicopters' (and their crews') capabilities to penetrate adverse weather.

Issue 15: Weather reconnaissance
Event. There was serious and justifiable concern about the ability to accurately forecast weather along planned routes to Desert One and the extraction site and less concern about forecast accuracy for Tehran because of the availability of weather predictions for major international airports. Forecasting difficulty was compounded by the need to predict acceptable weather for a two-day period. Accordingly, an AWS team was formed to gather data on Iran. It was tasked to forecast Iranian weather on a regular basis, and its predictions were checked for accuracy and reliability by comparing them with weather photos of the forecasted period. Over time, the team's ability to forecast with accuracy and reliability was validated by the JTF. Primary interest was focused on visibility, hazards to flight such as storms, ambient light and winds for navigation, and timing. Satellite imagery was extremely useful but incapable of revealing the presence of low-level clouds or other restrictions to visibility hidden beneath an overcast sky and was of limited value at night. Nevertheless, there was evidently sufficient confidence in the forecaster's ability to predict VMC (Visual Meteorological Conditions) and the frequency of VMC so that alternative means to VFR (Visual Flight Rules) flight procedures were not pursued. The weather forecast for the night of 24 April did not predict reduced visibility over extended distance of the helicopter route. Uninformed and unprepared to cope with the extremely low visibilities encountered, the leader paused, the flight became separated, Helicopter #5 aborted, and all helicopters reaching Desert One were appreciably late.

JTF Rationale. The JTF believed that the probability of VMC for the helicopter ingress was reasonably high, and that the AWS team could accurately forecast the en route weather. Therefore, the helicopter ingress would be accomplished by visual navigation using night vision goggles. If the helicopters encountered weather that could not safely be penetrated using visual navigation with night vision goggles, the flight—and mission—would be aborted. The use of a weather reconnaissance aircraft had the disadvantage of being one more sortie over the helicopter route that could arouse attention. This risk to OPSEC was considered to override any advantage to be gained, in view of what appeared to be a simple and straightforward approach to handling weather contingencies.

Alternative. COMJTF and his air component staff had the means to obtain more timely and accurate weather data. Weather reconnaissance is a proven and often used means of accurately determining weather along flight routes with a paucity of weather reporting stations and high risk of incomplete knowledge. In hindsight, a weather reconnaissance C-130 would have encountered the dust phenomenon in advance of the helicopters and assessed its magnitude and impact before the helicopters would have to penetrate the area of reduced visibility.

It is purely conjecture at this point, but full knowledge of what the helicopters would encounter, balanced against their planning and training for VMC flight, may have caused COMJTF to order an abort. Although useful in a macro sense, satellite weather imagery often has proven to be neither accurate nor timely enough to meet operational requirements on a high-risk mission. It is therefore believed that information provided by a C-130 weather reconnaissance of the RH-53D route could have reduced the risk margin.

Implications. On the negative side, the C-130 would have been one more sortie overflying the helicopter route and could have alerted ground watchers so that the helicopter flight would have been visually detected. On the positive side, weather reconnaissance could have provided COMJTF with more accurate and timely information on which to base a decision on whether or not to abort that night and try again within the available window.

Evaluation. Weather reconnaissance along the exact helicopter route would have provided COMJTF with precise information on the prevailing weather, and influenced a decision to continue at that juncture or to wait for more favorable conditions. The group considered that provisions for handling weather contingencies could and should have been enhanced. The weather reconnaissance was one option that cost nothing in additional aircraft, fuel, or crew requirements, although there were OPSEC considerations.

Issue 17: Helicopter aborts
Event. Eight mission-capable RH-53D helicopters departed *Nimitz* on the evening of 24 April 1980. Of these eight, only five arrived at Desert One capable of proceeding. One helicopter aborted in the Iranian desert short of Desert One, another turned back for loss of instruments due to electrical failure, and a third RH-53D aborted at Desert One as the result of a hydraulic leak that in turn failed a primary hydraulic pump. Because only five helicopters were available to proceed against a firm minimum requirement of six, the rescue mission was aborted. Accordingly, a post-mission analysis of the aborts was warranted.

JTF Rationale. Helicopter #6, the first abort, experienced a BIM indication approximately two hours into the flight. RH-53 rotor blade spars are pressurized with nitrogen, and the spar's ability to retain the nitrogen under pressure is an indication of spar integrity. A BIM warning indicates possible loss of nitrogen pressure in the blade but does not necessarily indicate that the pressure loss is the result of a crack in the spar. Nitrogen pressure loss can result from a leaky filler valve, a defective seal on the spar extrusion, or a crack in the spar that can ultimately result in rotor blade failure. The crew of #6 made a precautionary landing in the desert to investigate, verified the cockpit indication with the BIM indicator on the rotor blade, and based on normal operating procedures elected to abandon the helicopter. With regard to spar failures, the CH/HH-53 helicopter family has experienced 31 spar cracks, three of which have resulted in crashes. However, the RH-53D, equipped with an improved cockpit detection system, has not experienced a spar crack. To date, 210 RH-53 blades have been returned to Naval Air Rework Facility (NARF) for various inspections and repairs—43 of these were for BIM indications. All 210 RH-53D rotor blades inspected demonstrated spar integrity. Why this is true is unknown, but the fact remains that in 38,216 RH-53D flying hours (229,296 blade-hours) logged through December 1979 not one crack has been found in an RH-53D rotor blade spar. Moreover, an H-53 blade fatigue failure analysis conducted by Sikorsky in 1974 revealed that rotor blades with cracked spars would retain structural integrity for up to 79 flight hours from crack initiation. The time from crack initiation to spar failure is a function of airspeed, as indicated below.

Forward Speed	Time From Crack Initiation To Spar Separation
100 KTS	79.27 HRS
120 KTS	27.47 HRS
130 KTS	15.13 HRS
140 KTS	8.73 HRS
150 KTS	5.63 HRS
160 KTS	3.33 HRS
170 KTS	2.43 HRS

Note: based upon an aircraft maximum gross weight of 42,000lb

In 1974, as a result of the Sikorsky data, the US Air Force directed that the H-53 not be flown in excess of five hours beyond BIM indication at or below 130 KTS or for more than two hours above 130 KTS.

Helicopter #5 aborted four hours into the mission and returned to *Nimitz* because of failures to essential flight instruments that the pilots believed were critical to safely continuing the flight. At the abort point, #5 was within 25 minutes of exiting the dust cloud and about 55 minutes (110 nm) from Desert One. When the pilot was asked if he would have proceeded had he been fully aware that the dust cloud dissipated in 50 nm and the weather at Desert One was VMC, he said he probably would have.

The lead C-130 crew possessed essential information on Desert One weather and the dust cloud that was not passed to Helicopter #5. Based on the helicopter pilot's testimony, these data, had they been passed, could have altered his abort decision. Once at Desert One, Helicopter #5 could have continued in the VMC conditions existing and, moreover, would have had the opportunity to exchange equipment with the non-mission-capable helicopter. Helicopter #2 aborted at Desert One because of a hydraulic pump failure resulting from fluid depletion through a cracked "B" nut. Failures of this type usually result in metal contamination throughout the hydraulic system. Correcting the malfunction required replacing pump filters and thorough flushing of the system. The extensive maintenance required to repair a hydraulic pump malfunction justified the decision to not take a spare hydraulic pump along.

Alternative. In light of the circumstances surrounding helicopter aborts that led ultimately to the overall mission abort, it is apparent that the pilot of helicopter #5 lacked certain knowledge vital to reaching an informed decision to proceed or abort. Uncertainty regarding Iranian radar coverage and the dust phenomenon (see Issues 14 and 18) played important roles in Helicopter #5's decision to return to the carrier. However, the major factor in his abort decision was lack of readily available information on weather conditions further en route and at Desert One. Information on the number of mission-capable helicopters at Desert One or still en route also could have influenced his decision and should have been made known. Failure to pass this vital information back to the carrier and support bases and rebroadcast it via secure HF was the result of a very restrictive communications doctrine related to the overriding concern for OPSEC. However, there were ways to pass the information to C-130s and helicopters en route that would have small likelihood of compromising the mission.

A BIM indication was a likely occurrence on the mission and had been experienced in training. BIM indications and other likely malfunctions should have been identified and researched in detail and information provided to aircrews as part of their mission preparation.

Implications. The negative aspects of the proposed alternative are relatively insignificant. It is somewhat doubtful that secure retransmissions would have compromised OPSEC. In the positive vein, the proposed alternative would have provided for a covered and secure flow of vital information to the rescue force while en route to Desert One.

Evaluation. When considering the conflict that often arises between OPSEC and operational requirements, a prudent planner of a clandestine high-risk venture should always be conservative. However, in the narrow scope of this issue, the group concludes that restricted communications flow within the task force denied information essential to reach informed decisions. The additional information might have prompted Helicopter #5 to continue on to Desert One. One more flyable helicopter would have enabled the mission to proceed.

Issue 18: The enemy radar threat
Event. This issue, while stated in generalized fashion, derives from a single, highly explicit event in which unevaluated data has passed directly to helicopter aircrews. This data and its implications contradicted the final conclusions of intelligence analysts.

Implications. There exists the possibility that some helicopter pilot judgments regarding altitude selection were affected by the informal report.

Evaluation. It would be inappropriate to fault COMJTF and his staff in this instance, as he learned of the informal report after the mission had been concluded, obviously much too late to take corrective action. Furthermore, six helicopters did arrive at Desert One, and the abort at that point cannot be related to any alleged enemy capability along the penetration route. What is illustrated by this event deserves reemphasis, however. All concerned should refer raw information reports to the appropriate intelligence staff representative for confirmation, denial, or other qualification before accepting the report as factual.

Issue 19: Helicopter Communications
Event. The helicopter force planned and trained to operate in complete radio silence. Intraflight communication, where possible, was to be done with light signals. The absence of radio communication indicated to the helicopter pilots that all was well and to continue the mission. Subsequently, when helicopter flight became separated in the dust cloud, each separate element lacked vital information. The lead helicopter did not know that #8 had successfully recovered the crew from #6 and continued nor that #6 had been abandoned in the desert. More importantly, after he reversed course in the dust and landed, the lead could not logically deduce either that the other helicopters had continued or that they had turned back to return to the carrier. He did not know when the flight had disintegrated. He could have assumed that they had become separated before he reversed course and unknowingly proceeded. Alternatively, they could have lost sight of him after turning and, mistaking his intentions, continued back to the carrier. Lastly, #5 might have elected to continue had he known that his arrival at Desert One would have allowed the mission to continue and that VMC existed at the rendezvous.

JTF Rationale. In concert with the view that OPSEC was critical to achieving surprise, every effort was made to keep radio transmission to the absolute minimum.

Alternative. Capabilities existed to pass to the helicopter crews vital information that would have enabled them to make more informed judgments. On the night of 24 April, all information deemed vital to the helicopters could have been transmitted by *Nimitz*.

Implications. Negative implications of the proposed alternative are relatively minor. Secure communications would not likely have compromised OPSEC. On the positive side, the proposed procedures would have enabled helicopter crews to be better informed while en route.

Evaluation. A system providing secure intelligence to the helicopter crews would have significantly enhanced the probability of the mission proceeding beyond Desert One. By his own statement, if the helicopter commander aboard #5 had been aware that the weather at Desert One was VMC, he would have continued.

Issue 21: Command and control at Desert One

Event. The first aircraft to arrive at Desert One, carrying the on-scene commander, Combat Control Team, and Road Watch Team, executed a missed approach to avoid a vehicle traveling along the highway adjacent to the desert strip. As the aircraft landed on its third approach, the Road Watch Team disembarked to take up blocking positions on the roadway approaches to Desert One. They each encountered traffic, one a bus with a driver and 43 passengers, the other a small fuel truck followed closely by a pickup truck. All three vehicles showed no signs of stopping when signaled. Shots were fired, which resulted in the bus stopping and the fuel truck set on fire. The fuel truck driver jumped out, raced back to the pickup, and escaped—44 Iranians on the bus were detained. This had all taken place rather rapidly—the operation was becoming more complex, but these contingencies had been foreseen and planned for. As the site filled up with C-130s, more than had been exercised at a western United States training area, it took on new and larger dimensions than had been experienced, but was unfolding as planned. Then it became apparent the helicopters were late, but for reasons unknown at Desert One. As the helicopters started arriving in separate elements, concern increased that there would not be enough helicopters, fuel or time remaining to continue beyond Desert One. The setting in which all this took place was, at best, a difficult but manageable one. The noise generated by 16 C-130 and 12 RH-53D engines made voice or radio communications difficult. Personnel moving about Desert One were shadowy, somewhat fuzzy figures, barely recognizable. Then came the unfortunate accident, when Helicopter #4 crashed into a C-130 while repositioning to allow another helicopter to take on more fuel for the return flight to *Nimitz*.

As complex and difficult as the Desert One scenario was, it had not been fully rehearsed. A training exercise at the western training area conducted on 13–14 April with two C-130s and four H-53s was used to validate the Desert One concept. Perhaps because the scope and complexity of Desert One was not replicated in a full-dress rehearsal, the plan for this desert rendezvous was soft. There was no identifiable command post for the on-scene commander; a staff and runners were not anticipated; backup rescue radios were not available until the third C-130 arrived; and, lastly, key personnel and those with critical functions were not identified for ease of recognition. For example, when the Desert One on-scene commander's name surfaced during post-mission interviews with helicopter pilots, they stated that, in some cases, they did not know or recognize the authority of those giving orders at Desert One. In this regard, instructions to evacuate helicopters and board the C-130s had to be questioned to determine the identity of those giving the orders to establish their proper authority.

JTF Rationale. The overriding concern for OPSEC played heavily in the JTF's decision not to fully rehearse the Desert One scenario. Moreover, the JTF apparently believed that desert operations had been practiced sufficiently and that, although there were technical differences in the refueling, a full rehearsal was not justified. With regard to identification, members of the JTF, by their own testimony, were confident that personal recognition between the key players was adequate to facilitate command and control of Desert One.

Alternative. The review group concluded that the uncertainties of conducting a clandestine operation in a hostile environment argued for the strictest adherence to doctrinal command and control procedures. The on-scene and functional commanders, their alternates and personnel of every key function should have been designated with readily identifiable markings visible in artificial or natural light. This would have enabled everyone on the scene to easily identify and quickly seek out responsible authorities for guidance when contingencies arose and to immediately recognize the authority of those giving orders or directions.

The lack of effective command and control became evident when the helicopter flight leader did not arrive first at Desert One as scheduled. There was no way to quickly find out or locate who was in charge. When the on-scene commander happened to be away from his radio to consult with others, his radio operator broadcast that the RH-53 and the C-130 had collided. Unfortunately, the transmission was incomplete and no call sign was given. This resulted in several blind radio calls from support bases in an attempt to find out what had happened and where. These unnecessary transmissions blocked out other radio calls.

The on-scene commander's principal location should have been fixed and easily recognized. An alternate or second in command and runners to carry orders should have been available and identifiable. Armbands or some other easily recognizable device would have had to have been fabricated for the identification of key personnel and their agents. In addition, backup communications should have been carried on both the first and second C-130s to insure reliable and secure communications from Desert One as soon as possible. Lastly, although not central to the command and control issue, a full-dress training exercise at a comparable desert training site could well have surfaced some of these problems (see Issue 5.)

Implications. The review group's alternative would have reduced confusion and accelerated information flow at Desert One. Equally important, it would have virtually eliminated the disconnects that surfaced when principals such as the helicopter flight commander arrived last and the Deputy Commander for Helicopter Forces aborted.

Evaluation. Although the proposed alternative would have smoothed Desert One operations, it would not have influenced the outcome. Nevertheless, it is a significant lesson learned for application to future operations.

Issue 22: Classified material safeguard

Event. In the event of mission abort at Desert One, JTF guidance called for pilots, crews, and radio operators to return their helicopter and material to *Nimitz*, taking appropriate action to protect classified [material]. The plan proved unfeasible when one helicopter crashed into a C-130, resulting in fire, casualties, and an overall hazardous situation. The on-scene commander decided to withdraw the entire force by the remaining C-130 aircraft as soon as possible, leaving the five undamaged helicopters at Desert One. Two of the helicopters located in the southern refuel zone were properly sanitized of classified material by the individuals responsible. The other three helicopters were located in the northern refuel zone in close proximity (within 100–150 feet) to the crash and fire. Personnel responsible for the classified material in those helicopters attempted to return to them but were told to immediately board the C-130s to expedite withdrawal. Failure to sanitize the helicopters resulted in loss of classified material. There is no evidence or any indication that the on-scene commander was aware that classified material was being left behind.

JTF Rationale. JTF guidance, coupled with military SOP and training, appeared sufficient to provide for adequate protection of classified material. The decision by the Desert One on-scene commander to expedite withdrawal of personnel by the remaining C-130 aircraft was made in the interest of troop safety, to protect remaining assets, and to minimize risk of detection.

Alternative. The review group's alternative would have been to refine command and control procedures at Desert One to ensure adherence to provisions of the JTF plan for handling of classified material (see Issue 21).

Implications. An attempt to return to the helicopters and to sanitize them could have cost additional lives, increased the risk of discovery and of damage to the escape aircraft, and delayed departure. However, the helicopters were not destroyed, there remained a requirement to protect classified material, and a period in excess of 20 minutes was available to sanitize the helicopters.

Evaluation. The loss of classified material had no direct impact on the success of this mission. However, such loss reflects unfavorably on the performance of the personnel involved. Their actions resulted in possible enemy exploitation of sensitive material, including its use for propaganda ends.

The conclusions drawn in this chapter derive from the determination of fact presented in Chapter II and the analysis of issues discussed in Chapter III.

Specific Conclusions

The concept of a small clandestine operation was valid and consistent with national policy objectives.

The review group concludes that the concept of a small, clandestine operation was sound. A larger, overt attempt would probably have resulted in the death of the hostages before they could be reached. It offered the best chance of getting the hostages out alive and the least danger of starting a war with Iran. Further, the large-scale military thrust required by an overt operation would have triggered early hostile reaction, possibly resulting in widespread Iranian casualties and giving strong credence to probable Iranian allegations that the rescue attempt was an act of war. Conversely, a small operation with Iranian casualties essentially limited to the act of freeing the hostages would have better supported the contention that it was a rescue, not a punitive raid.

The operation was feasible and probably represented the plan with the best chance of success at the time the mission was launched.

Despite all the complexities, the inherent difficulties, and the human and equipment performance required, the review group unanimously concludes that the risks were manageable, the overall probability of success good, and the operation feasible. Under these conditions, decision to execute was justified.

The plan for the unexecuted portion of the mission was soundly conceived and capable of successful execution. It appeared to be better than other alternatives—a realistic option with the best chance for success at the time of mission execution. Based upon the review group's visit with the ground rescue force and a comparison with the capabilities of CT forces of other nations, it appears that selection, training, and equipment of the ground rescue forces were excellent.

The group believes it virtually impossible to precisely appraise the remaining part of the operation and to measure probability of success. During that portion of the mission, the inevitability of hostile reaction would have become a major factor. The dynamics inherent in a recovery of the type envisioned would have produced a level of complexity that makes the study of probabilities essentially a matter of conjecture.

The rescue mission was a high-risk operation.
The mission had to be considered high risk because people and equipment were called upon to perform at the upper limits of human capacity and equipment capability. There was little margin to compensate for mistakes or plain bad luck.

Furthermore, possible measures to reduce the high risk factor could conceivably introduce new elements of risk. For example, the JTF considered that adding more helicopters and crews to improve the chances of having more helicopters available en route would result in an unnecessary increase in the OPSEC risk. A delay in execution for additional training could increase the risk.

The first realistic capability to successfully accomplish the rescue of the hostages was reached at the end of March.

Confidence in the probability of mission success grew after the final training exercise in the western United States. With the possible exception of several items of communications equipment, essentially all mechanical means used in the rescue operation—helicopters, aircraft, and special equipment—were available on 4 November 1979.

OPSEC was an overriding requirement for a successful operation.

Rescue depended upon surprising the captors in the Embassy compound before the hostages could be harmed. If this surprise could not be achieved, the mission would fail—either canceled or aborted, with high probability of the hostages being removed or executed. Further, recognizing the importance of the element of surprise, the group is reluctant to criticize, even constructively, the OPSEC standards for being too strict, as secrecy was successfully preserved until after withdrawal of the aircraft from Iran.

Nevertheless, throughout the planning and execution phases, decisions were made and actions taken or not taken because of OPSEC that the group believed could have been done differently. Furthermore, most, if not all, of the suggested alternatives could have been implemented without an adverse OPSEC impact had there been a more precise OPSEC plan developed early after the formation of the JTF organization and with specific responsibilities assigned.

Command and control was excellent at the upper echelons, but became more tenuous and fragile at the intermediate levels.

The command and control arrangements at the higher echelons from the NCA through the Joint Chiefs of Staff to COMJTF were ideal. Further down the operational chain, command relationships were less well defined and not as well understood.

External resources adequately supported the JTF and were not a limiting factor.

The effectiveness of the special supply system for the helicopters was commendable, especially considering the problems imposed by OPSEC.

Planning was adequate except for the number of backup helicopters and the provisions for weather contingencies.

More helicopters aboard *Nimitz* would have increased the chances of the required number of "Up" helicopters being available at each stage of the operation. Additional RH-53Ds with crews could have been deployed to *Nimitz* without crowding or impacting other mission requirements of the carrier and without a reduction in OPSEC. The use of C-130 aircraft to lead the RH-53D flight to Desert One would have decreased the probability of a mission abort due to weather. C-130 pathfinders and spare RH-53Ds could have been added to the mission without requiring additional fuel at Desert One.

Preparation for the mission was adequate except for the lack of comprehensive, full-scale training.

OPSEC considerations mitigated [sic] against such a rehearsal and, while the review group recognized the inherent risk in bringing all of the forces together in the western US training site, the possible security disadvantages of such a rehearsal seem to be outweighed by the advantages to be gained:

Increasing familiarity of element lead elements with one another, both during the operation and in the ensuing debriefing critique.

Exposing the command and control relationships to the pressures of a full-scale combination of airplanes, helicopters, troops, and vehicles, maneuvering in the crowded parking area under the confusing conditions of noise, dust, and darkness.

Two factors combined to directly cause the mission abort: Unexpected helicopter failure rate, and low visibility flight conditions en route to Desert One.

If the dust phenomenon had not occurred, Helicopter #5 would have arrived at Desert One, or if one more helicopter had remained up, six would have arrived at Desert One despite the dust.

There were alternatives available that would have reduced the probability of an abort due to these factors, and they have been discussed in detail in terms of planning and preparation.

The siting of Desert One near a road probably represented a higher risk than indicated by the JTF assessment.

The intrusion of the Iranian vehicles at Desert One significantly increased the chances of the Iranians' identifying the intent and timing of the operation. Although there was a workable plan to handle the bus passengers, the burned-out truck, empty bus, and abandoned heavy-lift helicopter near a well-traveled road could have resulted in early discovery by Iranian authorities. The group, however, realizes that the location may have been the best available.

GENERAL CONCLUSIONS

Although the specific conclusions cover a broad range of issues relating to the Terms of Reference, two fundamental concerns emerge in the review group's consensus which are related to most of the major issues:

The ad hoc nature of the organization and planning is related to most of the major issues and underlies the group's conclusions.

By not utilizing an existing JTF organization, the Joint Chiefs of Staff had to start, literally, from the beginning to establish a JTF, find a commander, create an organization, provide a staff, develop a plan, select the units, and train the forces before attaining even the most rudimentary mission readiness.

An existing JTF organization, even with a small staff and only cadre units assigned, would have provided an organizational framework of professional expertise around which a larger tailored force organization could quickly coalesce.

The important point is that the infrastructure would have existed—the trusted agents, the built-in OPSEC, the secure communications. At a minimum, COMJTF would have had a running start and could have devoted more hours to plans, operations, and tactics rather than to administration and logistics.

Operations Security

Many things, which in the opinion of the review group could have been done to enhance mission success, were not done because of strict OPSEC considerations. The review group considers that most of these alternatives could have been incorporated without an adverse OPSEC impact had there been a more precise OPSEC plan. A carefully structured JTF organization would have inherently provided an OPSEC environment within which a selective process could have allowed a wider initial disclosure policy—still a very stringent need-to-know policy—but based upon selective disclosure rather than minimum disclosure.

V. RECOMMENDATIONS

It is recommended that a Counterterrorist Joint Task Force (CTJTF) be established as a field agency of the Joint Chiefs of Staff with permanently assigned staff personnel and certain assigned forces.

Mission. The CTJTF, as directed by the NCA, through the Joint Chiefs of Staff, would plan, train for, and conduct operations to counter terrorist activities directed against US interests, citizens, and/or property outside the United States.

Concept. The CTJTF would be designed to provide the NCA with a range of options utilizing US military forces in countering terrorist acts. Such forces might range from a small force of highly trained specialized personnel to a larger joint force.

Relationships. The Commander, CTJTF (COMCTJTF), would be responsible directly to the Joint Chiefs of Staff (JCS). The CTJTF staff should be filled with individuals of all four Services, selected on the basis of their specialized capabilities in the field of special operations of various types.

Forces. The organic forces permanently assigned to the JTF should be small and limited to those which have a unique capability in special operations.

RECOMMENDATION. It is recommended that the Joint Chiefs of Staff give careful consideration to the establishment of a Special Operations Advisory Panel, comprised of a group of carefully selected high-ranking officers (active and/or retired) who have career backgrounds in special operations or have served at the CINC or JCS levels and who have maintained a current interest in special operations or defense policy matters.

The purpose of the panel would be to review highly classified special operations planning to provide an independent assessment function, which might otherwise be lacking due to the absence of the echelons of Service staff planners who normally review and critique JCS planning of a less sensitive nature.

For example, the panel might consist of five to seven members, with a chairman and members representing the Army, Navy, Air Force, and Marine Corps, appointed to fixed terms not to exceed three years. Members of the panel would maintain current security clearances and meet at least annually for update briefings.

When planning is initiated in response to a crisis, several members of the panel, depending upon individual qualifications and availability on short notice, would be organized to provide independent review. In this capacity, the panel members would not participate in the actual planning. Their function would be to provide the Joint Chiefs of Staff with the most objective, independent review possible.

Initial terms of service for panel members would be for one, two or three years, so that wholesale turnovers will not occur. Subsequent appointments should be for not more than three years. The purpose of such a policy would be to keep a fresh viewpoint and to ensure that panel members have recent experience with Service conditions and emerging technologies.

FIRE MAGIC:
THE ASSAULT ON LH181

GSG9, Somalia, 1977

Their faces taught with tension under the black camouflage paint, the commandos of West Germany's Grenzschutzgruppe 9 (GSG9) edged slowly through the heat of the African night to the rear of the Boeing 737. Lightweight aluminium ladders were gently positioned against the aircraft, and the men climbed into position. Accompanying them were two men from Britain's 22 SAS Regiment on temporary attachment to GSG9. GSG9's leader, Colonel Ulrich Wegner, watched all these preparations without expression, but inside his head whirled one question: could he get all the seventy-nine hostages and crew off the hijacked airliner alive?

Wegner had commanded GSG9 from its creation in 1972, and had striven to make the sixty-man unit, recruited from Federal Border Police, an elite amongst Counter-Revolutionary Warfare forces. Rigorously selected, with 75 per cent of candidates failing entry, GSG9 operatives were equipped with some of the most sophisticated arms in the world, the shining jewel in the armoury being the Heckler & Koch MP5A2 sub-machine gun. After years of training, GSG9 was now on 18 October 1977 facing its first real test: the storming of the hijacked jet on the runway of Mogadishu airport.

Five days before, at 1 p.m. on 13 October, Lufthansa flight LH181 had lifted off from Majorca's Palma airport, with eighty-six passengers and five crew, and headed towards its destination, Frankfurt. It never made it. Shortly after take-off four terrorists, two men and two women, had broken into the flight deck and, with pistols smuggled aboard in their hand luggage, threatened the pilot, Captain Jurgen Schumann, and his co-pilot Jurgen Vietor.

The terrorists – Zohir Youssif Akache (aka "Captain Martyr Mahmoud"), Suhaila Sayeh, Wabil Harb and Hind Alaheh – were a joint cell of the Popular Front for the Liberation of Palestine and the Red Army Faction called the "Martyr Halimeh Commando Unit". They demanded the release of eleven members of the Red Army Faction, together with a $15 million ransom.

A wild career across the skies of Europe, the Middle East and the Horn of Africa ensued, as the skyjackers sought a safe haven for their commandeered plane. Meanwhile, the West German Chancellor, Herr Schmidt, approached Britain for help – specifically whether 22 SAS would aid GSG9 in a hostage-rescue. Major Alistair Morrison, then second-in-command of 22 SAS, and Sergeant Barry Davies, one of the Regiment's counter terrorism experts, were duly dispatched to Dubai, where the GSG9 team was assembling and where the hijacked plane was about to land. Morrison and Davies took a box of "flash-bangs", the SAS-invented magnesium-based concussion grenades, with them.

Morrison and Davies flew out to Dubai, where they found Wegner and two of his men under virtual arrest. No sooner was this problem sorted out, than the hijacked aircraft flew on to the Republic of Yemen. There the terrorist's leader, Mahmoud, killed the captain of the liner, Schumann, for communicating with the security forces. The wild goose flight set off again, the Lufthansa Boeing now proceeding to Somalia on 17 October, with co-pilot Vietor in the control seat. Shortly after landing, the terrorists threatened to blow up the aircraft unless all their demands were met. They then threw Schumann's body on the runway of Mogadishu airport. Short of erecting a sign saying "We Mean Business" the terrorists could not have been more obvious in their implacability. There was now no real possibility of a peaceful outcome, short of conceding every want of the terrorists. As a ruse to gain some time for the GSG9 team to organize themselves, negotiators told the terrorists that eleven Red Army Faction members were being released. Even as this misinformation was being fed to the terrorists, the main body of the GSG9 team was flying in from Turkey, and Wegner, Morrison and Davies were thrashing out the plan to storm the airliner. The operation was codenamed "Fire Magic" – *Feuerzauber.*

At 1 a.m. on 18 October, GSG9 assembled for the assault, and the team's snipers moved into position. Morrison and Davies prepared their "fireworks". Thirty minutes later the twenty-two-man assault team began creeping forward half-crouched, off the edge of the runway directly behind LH181. This was the aircraft's blind spot. To divert the attention of the leader hijacker, "Captain" Mahmoud, the control tower engaged in intense conversation about the fictitious release of the Red Army Faction members; while Mahmoud was on the radio the assault ladders were erected against the Boeing's metal body. Morrison and Davies climbed cautiously on to the wings on either side of the aircraft, and the three GSG9 teams climbed to the emergency doors. At 2.07 a.m. – twenty-three minutes before Mahmoud's final deadline – an oil drum was rolled onto the runway in front of the aircraft and set alight. While two of the terrorists rushed forward into the cockpit to see the diversionary pyrotechnics, there was a massive blinding flash, courtesy of the SAS men who threw their flash bangs over the emergency exit and cockpit.

Barry Davies takes up the story:

The last thing I heard Ulrich Wegner say was, "Three, two, one, GO!"

Instinctively, I stepped away from the aircraft, having already pulled the pins from the two stun grenades which I was clutching. I tossed the first one casually in an arc over the starboard wing. It exploded about three feet above the two GSG9 soldiers waiting there, causing them great surprise! Just as it exploded, they punched in the panel which released the small hatchway into the aircraft. Taking a better swing, I threw the second grenade high over the cockpit. It actually exploded about two feet above the flight deck, to dramatic effect.

After throwing the second grenade, I whipped round to see the GSG9 soldier on my left turn the handle of the rear starboard door and with a kick throw his body clear of the ladder, still hanging on to the handle and pulling the door open on its hydraulics. The moment he did this the internal lights of the aircraft revealed one of the female terrorists standing there in a Che Guevara tee-shirt, wearing an expression of utter astonishment. At that instant the soldier on the right rung of the ladder fired a burst and stitched her with at least six rounds. She fell to the floor, dead, and the soldier disappeared into the aircraft.

Returning my attention to the starboard wing, I ran forward and scaled the small ladder, positioning myself by the open hatchway where the two GSG9 had already entered. As I looked into the aircraft I saw that the hatchway had fallen on the laps of the two passengers sitting there. They sat frozen, their eye closed tightly. Continuous gunfire rattled up and down the aircraft for what seemed a lifetime. I can remember saying to myself, "Come on, do it, do it – get it done!" Then came a couple of low thuds as two of the terrorists' grenades exploded.

The grenades had been thrown by the terrorist leader, Mahmoud, from the cabin towards the first-class passenger lounge; they exploded almost harmlessly.

Shouting in German for passengers and crew to get down, the GSG9 teams began to tackle the remaining terrorists. In the confusion, no one saw the terrorist Soraya dive into a rear toilet, from where she began shooting. In a return of fire from an MP5 she was wounded and incapacitated.

With the rear of the aircraft secure, the remainder of the fighting centred on the cockpit. It was soon over. Mahmoud was brought down by an MP5 burst, and Wegner shot the last terrorist in the head with a pistol.

As the joint GSG9–SAS team had calculated, the passengers, strapped to their seats, were below the line of fire. Save for the fragments of white metal from Mahmoud's grenades which caused minor injuries to stewardess Gabriele Dillmann, two passengers and one GSG9 operative, there were no "friendly" casualties. Hurriedly, the passengers and crew were disembarked and escorted to the passenger lounge. Major Morrison, Davies, recalled, was particularly courteous to one of the eleven German beauty queens who happened to be amongst the passenger complement.

Of the hijackers, Mahmoud died of his wounds, leaving Suhaila Sayeh as the sole terrorist survivor.

Watching the operation from the control tower was the German Minister of State, Herr Wischnewski. Immediately the assault was confirmed as successful by Wegner radioing the code "Frühlingszeit! Frühlingszeit!" ("Springtime! Springtime!"), Wischnewski in turn radioed the West German capital, Bonn: "Tell the world Germany has done it, the job's done."

It was.

There was, however, a blackly traumatic postscript. On the same day that the news of the rescue hit the world's media, the three leaders of the Red Army Faction – Andreas Baader, his girl-friend Gudrun Ensslin, and Jan Carp Raspe – committed suicide in Stammheim maximum security prison. Ennslin hanged herself, and the two men shot themselves. (Well, allegedly they did. Questions still linger as to where they got the guns to do so.) A fourth terrorist, Irmgard Moller, stabbed herself with a bread knife, but later recovered in hospital.

The Red Army Faction had one last rabid bite left. The terrorist outfit had kidnapped the German industrialist Hanns-Martin Schleyer some weeks before. In revenge for the assault on LH181 and the deaths of Baader, Ensslin and Raspe, Schleyer was executed. His body was found in the trunk of a green Audi at Mulhouse in Eastern France on 19 October.

DOCUMENT: Otto Skorzeny:
The Rescue of Mussolini from Gran Sasso

Otto Skorzeny was a junior Waffen SS officer serving in Berlin when a chance decision resulted in his overnight appointment as Chief of Germany's Special Troops. Prompted by the success of the raid on St Nazaire by British Commandos, Hitler ordered the setting up of a German equivalent. The Army High Command, however, regarded the order as another Hitler whim, and pushed it around departmental pending trays. Eventually, it landed up on the desk of someone who remembered a university acquaintance who might do as leader of the new unit. And so Otto Skorzeny found himself plucked from behind a desk and brevetted Chief of Special Troops. To mark the occasion he was promoted – to the rank of Captain.

As the world was soon to discover, the German army had inadvertently appointed a man who not only believed in the commando concept, but had the ability to carry it out. Born in Austria in 1908, Skorzeny was physically imposing (6 feet 4 inches, with a duelling scar from ear to chin), charismatic, and daring. Within six months of his appointment, Skorzeny had not only welded together a commando force, but had brought off the most improbable exploit of the war – the rescue of the Italian dictator, Mussolini, in September 1943 from the mountain prison where he was held by Italian forces intent on surrender to the Allies.

Skorzeny's rescue of Mussolini remains the gold standard in covert rescue missions.

September 10th, 1943. We had not been out of our uniforms for two nights and days, and though our general was in the same case it was essential that I should see him with a view to making the great decision.

But first I discussed all the possibilities with Radl. We both fully realized that speed was absolutely vital. Every day, every hour that we delayed increased the danger that the Duce might be removed elsewhere, nay even worse, delivered over to the Allies. This supposition subsequently turned out to be most realistic. One of the terms of the armistice agreed by General Eisenhower was that the Duce should be handed over.

A ground operation seemed hopeless from the start. An attack on the steep, rocky slopes would have cost us heavy losses, as well as giving good notice to the enemy and leaving them time to conceal their prisoner. To forestall that eventuality, the whole massif would have to be surrounded by good mountain troops. A division at least would be required. So a ground operation was ruled out.

The factor of surprise could be our only trump as it was to be feared that the prisoner's guards had orders to kill him if there was any danger of rescue. This supposition later proved well founded. Such an order could only be frustrated by lightning intervention.

There remained only two alternatives – parachute landings or gliders.

We pondered long over both and then decided in favour of the second. At such altitudes, and in the thin air, a parachute drop would involve too rapid a state of descent for anyone equipped with the normal parachute only. We also feared that in this rocky region the parachutists would be scattered too widely, so that an immediate attack by a compact detachment would not be possible.

So a glider remained the only solution. The final decision was in the hands of the Parachute Corps experts and General Student.

What were the prospects of success with glider landings? When we took our air photographs to the big laboratory at Frascati on the afternoon of the 8th, we had found it completely destroyed. I asked one of my officers to look somewhere else and he eventually found an emergency laboratory at an airstrip. Unfortunately, we could not have the usual big stereos which would have shown up all the details of the mountain zone. We would have to be content with ordinary prints approximately 14 by 14 cm.

These proved good enough to enable me to recognize the triangular meadow which I had noticed as we flew over. On the suitability of this meadow as a landing-ground we based our whole plan and I accordingly drew up detailed orders for the individual parties.

General Student suggested that a parachute battalion infiltrate by night into the valley and seize the lower station of the funicular at the hour appointed for the landing. In that way we should have cover on that side and also a line of retreat if withdrawal became necessary after the operation was complete.

The talk with General Student had the desired result. Of course he realized that there were many most serious objections but he agreed that there was only one possible way short of abandoning the enterprise altogether. Then the experts in air landings – the Chief-of-Staff and the Ia Air of the Parachute Corps – were called in to give their reactions.

These two officers were at first wholly averse to the plan. They objected that an air landing of this kind at such an altitude and without a prepared landing-ground had never been attempted before. In their view the projected operation would result in the loss of at least 80 per cent of the troops employed. The survivors would be too few to have any chance of success.

My answer was that I was fully aware of this danger, but every novel venture must have a beginning. We knew the meadow was flat and a careful landing should enable us to avoid serious casualties. "Of course, gentlemen, I am ready to carry out any alternative scheme you may suggest."

After careful consideration, General Student gave his final approval and issued his orders: "The twelve gliders required are to be flown from the south of France to Rome at once. I fix 6 a.m. on the 12th September as zero-hour. At that moment the machines must land on the plateau and the funicular station be seized by our battalion. We can assume that at that early hour the dangerous air currents so common in Italian mountain regions will be relatively weak. I will instruct the pilots personally and impress upon them the importance of the utmost care in landing. I am sure you are right, Captain Skorzeny. The operation cannot be carried out in any other way!"

After this decision had been given, Radl and I worked out the details of our plan. We had to make careful calculations of the distances, make up our minds as to what arms and equipment the men should carry and, above all, prepare a large-scale plan showing the exact landing-place for each of the twelve gliders. Each glider could take ten men, i.e., a group, in addition to the pilot. Each group must know exactly what it had to do. I decided that I would go myself in the third glider so that the immediate assault by my own and the fourth group could be covered by the two groups already landed.

At the conclusion of these labours we spent a little time discussing our chances. We did not bluff ourselves that they were other than very slim. No one could really say whether Mussolini was still on the mountain and would not be spirited away elsewhere before we arrived. There was the further question whether we could overpower the guards quickly enough to prevent anyone killing him first, and we had not forgotten the warning given by the staff officers.

We must, in any event, allow for casualties in the landings. Even without any casualties we should only be 108 men and they could not all be available at the same moment. They would have to tackle 150 Italians who knew the ground perfectly and could use the hotel as a fortress. In weapons the two opponents could be regarded as approximately equals, as our parachutists' tommy-guns gave us an advantage, compensating to some extent for the enemy's superiority in numbers, particularly if we had not suffered too badly at the outset.

While we were immersed in these calculations Radl interrupted: "May I suggest, sir, that we forget all about figures and trying to compute our chances; we both know that they are very small, but we also know that, however small, we shall stake our lives on success!"

One more thought occurred to me: how could we increase the effect of surprise, obviously our most potent weapon? We racked our brains for a long time and then Radl suddenly had a bright idea: "Why not take with us an Italian officer, someone who must be reasonably well known to the Carabinieri up there? His very presence will bluff the guards for a short time and restrain them from immediately reacting to our arrival by violence against the Duce. We must make the best possible use of the interval."

This was an excellent idea, which I promptly approved and considered how best to exploit. General Student must confer with the officer in question during the evening before the operation and somehow persuade him to come with us.

To prevent leakage or betrayal, he must remain with us until the following morning.

We discussed the choice of the most suitable person with someone who knew the situation in Rome and decided upon some high-ranking officer of the former Italian headquarters in that city who had adopted a substantially neutral attitude during the recent disturbances. He must be invited to a conference at Frascati after General Student had approved the idea.

Fresh troubles now descended upon us. The reports we received during the 11th September about the movements of the gliders was very unsatisfactory. Owing to enemy air activities they had had to make various detours and bad weather had not helped. Despite these misfortunes, we hoped to the last that they would arrive in time, but we hoped in vain.

The selected Italian officer, a general, appeared punctually, but had to be politely put off till the next day and invited to a conference with General Student for 8 p.m. at the Practica di Mare airfield. Zero-hour had to be postponed, as we received news that the gliders could not arrive in Rome before the early hours of the 12th. General Student fixed it for 2 o'clock on the Sunday (12th September) as we certainly could not wait another twenty-four hours. This postponement involved awkward changes in our plans and further prejudiced our chances. Owing to the air currents and local winds to be anticipated in the middle of the day the landing would be more dangerous, and the fact that the assault was to be made at 2 p.m. (i.e., in broad daylight) set a difficult task for the detachment operating in the valley. Various changes were necessary and had to be made with the utmost speed.

In the afternoon of the Saturday I visited the garden of a monastery in Frascati where my own men and the Mors battalion had pitched their tents. For this enterprise I meant to take volunteers only, and I had no intention of keeping them in the dark as to the dangers involved. I had them paraded and made them a short speech: "The long waiting-time is over. We have an important job to do to-morrow.

Adolf Hitler has ordered it personally. Serious losses must be anticipated and, unfortunately, cannot be avoided. I shall of course lead you and can promise you that I will do my utmost. If we all stick together the assault will and must succeed. Anyone prepared to volunteer take one step forward!"

It gave me the greatest pleasure to see that not one of my men wanted to be left behind. To my officers and von Berlepsch commanding the one parachute company, I left the disagreeable task of refusing some of them, as the party must not exceed 108 in all. I myself selected 18 of my Waffen SS men. A small special commando was chosen for the valley detachment and another for an operation to rescue the Duce's family. I remained at the camp a little longer and was delighted with the spirit and enthusiasm everywhere displayed.

At that moment we got a terrible shock from an Allied wireless message which came through. It was to the effect that the Duce had arrived as a prisoner in Africa on board an Italian man-of-war which had come from Spezia. When I recovered from the fright I took a map and compasses. As we knew the exact moment when part of the Italian fleet left Spezia I could easily calculate that even the fastest ship could not possibly have reached Africa so soon. The wireless message must, therefore, be a hoax. Was I not justified in regarding all news from enemy sources with the greatest suspicion ever after?

Sunday, the 12th September, 1943. At 5 a.m. we marched in close order to the airfield. There we learned that the gliders were expected at 10 a.m.

I again inspected the equipment of my men, who were all wearing parachute uniform. Parachute rations for five days had been issued. I had arranged that several boxes of fruit should be sent up and we sat about, pleasantly idle, in the shade of the buildings and trees. There was an atmosphere of tension, of course, but we took care to prevent any manifestation of apprehension or nerves.

By 8 o'clock, the Italian officer had not showed up so I had to send Radl off to Rome, telling him that the man had to be produced, alive, in double quick time. The trusty Radl duly produced him, though he had the greatest difficulty in finding him in the city.

General Student had a short talk with him in my presence, Lieutenant Warger acting as interpreter. We told him of Adolf Hitler's request for his participation in the operation, with a view to minimizing the chance of bloodshed. The officer was greatly flattered by this personal request from the head of the German state and found it impossible to refuse. He agreed, thereby placing an important trump in our hands.

About eleven the first gliders came in. The towing planes were quickly refuelled and the coupled aircraft drawn up in the order in which they were to start. General Student dismissed the men of Berlepsch's company and then my own.

The pilots and the twelve group commanders were summoned to an inner room, where General Student made a short speech in which he again laid great stress on the absolute necessity for a smooth landing. He categorically forbade crash landings, in view of the danger involved.

I gave the glider commanders detailed instructions and drew a sketch on a blackboard showing the exact landing-place of each craft, after which I cleared up all outstanding points with the commanders of each group and explained the tasks allotted to them. The men had decided on their password, something guaranteed to shift all obstacles. It was "Take it easy", and the battle cry remained the watchword of the SS commandos right up to the end of the war.

Flying times, altitudes, and distances were then discussed with the Ic (Intelligence officer) of the Parachute Corps, who had been on the photographic expedition with us. He was to take his place in the first towing plane as, apart from Radl and myself, he alone knew the appearance of the ground from the air. The flying time for the 100 kilometres to be covered would be approximately one hour, so it was essential that we should start at 1 o'clock prompt.

At 12.30, there was a sudden air-raid warning. Enemy bombers were reported and before long we were hearing bomb bursts quite near. We all took cover and I cursed at the prospect of the whole enterprise being knocked on the head at the last moment. Just when I was in the depths of despair, I heard Radl's voice behind me: "Take it easy!" and confidence returned in a flash. The raid ended just before 1 o'clock. We rushed out to the tarmac and noticed several craters, though our gliders were unharmed. The men raced out to their aircraft and I gave the order to emplane, inviting the Italian General to sit in front of me on the narrow board, which was all that was available in the cramped space into which we were packed like herrings. There was in fact hardly any room for our weapons. The General looked as if he were already regretting his decision and had already shown some hesitation in following me into the glider. But I felt it was too late to bother about his feelings. There was no time for that sort of time!

I glanced at my watch. 1 o'clock! I gave the signal to start. The engines began to roar and we were soon gliding along the tarmac and then rising into the air. We were off.

We slowly gained altitude in wide circles and the procession of gliders set course towards the north-east. The weather seemed almost ideal for our purpose. Vast banks of white cloud hung lazily at about 3,000 metres. If they did not disperse we should reach our target practically unobserved and drop out of the sky before anyone realized we were there.

The interior of the glider was most unpleasantly hot and stuffy. I suddenly noticed that the corporal sitting behind me was being sick and that the general in front had turned as green as his uniform. Flying obviously did not suit him; he certainly was not enjoying himself. The pilot reported our position as best he could and I carefully followed his indications on my map, noting when we passed over Tivoli. From the inside of the glider we could see little of the country. The cellophane side-windows were too thick and the gaps in the fabric (of which there were many) too narrow to give us any view. The German glider, type DFS 230, comprised a few steel members covered with canvas. We were somewhat backward in this field, I reflected, thinking enviously of an elegant aluminium frame.

We thrust through a thick bank of clouds to reach the altitude of 3,500 metres which had been specified. For a short time we were in a dense grey world, seeing nothing of our surroundings, and then we emerged into bright sunshine, leaving the clouds below us. At that moment the pilot of our towing machine, a Hentschel, came through on the telephone to the commander of my glider: "Flights 1 and 2 no longer ahead of us! Who's to take over the lead now?"

This was bad news. What had happened to them? At that time I did not know that I also had only seven machines instead of nine behind me. Two had fallen foul of a couple of bomb craters at the very start. I had a message put through: "We'll take over the lead ourselves!"

I got out my knife and slashed right and left in the fabric to make a hole big enough to give us something of a view. I changed my mind about our old-fashioned glider. At least it was made of something we could cut!

My peephole was enough to let us get our bearings when the cloud permitted. We had to be very smart in picking up bridges, roads, river bends and other geographical features on our maps. Even so, we had to correct our course from time to time. Our excursion should not fail through going astray. I did not dwell on the thought that we should be without covering fire when we landed.

It was just short of zero-hour when I recognized the valley of Aquila below us and also the leading vehicles of our own formation hastening along it. It would clearly be at the right place at the right time, though it must certainly have had its troubles too. We must not fail it!

"Helmets on!" I shouted as the hotel, our destination, came in sight, and then: "Slip the tow-ropes!" My words were followed by a sudden silence, broken only by the sound of the wind rushing past. The pilot turned in a wide circle, searching the ground – as I was doing – for the flat meadow appointed as our landing-ground. But a further, and ghastly, surprise was in store for us. It was triangular all right, but so far from being flat, it was a steep, a very steep hillside! It could even have been a ski-jump.

We were now much nearer the rocky plateau than when we were photographing it and the conformation of the ground was more fully revealed. It was easy to see that a landing on this "meadow" was out of the question. My pilot, Lieutenant Meyer, must also have realized that the situation was critical, as I caught him looking all around. I was faced with a ticklish decision. If I obeyed the express orders of my General I should abandon the operation and try to glide down to the valley. If I was not prepared to do so, the forbidden crash-landing was the only alternative.

It did not take me long to decide. I called out: "Crash landing! As near to the hotel as you can get!" The pilot, not hesitating for a second, tilted the starboard wing and down we came with a rush. I wondered for a moment whether the glider could take the strain in the thin air, but there was little time for speculation. With the wind shrieking in our ears we approached our target. I saw Lieutenant Meyer release the parachute brake, and then followed a crash and the noise of shattering wood. I closed my eyes and stopped thinking. One last mighty heave and we came to rest.

The bolt of the exit hatch had been wrenched away, the first man was out like a shot and I let myself fall sideways out of the glider, clutching my weapons. We were within 15 metres of the hotel! We were surrounded by jagged rocks of all sizes, which may have nearly smashed us up but had also acted as a brake so that we had taxied barely 20 metres. The parachute brake now folded up immediately behind the glider.

The first Italian sentry was standing on the edge of a slight rise at one corner of the hotel. He seemed lost in amazement. I had no time to bother about our Italian passenger, though I had noticed him falling out of the glider at my side, but rushed straight into the hotel. I was glad that I had given the order that no one must fire a shot before I did. It was essential that the surprise should be complete. I could hear my men panting behind me. I knew that they were the pick of the bunch and would stick to me like glue and ask no explanations.

We reached the hotel. All the surprised and shocked sentry required was a shout of "*mani in alto*" (hands up). Passing through an open door, we spotted an Italian soldier engaged in using a wireless set. A hasty kick sent his chair flying from under him and a few hearty blows from my machine-pistol wrecked his apparatus. On finding that the room had no exit into the interior of the hotel we hastily retraced our steps and went outside again.

We raced along the façade of the building and round the corner to find ourselves faced with a terrace 2.50 to 3 metres high. Corporal Himmel offered me his back and I was up and over in a trice. The others followed in a bunch.

My eyes swept the façade and lit on a well-known face at one of the windows of the first storey. It was the Duce! Now I knew that our effort had not been vain! I yelled at him: "Away from the window!" and we rushed into the entrance hall, colliding with a lot of Italian soldiers pouring out. Two machine guns were set up on the floor of the terrace. We jumped over them and put them out of action. The Carabinieri continued to stream out and it took a few far from gentle blows from my weapon to force a way through them. My men yelled out "*mani in alto*". So far no one had fired a shot.

I was now well inside the hall. I could not look round or bother about what was happening behind me. On the right was a staircase. I leaped up it, three steps at a time, turned left along a corridor and flung open a door on the right. It was a happy choice. Mussolini and two Italian officers were standing in the middle of the room. I thrust them aside and made them stand with their backs to the door. In a moment my Untersturmfuehrer Schwerdt appeared. He took the situation in at a glance and hustled the mightily surprised Italian officers out of the room and into the corridor. The door closed behind us.

We had succeeded in the first part of our venture. The Duce was safely in our hands. Not more than three or four minutes had passed since we arrived!

At that moment the heads of Holzer and Benz, two of my subordinates, appeared at the window. They had not been able to force their way through the crowd in the hall and so had been compelled to join me via the lightning-conductor.

There was no question of my men leaving me in the lurch. I sent them to guard the corridor.

I went to the window and saw Radl and his SS men running towards the hotel. Behind them crawled Obersturmfuehrer Merzel, the company commander of our Friedenthal special unit and in charge of glider No. 4 behind me. His glider had grounded about 100 metres from the hotel and he had broken his ankle on landing. The third group in glider No. 5 also arrived while I was watching.

I shouted out: "Everything's all right! Mount guard everywhere!"

I stayed a little while longer to watch gliders 6 and 7 crash-land with Lieutenant Berlepsch and his parachute company. Then before my very eyes followed a tragedy. Glider 8 must have been caught in a gust, it wobbled and then fell like a stone, landed on a rocky slope and was smashed to smithereens.

Sounds of firing could now be heard in the distance and I put my head into the corridor and shouted for the officer-in-command at the hotel. A colonel appeared from nearby and I summoned him to surrender forthwith, assuring him that any further resistance was useless. He asked me for time to consider the matter. I gave him one minute, during which Radl turned up. He had had to fight his way through and I assumed that the Italians were still holding the entrance, as no one had joined me.

The Italian colonel returned, carrying a goblet of red wine which he proffered to me with a slight bow and the words: "To the victor!"

A white bedspread, hung from the window, performed the functions of a white flag.

After giving a few orders to my men outside the hotel I was able to devote attention to Mussolini, who was standing in a corner with Untersturmfuehrer Schwerdt in front of him. I introduced myself: "Duce, the Fuehrer has sent me! You are free!"

Mussolini embraced me: "I knew my friend Adolf Hitler would not leave me in the lurch," he said.

The surrender was speedily carried out. The Italian other ranks had to deposit their arms in the dining room of the hotel but I allowed the officers to keep their revolvers. I learned that we had captured a general in addition to the colonel.

I was informed by telephone that the station of the funicular had also fallen undamaged into our hands. There had been little fighting, but the troops had arrived to the second and the surprise had been complete.

Lieutenant von Berlepsch had already replaced his monocle when I called to him from the window and gave orders that reinforcements must be sent up by the funicular. I wanted to make insurance doubly sure and also show the Italian colonel that we had troops in the valley as well. I then had our wireless truck in the valley called up on the telephone with instructions to send out a message to General Student that the operation had succeeded.

The first to arrive by the funicular was Major Mors, commanding the parachute formation in the valley. Of course the inevitable journalist put in an appearance. He immediately made a film to immortalize the hotel, the damaged gliders and the actors in the drama. He made a mess of it and later on I was very annoyed that the pictures in the magazine suggested that he had himself taken part in the operation. We certainly had too much to do in the first moments to find time to pose for reporters.

Major Mors then asked me to present him to the Duce, a request I was very pleased to comply with.

I was now responsible for Mussolini and my first anxiety was how we were to get him to Rome. Our plan had provided for three possibilities.

Both he and I considered that it would be too dangerous to travel 150 kilometres by road through an area which had not been occupied by German troops since the defection of Italy. I had therefore agreed with General Student that Plan A should be the sudden *coup de main* against the Italian airfield of Aquila de Abruzzi, at the entrance to the valley. We should hold it only a short time. I would give the zero-hour for this attack by wireless and a few minutes later three German He 111s would land. One of them would pick up the Duce and myself and leave at once, while the two others gave us cover and drew off any aircraft pursuing.

Plan B provided that a Fieseler-Storch should land in one of the meadows adjoining the valley station. Plan C was for Captain Gerlach to attempt a landing with the Fieseler-Storch on the plateau itself.

Our wireless truck got through to Rome with the report of our success, but when I had fixed up a new time-table with Lieutenant Berlepsch and tried to give the parachutists the zero-hour, 4 o'clock, for the attack on the airfield we found we could not make contact. That was the end of Plan A.

I had watched the landing of one of the Fieseler-Storchs in the valley through my glasses. I at once used the telephone of the funicular to have the pilot instructed to prepare to take off again at once. The answer came back that the aircraft had suffered some damage on landing and could not be ready straight away. So only the last and most dangerous alternative, Plan C, remained.

After they had been disarmed, the Italian other ranks showed themselves extremely helpful and some of them had joined with the men we had sent out to rescue the victims of the glider crash. Through our glasses we had seen some of them moving, so that we could hope that it had not been fatal to all its occupants. Other Carabinieri now helped in clearing a small strip. The biggest boulders were hastily removed, while Captain Gerlach circled overhead and waited for the agreed signal to land. He proved himself a master in the art of emergency landing, but when I told him how we proposed to make a getaway with his help he was anything but pleased with the prospect, and when I added that there would be three of us he said bluntly that the idea was impracticable.

I had to take him aside for a short but tense discussion. The strength of my arguments convinced him at last. I had indeed considered every aspect of the matter most carefully and fully realized my heavy responsibility in joining the other two. But could I possibly justify letting the Duce go alone with Gerlach? If there was a disaster, all that was left for me was a bullet from my own revolver: Adolf Hitler would never forgive such an end to our venture. As there was no other way of getting the Duce safely to Rome it was better to share the danger with him, even though my presence added to it. If we failed, the same fate would overtake us all.

In this critical hour I did not fail to consult my trusty friend, Radl. I then discussed with him and Major Mors the question of how we were to get back. The only men we wanted to take with us were the general and the colonel, and we must get them to Rome as soon as possible. The Carabinieri and their officers could be left at the hotel. The Duce had told me that he had been properly treated, so that there was no reason not to be generous. My pleasure at our success was so great that I wanted to spare my opponents.

To guard against sabotage to the cable railway I ordered that two Italian officers should ride in each cage and that after we had got away the machinery should be damaged sufficiently to prevent its being put in working order again for some time. All other details I left to Major Mors.

Now at last, I had time to pay a little attention to the Duce. I had seen him once before, in 1943, when he was addressing the crowd from the balcony of the Palazzo Venezia. I must admit that the familiar photographs of him in full uniform bore little resemblance to the man in the ill-fitting and far from smart civilian suit who now stood before me. But there was no mistaking his striking features, though he struck me as having aged a lot. Actually he looked very ill, an impression intensified by the fact that he was unshaved and his usually smooth, powerful head was covered with short, stubbly hair. But the big, black, burning eyes were unmistakably those of the Italian dictator. They seemed to bore right into me as he talked on in his lively, southern fashion.

He gave me some intensely interesting details about his fall and imprisonment. In return I managed to give him some pleasant news: "We have also concerned ourselves with the fate of your family, Duce. Your wife and the two youngest children were interned by the new government in your country place at Bocca della Caminata. We got in touch with Donna Rachele some weeks ago. While we were landing here another of my commandos, under Hauptsturmfuehrer Mandel, was sent to fetch your family. I'm sure they are free by now!"

The Duce shook my hand warmly. "So everything's all right. I'm very grateful to you!"

Donning a loose winter overcoat and a dark, soft hat, the Duce came out of the door. I went ahead to the waiting Storch. Mussolini took the rear seat and I stowed myself in behind. I noticed a slight hesitation before he climbed in and recollected that he was a pilot himself and could well appreciate the risks he was running.

The engine worked up to full speed and we nodded to the comrades we were leaving behind. I seized a stay in each hand and by moving my body up and down, tried to give the aircraft more thrust or lessen the weight. Gerlach signalled the men holding the wings and tail to let go and the airscrew drew us forward. I thought I heard a mixture of "Evivas" and "Heils" through the cellophane windows.

But, although our speed increased and we were rapidly approaching the end of the strip, we failed to rise. I swayed about madly and we had hopped over many a boulder when a yawning gully appeared right in our path. I was just thinking that this really was the end when our bird suddenly rose into the air. I breathed a silent prayer of thanksgiving!

Then the left landing-wheel hit the ground again, the machine tipped downwards and we made straight for the gully. Veering left, we shot over the edge. I closed my eyes, held my breath and again awaited the inevitable end. The wind roared in our ears.

It must have been all over in a matter of seconds, for when I looked around again Gerlach had got the machine out of its dive and almost on a level keel. Now we had sufficient airspeed, even in this thin air. Flying barely 30 metres above the ground, we emerged in the Arrezzano valley.

All three of us were decidedly paler than we had been a few minutes earlier, but no words were wasted. In most unsoldierly fashion I laid my hand on the shoulder of Benito Mussolini whose rescue was now beyond doubt.

Having recovered his composure, he was soon telling me stories about the region through which we were flying at an altitude of 100 metres, carefully avoiding the hilltops. "Just here I addressed a huge crowd twenty years ago." . . . "Here's where we buried an old friend" the Duce reminisced.

At length Rome lay below us, on our way to Practica di Mare. "Hold tight! Two-point landing," Gerlach shouted, reminding me of the damage to our landing-gear. Balancing on the right front and tail landing-wheels, we carefully touched down. Our trip was over.

Captain Melzer welcomed us in the name of General Student and congratulated us warmly on our success. Three He 111s were waiting for us, and after the conventions had been observed by my formally presenting their crews to the Duce, I gratefully shook Gerlach's hand on parting. There was no time to lose if we were to reach Vienna before dark.

Hitler was ecstatic with the news of Mussolini's rescue, and danced for the first time since the Fall of France. He awarded Skorzeny the Knight's Cross personally.

Other dazzling adventures for Skorzeny quickly followed. In September 1944 Skorzeny kidnapped the son of the Hungarian Regent and occupied the Citadel of Budapest (a move which prevented Hungary concluding a separate peace with the USSR, and rescued a million encircled German troops). During the Ardennes offensive, December 1944, he organized "American Brigades" of disguised Germans to cause havoc behind Allied lines. Eisenhower was a prisoner in his own HQ for a week.

With the conclusion of the war in Europe, Skorzeny (now a Major-General) was declared by the Allied Prosecutor to be "the most dangerous man in Europe", and charged with war crimes. The most serious of these related to "fighting in enemy uniform" during the Ardennes Offensive.

At one stage it looked as though Skorzeny would hang. This fate, however, was averted when his defence lawyer called as a witness the British war hero, Wing Commander Forrest

Yeo-Thomas, who revealed that the British had done the same thing in reverse as a matter of course. Skorzeny was duly acquitted.

On his release from POW camp he settled in Spain, where he returned to his pre-war occupation of engineering. One of the most influential pioneers of special forces, Skorzeny died in 1975.

THE SON TAY RAID

US Special Forces, North Vietnam, 1970

Sorting through aerial reconnaissance photographs on 9 May 1970, an NCO of the USAF 1127th Field Activities Group, based at Fort Belvoir, spotted something that took his breath away. In a complex of buildings in North Vietnam there were POW uniforms arranged in the shape of the letters "SAR" – standing for "Search and Rescue". On closer examination, he could see rocks arrange in morse code: the message they spelled was that six US prisoners in the camp would die soon if they did not get help.

So began what would turn out to be one of the boldest covert operations of the Vietnam War – a night-time raid into the heart of Communist Vietnam to rescue US POWs from Son Tay prison camps just 23 miles west of the capital, Hanoi. Throughout the remainder of May 1970 a dedicated team of experts from the Defense Intelligence Agency (DIA) poured over photographs of Son Tay taken from satellite reconnaissance, RF-4 aircrafts missions. The imagery suggested that seventy American POWs were being held at the isolated compound in the heart of North Vietnam. The Joint Chiefs of Staff, having evaluated the information, decided that a raid to rescue the POWs was both desirable and achievable. The go-ahead was given to Special Assistant for Counter-Insurgency and Special Activities, Brigadier-General Donald Blackburn, to plan the mission. An old-style fire-eater, Blackburn, who had led Philippine guerrillas on Luzon during World War II, wanted to head the raid himself, but because he knew too many secrets – he'd recently commanded Military Assistance Command, Vietnam – Studies and Observations

Group (MACV-SOG) in 'Nam – he was barred. The job instead fell to Colonel Arthur "Bull" Simons, a seasoned special forces officer. The operation was code-named Ivory Coast, and the rescue force known as the Joint Contingency Task Group.

The vagaries of the monsoon season dictated that the "weather window" would be most favourable between 20 and 25 October, when there would also be a quarter moon to aid visibility. At Fort Bragg special forces troopers were asked to volunteer for a mission, about which all they were told was that it was to be "hazardous" and under the leadership of "Bull" Simons. Some fifteen officers and eighty-two NCOs, mainly from the 6th and 7th Special Forces Groups, were chosen from the 500 volunteers. Meanwhile, under the command of Major-General Leroy Manor, a US air force component was selected. The aviators participating in the raid flew 368 sorties in practice for the mission.

If anything the training undergone by the assault team was even more demanding. To carry out realistic training for Son Tay a complete mock-up of the compound was built at Eglin's Duke Field base, Florida. So that Soviet satellite overflights would not discover its existence, the mock-up was made to be dismantled during the day and re-made at night. A $60,000 highly detailed table-top model of the camp was also constructed.

Under the most realistic conditions possible, including live-fire exercises, the raid was rehearsed 170 times. During training it became apparent that the raiders would have trouble suppressing fire from the watchtowers at the compound; to negate this threat, Simons added a HH-53 Super Jolly Green Giant to the mission complement. The HH-53 was to annihilate the towers with its 7.62mm miniguns. Also, even the best Green Beret sharpshooters were having trouble achieving an accuracy rate of more than 25 per cent in the dark; the problem was solved by acquiring "Singlepoint Nite Sights" from a commercial supplier for the M16s. Aside from the M16s the assault team carried 12-gauge shotguns, .45 automatic pistols, an M-79 grenade launcher, CAR-15s, M72 light anti-tank weapons (LAWs), and 213 grenades.

The raiding force was comprised of three platoons: fourteen Green Berets in team "Blueboy" would land inside the compound in an intentional HH-3 helicopter crash; a main support group, "Greenleaf", comprising twenty-two men, including Bull Simons himself, would provide immediate support; a further group, "Redwine", of twenty men, would protect the perimeter and provide support to either of the other two groups if needed.

Starting on 28 September, the Green Beret assault force practised the assault with the actual air force crews and their machines. These were the HH-3 chopper that was to land in the compound, five HH-53s to carry the rest of the assault force, A-1 strike aircraft, and three C-130s. Although the mission force was ready by 7 October, bang on schedule, approval from the White House was delayed for at least several weeks due to "ongoing political discussions." These were the overtures towards communist China by the administration of Richard Nixon, which the Oval officer considered would be wobbled by an incursion into China's semi-ally, North Vietnam. In expectation that the mission would get the green light, the raiding force began to deploy to Thailand on 12 November. Information had come through to Washington that six POWs had died while in captivity in North Vietnam. The mission became urgent. On 18 November the President authorized transmission of the "execute" message. The next weather window was 20 November.

At this point "HUMINT" (Human Intelligence) reached the planners that the estimated sixty to seventy prisoners at Son Tay had been moved. After twelve hours of deliberation, General Blackburn, DIA Director Lieutenant General Donald Bennett, and Secretary of Defense Laird (among others) recommended that the mission proceed. The evidence that the POWs were still at Son Tay seemed as compelling as the evidence that they had been relocated. And why not err on the side of doing the right thing? As Colonel Simons said in his pre-mission speech to the raiders: "We are going to rescue seventy American prisoners of war, maybe more, at a camp called Son Tay. This is something that American prisoners have a right to expect from their fellow soldiers."

On the evening of 20 November, the strike force launched from Thailand. Two MC-130 Combat Talons led the low-level ingress into North Vietnamese airspace; these had to fly at just

105 knots, 10 knots above their stalling speed, for the entire three-hour, twenty-three-minute trip to the target.

The strike force approached Son Tay undetected at 2.18 a.m. on 21 November 1970. Simultaneously, the US Navy began a massive diversion operation over Haiphong Harbor. As planned, one of the Combat Talons dropped illuminations flares, then an HH-53 helicopter overflew the Son Tay compound and destroyed the two guard towers with its side mini-guns. Next, the HH-3 intentionally crashed inside the prison courtyard. Captain Richard J. Meadows used a bullhorn to announce to the POWs they were about to be rescued, while the team rushed in four elements to assault the prison and search the blocks cell by cell.

Seconds later came the only mistake of the mission. A navigation error landed the largest part of the strike force – Simons' support group – at the "Secondary School" 440 yards south of the main Son Tay compound. While the raiders encountered minimal resistance at the Son Tay compound itself, Simons' team at the Secondary School found themselves engaged in a firefight with soldiers who were "much taller than Orientals and not wearing normal NVA [North Vietnamese Army] dress." Despite all the imagery analysis of the Son Tay compound no one had noticed that the Secondary School was a garrison; Simons and his men had stumbled on a whole force of Chinese or Russian advisers. In an eight-minute firefight the Green Berets killed, in Simon's estimate, between 100 and 200 enemy occupants before fighting their way to join the main strike force.

In the main compound Captain Meadows had ordered a second search of the cells, before transmitting the code "Negative Items". No POWs found. The assault force then began exfiltration.

The HH-53s returned singly to the extraction LZ beside the compound. To avoid a rain of SAM missiles the helis came in at treetop height, with the first landing at 2.37 a.m. Apple 03, the last aircraft out, lifted off at 2.48 a.m.

Only two US servicemen were wounded in the raid; one aircrew broke his ankle in the intentional crash landing in the compound and one trooper suffered a bullet wound in the leg – the only casualty to enemy fire.

The raiding force was on the ground in North Vietnam for twenty-seven minutes.

Three days after the raid, Secretary of Defense Melvin Laird convened a Pentagon news conference to announce that a raid had been attempted, but "regrettably no prisoners were found."

Despite the strike force's daring penetration of the heart of North Vietnam, public reaction to the raid was one of disappointment for its failure to rescue any POWs. While this is not surprising, the odds of a successful POW rescue were always slim. The US had mounted some forty-five previous raids in Laos, Cambodia and South Vietnam to rescue American POWs and had managed to bring out one sole prisoner, who died shortly afterwards from the injuries inflicted upon him by his captors.

The Son Tay raid is also the proof that the affairs of war are ruled by what King Frederick of Prussia called "His Sacred Majesty Chance". Luck, in other words. It was bad luck that the POWs had been moved from Son Tay; it was good luck Simons' strike force landed on the Secondary School and were able to neutralize the threat posed by the advisers immediately. Otherwise the advisers would have been able to interdict the raiders en masse.

Yet the failed mission did bring success of a sort. The Son Tay raid brought the world's attention to the inhumane treatment of the American POWs. After Son Tay the North Vietnamese improved the conditions in which the POWs were kept.

The Special Forces Creed

I am an American Special Forces soldier. A professional! I will do all that my nation requires of me. I am a volunteer, knowing well the hazards of my profession.

I serve with the memory of those who have gone before me: Roger's Rangers, Francis Marion, Mosby's Rangers, the first Special Service Forces and the Ranger Battalions of World War II, The Airborne Ranger Companies of Korea. I pledge to uphold the honor and integrity of all I am – in all I do.

I am a professional soldier. I will teach and fight wherever my nation requires. I will strive always to excel in every art and artifice of war.

I know that I will be called upon to perform tasks in isolation, far from familiar faces and voices, with the help and guidance of my God.

I will keep my mind and body clean, alert and strong, for this is my debt to those who depend upon me.

I will not fail those with whom I serve. I will not bring shame upon myself or the forces.

I will maintain myself, my arms, and my equipment in an immaculate state as befits a Special Forces soldier.

I will never surrender though I be the last. If I am taken, I pray that I may have the strength to spit upon my enemy.

My goal is to succeed in any mission – and live to succeed again.

I am a member of my nation's chosen soldiery. God grant that I may not be found wanting, that I will not fail in this sacred trust.

DOCUMENT: Vietnam Studies: U.S. Army Special Forces, 1961–1971, CMH Publication 90-23, Department of the Army

The Balance Sheet

An elite group has always appeared within the Army during every war in which the United States has been engaged. The Minutemen in the Revolution, the Cavalry in the Civil War, the Rough Riders in Cuba, the Lafayette Escadrille in World War I, the Rangers in World War II, and the Helicopter Pioneers in Korea—always some group has captured the imagination of the American public and has embodied the national ideals of the American fighting man.

As surely as such groups arose, there arose also the grievances of the normally conservative military men who rejected whatever was distinctive or different or special. The conservative approach to military matters is, of course, by and large the safest, most effective, and most practical. It is in the American character, however, to attack problems vigorously, to attempt rapid and complete solutions, and to accomplish the business at hand with a certain amount of independent daring and courage. Thus, the emergence of Army units combining these characteristics is not unusual but is the historical pattern. Future planners would do well not only to recognize this American military phenomenon but also to capitalize on it.

In the conduct of conservative military affairs, revisions of current military modes are frequently resisted with missionary zeal and emotional fervor simply because they mean change, they are different. In the complexities of handling national defense matters, a defender of the status quo can find many reasons for not doing something. If a new military program or unit is being developed in order to meet new needs, new threats, or new tactics, consideration should be given to the use of elite U.S. Army units, despite the customary resistance to change or elitism usually found in conservative establishments.

The U.S. Army Special Forces had the continuous and unswerving support of each commander of the U.S. Military Assistance Command, Vietnam. Generals Harkins, Westmoreland, and Abrams recognized the value of the Special Forces operations and consistently provided the unit with maximum support, direction, and guidance. Because Special Forces was a unique organization with many talents and demonstrated capabilities, each commander had somewhat different ideas on how to use it. Regardless of the employment, however, each commander was completely receptive to new tactics and techniques, new plans and programs, and new operational possibilities. Operational requests, personnel requisitions, and administrative and logistical demands were promptly and carefully attended to and authorized whenever possible. Whatever shortfall in Special Forces operations may have occurred, it never came as a result of lack of support from the head of the Military Assistance Command.

One single statutory action that proved most beneficial to the Special Forces was the approval in September 1963 of an Army regulation which dealt with the administrative, logistical, and financial support for paramilitary forces and provided the means by which such support could be obtained, managed, controlled, and accounted for. Before that date support arrangements were accomplished on an *ad hoc* basis, leaving no firm, acceptable method for accomplishing these requirements on an approved, departmental, permanent basis. The publication of this regulation for the first time placed Department of the Army support for paramilitary activities on a sound, respectable, businesslike footing.

Support by the U.S. Air Force in the Republic of Vietnam was superb. The tactical air force and airlift command elements performed outstanding feats in support of Special Forces. For example, airlift for the first of the three combat parachute assaults conducted by the Special Forces in South Vietnam consisted of nine C-130 aircraft. These planes were assembled, rigged, operationally prepared, spotted, and ready for take-off within a few hours after the approval of the operation was given. The first aircraft crossed the intended drop zone exactly on the minute prescribed. In October 1966 tactical aircraft, hastily scrambled, provided the firepower to rescue a sizable contingent of Special Forces in the Plei Trap Valley. Without these fighters, the force stood to receive staggering casualties. Tactical aircraft provided instant response to missions generated by the mobile guerrilla forces, including resupply of vital necessities. Airlift command was largely responsible for the movement each month of 17,000,000 pounds of supplies in 500-pound lots to Special Forces camps throughout Vietnam. The armed C-47 gunship was a tremendous help to camps under attack and accounted for the continued existence of camps many miles removed from immediate relief forces or firepower.

The U.S. Navy contributed significantly to the successful operations of the 5th Special Forces Group, and this assistance took many forms. For instance, the Navy provided its entire inventory of patrol air cushion vehicles in the theater during the monsoon operations in IV Corps in 1966–1967. These craft, together with the Special Forces airboats and motorized sampans, raised havoc with enemy forces slowed down or stopped by the floodwaters in the Mekong Delta.

Navy personnel also acted as instructors for the irregulars piloting the airboats and sampans. Navy river patrol craft worked harmoniously and successfully in joint land operations with troops of the Civilian Irregular Defense Group and the Special Forces advisers. Navy SEAL (sea, air, land) teams conducted joint training and exercises with scuba teams from the Special Forces.

The U.S. Marine Corps, especially in the 1962–1964 period, developed an outstanding relationship with the Special Forces. The Special Forces camps in the I Corps area literally lived or died depending on Marine helicopter support in those early days, when supply runs were made into the most rugged areas. Marine helicopters evacuated the survivors of Camp A Shau in early 1966. Joint operations using Marine reconnaissance units with civilian irregular and Special Forces units were most successful, as were certain innovative tactics devised together, such as airlifting 105-mm. howitzers to predetermined meeting sites to attack enemy units preparing to assault outgunned friendly forces. In May 1967 civilian irregulars, Special Forces troops, and U.S. marines fought side by side in defense of the camp at Con Thien administering a blistering defeat to the North Vietnamese Army.

The instances of co-operation and mutual support listed above are very few and do not reveal the deep confidence each service had in the other. Rather, they are random examples of common effort, intended to emphasize the truism that service rivalries diminish in inverse proportion to the nearness of the firing line.

In Vietnam there were certain factors that operated against the efforts of the U.S. Special Forces, and over which the Special Forces had little or no control. For the first time in its history the United States found itself waging a military and a political contest simultaneously. The Korean War was limited, as were the numerous incidents between 1945 and 1960. The new factor encountered in the Vietnam conflict was the departure from the sequential "military-then-political" actions of previous wars, in which the military effort was primary and foremost. Decisions to be made were evaluated principally in terms of military consequences, with political implications incorporated as part of a long-range integration of effort. As territory was rolled up, military government forces followed, to be supplanted later by civilian agencies restoring civilian control and development. In Vietnam military decisions were viewed in terms of the political consequences they might have, a situation to which the average military professional was unaccustomed. The usual primary military objectives of "closing with the enemy and defeating him" were limited by political decisions. The immediate impact on the military unit often took the form of misunderstanding, aborted tactical plans, and communication gaps.

There was a lack of understanding throughout all ranks on the nature of insurgent wars and of that in Vietnam in particular. Most U.S. Army schools had failed to incorporate many of the lessons learned in the Korean War. The march and countermarch across the European plain were still the staples for instruction well into the 1960s. Reports from Vietnam that the enemy was a mighty jungle fighter of indomitable prowess, spurred on and nurtured by the knowledge that his political convictions were right, caused the military service schools to juggle hastily the instructional units in the curriculum to accommodate this type of foe. Despite these efforts, the elemental lessons of infiltration, scouting and patrolling, reconnaissance, ambush tactics, night fighting, and unorthodoxy in tactics and logistics had to be learned and relearned on the ground in Vietnam. The twelve-month tour of duty operated against any one commander's accumulating very much experience or passing it on to his successors. The experience of the Special Forces ultimately proved that the night and the jungle belonged to the fighter who could use them best.

The fundamental communications gap stemmed in great part from the education gap. The cliché that the American soldier is the best informed soldier in the world was often repeated but it was sometimes dubious whether he was informed at all. Certainly, in terms of proportionate time, very little effort was made to explain to him Vietnamese or Oriental culture and customs; had the average American soldier been better informed, many actions of the Vietnamese would have been at least understandable, if not palatable to him. So acute was the lack of information that in 1962 special courses on countering insurgencies were hurriedly devised for senior officers, but the course content was a long time getting down to the individual foot soldier. The advice of foreign experts in insurgency and counterinsurgency was sought and followed even though their expertise, for the most part, had been acquired in different locales under totally different ground rules. As a result the random and usually irrelevant courses of action that were taken had little or no bearing on the Vietnam struggle.

The lack of adequate preparation for the Vietnam War within the active Army took many forms. Not only were the political and sociological aspects of the war given less than full attention, but also the related areas of language training, civil affairs (or civic action, as it became known), psychological operations, and interdepartmental co-ordination received little emphasis. The personnel actions which bothered the Special Forces members most were the complete and continual disregard by departmental personnel officials of the comparative combat responsibilities of Special Forces people. Because the table of equipment for a Special Forces group specified the position of a Special Forces lieutenant colonel as the commander of a Special Forces company, no amount of correspondence ever really convinced the personnel managers at Department of the Army that this position was really the equivalent of that of a battalion commander in terms of combat responsibility.

Command and control rules, procedures, and adjustments suffered because of the lack of understanding of the nature of the war, the lack of education in fighting it on a daily basis, the lack of communication throughout the chain of command, and the inbred convictions acquired during combat operations in World War II and Korea. The lack of preparation for this war had certain effects. For one thing, it led to a preoccupation with statistics. In many instances the success or failure of an operation was validated by the statistical considerations attending it. The usual method of determining the efficacy of psychological operations, for example, was by counting the number of leaflets dispensed or the number of loudspeaker broadcasts made. Often preconceived operational methodologies were a handicap. Senior U.S. Army commanders arrived with combat methods for the conduct of operations firmly in mind. That the methods did not fit the times or the struggle did not keep the commanders from using them. It often took a substantial period of time to educate such commanders to the facts of life. For example, they were slow to learn that the Vietnamese troops were allies, not subordinates; that the CIDG forces were indeed civilians and irregulars, and CIDG companies did not equate in terms of numbers, firepower, or training with U.S. Army infantry companies; and that all troops of whatever national origin in a given tactical area of responsibility did not automatically come under the command of the U.S. area commander.

There was, too, a certain lack of imagination in the development of new tactics. Deviations from current doctrine, however outdated that doctrine might be, were not systematically sought or encouraged. Unusual formations such as the mobile guerrilla forces and the clandestine resupply methods were accepted because of their demonstrated success. Long-range reconnaissance units, such as Projects Delta, Sigma, and Omega, were welcomed because of their exceptional record of performance, yet reconnaissance teams in major U.S. combat units continued to scout and patrol only as far out as the organic weapons of their units could cover them. The search for combat intelligence still followed the stereotyped pattern of seeking and reporting information, analyzing it so that it became useful intelligence, then seeking more of the same; seldom was a unit concerned with information about the interior control organization—the so-called infrastructure—of the enemy. Fighting camps, floating camps, and waterborne operations in conjunction with helicopters were accepted more as oddities than as adaptations to particular conditions. Night operations were the exception in most units, though as early as October 1966 all irregular operations supervised by the Special Forces began and, where practicable, ended during the hours of darkness.

A sound principle of war deals with the chain of command. This principle holds that orders are best carried out and control and discipline are best maintained by making each level of authority aware of its responsibility for carrying out a mission. The ubiquitous helicopter damaged the chain severely since the temptation to deal with subordinates several layers down was too great to resist. Indeed, the war became known as the "small unit commander's war," quarterbacked by a senior commander circling overhead. With a platoon leader, for example, getting precise instruction from a division commander, the teamwork and leadership development between the platoon leader, the company commander, the battalion commander, and the brigade commander were bound to be disrupted.

Certain factors were controlled by the 5th Special Forces Group in Vietnam and contributed positively to the success of the group effort. The table of organization and equipment remained flexible. Personnel, organizational detachments, equipment, and administrative arrangements could be easily adjusted within the personnel or fiscal ceilings imposed. The Special Forces had many military occupational specialties in its tables. Additional units not of the Special Forces but with similar occupational roles, such as medical or engineer, were easily added, controlled, and supervised. The fragmented, independent operation of the group facilitated ad hoc attachments where and when required. The volunteer status of members of the Special Forces effectively weeded out many unqualified men.

Training programs within the Special Forces were of long term, forty-four to sixty-two weeks. Such training combined with follow-up training in a secondary specialty produced soldiers of high professional standing.

The requirement that a man volunteer for both parachute and Special Forces training, the high training standards, the premium on independence and reliability, the emphasis on team loyalty and dedication, and the development of a sense of belonging to an exceptional unit tended to produce the most professional and most capable noncommissioned officers in the U.S. Army. The record of combat decorations, repeated tours in Vietnam, combat efficiency, and manifest pride in the organization reflect this professionalism.

Command of the 5th Special Forces group was placed in the hands of Special Forces officers. In the early days this empirical requirement was not a prerequisite for assignment. Beginning in 1966, the normal policy became a succession of assignments, starting with command of the 1st Special Forces Group in Okinawa and concurrent orientation tours in Vietnam; thereafter, the commanding officer of the 1st Special Forces Group succeeded to command of the 5th Special Forces Group.

There were also present within the structure of the 5th Special Forces Group in Vietnam certain factors that worked against the efficiency of the group.

In the early years, their role as advisers rather than operators was not made clear to most Special Forces troops. In their desire to accomplish positive gains and as a result of their concern for the welfare of the irregulars, attachments were formed between the Americans and the irregulars which adversely affected the Special Forces effort. The Vietnamese Special Forces initially resented the "big brother" role assumed by many U.S. Special Forces troops; the irregulars, who had relatively little empathy with the Vietnamese, assumed that the U.S. Special Forces would stand with the irregulars against the Vietnamese. These misplaced assumptions were partly responsible for the Montagnard uprising in September 1964. In time both the Americans and the irregulars came to understand and respect the Special Forces advisory role.

It is usually accepted by the military that U.S. Special Forces detachments were more successful in advising local governments than were other U.S. advisory elements. When the full circumstances were known, it was seen that much of the success of the detachments stemmed from their access to "more supplies, more quickly obtained." Detachments doing double duty as advisers for the Vietnamese Special Forces and advisers to local civil government agencies did either job well but seldom both successfully.

The buildup in South Vietnam from 1965 to 1967 outstripped the capability of the continental United States replacement system to furnish trained men. Standards dropped—in the field of communications, for example, the ability to perform at a high rate of speed in continuous wave communications declined—and it became necessary to give each new arrival an examination in his specialty before sending him out to a camp. This additional burden slowed down the operational pace because men had to be diverted to conduct the tests. Lowered standards invited less competent men who could not stand the rigors of the independent, isolated, and perilous life of a camp. From 1966 to 1967 a study was undertaken by the Walter Reed psychiatric unit in conjunction with the 5th Special Forces Group to determine whether it was possible to devise a test or examination that could predict which Special Forces soldiers were likely to break down in a camp environment. After a year of intense and careful study, it was concluded that the best indicator of who would or would not succeed as a positive member of a detachment in the field was the judgment of the senior Special Forces noncommissioned officer who trained or supervised the man. Frequently a Special Forces man would be dropped from the force as not suitable, but by one device or another would regain a position in the Special Forces.

The practice of placing the Civilian Irregular Defense Group camp forces, together with the U.S. and the Vietnam Special Forces detachments, under operational control of Vietnamese and U.S. military commanders was a throwback to conventional lines of command and control. The reasons for such control lines are obvious, but they proved less successful than when the group commander controlled all his men. Aside from the technical, communications, and operational reasons that could be advanced, the average Special

Forces man in a camp had better morale and esprit when under group command.

Credits

The U.S. Army Special Forces made significant progress in many areas during its term of service in the Republic of Vietnam. As a tactical combat unit, the U.S. Special Forces dealt with the Vietnamese Special Forces in both an advisory and an operational capacity. This primary relationship did not impair or preclude other working relationships with U.S. armed forces, Free World Military Assistance Forces, U.S. government agencies, or Vietnamese government agencies.

Positive contributions were made by the Special Forces over the years to the American national effort to defeat the North Vietnamese Army and the Viet Cong. These contributions were made not only to the immediate operations of the war, but also to the development of the Special Forces as a general purpose unit within the U.S. Army troop structure. As a result, any doubts about the value or practicality of having this type of unit in the permanent U.S. Army force structure were removed.

The record of service performed in the past becomes doubly valuable when viewed in the light of possible combat in the future. If, as predicted, the cycle of wars continues to emphasize the limited-objective, political-military struggle and to avoid massive dispositions of regular forces, the U.S. Army Special Forces will not have to prove its claim as an exceptionally effective combat unit in the limited conflict.

Starting with a relatively austere organization and lacking clear objectives and co-ordinated support programs, and improvising tactics and techniques at widely scattered locations, the U.S. Special Forces in Vietnam achieved notable success. Its members demonstrated repeatedly their combat ability, esprit de corps, determination, and willingness to sacrifice. Remarkable is the fact that this level of effort was just as strong and effective at the end of the campaign as it was ten years earlier in the beginning.

The conceptual soundness of the organization for Special Forces was tested thoroughly. Though the force was never intended for conducting such programs as the Civilian Irregular Defense Group projects the flexibility of its detachments, the ability of the force to use support in many forms and from many sources, and the number of specialties represented in each detachment enabled small detachments operating independently to achieve a variety of objectives.

Within its own organizational and support limits, the U.S. Special Forces successfully practiced a number of new tactics and techniques of the highest professional caliber. Notably the force was responsible for the formation and employment of the mobile guerrilla forces—BLACKJACK Operations—and of extended distance reconnaissance and security forces—Projects Delta, Sigma, and Omega; the constant circulation of Special Forces resources from pacified to contested geographic areas of Vietnam; successful operations with other Free World Military Assistance Forces and joint operations with other armed forces; the construction of fighting camps, and in the Mekong Delta region, floating camps; the full-scale employment of irregulars in night operations exclusively; the conduct of waterborne operations in a carefully planned flood campaign, using the Special Forces "navy"—some 400 water craft consisting of airboats, sophisticated U.S. Navy craft, and locally acquired motorized sampans; and the formation and development of airborne-qualified irregular forces as a mobile strike force for use as reserves or as exploitation forces.

The Special Forces founded and operated the theater school, known as the MACV Recondo School, for training reconnaissance troops for all U.S. and Free World forces. It also developed a decentralized form of logistic support featuring direct sea, air, and road shipments to forward supply points in all corps tactical zones. The Special Forces produced a series of handbooks, describing in detail how to carry out any portion of the group's business, from building a camp to serving as an investigating officer. The group developed a civic action program which placed the emphasis on performance rather than philosophy, and on self-help rather than charity; a flexible and controlled accounting system for supplies and funds; and an annual Special Forces campaign plan for utilization of the force in furtherance of announced objectives of the Military Assistance Command, Vietnam. The group also developed a body of lessons learned for review by the Continental Army Command, and, where appropriate, insertion into its training programs.

The Special Forces made recommendations for future doctrine, organization, and equipment. Doctrinally, it was suggested that the mission of Special Forces be expanded beyond the rather narrow specialty of unconventional warfare. Organizationally, recommendations were made to rearrange the detachments to provide greater administrative and logistic capabilities; to add Judge Advocate, Inspector General, Comptroller, and Engineer personnel; to revise drastically the intelligence section; and to give greater responsibility to the noncommissioned officers.

Debits

The U.S. Army Special Forces performance in Vietnam revealed several shortcomings that were constantly under review and analysis, but were still thorny problems at the termination of operations. For instance, psychological operations continued to fail for a number of reasons. There were not enough trained people in the field. Further, the attitude toward integration of psychological operations into tactical plans was indifferent at many levels of command. Direction of the psychological operations effort from the MACV level seemed to emphasize the civic action support theme, to the exclusion of unit level psychological operations tactics and techniques.

Policy direction for the integration of U.S. and Vietnamese psychological operations at the brigade and group level was ambivalent. When guidance did come, it was usually too proscribed to be usable at the lower levels of command. Psychological operations were essentially defensive in nature. Opportunities or suggestions for offensive psychological operations were usually buried in the useless and meaningless statistics of numbers of leaflets delivered or broadcasts made.

The American soldier is the most generous person on earth. It follows that he runs the risk of exhibiting too much concern or extreme paternalism. Since the military and political struggles in Vietnam were being waged simultaneously, the less privileged members of local society made unwarranted assumptions from this display of generosity as to the amount and depth of American support for their cause. The genuine American concern for improving the lot for the underprivileged was given free rein in the early days of the Special Forces in Vietnam; nor was any attempt made by the group to control or limit this generosity firmly up to the time of the group's departure from the country. The sympathy for the minority groups was construed by some as interference to the point that it weakened the American position of rendering advice and assistance to the Vietnamese Special Forces counterparts. Add to this the American characteristic of impatience to get a job done, and the result was a further gap between the Vietnamese Special Forces and the civilian irregulars.

Despite the successful accomplishment of its role of advising, assisting, supporting, arming, clothing, feeding, and shepherding 42,000 irregulars at the peak CIDG strength, and an additional 40,000 Regional Forces and Popular Forces in the local government advisory role, the Special Forces troops were continually conscious of mistrust and suspicion on the part of many relatively senior field grade U.S. military men. This state of affairs, which came about chiefly from a lack of knowledge of Special Forces operations, their limitations and their capabilities, gave rise to many discrete efforts to bring the Special Forces either totally or in separate parts within the operational control of a U.S. senior official. This desire to control Special Forces assets was not restricted to operational commanders, but was evident in many staff officers as well. The most difficult operational control demands came from staff sections at Headquarters, Military Assistance Command, Vietnam. It is also true that some senior Special Forces officers endorsed divided control, since the division of authority,   responsibility,   and   command   and   control encouraged a situation where both sides, the regular U.S. military chain and the group headquarters, could be played against one another to the advantage of the local U.S. Special Forces commander. To some Special Forces men, the notion of transferring operational control of field detachments to other U.S. Army elements was attractive since it removed a great deal of responsibility for day-to-day operations from the group headquarters. It is a matter of record that the group was most successful when operated as a group, under strong central Special Forces leadership.

Although it has been suggested that had the group been commanded by a general officer many of these travails would have been avoided, there is nothing in the Special Forces experience to validate that speculation. Indeed, if the position of commander were upgraded simply to counter the adverse attitudes, then the more likely consequence would have been continued distrust but under more circumspect approaches. A valid case could be made on an exception basis that the position of group commander exceeded in terms of mission responsibility and liabilities the position of any U.S. brigadier in Vietnam. Should a future commitment of U.S. military forces require the same scale of investment of Special Forces as occurred in Vietnam, the feasibility and desirability of a general officer command of Special Forces should be examined at that time.

The Future of the Special Forces
Certain hard facts have emerged from the experience gained by the Special Forces in the Vietnam War. The Special Forces, for example, can function expertly and efficiently under adverse conditions for long periods of time, as demonstrated by the performances of men stationed in remote camp locations for one-year tours. That Special Forces troops are highly motivated and determined to accomplish their missions as professional soldiers is shown by their repeated tours of duty in the combat zone. The Special Forces organization is very flexible; despite its original focus on unconventional warfare, it adjusted remarkably well to the significantly different

methods of countering insurgency by use of conventional forms of warfare with civilian irregulars.

Several questions as to the future role of the Special Forces arose even before the unit departed from Vietnam. Were the tables of organization and equipment adequate and comprehensive? Should the mission of the Army Special Forces be changed to include more than the single mission of waging unconventional warfare? Should there be a permanent branch of service for Special Forces officers and men, as opposed to the detailed, temporary duty nature of their current assignments? Some of these questions are readily answered, some require substantial study.

The tables of organization and equipment have already been modified to incorporate changes brought about by the lessons learned in Vietnam. The new organization has resulted in greater flexibility of employment and more efficient operational capability for the revised group. The doctrinal mission statement of the Special Forces has been revised officially to indicate that the roles and missions are really a function of Special Forces capabilities rather than simply a single unconventional warfare role. This revision permits a broad range of possibilities from the individual in a direct action role to the entire group involved in a guerrilla war.

The question of the feasibility or desirability of authorizing a permanent branch of service for Special Forces officers and men can best be answered by a comprehensive, objective study. The temporary nature of an assignment to Special Forces has created an atmosphere of uncertainty for potential volunteers that has worked to the detriment of the program. Other arms and services quite naturally are reluctant to lose members to the Special Forces for periods up to three years. Within an arm or service, the necessity for formal evaluation of all members of that arm or service within a general pattern of development works to the detriment of the careers of those inclined to Special Forces assignments.

It is impossible to equate combat and command duties between Special Forces officers and their contemporaries in various arms and services. Special Forces duties and assignments exceed the norm for other arms and services, partly because of the variety of skills and talents embodied in a small force. Quite a few Reserve officers refused to apply for Regular commissions because such action, if approved, took them out of Special Forces immediately and placed them in a career pattern of assignments which were, in their opinion, less appealing than the Special Forces.

As for enlisted men, the education and training necessary to qualify as a Special Forces man led individuals into rather parochial fields. Yet as centralized promotions and proficiency pay criteria became more demanding, the tests for proficiency and standing focused on regular unit performance to the disadvantage of the Special Forces noncommissioned officer. An operations sergeant trained by Special Forces is now competing with an infantry unit operations sergeant through a test mechanism that is focused on the infantry unit, with no allowance for the Special Service unit.

The usual arguments against a permanent branch for Special Forces center on the number of men in the program, the similarity with other combat arms in terms of duties, and a variety of clichés designed to avoid the possibility of setting a precedent for other specialists. If the overall troop basis of the future contains the permanent feature of Special Forces units, then an analysis in depth should be made to determine the feasibility and desirability of authorizing a permanent branch of service for the members of those units.

One inescapable fact has clearly emerged. The Special Forces men earned on the battlefield their rightful place in the United States Army. Tough, resourceful, dedicated, and efficient, the men of the Special Forces stood and fought as well and as bravely as those of any fighting unit in our country's history. They are firmly committed to their official motto of "Free the Oppressed" and with equal firmness to their unofficial yardstick: "We are known by what we do, not by what we say we are going to do."

The Special Forces men did their duty well and honorably in Vietnam. They kept faith with the Army and with the United States of America.

SCUD-HUNTING

22 SAS, Iraq, 1991

1941. The Special Air Service – destined to become the world's most famous and most feared special forces unit – was conceived in the most unlikely of places: a hospital bed in Egypt. Injured while undertaking some unofficial parachute training, David Stirling, a twenty-six-year-old subaltern in No. 8 (Guards) Commando, used his enforced sojourn in 15th Scottish Military Hospital in Cairo to conjure a scheme for hit-and-run operations against the Germans in the North African desert.

On his release from hospital in July, Stirling decided to take his idea to the top. To present the plan through the usual channels would only mean it getting buried in what Stirling thought of as "fossilized shit" – bureaucracy, in other, politer, words. Although generals are not, by and large, in the habit of granting interviews to second-lieutenants, Stirling hobbled on crutches to General Headquarters Middle East in Cairo's leafy Tonbalat Street; after failing to show a pass at the security barrier, he went around the corner, jumped over the fence and careered inside the building, the warden's bellowed alarms close behind him. Up on the third floor, Stirling found his way into the office of Major General Neil Ritchie, Claude Auchinleck's Deputy Chief of Staff. Stirling breathlessly apologized to the surprised Ritchie for the somewhat unconventional nature of his call, but insisted that he had something of "great operational importance" to show him. Stirling then pulled out the pencilled memo on small-scale desert raiding he had prepared in hospital. "He [Ritchie] was very courteous,"

Stirling remembered years later, "and he settled down to read it.

About halfway through, he got very engrossed, and had forgotten the rather irregular way it had been presented." It was Stirling's turn to be surprised. Looking up, Ritchie said matter-of-factly, "I think this may be the sort of plan we are looking for. I will discuss it with the Commander-in-Chief and let you know our decision in the next day or so." The Commander-in-Chief was General Claude Auchinleck, new to his post, and under immense pressure from Churchill to mount offensive operations. Stirling's plan was a gift for Auchinleck; it required few resources, it was original, and it dovetailed neatly with Churchill's own love of commandos. Stirling's memo went under the cumbersome title of "Case for the retention of a limited number of special service troops, for employment as parachutists", but there was nothing ungainly about its concept; on the contrary, Stirling understood that small can be beautifully lethal in wartime. The unit Stirling proposed was to operate behind enemy lines and attack vulnerable targets such as supply lines and airfields at night. What is more, the raids were to be carried out by groups of five to ten men, rather than the hundreds of a standard commando force, the very numbers of which made them susceptible to detection by the enemy. Since these special service commandos were to be inserted by air, they had greater range than seaborne troops and did not require costly (and reluctant) Royal Navy support. Stirling wrote later:

> I argued the advantage of establishing a unit based on the principle of the fullest exploitation of surprise and of making the minimum demands on manpower and equipment . . . a sub-unit of five men to cover a target previously requiring four troops of commando, i.e. about two hundred men. I sought to prove that, if an aerodrome or transport park was the objective of an operation, then the destruction of fifty aircraft or units of transport was more easily accomplished by a sub-unit of five men than by a force of two hundred.

While Auchinleck pondered Stirling's memo, Ritchie looked into David Stirling's background. He was equally pleased and displeased by what he found. On graduation from the Guards' depot at Pirbright, David Stirling had been classed as an "irresponsible and unremarkable soldier". He was dismissive of authority. He overslept so much he was nicknamed "the Great Sloth". In Egypt his partying had become legendary, and he had more than once revived himself from hangovers by inhaling oxygen begged from nurses at the 15th Scottish Military Hospital.

But it wasn't all bad. David Stirling, born in 1915, came from "good stock"; he was the youngest son of Brigadier Archibald Stirling of Keir; his mother was the daughter of the 16th Baron Lovat. After Ampleforth and three years at Cambridge, Stirling had enthusiastically joined the Scots Guards, before transferring to No. 8 Commando. Like many a commando officer, he was recruited over a pink gin at White's Club by Lieutenant-Colonel Bob Laycock, 8 Commando's Commanding Officer. As part of the "Layforce" brigade, No. 8 Commando had been dispatched to North Africa, where its seaborne raids had been embarrassing wash-outs. On the disbandment of Layforce, Stirling had jumped – literally – at the chance of joining an unofficial parachute training session organized by another officer in No. 8 Commando. Many people over the years mistook Stirling's diffidence, abetted by the slight stoop common to the very tall (Stirling was 6 feet 6 inches) for a lack of ambition; on the contrary, Stirling possessed a core of steely resolve. (Churchill, who met Stirling later in the war, borrowed an apposite couplet from *Don Juan* for his pen portrait of the SAS leader as "the mildest manner'd man that ever scuttled ship or cut a throat".) This inner determination was the reason why Stirling participated in the impromptu parachutejumping trials at Fuka: he wanted to get on with the war. Unfortunately, the aircraft used, a lumbering Valencia bi-plane, was not equipped for parachuting and the men had secured the static lines which opened the silk canopies to seat legs.

Stirling's parachute caught on the door and snagged; he descended far too rapidly and hit the ground so hard that he was temporarily paralysed from the waist down. Thus he had ended up as a bed patient in the Scottish Military Hospital.

Three days after his meeting with Ritchie, Stirling was back at Middle East Headquarters, this time with a pass. Auchinleck saw him in person. Stirling was given permission to recruit a force of sixty officers and men. The unit was to be called "L Detachment,

SAS Brigade". The "SAS" stood for "Special Air Service", a force which was wholly imaginary and whose nomenclature was devised by Brigadier Dudley Clarke, a staff Intelligence officer, to convince the Germans that Britain had a large airborne force in North Africa.

To mark his new appointment as the Commanding Officer of L Detachment, Stirling was promoted to captain. There were two particular officers Stirling wanted for his outfit.

The first was John "Jock" Lewes, whom Stirling found at Tobruk, where he was leading raids on the Axis lines. British by birth, Lewes had been brought up in Australia, and was an Oxford rowing "blue" who had led his university eight to a historic win over Cambridge. It had been Lewes who had organized the parachute jump at Fuka during which Stirling had crashed. Lewes's influence on the formation of the SAS was paramount; on a visit to Stirling in hospital, Lewes had voiced proposals and queries which did much to further the embryonic idea of a desert raiding force that was circling around in Stirling's head. Stirling said later: "The chat with Jock was the key to success. I knew I had to have all the answers to the questions he raised if I was to get anywhere."

When Stirling asked Lewes to become the first recruit of "L Detachment" Lewes refused point blank. He did not trust Stirling's commitment. But Stirling, as everyone agreed, could be very persuasive. Besides, he was displaying more grit than Lewes had seen in the party boy hitherto. After a month of cajoling, Lewes agreed to join. So did Captain R. B. "Paddy" Mayne. Before the war, Mayne had been a rugby player of international rank, capped six times for Ireland and once for the British Lions. He was also a useful boxer and had reached the final of the British Universities' Championship heavyweight division. Unfortunately, when taken by drink Mayne was not too fussy whom he fought; in June 1941 he'd been returned to unit from 11 Commando for attacking his commanding officer.

However, Paddy Mayne was much more than a 6-feet-2-inch drinker and brawler. A former law student, he had a "Dr Jekyll" side, and was sensitive, literate, modest and painfully shy.

Unquestionably he was brave; he'd won a Mention in Dispatches for his baptismal combat – 1 Commando's raid on the Litani River in Syria. He would end up as one of the four most decorated British officers of World War II, with a Distinguished Service Order (DSO) and three Bars. As "brave as ten lions, a tactical genius", is how George Jellicoe, a fellow SAS officer (and later a commanding officer of the Special Boat Squadron), remembered Mayne. Nevertheless, before accepting Mayne into L Detachment, Stirling extricated a promise that he would not attack his new commanding officer. As Stirling noted years later, Mayne "kept the promise, at least in respect of myself, though not with others".

Like Lewes and Mayne, most of the rest of the officers and men of L Detachment, who would later be known as "the Originals", were volunteers recruited from commandos beached at the Infantry Base Depot at Geneifa following the disbandment of Layforce.

Selection was based on Stirling's personal impression of the men at brief interviews. He also told them that if they failed to make the grade in training they would have to return to their units. Why did they join? Captain Malcolm Pleyell, L Detachment's first medical officer, wrote, doubtless accurately:

> This sort of warfare possessed a definite flavour of romance.
> It conjured up visions of dashing deeds which might become
> famous overnight.

By August 1941, Stirling had established a base at Kabrit, 100 miles south of Cairo in the Canal Zone. Equipment was conspicuous by its absence, due to the parsimony of Q Branch.

Arriving by truck at Kabrit, Johnny Cooper, recruited from No. 8 Commando, found:

> Only two medium-sized marquees and three 180-lb tents
> piled up in the middle of the strip of bare desert allocated to
> us. No camp, none of the usual facilities, not even a flagpole.
> A wooden sign bearing the words "L Detachment – SAS"
> was the sole clue that this was base camp.

Being, in his own words, a "cheekie laddie", Stirling had a plan to secure the necessary equipment to complete the camp – which

was to "borrow" it from a New Zealand camp down the road.
Thus the first – and highly unofficial – attack of L Detachment
was a night raid on the camp of 2nd New Zealand Division. They
filled up L Detachment's one and only three-ton truck with
anything useful that could be found – including tents and a piano
for the sergeants' mess. The next day, L Detachment boasted one
of the smartest and most luxuriously furnished British camps in
the Canal Zone.

Training then began in earnest. From the outset, Stirling
insisted on a high standard of discipline, equal to that of the
Brigade of Guards. In his opening address to L Detachment on 4
September, he told the men: "We can't afford to piss about disci-
plining anyone who is not a hundred per cent devoted to having
a crack at the Hun." L Detachment required a special discipline:
self-discipline. Stirling told the L Detachment volunteers that
control of self was expected at all times, even on leave:

> When anyone is on leave in Cairo or Alexandria, please
> remember that there's to be no bragging or scrapping in bars
> or restaurants. Get this quite clear. In the SAS, all toughness
> is reserved exclusively for the enemy.

In return, the usual Army "bullshit" of parades and saluting officers every time they loomed into sight was to be dropped. This
informal style was to become a hallmark of the SAS. Stirling
expected personal initiative, independence and modesty. Any
"passengers" would be returned to their units.

David Stirling also demanded the utmost physical fitness, but
it was Jock Lewes who translated the master's ideas into practi-
calities. The early L Detachment training devised by Lewes was,
in essence, commando training adapted to desert conditions,
especially those encountered at night. The emphasis was on navigation, weapons training, demolition training and punishing
physical training sessions. Endurance marches became mara-
thons of up to thirty miles a night, carrying packs crammed with
sand or bricks.

Everyone joining the SAS had to be a parachutist, since Stirling
envisaged insertion by air for his force. No parachute training

instructors were available (the only British parachute-training schools extant were Ringway, near Manchester, and Delhi, in India), so the SAS under Jock Lewes developed its own parachute training techniques. These involved jumping from ever higher scaffold towers and from the tailboard of a 112-pound Bedford truck moving at 30 miles per hour across the desert. More than half "the Originals" of L Detachment sustained injuries launching themselves off the back of the Bedford. After this very basic parachute training, the L Detachment recruits made their first live drop, from a Bristol Bombay aircraft. There were no reserve parachutes. Two men, Ken Warburton and Joseph Duffy, died when the snap-links connecting the strops on their parachutes to the static rail in the Bombay twisted apart. Consequently, when they jumped they were no longer attached to the aircraft – and there was nothing to pull the canopies out. Afterwards, Bob Bennett recalled:

> We went to bed with as many cigarettes as possible, and smoked until morning. Next morning, every man (led by Stirling himself) jumped; no one backed out. It was then that I realized that I was with a great bunch of chaps.

The drop on the morning of 17 October was a key moment in SAS history. Stirling displayed leadership; he took the men through the doubt and the darkness.

To replace the faulty clips on the Bombay had been straightforward; however, another engineering problem facing L Detachment proved harder to solve. What bomb should the patrols carry to blow up German aircraft? The bomb had to be small enough to be easily transportable but powerful enough to do the job of destruction. Most SAS men infiltrating on foot from a drop zone could only be expected to carry two of the widely available five-pound charges, which would only inflict superficial damage. Once again it was Jock Lewes to the rescue. After weeks of experiments in a small hut at Kabrit, Lewes invented the requisite device – henceforth known as the "Lewes bomb" – which was a mixture of plastic explosive, thermite and aluminium turnings rolled in engine oil. Likened to a "nice little black pudding" by L Detachment's Sergeant John Almonds (known to all as "Gentleman Jim"), the Lewes bomb was sticky and could quickly be placed onto the side of an aircraft. Just a pound of "Lewes bomb" could annihilate an aircraft, meaning that each trooper could carry the means of dispatching ten.

By the end of August, L Detachment was ready for its final exercise, a dummy attack on the large RAF base at Heliopolis, outside Cairo. Stirling had been bluntly told by an RAF Group Captain that his plan to sabotage German aircraft on the ground was far-fetched. So far-fetched, indeed, that he bet Stirling $16 that L Detachment could not infiltrate the Heliopolis base and place labels representing bombs on the parked aircraft. Now, Stirling decided, it was time to pay up. The entire orbat (order of battle) of L Detachment, six officers and fifty-five men, trekked ninety miles across the desert from Kabrit over four days, on four pints of water each, and carrying weights to simulate Lewes bombs. Although the RAF knew the SAS were coming, and even set up air patrols, Stirling and his men successfully infiltrated the base on the fourth night and adorned the parked aircraft with sticky labels marked "BOMB". Stirling collected his $16.

The first operational raid by the SAS was planned for the night of 17 November 1941. Five parties were to be dropped from Bristol Bombays, to attack Axis fighter and bomber strips at Gazala and Timini. The drop zones were about twelve miles from the objective, and the teams were to spend a day in a lying-up position observing their targets before a night attack with Lewes bombs, to be detonated by time-delay pencils. After the attack, the teams were to rendezvous south of the Trig al'Abd track with a motor patrol of the Long Range Desert Group (LRDG). Reconnaissance behind enemy lines was the stock-in-trade of the LRDG, which had been founded by Major Ralph Bagnold, an amateur pre-war explorer of the Sahara.

Stirling's attack had a purpose beyond the destruction of enemy aircraft; it was designed to divert enemy attention on the eve of Operation Crusader, Auchinleck's offensive to push Rommel out of Cyrenaica in North Africa. The same evening was to see No. 11 Commando attack Rommel's house in Beda Littoria (now Al Baydá).

Like so many previous commando raids, that on Rommel's headquarters was a seamless disaster, resulting in the loss of thirty men for no gain whatsoever; the house raided by 11 Commando had never even been used by Rommel. Not that Stirling's debut raid garnered a better result, though. Following a Met Office forecast of 30-knot winds and rain in the target area, Stirling toyed with cancelling the *Squatter mission*, since airborne operations in anything above 15 knots invariably ended in the scattering and injuring of the parachutists. On further thought, though, Stirling decided to go ahead, as he believed that a cancellation would affect L Detachment's bubbling-over morale. Moreover, in his sales talk on behalf of his intended parachute force, Stirling had promised general headquarters that the unique quality of his unit was that "the weather would not restrict their operations to the same extent that it had done in the case of seaborne special service troops". To Stirling's relief, the officers of L Detachment, assembled ready to go at Baggush airfield, backed his decision to go ahead. So did the enlisted men. "We'll go because we've got to," Stirling told them. Any man who wanted to could leave. No one did.

Of the fifty-four SAS men who jumped out into the windswept night of 16 November, only twenty-one made the rendezvous with the LRD Group. The plane carrying Lieutenant-Charles Bonnington's stick was hit by flak, after which a Me-109 fighter delivered the *coup de grâce*; all the SAS men aboard were injured, one fatally. Meanwhile, Lieutenant Eoin McGonigal had been killed on landing, and when his stick set out towards the rendezvous they were captured by an Italian patrol. Nearly every man in Stirling's, Mayne's and Lewes's sticks suffered concussion, sprains or broken bones; Mayne's troop sergeant, Jock Cheyne, broke his back. Since all their gear had been dropped separately, even the walking able found themselves lacking bombs and fuses. What fuses were recovered were then wrecked by the driving rain. The storm of 16 and 17 November 1942 was one of the worst of the war in the western desert. Demoralized, the survivors trekked to the rendezvous not through blistering heat, as they had expected, but through mud and floods. Stirling and Bob Tait were among the last to arrive. Waiting for them on the Trig al'Abd was Captain David Lloyd Owen of the LRDG's Y patrol:

> One very interesting thing arose from my meeting with David Stirling that morning. David told me all about the operation and that it had been a total failure. He was a remarkable man. He never gave in to failure and was determined to make the next operation a success. I turned over in my mind, "Why the hell do this ridiculous parachuting, why didn't they let us take them to where they wanted to go? We could take them like a taxi to do the job. We could push off while they did their task, and then pick them up at an agreed rendezvous." We discussed this while having a mug of tea laced with rum in the dawn. He was a little doubtful. I then took him to the next RV to meet up with Jake Easonsmith who was detailed to take him to Siwa and thence to Cairo. A week or so later David told me he had been so immensely impressed by Jake and his patrol, he decided that he would work with us, and they did until the end of 1942, when they got their own transport. These were months of great success.

They were. Although Stirling thought his L Detachment SAS might be killed off as a result of *Squatter*'s failure, no one at general headquarters seemed to care much. General headquarters had bigger problems on its collective mind than the loss of thirty-four parachutists; Rommel was making his famous "dash to the wire" and a counter-thrust was needed. It would help the counter-thrust if the Axis aircraft at Tamet, Sirte, Aghayala and Agedabia aerodromes were destroyed. Stirling was given another chance and he took it with both hands. This time there was to be no parachute drop; the SAS were to be taxied to the target by the LRDG.

On 8 December, Stirling, Mayne and eleven other SAS men departed their temporary headquarters at Jalo oasis accompanied by the LRDG's Rhodesian patrol under the command of Captain Gus Holliman. Stirling and Mayne were set to raid Sirte and Tamet airfields, which were about 350 miles from Jalo, on the

night of 14 December. At the same time, Jock Lewes was to lead
a section in an attack on Aghayla. A fourth SAS patrol, comprising four men under Lieutenant Bill Fraser, was to raid Agedabia
a week later. Sitting aboard the LRDG's stripped-down Ford
trucks, the SAS men were overcome by the vastness of the Sahara.
There was no sign of life, and Stirling found the brooding soli-
tude like being on the high seas. Courtesy of dead-on navigation
by the LRDG's Corporal Mike Sadler, the SAS were just 40
miles south of Sirte by noon on 11 December. Then their luck
changed: an Italian Ghibli spotter plane appeared out of the haze
to strafe and bomb them. Holliman ordered the patrol to make
for cover in a thorn scrub 2 miles back, and there they lay as two
more Ghiblis came hunting, but failed to see the patrol. The
element of surprise, the *sine qua non* of the SAS, was lost. Even so,
Stirling determined to press on, and the obliging LRDG dropped
the SAS off not at the agreed 20 miles from Sirte, but a mere 3
miles. Knowing that a reception committee was likely to be waiting, Stirling chose not to risk his whole section but instead to
infiltrate the airfield with just one companion, Sergeant Jimmy
Brough. The rest of the team, under Mayne, was sent to a satellite
airfield 5 miles away at Wadi Tamet.

Unfortunately, during their recce of the airfield Stirling and
Brough stumbled over two Italian sentries, one of whom began
firing off bullets, causing the SAS men to sprint away into the
desert night. Next day, as they lay up near the base, Stirling and
Brough watched in bitter frustration as Italian Caproni bomber
after bomber flew away. Alerted and suspicious, the Italians were
evacuating the airfield.

At nightfall, Stirling and Brough tramped in silence to the
rendezvous with the LRDG. Once again, an SAS operation had
been a washout. Stirling knew that unless Mayne and Lewes
triumphed, the disbandment of the SAS was likely. Mayne's
attack was to take place at 11 p.m.; the hour came and went, unlit
by explosions, and then there was a great *whumph* and a bolt
flame in the west, followed by explosion upon explosion. The
SAS was in the sabotage business. Stirling and Brough almost
danced with delight. "It almost makes the army worthwhile,"
shouted Brough. There had, it turned out, been a good reason for

Mayne's slight delay at Wadi Tamet. Approaching the airfield, Mayne had noticed a chink of light and the sound of laughter coming from a hut; on putting his ear to the door he realized that it was the pilots' mess and a party was in full swing. Deciding that the party should come to an end, Mayne kicked open the door and hosed the room with bullets from his .45-calibre Tommy gun. For good measure, he shot out the lights, leaving the room in chaos. Crouching outside were the rest of his section – McDonald, Hawkins, Besworth, Seekings and White. Reg Seekings recalled:

> As soon as Paddy cut loose . . . the whole place went mad – [they fired] everything they had including tracer . . . They had fixed lines of fire about a couple of feet from the ground. We had either to jump over or crawl under them . . . Besworth came slithering over to us on all fours. I can still see him getting to his feet, pulling in his arse as the tracer ripped past his pack, missing him by inches. On a signal from Paddy, we got the hell out of it.

They dashed to the airfield, setting Lewes bombs as they passed down the rows of aircraft. Finding himself a bomb short, Mayne clambered into one aircraft's cockpit and tore out the instrument panel with his bare hands. Corporal Seekings takes up the story:

> We had not gone fifty yards when the first plane went up. We stopped to look but the second one went up near us and we began to run. After a while we felt fairly safe and stopped to take another glance. What a sight! Planes exploding all over, and the terrific roar of petrol and bombs going up.

Jock Lewes had not enjoyed good hunting, but when Bill Fraser's party reached their rendezvous they reported the most astounding success of all. They had blown up thirty-seven aircraft at Agedabia aerodrome. In this week-long sequence of raids, the SAS had accounted for no less than sixty-one enemy aircraft destroyed, together with petrol, stores and transport.

His tail up, Stirling could not wait to have another go at the enemy. On the presumption that the enemy would not expect another attack so soon, Stirling and Mayne set off from their Jalo desert base on Christmas Day 1941 to revisit Tamet and Sirte. Their second attack was a mirror image of the first. Mayne destroyed twenty-seven aircraft at Tamet; Stirling was unable to reach the airfield because of the crush of German armour and vehicles around it. He was fortunate to escape with his life; an Italian guard tried to shoot him, only to discover he had a faulty round in the barrel of his rifle.

Meanwhile, Fraser and Lewes were taken by Lieutenant Morris's LRDG patrol to raid airstrips at Nofilia and Ras Lanuf. At the latter location, Mussolini had built a grandiose triumphal arch to commemorate his African conquests; to the Tommies it looked similar to the arch at the end of Oxford Street, and "Marble Arch" it became known to one and all throughout the British Army. Lewes had a difficult time at Nofilia when a bomb he was placing on an aircraft exploded prematurely. Withdrawing under heavy fire, Lewes and his party were picked up by their LRDG escort, only to come under attack by Messerschmitts and Stukas in the open desert. Jock Lewes was killed, the survivors scattered.

The death of Lewes was a heavy blow to Stirling, as there was no one else on whom he so heavily relied. There was more bad news: Captain Fraser's patrol was missing.

To this episode, at least, there was a happy ending. On finding the Marble Arch strip bereft of aircraft, Fraser and his section had waited for Morris's LRDG patrol. When, after six days, Morris failed to arrive, the SAS men decided to walk the 200 burning miles to Jalo. Their walk, which took eight days, was the first of several epic peregrinations in the SAS annals, to rank alongside that of Trooper John Sillito the following year (again, 200 miles in eight days, drinking his own urine for hydration).

Fraser's walk and the unit's bag of nearly ninety aircraft in a month were an emphatic vindication of Stirling's concept of small-scale raiding by a volunteer elite.

It was Stirling's gift as a leader to see the big picture, and where the SAS fitted into that scene. He was also, due to his social background and boundless confidence, possessed of friends in the highest places. Both attributes came together in early January 1942, when Stirling sought a personal interview with Auchinleck, the Commander-in-Chief, during which he proposed that L Detachment should switch from striking airfields to ports.

Although the *Crusader* operation had pushed Rommel west-wards, the Afrika Korps remained a potent force, not least because it continued to receive supplies of Panzers through the coastal harbours. Stirling pointed out to Auchinleck that Bouerat would become the likely main supply harbour for the Afrika Korps, and that the fuel dumps there could and should be blown up. Auchinleck agreed. When Stirling asked for men for L Detachment, Auchinleck gave him permission to recruit a further six officers and thirty to forty men, some of whom could be drawn from the Special Boat Section of No. 8 Commando. For good measure, Auchinleck promoted Stirling to major.

There was one final thing: Stirling's enemies in general head-quarters (who were the sort of literal-minded men who thought irregular forces were a diversion from the "real" war) had bluntly informed him that L Detachment, because it was a temporary unit, could not have its own badge. Nonetheless, Stirling brashly wore SAS wings and cap badge to meet the Commander-in-Chief. Stirling had calculated correctly; Auchinleck liked and approved of the badge. The SAS badge was more than a mark of an elite unit, it was a debt Stirling felt he owed Lewes, who had been instrumental in its design. The so-called "Winged Dagger" was modelled by Bob Tait on King Arthur's sword Excalibur, while the wings were probably taken from an ibis on a fresco in Shepheard's Hotel. The colours of the wings, Oxford and Cambridge blue, were selected because Lewes had rowed for Oxford, and Tom Langton, another early L-Detachment officer, for Cambridge. It was Stirling himself who came up with the motto "Who Dares Wins". The badge was worn on berets – which at first were white, but when these attracted wolf whistles they were changed to a sand colour, which they still are.

On the way back to Jalo, Stirling came across fifty French parachutists at Alexandria who, after some vigorous appeals to the Free French commander in Cairo, General Catroux, Stirling annexed for the SAS. He also recruited Captain Bill Cumper of the Royal Engineers, a Cockney explosives expert who would take on the vacancy of demolitions instructor left open by Lewes's death. But Cumper could not take on the whole gamut of training the SAS recruits who were now so numerous the camp at Kabrit was overflowing with them; that mantle, Stirling resolved, should be taken by Paddy Mayne. Sitting in his tent, Stirling explained his thinking to Mayne, who accepted with bad grace verging on insubordination. He would only "do his best", and then only on a temporary basis. Mayne even hinted that Stirling was green-eyed about his success in blowing up aircraft, and pinning him to a desk was a way of stealing the glory.

With a moody Mayne left sulking in Kabrit, Stirling launched a raid on Bouerat from Jalo on 17 January. Taxiing the SAS team out was the Guards patrol of the LRDG, led by Captain Anthony Hunter. As on previous missions, Stirling seemed chained to ill luck. On the sixth day out, the patrol was strafed and bombed in the Wadi Tamrit, with the loss of the radio truck and three men. Then Stirling instructed the two Special Boat Section men in the party to assemble their *folbot* (a type of collapsible canoe) before the final approach – the plan being for the SBS men to paddle out and set limpet mines on ships in the harbour. As their 1,680-pound Ford truck neared Bouerat, it lurched down a pothole and the *folbot* shattered. Not that it mattered; there were no ships in the port. Instead, Stirling had to satisfy himself with detonating petrol bowsers and the wireless station.

Picked up by an LRDG truck driven by Corporal "Flash" Gibson, Stirling and his crew rode around, stopping to plant bombs on parked trucks. They then made off to the main rendez-vous. Mounted on the back of the Ford V-8 truck was a novelty – a Vickers K aircraft-type machine gun, whose .303-inch barrels could spew out bullets at 1,200 rounds per minute. Johnny Cooper was the man with his finger on the trigger:

As we motored at speed along the track, we suddenly noticed flashing lights up ahead of us and a few isolated shots whizzed through the air. Whether they were warning shots or the enemy clearing their guns we did not know, but as our truck accelerated down a slight incline it became painfully obvious that an ambush had been set up . . . I slipped off the safety catch and let fly with a devastating mixture of tracer and incendiary, amazed at the firepower of the Vickers. At the same time, Reg [Seekings] opened up with his Thompson, and we ploughed through the ambush, completely outgunning and demoralizing the Italians. Gibson, with great presence of mind, switched on the headlamps and roared away at about 40 mph, driving with absolute efficiency and coolness to extricate us from a difficult position.

Gibson was awarded the Military Medal (MM) for the operation, and Johnny Cooper the Distinguished Conduct Medal. Vickers K, fired for the first time in action by the SAS, became the unit's weapon of choice for the rest of the war.

* * *

Aside from the constant struggle with Middle East Headquarters to preserve, let alone expand, L Detachment, Stirling threw himself into the planning of another raid – one which tested the soundness of his strategic vision. This raid was intended to assist in the battle of Malta. Perched in the middle of the Mediterranean, British-controlled Malta posed a mortal threat to Rommel's line of supply back to Italy. Consequently, the Axis was trying to bomb and blockade the island into submission. Announcing that the loss of Malta would be "a disaster of the first magnitude to the British Empire, and probably fatal in the long run to the defence of the Nile Valley", Churchill decreed that two supply convoys must get through in the June dark-phase. Since these convoys would almost certainly be attacked by Axis aircraft operating from Cyrenaica and Crete, Stirling proposed that L Detachment would mount a synchronized attack on Axis aerodromes in these locations on 13 and 14 June 1942. Fortunately for L Detachment, its ranks had been modestly enlarged by the annexation of the Special Interrogation Group. This had been formed by Captain Buck and consisted of German-speaking Jews and a couple of Afrika Korps deserters, all of whom were prepared to masquerade in German uniform, knowing all too well their fate if caught.

The various L Detachment teams who were to carry out the raids in North Africa gathered at Siwa, before being escorted to within striking distance of their targets by the LRDG. Stirling, accompanied by his familiars, Cooper and Seekings, headed for Benina aerodrome. For once, Stirling had good hunting. Johnny Cooper later wrote:

We were about a thousand feet above the airfield and were able to look down on the coastal plain towards Benghazi. We lay up during the day in a patch of scrub and bushes, making our plans and checking compass bearings for the night approach. David told us that he had laid on an RAF raid on Benghazi that night to act as a diversion, and that this would determine the time of our attack. At last light the three of us, with David in the lead, started to descend the escarpment.

This was quite difficult as our way was criss-crossed by numerous small wadis. Slithering and stumbling over the rocks, grabbing hold where we could in order not to break our necks or legs, we managed to complete this section before total darkness fell. We got on to the airfield without difficulty and simply walked out into the middle. Dead on time, the RAF arrived over the town and started their bombing runs, while we sat there in the dark. As we were a long way from the main buildings we were able to talk quite freely about all sorts of subjects. David gave us a long lecture on deer stalking, including methods of getting into position to stalk, the problems of wind and the necessity for camouflage and stealthy movement. Absorbed in his Highland exploits we could forget the job in hand and time passed very quickly.

Glancing at his watch, David brought the lecture to a close. "Right," he said, "squeeze the time pencils. We're ready to go." We each had twenty bombs and the whole operation only took a few minutes. We crept forward for about five hundred yards when we found ourselves in the middle of a dug-in dump of aviation fuel which was about six feet deep and extended over quite a large area. We left two bombs there so that we would have illumination later, then moved on. Reg suddenly grabbed David by the arm. We all heard the heavy tread of a sentry on the tarmacadam perimeter track between the hangars and the office block. He was ambling along quite

nonchalantly and his hobnailed boots gave us plenty of warning. We crouched down and waited until he had passed the
hangars and then crept up to the closed doors. Reg and I
managed to prise them open rather noisily, but no alarm was
given. Leaving Reg outside with his Tommy gun, David and
I went inside. As our eyes grew accustomed to the darkness
we saw that the hangar was full of German aircraft. Motioning
me to go to the right, David set off to the left, and we busily
placed our bombs on the Stukas and Messerschmitts that
were in there for repair.

I came across a Me110, a large twin-engined fighter-
bomber, and had to stand on tiptoe to try to place my bomb
on the wing. But David, who was so much taller than I, stole
up from behind. "All right, Cooper, this one's mine. You go
into the far corner and fix that JU52." I reluctantly withdrew
my bomb and went over to do justice to the Junkers. We then
continued to the second hangar and dealt with more aircraft
while Reg discovered a mass of spare aero engines and highly
technical-looking equipment. All this accounted for our full
stock of sixty bombs. As each weighed nearly two pounds,
fifteen were all that could be carried easily, in addition to
personal weapons and other kit. Further down the track
between the hangars we came across a small guard house and
we observed that occasionally the door opened as the sentries
were changed. David said that he would give them something
to remember us by, and with Reg and myself covering him,
he kicked open the door. We saw that the room was crowded
with Germans, many of whom were asleep. David calmly
bowled a grenade along the floor, saying "Share this among
you." He slammed the door and jumped clear. The delay was
only four seconds and the explosion shattered the guard
house while we rapidly made our escape behind the hangars.
We never knew what casualties we had caused, but they must
have been considerable in such a confined space. While still
behind the last hangar we heard our first bomb go off, to be
followed in rapid succession by all the rest.

Although all the time pencils had been activated at the
same time, there was always a slight difference due to

differing acid strengths. Almost deafened by the noise, we struggled through a gap in the wire, crossed the main road and scrambled up the escarpment.

Climbing up the escarpment on the edge of the Jebel, Stirling called a halt; he was suffering one of his frequent migraine attacks. Eventually Cooper and Seekings led Stirling, staggering and half blind, into a concealed position in the scrub, where they watched "the fantastic fireworks display". Cooper thought it difficult to believe that such destruction could be wrought by just three men and the contents of their knapsacks.

The natural environment of the SAS, it might be said, was the desert. Fifty years later it was back there with a vengeance.

*   *   *

"Stormin' Norman" Schwarzkopf, the American in command of the Coalition gathered to evict Saddam Hussein from Kuwait, was notoriously no friend of special forces. Encountering a group of US special forces in the Gulf, Schwarzkopf barked: "I remember you guys from Vietnam . . . you couldn't do your job there, and you didn't do your job in Panama. What makes you think you can do your job here?" The one British member of Schwarzkopf's planning staff, CENTCOM, knew what British special forces at least could do. For weeks ex-SAS CO Peter de la Billière sought a role for 22 SAS, before finally persuading Schwarzkopf to sit down for a presentation by the Regiment on the benefits of its insertion deep behind the lines to cut roads and cause diversions to draw Iraqi troops from the front. Convinced, Schwarzkopf gave 22 SAS the go-ahead to cross the Iraqi border at the beginning of the air campaign against Iraq, scheduled for 29 January 1991.

The Regiment was as surprised as most people outside the US clique running the war when, at dawn on 17 January, hundreds of Allied aircraft and Tomahawk Cruise began bombarding targets in Iraq. Within twenty-four hours the Iraqi airforce was all but wiped out and Saddam's command and communications system heavily degraded. The only nagging area of doubt was Iraq's surface-to-surface missile capacity. Though an outdated technology, being little more than a Soviet version of Hitler's V2, the

Scud was capable of carrying nuclear and bio-chemical warheads. On the second night of the air campaign, Saddam answered all the speculation about "would he?" and "could he?" by launching Scuds (with conventional warheads) at Israel. Although the Scuds failed to cause any injuries, they were politically lethal; if the Israelis retaliated, the fragile anti-Saddam coalition would likely blow apart. No Arab state could afford to be seen to side with "Zionists" or their friends. Suddenly, the Scud-hunt was on, with the coalition diverting 30 per cent of its air capability to tracking Scuds and their mobile launchers in the vast Iraqi desert. Even the preternaturally upbeat Schwarzkopf could only say before the world's media on 19 January that seeking Scuds in the desert was like seeking the proverbial needle in a haystack.

Peter de la Billière, meanwhile, realized that the Scud menace offered 22 SAS a clear-cut mission in the war, signalling the Regiment that "all SAS effort should be directed against Scuds". That same day, the 300 troopers from A, B and D Squadrons already gathered in the Gulf were rushed over 900 miles from their holding area to a forward operating base just inside the Saudi border with Iraq.

The Regiment decided on two principal means of dealing with the Scud menace. Firstly, it would insert into Iraq three covert eight-man static patrols to watch roads (what the Regiment calls Main Supply Routes, or MSRs) and report on the movement of Scud traffic. When Scud sites and launchers were identified, US F15 and A10 airstrikes would be called down to destroy them, with the SAS identifying the targets using a tactical airlink or laser designator. Alongside the road-watch patrols, the Regiment would infiltrate into Iraq four columns of heavily armed "Pink Panther" Land Rovers, Unimogs and Cannon motorcycle scouts. The columns were to penetrate the "Scud Box", the area of western desert bordering Jordan which was thought to contain around fourteen mobile launchers.

The South and Central road-watch teams were inserted on 21 January, and both found that the spookily featureless desert offered no possibility of concealment. The South road-watch team aborted their mission immediately and flew back on their insertion helicopter. Meanwhile, the Central team called down an airstrike on two Iraqi radars, before they too "bugged out", driving their Land Rovers through 140 miles of biting cold desert before reaching Saudi Arabia.

Road-watch North, codenamed "Bravo Two Zero", was landed by Chinook at night 100 miles north-west of Baghdad. The weather was appalling from the start, with driving wind and sleet in what turned out to be the worst winter in the area for thirty years. As is traditional in the SAS, the decision on how to deploy was left to the patrol. Despite the urging of the Regiment's commanding officer and the regimental sergeant major, Peter "Billy" Ratcliffe, Bravo Two Zero, led by Sergeant "Andy McNab", decided not to take a "dinky" (a short-wheel-base Land Rover) with them. They did decide to take an Everest of kit: water and rations for fourteen days, explosives, ammunition, extra clothes, maps, compasses, survival equipment, 203 rifles, guns, empty sandbags, LAW66mm anti-tank launchers, communications gear, camouflage nets, Minimi machine guns – so much kit, indeed, that each man was carrying 176 pounds of it.

As dawn broke on their first day, the Bravo Two Zero team saw that their map failed to show some significant local features. Aside from a small farm across from the wadi they were lying in, there was an Iraqi S60 anti-aircraft battery less than a mile away. Unfortunately the ground was so hard they could not dig a hide, either for cover from the enemy or the cutting wind. The morning had not done with unpleasant surprises for Bravo Two Zero; when the patrol's signaller, Trooper Steven "Legs" Lane went to use the PRC 319 radio he could not get communications with the Regiment's forward base at al-Jauf. Over the next hours, everybody had a go at "fixing" the wireless; nobody could. At noon, McNab called the patrol together and explained he would instigate loss-comms drill, which involved the patrol relocating to the helicopter drop-off, where a helicopter would bring them in a new radio.

In the lying-up place in the wadi the next day, while the patrol waited to move out, they heard the jingle of sheep bells. Once before the sheep and their boy herder had come close to the wadi, but not so close as to see them. This time the boy herder reached the edge of the wadi, and looked down. The patrol froze. Sergeant Vince Phillips, the patrol second in command, believed he made eye contact with the boy, but wasn't certain.

The patrol had to assume they had been compromised. As Lane sent a message "High possibility compromise. Request relocation or exfil" on the emergency guard-net, the rest of the team prepared to move out, gathering kit and gulping down water. Exiting the bottom of the wadi, they heard the sound of a tracked vehicle and a diesel engine. The SAS team thought a tank or Armoured Personnel Carrier was being sent in after them and broke out their LAW 66mm rocket-launchers. Corporal Chris Ryan recalled:

There we were, waiting for this tank to come into view round the corner. Every second the squealing and grinding got louder. We were stuck, pinned like rats in the dead-end of the ravine. We couldn't tell what else might be coming at us over the flat ground above. The chances were that the Iraqis were deploying behind us, too; even at the moment, they were probably advancing on our position. A couple of hand grenades tossed over the edge would make a nice mess of us. Even so, if the tank came into view and levelled its gun on us, we'd have no option but to run up on to the plain, and chance it with the AA positions on the high ground.

By then it was 1700 hours, but still full daylight. Someone said, "Let's get some water down our necks, fellers," and everyone started drinking, because we knew that if we had to run for it, we'd need the liquid inside us. Other guys began frantically repacking their kit, pulling off the warm jackets they'd been wearing and stuffing them into their Bergens. A couple of the lads struggled out of their NBC suits and stowed them.

No one gave any orders about what to do. We just decided that if a tank or armoured personnel carrier came round the corner, we'd try to take it out, and then go past it down the wadi, using the dry watercourse as our escape-route. The rockets wouldn't have been much use against a tank, but they might have disabled it by blowing off a track.

So there we were, getting water down our necks and having something to eat. Then I looked round at the tail ends of the rocket launchers in front of me and said, "Hey, fellers – watch the fucking back-blast on these things. I don't want my face burned." When a 66 is fired, the danger area behind the tube extends for twenty metres. There was silence for a minute. Then, suddenly, out of fear and tension, everyone started laughing. They couldn't stop. I thought, "This is bloody ridiculous. There's a tank coming round the corner, and here we all are, giggling like schoolgirls."

Dinger pointed at my German Army cap and shouted, "Hey, Chris, you look like Rommel."

"Fuck off, Dinger," I yelled back. He was dragging desperately on his fag. "Put that fucking thing out!"

"Ah – fuck the SOPs," he said, and everyone laughed some more.

I checked my 203 magazines again, tapping them on the bottom to make sure the lip was properly engaged in the breech. I had the mags taped together in pairs, head to toe, so that I could load the second instantly by turning the empty one upside down. Each could hold thirty rounds, but I'd only loaded them with twenty-eight, to leave the springs a bit looser and cut down the chance of a stoppage. The spares were in my left-hand lower pouch.

Then suddenly round the corner came . . . not a tank, but a yellow bulldozer. The driver had the blade high up in front of him, obviously using it as a shield; he looked like an Arab, wearing a green parka with the hood up. We all kept still, lying or crouching in firing positions, but we knew the man had seen us. He was only 150 metres away when he stopped, stared, and reversed out of sight before trying to turn round.

Obviously a local, he must have known that the wadi came to a dead-end, and his only purpose in coming up it had been to find out who or what was in there. We held our breath as the squealing and grinding gradually died away.

For a minute or two we felt more relief than anything else. Then it was, "Get the radio away, Legs," and everyone was saying, "We've got to go. We've got to go." Dinger lit another

fag and sucked on it like a dying man. Now we felt certain that
the local militia must be deploying behind us, and one or two of
the lads were being a bit slow, so it was "Get a fucking move
on" all round. We'd already decided to ditch the surplus kit we
couldn't carry, but we pulled our Bergens on and were ready
for the off. As we were about to leave, I called, "Get your
shamags round your heads." So we all wrapped our heads in
shawls, in case we could bluff our way and pass as Arab soldiers,
even for a few minutes. As soon as Legs was ready, we started
walking southwards, down the wadi, towards our emergency
rendezvous point. Finding myself at the front, I led the patrol
out. Call it arrogance, if you like, but I didn't trust anyone else
to go first. Dusk was already coming on, and I was hoping we
could reach the drop-off point, less than two kilometres to the
south, and put down enough fire to defend ourselves until dark
fell – and then we'd have to wait until the chopper came in.

Moving out, I kept close in to the left-hand wall of the
wadi, because that was the steepest, and in the lee of it we
were out of sight of the AA guns. When I turned round, I
found that the guys had opened up to a tactical spacing of
maybe twenty metres between each; but I was thinking, "If
we have a nonsense here, we want to be tight together." So I
yelled back, "Close up!"

The bulldozer had gone out of sight, but we were moving
towards where we'd last seen it. All too soon the wadi began
to flatten out, and on our left a long slope ran up to the plain
above. As we came clear of the steep part of the wadi wall, I
suddenly saw two Arabs on the high ground above us, guns
down by their sides. They were barely 200 metres away, and
were standing motionless. There was something oddly inert
about their appearance; they showed no surprise and did not
move as we walked into their view. Both were wearing dark
overcoats on top of their dishdashes (native cotton robes),
which reached down to their ankles. Also they had red-and-
white shamags done up on top of their heads like turbans. I
reckoned they were civilians or possibly militia.

"It's that sodding boy," I said to myself. "He's run like hell
and tipped them off."

"Close up!" I yelled again, because it was obvious the shit was going to go down. Next behind me was Bob Consiglio, and I shouted back to him, "Fucking hurry! Catch up!"

We kept going. But the two Iraqis began to parallel us, moving forward. In case anybody hadn't seen them, I called back, "We've got two on the high ground to the left, and they're walking down. Keep going."

Behind me everyone started cursing. The tension in the patrol was electric. I felt fear rising in my chest. Afterwards, I realized that the two Iraqis were waiting for reinforcements to come up; also, they were probably a bit confused, not knowing who the hell we were. But at the time I was wondering if we could outrun them, or lose them somehow, without starting a firefight.

Then I blew it in a big way. I thought, "I'm going to try the double bluff here," and I waved at them. Unfortunately I did it with my left hand, which to an Arab is the ultimate insult – your left hand being the one you wipe your arse with. The reaction was instantaneous: one of them brought up his weapon and opened fire. Suddenly he was putting rounds down on us. We swung round and put a couple of short bursts back at them. Both dropped on to one knee to continue firing. As I stood there, I saw Vince take off down the wadi. In spite of the danger, there was something ridiculous about his gait: a pair of legs, going like the clappers under a Bergen, and not making much progress either.

"Stay together!" I yelled. "Slow down!" We began to run, turning to fire aimed bursts. The secret is to keep them short – no more than two or three rounds at a time. Otherwise the recoil makes the weapon drift up, and the rounds go high. We ran and fired, ran and fired.

Within seconds a tipper truck with metal sides screeched to a halt beside the two Arabs, and eight or ten guys spilled out of it. Stan also saw an armoured car carrying a .50 machine gun pull up. Somehow I never saw that; it may have been behind a mound from where I was standing. Some of the Iraqis began firing from the back of the truck, others from positions behind it.

Running and shooting, the SAS team found their Bergens too heavy and cumbersome and began ditching them. Eventually, Bravo Two Zero lost the pursuing Iraqis in the gloom of the early winter afternoon. Stopping to get their breath, the patrol decided to make for the Syrian border, 75 miles away, via the Euphrates. The Iraqis, they calculated, would expect them to head south for Saudi. Bravo Two's decision to go for Syria may well have put the Iraqis off the scent; it certainly deceived SAS commanders at al-Jouf, because the emergency route the team had filed was different. Consequently, any search and rescue mission would look in the wrong place.

Bravo Two Zero walked 50 miles that night through sleet, pausing to rest only four times. Two of the team were in a bad way; Vince Phillips had injured his leg in the contact with the enemy, while Trooper "Stan" was dehydrated because of sweat loss from his thermal clothing. Everybody else, meanwhile, was freezing to death.

Setting off again, the patrol staggered single file into the night. At the back of the patrol, McNab stopped to use his TACBE personal rescue beacon, and got a confused response from an American pilot. By the time McNab put the TACBE back in its pouch, Ryan, Phillips and Trooper Mal had disappeared into the night; McNab and the remainder of the patrol had no option but to carry on without them, hoping they would meet later. The sleet turned to snow. The wind-chill was starting to kill them; lying up in a hollow the next day McNab likened to "lying in a freezer cabinet, feeling your body heat slowly slip away". By dawn on 26 January McNab reckoned they might not survive another twenty-four hours in the open. They were next to the al-Haqlaniyya–Krabilah highway, so they decided to hijack a vehicle.

With shamags wrapped around their swarthy faces, Trooper Bob Consiglio and McNab could pass for Arab. The plan then was for Consiglio to be an injured Iraqi soldier and McNab his Samaritan helper, who would stumble into the road and flag down a suitable car. McNab recalled:

After about twenty minutes, vehicle lights came over the small crest and drove towards us. Satisfied that it was not a troop truck, we stood up. The vehicle caught us in its head-lights and slowed down to a half a few metres down the road. I kept my head down to protect my eyes and to hide my face from the driver. Bob and I hobbled towards it.

"Oh shit," I muttered into Bob's ear. Of all the vehicles in Iraq that could have come our way that night, the one we had chosen to hijack and speed us to our freedom was a 1950s New York yellow cab. I couldn't believe it. Chrome bumpers, whitewall tires, the lot. We were committed. Bob was in my arms giving it the wounded soldier. The blokes were straight up from the ditch.

"What the fuck have we got here?" Mark shouted in disbelief. "This is the story of our lives, this is! Why can't it be a fucking Land Cruiser?"

The driver panicked and stalled the engine. He and the two passengers in the back sat staring open-mouthed at the muzzles of Minimis and 203s. The cab was an old rust bucket with typical Arab decoration – tassels and gaudy religious emblems dangling from every available point. A couple of old blankets were thrown over as seat covers. The driver was beside himself with hysteria. The two men on the back seat were a picture, both dressed in neatly pressed green militia fatigues and berets, with little weekend bags on their laps. As the younger of the two explained that they were father and son, we had a quick rummage through their effects to see if there was anything worth having. We had to move quickly because we couldn't guarantee that there wouldn't be other vehicles coming over. We tried to shepherd them to the side of the road, but the father was on his knees. He thought he was going to get slotted.

"Christian! Christian!" he screamed as he scrabbled in his pocket and pulled out a keyring with the Madonna dangling from it. "Muslim!" he said, pointing at the taxi driver and trying to drop him in it. Now the driver sank to his knees, bowing and praying. We had to prod him with rifle barrels to get him to move.

"Cigarettes?" Dinger enquired.

The son obliged with a couple of packs. The father got up and started kissing Mark, apparently thanking him for not killing him. The driver kept praying and hollering. It was a farce.

Driving towards Krabilah, McNab at the wheel, the SAS men in the taxi made good progress for nearly an hour. In the warmth and comfort of the car some of them began sleeping. They then hit a vehicle checkpoint, which they decided to bypass on foot. By now the dumped occupants of the taxi had raised the alarm. The Iraqis were hunting for McNab and his patrol.

On the other side of the checkpoint, McNab and Consiglio tried their old flag-down-a-car trick. They were spotted by an Iraqi police patrol, who opened fire. After a quick return salvo, the SAS men legged it into the night, heading towards the Euphrates and the border. An air raid proved a useful diversion, as the patrol cautiously edged along the alleyways of a town down to the Euphrates' bank. The river was in full spate, and McNab rated their chances of swimming across as slim. They were just 6 miles from the border, so they decided to push along the bank looking for a crossing place. At around 4 miles from the border, an Iraqi patrol started blasting at the SAS men from the side of a wadi running into the Euphrates. A running firefight broke out. Bob Consiglio, a Swiss-born former Royal Marine, held off the Iraqis with his Minimi until he ran out of ammunition; separated from the remainder of the patrol, he ran down a track towards the Euphrates.

A group of militiamen hidden in a clump of trees opened fire; one of their bullets felled Consiglio. Another round ignited a phosphorus grenade Consiglio was carrying. Awarded a posthumous Military Medal, Consiglio was the first SAS soldier of the campaign to die from enemy fire. Troopers Lane and Lance Corporal "Dinger", at the back of the patrol, edged down to the black Euphrates, where Lane urged Dinger to join him and swim across, with pieces of thrown-away polystyrene stuffed in their smocks for buoyancy. Lane emerged on the far bank in a state of collapse; Dinger hid him in a bankside hut and tried to warm him up. They were spotted and locked inside. Dinger broke through the roof, but was soon surrounded and captured. As he was taken away on a tractor-drawn cart, he saw Lane's body being brought out of the hut on a stretcher. Lane was dead.

While Lane and Dinger were swimming the Euphrates, McNab and Trooper Mike Coburn crawled across the bed of a wadi. As they emerged, a group of Iraqi police opened up. Coburn, by now left only with a bayonet in his armoury, was hit by rounds in the arm and leg. Captured, he was dragged through the mud to a Land Cruiser, to be taken away for interrogation. McNab, meanwhile, wormed along the ground, until he found an irrigation pipe and holed up. The next morning he was spotted by a labourer, who reported to the police. Screeching up in a Land Cruiser, the police pulled McNab out and bundled him into the back of a Land Cruiser. He was taken to the same barracks as Dinger. Like other captured Coalition personnel, they were subjected to days of torture.

On 26 January, the same day that McNab was dragged out of the water pipe, Chris Ryan and Mal split up when the latter decided to approach a shepherd's cottage and find some transport. A man in the cottage alerted the police. Mal was surrounded and captured.

Now alone, Ryan struck out for the border, with only two packets of biscuits for food. Five days later, desperately short of water, he filled his bottles from a stream. Hiding away in a culvert, he sat down to slake his thirst:

I was desperate for a drink, and looking forward to one with incredible anticipation. But when I went to compress the plastic clip that held the buckle on my webbing pouch, I found that my fingers were so sore and clumsy that I could scarcely manage the simple task. Gasping with pain, I used all my strength to force the clips together. Then came a horrendous disappointment. Bringing out one bottle at last, I opened it and raised it to my lips – but the first mouthful made me gasp and choke. Poison! The water tasted vicious and metallic, as if it was full of acid. I spat it straight out, but the inside of my mouth had gone dry, and I was left with a burning sensation all over my tongue and gums. I whipped out my compass-mirror, pointed the torchbeam into my mouth and looked round it. Everything seemed all right, so I took another sip, but it was just the same. I remembered that when Stan had collapsed during the first night on the run I'd put rehydrate into my bottles, to bring him round, and I wondered if the remains of it had somehow gone off. Then I tried the second bottle, and found it exactly the same. I couldn't make out what the hell had gone wrong. Whatever the problem, the water was undrinkable, and I emptied the bottles out.

"Now I *am* fucked," I thought. I was in a really bad state. It was eight days since I'd had a hot meal, two days and a night since I'd had a drink. My tongue was completely dry; it felt like a piece of old leather stuck in the back of my throat.

My teeth had all come loose; if I closed my mouth and sucked hard, I could taste blood coming from my shrunken gums. I knew my feet were in bits, but I didn't dare take my boots off, because I feared I'd never get them on again. As for my hands – I could see and smell them all too well. The thin leather of my gloves had cracked and split, from being repeatedly soaked and dried out again, so that my fingers hadn't had much protection. I'd lost most of the feeling in the tips, and I seemed to have got dirt pushed deep under my nails, so that infection had set in. Whenever I squeezed a nail, pus came out, and this stench was repulsive. With my extremities suppurating like that, I wondered what internal damage I might be suffering, and could only hope that no permanent harm would be done. With the complete lack of food, I'd had no bowel movement since going on the run, and I couldn't remember when I'd last wanted to pee. I yearned for food, of course, but more for drink – and when I did think about food, it was sweet, slushy things that I craved. If ever I found myself back among rations packs, I would rip into the pears in syrup, ice cream and chocolate sauce.

I felt very frightened. First and most obvious was the danger of being captured – the fear of torture, and of giving away secrets that might betray other guys from the Regiment. Almost worse, though, was the fact that I could see and feel my body going down so fast. If I didn't reach the border soon, I would be too weak to carry on.

Setting off again, he stumbled towards the border, which he reached on the night of 30 January. Only he wasn't sure he was at the border:

I reached a refuse heap, where loads of burnt-out old cans had been dumped in the desert, and sat down among them to do yet another map-study. I couldn't work things out. Where was the town, and where was the communications tower which the map marked? Where, above all, was the bloody border?

I started walking again, on the bearing, and as I came over a rise I saw three small buildings to my front. With the naked eye I could just make them out: three square bulks, blacked out. But when I looked through the kite-sight, I saw chinks of light escaping between the tops of the walls and the roofs. As I sat watching, one person came out, walked round behind, reappeared and went back indoors. I was so desperate for water that I went straight towards the houses. Again, I was prepared to take out one of the inhabitants if need be. I was only fifty metres away when I checked through the kite-sight again and realized that the buildings were not houses at all, but sandbagged sangars with wriggly tin roofs. They formed some sort of command post, and were undoubtedly full of squaddies. Pulling slowly back, I went round the side and, sure enough, came on a battery of four anti-aircraft positions. If I'd walked up and opened one of the doors, I'd almost certainly have been captured. Once more the fright got my adrenalin going and revived me.

On I stumbled for another hour. My dehydration was making me choke and gag. My throat seemed to have gone solid, and when I scraped my tongue, white fur came off it. I felt myself growing weaker by the minute. My 203 might have been made of lead, such a burden had it become, so much of the strength had ebbed from my arms. My legs had lost their spring and grown stiff and clumsy. My ability to think clearly had dwindled away.

At last I came to a point from which I could see the lights of a town, far out on the horizon. Something seemed to be wrong. Surely that couldn't be Krabilah, still such a distance off? My heart sank: surely the border couldn't still be that far? Or was the glow I could see that of Abu Kamal, the first town inside Syria, some twenty kilometres to the west? If so, where the hell was Krabilah? According to the map, Krabilah had a communications tower, but Abu Kamal didn't. The far-off town *did* have a bright red light flashing, as if from a tower – and that made me all the more certain that the place in the distance was Krabilah.

Morale plummeted once more. Like my body, my mind was losing its grip. What I *could* make out was some kind of straight black line, running all the way across my front. Off to my left I could see a mound with a big command post on it, sprouting masts. Closer to me were a few buildings, blacked out, but not looking like a town.

I sat down some 500 metres short of the black line and studied the set-up through the kite-sight. Things didn't add up. With Krabilah so far ahead, this could hardly be the border. Yet it looked like one. I wondered whether it was some inner frontier-line which the Iraqis had built because of the war, to keep people back from the border itself. Suddenly I thought of the Int guy back at Al Jouf, unable to tell what the border looked like. "What an arsehole!" I thought. "He should have known. That's his fucking job."

Whatever this line ahead of me might be, all I wanted to do was get across it. I was gripped by a terrific sense of urgency, but I forced myself to hold back, sit down and observe it. "This is where you're going to stumble if you don't watch out," I told myself. "This is where you'll fall down. Take time over it."

There I sat, shivering, watching, waiting. A vehicle came out of the command post and drove down along the line – an open-backed land-cruiser. Directly opposite my vantage-point two men emerged from an observation post, walked up to the car, spoke to the driver, jumped in, and drove off to the right. It looked as if the Iraqis were putting out roving observers to keep an eye on the border. I couldn't tell whether this was routine, or whether they suspected that enemy soldiers were in the area; but after a few minutes I decided that the coast was clear, and I had to move.

At long last I came down to the black line. Creeping cautiously towards it, I found it was a barrier of barbed wire: three coils in the bottom row, two on top of them, and one on top of that. Having no pliers to cut with, I tried to squeeze my way through the coils, but that proved impossible: barbs hooked into my clothes and skin and held me fast. I unhooked myself with difficulty, and decided that the only way to go was over the top. Luckily the builders had made the elementary mistake, every twenty-five metres, of putting in three posts close to each other and linking them together with barbed wire.

Obviously the idea was to brace the barrier, but the posts created a kind of bridge across the middle of the coils. I took off my webbing and threw it over, then went up and over myself, sustaining a few lacerations but nothing serious. Still I could not believe I was clear of Iraq. The barrier seemed so insignificant that I thought it must only be marking some false or inner border, and that I would come to the true frontier some distance further on. The real thing, I thought, would be a big anti-tank berm, constructed so that vehicles could not drive across. Maybe this was why I had no feeling of elation; for days I had been thinking that, if I did manage to cross the frontier, it would be the climax of my journey, but now I felt nothing except utter exhaustion.

Ryan was in Syria. His marathon walk of 186 miles almost equals that of Jack Sillito in 1942.

While Bravo Two Zero were struggling their way to the frontier, the mobile fighting columns were having their own dramas. Three of the columns, which comprised a half-squadron each, were operating efficiently inside Iraq; however, Alpha One Zero, under an SBS major, seemed lacking in purpose. To the steaming ire of the regiment's commanding officer, the column couldn't actually find a way across the berm dividing Iraq from Saudi. At length, Alpha One Zero crossed into Iraq via a dash through a checkpoint. Almost immediately the column had a contact with the enemy. Its vehicles under cam-nets, the patrol had laagered up and Sergeant Cameron "Serious" Spence was among those with drooping eyelids:

I sat there, taking my time over the smoke and the brew, until I felt my eyelids dropping. After three days and nights with scarcely a moment's shut-eye, I staked out my own patch around the forward wheel that Tom had vacated, ticking off those last few things I needed to know before I could sleep. Jeff was getting some kip at the next wheel. The visibility was good – out to ten kilometres, a mixed blessing. We were just about set for the rest of the day. All Tom had to do was clean his M16 and he was done, too. Buzz had taken the forward sentry position. Everything was as it should be. I adjusted my webbing under my head, got comfortable, and within seconds had lapsed into sleep.

After what passed for five minutes – I later found out it was an hour – I heard Buzz's voice go off in my head. He could only have whispered the warning, but it sounded like a fucking siren going off in some deep recess of my brain. The words tumbled over and over. There was something faintly hypnotic about them. For a moment, they held me in the grip of a dreamy kind of paralysis. Then, Tom was shaking me. The words came back to me and I knew it was no dream.

Stand-to, stand-to. Enemy.

Fuck. A pang of fear hit me in the gullet, followed by a weird moment of doubt. Could this be some kind of wind-up? The fear redoubled and hit me again. Nobody, not even Tom or Buzz, would pull a stunt like this on our third day. This was for fucking real. I was up and out of the sleeping bag in a second, fumbling for my Bergen and my M16. For a few seconds more, chaos reigned, then we were taking up position. Suddenly, a vehicle appeared. It slowed, then stopped, sitting there 700 metres out; watching us, watching them. And then, it came towards us, and kept coming, until it drew up right outside our cluster of cam-nets. Two Iraqis got out. They paused to pick up their helmets, then divided. The driver moved for Tony's vehicle, the commander headed straight for the front of our Land Rover, where Tom and I had taken up station. The officer bent down and picked up the cam-net. That was when he saw me.

The last thing I remember thinking was that it shouldn't be like the fucking movies, but that's how it was – the whole thing moved in excruciating slow-time like a Sam Peckinpah Western.

I had a moment to register the look of blank surprise on the Iraqi's face as he came up under the cam-net and twigged me. He started to raise his weapon, but I fired, quick double-tap – *ba-bam* – and he went down. As he fell, his body was hit by at least six more rounds – bullets from other weapons that had been trained on him from the moment he'd got out of the vehicle – and he pirouetted in a macabre death-dance before hitting the dirt, face-down.

I heard more firing and saw bullets striking the second man. Several punched into his chest. One all but removed the side of his head. A voice in the back of my head started telling me over and over that I'd killed a man – *bam*, just like that.

But it was a small voice. And it was rapidly drowned by a chorus of other thoughts. What about the GAZ? Who else was in there? Had Jeff made it with the phosphorus grenade? Training, thank God, takes over. You're not left long with the moral consequences of your actions.

I was out from under the cam-net before I even knew it. As I moved towards the still-twitching body of the man I'd shot, I could see a flurry out of the corner of my eye as Buzz and Jeff tore into the back of the GAZ. Your training doesn't allow you to look, even though your instincts want to. I was on the body in a second, pulling it over, one hand tugging at his arms in the search for firearms, grenades, knives; you never know what the fucker might still have up a sleeve, even in his death-throes.

I looked up and saw a similar scene being played out around the other body.

No doubt about it, they were both dead. And then there's a blood-curdling cry from the GAZ. I spun around to see Buzz and Jeff dragging something – someone – out of the

Iraqi vehicle. Another man had been in the back, but they'd got the drop on him. As far as I could tell, the guy was uninjured, but he was squealing like a stuck pig all the same.

Jostling, blurred action as Buzz and Jeff threw their captive to the ground, both of them yelling at the top of their voices: "Shut the fuck up."

The Iraqi doesn't get it and starts jabbering and wailing louder than ever. And then he opens his eyes and sees the muzzle of Buzz's Commando a moment before it grinds into the thin skin between his eyebrows. At the same time, Buzz is shouting again, only now the tone is different. The shrillness that had been there in the initial adrenalin rush is gone. There's depth and authority in his words. Be quiet, he's telling him, or he'll blow his fucking brains to Babylon.

This time the Iraqi makes the connection and zips it. Silence. In the stillness that followed, there was a fraction of a moment in which my heightened senses registered the blueness of the sky and the sound of the cam-net flapping in the wind behind me. And then it started all over again. Shouts, movements, oaths, orders, as blokes from the other vehicles pounded over to our two 110s to join the fray. I left a group of the boys to go through the uniform of the body at my feet as I searched the scene for Alec, Tony and Graham. It was time for a fucking "head shed" meeting, the fastest we'd ever had. Two, maybe three minutes had elapsed since the first shots had been fired. Everybody recognized the situation for what it was. True, we had things under control, but you could hear traces of panic in the shouts and rasped commands around you.

The situation had turned to rat-shit and no mistake.

Back in al-Jouf the commanding officer was cock-a-hoop that Alpha One Zero had negotiated its first contact. The commanding officer's delight died when he realized that the major commanding the column was now heading south, taking it away from its designated area of action. Turning to Regimental Sergeant Major Ratcliffe, the commanding officer informed him that he, Ratcliffe, would be relieving the major of his command.

Never in the history of the Regiment has a squadron commander been relieved in the field and replaced by a non-commissioned officer.

The next day Ratcliffe flew into Iraq on the Chinook resupplying Alpha One Zero. He wrote later:

As I walked down the tail ramp I found myself buffeted by a strong wind that had sprung up from the north and which, because of the wind-chill factor, had sent the temperature plummeting well below zero. I could see at once why the men running down the nearby slope towards the Chinook didn't look much like the crack desert patrol I had last seen in Victor. They were mostly wrapped in their chemical-warfare suits with extra jackets on top, and had shamags, Arab headdress of the kind favoured by Yasser Arafat, wound around their heads and the lower parts of their faces. The noise from the two rotors, which continued to turn and had formed twin dust halos from the sand being sucked up from the desert floor, was almost deafening. RAF aircrew never switch off their engines during a supply run or insertion into hostile territory, in case they come under attack and have to make a quick getaway.

I grabbed one of the men as he trotted past, put my mouth close to where I thought his ear should be beneath the shamag, and yelled, "Where's the OC?" He pointed up the slight incline down which they had come and shouted something I couldn't make out. I set off in the direction he had indicated, and on the way passed a strange-looking vehicle that had been parked with a couple of its wheels in a kind of natural ditch. It was giving off an awful stench which I vaguely recognized, but which I didn't have the time to investigate right then.

At the crest of the slope I came across another small gang of troopers gathered around two Land Rovers. They looked amazed suddenly to see the RSM, but I didn't give them time to ask me what I was doing there. Without preamble, I said, "One of you go and find the OC and bring him here to me."

A few minutes later the commander appeared. He looked at me quizzically, but before he could say anything I said, "I'm sorry," and handed him the CO's letter. There was enough moonlight for him to read it without a torch. When he'd finished he looked up, his face working with some powerful emotion which he somehow managed to keep bottled up. Then he walked away. I set off back for the chopper, wondering what he would do. I needn't have worried. He fetched his Bergen and rifle and joined me at the tail ramp of the helicopter. The unloading had been completed. The Iraqi officer the patrol had captured the previous day was brought down and I went across and walked with him over to the helicopter. I could guess what he must be feeling, especially after seeing three of his fellow officers killed, and even felt a pang of sympathy for him.

While this was happening the outgoing OC had located his number two, Pat, and was explaining to him that he had been relieved of his command. Then the two men hugged each other as though they were brothers.

The worst part of my job was over. The pilots needed to get on their way as soon as possible, and I wanted to get started. Recognizing that there was no point in wasting more time, I hustled the patrol's former OC aboard the helicopter and gave Jim the thumbs-up signal. Now the handover was complete I couldn't help feeling sorry for the departing major. He had accepted the order without argument, and his behaviour had been impeccable. Moments later the tail ramp winched shut, and with enough racket to wake every Arab – not to mention his goats, dogs and camels – within three miles, the engines wound up to full power and the Chinook was away into the star-studded sky.

After arranging the burning of the GAZ and the Iraqi bodies, Ratcliffe ordered the patrol 30 miles back towards the action. At the lying-up position, Ratcliffe told the half-squadron they were "about to find out what it's really like to be involved in a war".

Regimental Sergeant Major Peter Ratcliffe did not disappoint. On 8 February Alpha One Zero carried out a raid on a microwave Scud-control station, codenamed Victor Two, alongside the Baghdad–Amman highway:

I led my demolition team and six other men off to the left, to make use of whatever shadow cover was available close to the berm, and then headed north towards the road junction and the final jumping-off point for the target. Pat and his three Land Rovers drove along the same route after us. The crew of the wagon carrying the Milan, which only had thirty metres to travel, had been told to move into position ten minutes after the rest of us had left. The demolitionists were Mugger and Ken and a quiet Yorkshire corporal named Tom. A tall guy, very fit and strong, it was he who had driven the GAZ containing the bodies of the three dead Iraqis back to where I was flown in, apparently prepared to put up with the corpses in exchange for having a closed vehicle with a heater. As backup there was myself, Des and Captain Timothy, the young officer who had joined us from the infantry. Each of us carried one of the explosive charges that had been made up back in the LUP. I had the shaped charge for the fence and Des the charge for the wall, while Timothy had the charges we would use to blow the doors in the bunker. In addition, each of us was carrying a powerful high-explosive charge with which we would take out the switching gear. When we reached our jumping-off point we were just 200 metres from the relay station. From there all we could see of the building was the wall around it and, behind it, the steel antenna soaring into the night sky. The wall seemed to be of concrete, grey in color apart from one section, a few metres wide, which appeared to be a different shade. From that distance, however, even with the moonlight, we couldn't make it out properly.

The six men who had moved forward with us – one of them with a LAW80 – had already broken away and crossed the road to come up on the two trucks. To the right and less than fifty metres beyond them was the large bunker, where I could easily make out the enemy coming and going. Even though it was late there seemed to be quite a lot of activity.

About 150 metres to our left the other bunker was now clearly visible. It too was brightly lit inside and had enemy personnel moving about. There were other, smaller buildings behind the left-hand bunker, and about 100 metres beyond the target was the large military encampment that we had spotted during the recce.

"A few more than the thirty guys we expected," breathed Des.

"Yeah, but by the time they realize what's going on we'll be back at our LUP," I answered softly. "So let's just brass it out and get it over with." I looked at the other five, then nodded. Time to go.

As we stepped out in single file, slightly crouched but moving fairly quickly, I could see to our left, where the low growl of the Land Rovers had died away, that Pat had the wagons parked a few metres apart and facing the different directions from where trouble might be expected to come.

We pressed on, slinking over the MSR and past the right-hand bunker.

Whether the Iraqis in the right-hand bunker actually saw us or not I don't know. But no one shouted or challenged us and in less than a minute we had reached the wall. Ken, whose job it was to blow this first obstacle, led the way, followed by Des, who was carrying the charges. Mugger, who would bring down the fence, was next, and then me with his charges. Behind me was Tom, who would blow the bunker's main door, and Captain Timothy carrying his charges. Close to, we could see straight away what made one section a different shade from the rest of the wall. It was plastic sheeting. An already dodgy mission was growing stranger by the minute.

"Pull the stuff back and let's see what's behind it," I hissed.

At once Ken and Des peeled back one edge, then Des turned and said, "The wall's already been blown. There's a bloody great hole here."

"Well, let's get through it," I said. We were crouched down by the wall, but with the moonlight we would be immediately visible to anyone who looked hard enough from the trucks, the bunkers, or even the smaller buildings to our left. It felt as though we were standing in the spotlights on stage in a packed theatre.

Within thirty seconds all six of us were through the gap and had pushed the plastic sheeting back in place. Inside, there was total chaos. The place had obviously suffered a direct hit from an Allied bomb or missile. In places the fence was twisted and flattened, and in others completely torn from its cement base. Of the main bunker there was almost nothing left. There were buckled steel girders and shattered concrete everywhere. Some of the wreckage was so precariously balanced that it looked likely to crash down at any moment. I took a look around for an entrance to the three underground rooms, but the stairway and the rooms had been completely buried beneath the rubble. The whole site was extremely hazardous, and I realized that one or more of us could get badly injured simply walking in the ruins, especially since the moonlight on the wreckage left large areas in deep shadow. It was perfectly certain, too, that there wasn't any switching gear left for us to destroy. Curiously, I felt a sense of anti-climax. Still, there was one thing we could do.

"Des, you and Timothy dump all your explosives here and get back to the gap in the wall and wait for us there. Now we're here we'd better bring down the mast, if nothing else."

Since the mast was still up, it could still receive and transmit signals via the antennae and dishes on it – which meant the site could still get Scuds off towards Israel. Thinking quickly, I offloaded my own explosives and told Mugger, "Let's blow the mast and get out of here."

"These charges are not really suitable," he replied mournfully. "They're no good for cutting steel."

This was too much. First we had intelligence that told us the place was defended, if at all, by about thirty Iraqis. Then Intel had failed to tell us that there were a military camp and fortified defensive positions around the relay station. Meanwhile, somebody had neglected to tell us, or RHQ, that the site had already received an extremely accurate air or missile raid. Finally, having successfully reached our target unseen with more than 100 pounds of explosive charges, we found that those charges probably would not do the one job that still needed doing. Well, we were bloody well going to do something, I thought.

"Surely you can do something?" I asked Mugger. He considered for a while, and finally nodded. "If we pack a charge and a third of the other explosives around each of three of the mast's four legs, then it will give us about thirty-five pounds per leg. With luck that will do the job."

"Okay. Let's do it," I said. "It sounds much too damned quiet out there for it to last." By now we had been almost in the centre of an enemy installation for ten or fifteen minutes. It seemed incredible that nobody had noticed us, but how much longer could we trust our luck to last? I had a strong suspicion that the answer was "not much", but the demolitionists were already on the case. Mugger, Ken and Tom quickly divided the explosives into three piles, then each of them grabbed one pile and headed in a crouch for one of the steel legs of the mast. I waited between two of the legs, aware that these three guys were playing with high explosives that could blow us all to atoms in a millisecond if anything went wrong. So while I hoped that they wouldn't take too long, I also didn't want them to be foolishly hasty. Ken was the first to finish, then, thirty seconds later, Tom came over to join us.

"What's keeping Mugger?" I asked.

"He's going to pull the three switches," Ken answered. By now we were scarcely bothering to lower our voices.

"Right," I told them. "You two go and join Des and Timothy and all of you get through the wall and wait there. We'll be right with you."

A minute later Mugger appeared out of the darkness and gave me a big grin. "Okay, Billy," he said. "They're each on a two-minute delay, so let's head for the great outdoors." He was, as usual, as cool as a cucumber and, like any artist, supremely happy in his work. I didn't need any extra prompting, and we lit out for the wall like greyhounds. At which point our good fortune took a nosedive. We were through the tangled fence and close to the gap in the wall when all hell broke loose. There were several single shots followed by a burst of automatic fire, then the enormous *whoosh* of a Milan going in and, seconds later, a huge explosion as the missile struck home. Then everyone seemed to let rip together. Rounds were zipping overhead and we could hear them smacking into the other side of the wall.

There were bullets flying everywhere, riddling the sheeting covering the gap while, above, tracers created amazing patterned arches. We were safe enough on our side of the wall, but not for long. Behind us, no more than ten metres away, was over 100 pounds of high-explosive getting ready to blow in less than ninety seconds.

"What do you reckon, Mugger?" I asked.

"We haven't got much fucking choice, have we?" he replied.

I grinned at him. "No. I suppose not. So let's go." And with that I ducked round the plastic sheet and into the other area on the other side. The other four were all lying by the wall outside.

"Line abreast and back to the jumping-off point," I yelled.

"And let's move it. It's all going to blow in a few seconds."

Surging forward, we spread out like the three-quarter line in a rugby game and belted towards the dark, looming mass of the north end of the berm. Though I swear that not even the finest line-up ever made it from one end of a rugby pitch to the other at the speed we travelled that night. Of course, we were all as fit as professional athletes, and given the amount of adrenalin fizzing around in our muscles we'd have been good for a few world records – if anyone could have spared the time to clock us.

As Ratcliffe and his team reached the Land Rovers, Iraqis on top of a nearby berm started popping them. The drivers started up, the gunners on the back loosing off Gimpies, Brownings and Mk19 grenade-launchers. A swerving Land Rover knocked Ratcliffe down, his rifle went flying into the dark. He was about to search for it – and the twenty gold "escape" sovereigns hidden in the butt – when a voice yelled "Jump on or we're fucking going without you." He jumped on. Bullets snipped the bodywork as they roared away.

A motorcycle recce next day confirmed that the tower had fallen. Every SAS man had got out alive.

Regimental Sergeant Major Ratcliffe was later awarded the DCM for his bravery and leadership at Victor Two.

With the columns running short of supplies, the commanding officer of the Regiment organized a convoy of three-tonners to take in the goods. Escorted by spare B Squadron troopers in Pink Panthers, the resupply convoy arrived at the Wadi Tubal deep in Iraq. Assembled in the wadi were three full SAS sabre-squadrons, together with R Squadron reserves and headquarters' personnel. With the biggest gathering of the SAS in the field since 1942 around him, Peter Ratcliffe decided to mark the occasion by holding a meeting. Cameron Spence recalled:

Soon after I got back to our vehicle, word came down that Roger (Peter "Billy" Ratcliffe) wanted all senior ranks to gather for a talk later in the afternoon in an area away from the resupply wagons.

"It can't be haircuts," Nick said, preening himself in the reflection of his goggles.

"Or our beards," Tom added, scratching the growth on his chin. "We're at fucking war."

"Maybe you're not allowed into theme parks with stubble," Nick said. "They think you're a bender or something."

"Who knows?" I chipped in. A talk with the RSM was serious. Something was in the wind.

"Do you think this could be it?" Tom said, later. "The big one."

"Maybe," I nodded. "Let's just hope it's a worthwhile target."

Later that afternoon, I grouped with the senior NCOs from A and D Squadron. While we waited for Roger to open the meeting, you could taste the excitement in the narrow gully where we'd all gathered. No question about it, this had to be the regimental work-out half of us had anticipated. It was then that I glanced over my shoulder and saw Phil. I was still trying to work out why the Regimental Quarter Master Sergeant – our food-king – was at a planning conference that had all the makings of a war-party pow-wow when Roger stood on a boulder and the meeting kicked off. It took a few minutes before we got the gist of what was happening here. It was a case of our ears working fine, but our sodding brains not believing the inbound message.

"Fuck," I heard Tony say behind me. "It can't be."

I turned around. "It is."

One hundred kilometres inside Iraq, Britain's biggest war since Korea going on around us, and the warrant officers and sergeants of the Special Air Service had been called to a mess meeting.

It was serious business. Definitely no laughing matter. Top of the agenda was the forthcoming summer ball, followed by an outstanding mess account and the weighty matter of whether or not the sergeant's mess could afford a new suite and some nice blue curtains.

The motions were discussed, passed and the minutes recorded in a notebook so they could be transferred back to Hereford. On my return to the vehicle, I stopped cursing and burst out laughing.

"What is it?" Nick asked.

I tried to get the words out, but the tears kept rolling down my face.

Nick, Tom and Jeff stared at me like I'd flipped. They must have been thinking: poor old sod. A month behind the lines and he's gone, a headcase.

Eventually, I managed to tell them about the meeting in the gully.

Their reaction was pretty much the same as mine. Disbelief. Anger. Laughter. Hysteria. It took us most of the rest of the afternoon to stop crapping ourselves.

Later, I managed to see this side-show in its true light. Who cared if it was British bureaucracy at its worst? It showed that even in the enemy's backyard, we were in control. Totally relaxed. Life went on and nothing was going to interfere with it.

The SAS had some new curtains to choose. Saddam could go swivel.

On 23 February the SAS columns were ordered to return to Saudi Arabia. The Coalition's ground offensive had started, and there was no longer a role for the SAS behind the lines. Crossing the border back into Saudi Arabia, some of the drivers looked at their mileage clocks; the pinkies, Unimogs and motorcycles had done more than 1,500 miles. Some of the men had been behind Iraqi lines for forty-two days. Even the cynical General Schwarzkopf was impressed by the achievements of 22 SAS, to the extent of writing them a personal letter of commendation. Alpha One Zero's destruction of the mast at Victor Two was only one hit in a list that included the same unit's wrecking of a military fibre-optics network, Delta Two Zero's laser-painting of two Scuds for an F-15 airstrike, Delta Two Zero's demolition of a Scud-control tower, a D Squadron patrol's "painting" of a Scud convoy for another US airstrike, plus its own Milan guided-missile attack on the convoy. (Troopers from the same half-squadron also made a bug-out to rival Bravo Two Zero's, going five days across the desert, despite Lance Corporal Taff Powell having a bullet in the guts.) After the SAS entered the Iraqi desert, Scud launches fell by 50 per cent.

DOCUMENT: General H. Norman Schwarzkopf: "Letter of Commendation for the 22 Special Air Service (SAS) Regiment"

SUBJECT

Letter of Commendation for the 22 Special Air Service (SAS) Regiment.

1. I wish to officially commend the 22 Special Air Service (SAS) Regiment for their totally outstanding performance of military operations during Operation Desert Storm.

2. Shortly after the initiation of the strategic air campaign, it became apparent that the Coalition forces would be unable to eliminate Iraq's firing of Scud missiles from western Iraq into Israel. The continued firing of Scuds on Israel carried with it enormous unfavorable political ramifications and

could, in fact, have resulted in the dismantling of the carefully crafted Coalition. Such a dismantling would have adversely affected in ways difficult to measure the ultimate outcome of the military campaign. It became apparent the only way that the Coalition could succeed in reducing these Scud launches was by physically placing military forces on the ground in the vicinity of the western launch sites. At that time, the majority of available Coalition forces were committed to the forthcoming military campaign in the eastern portion of the theater of operations.

Further, none of these forces possessed the requisite skills and abilities required to conduct such a dangerous operation. The only force deemed qualified for this critical mission was the 22 Special Air Service (SAS) Regiment.

3. From the first day they were assigned their mission until the last day of the conflict, the performance of the 22 Special Air Service (SAS) Regiment was courageous and highly professional. The area in which they were committed proved to contain far more numerous enemy forces than had been predicted by every intelligence estimate, the terrain was much more difficult than expected and the weather conditions were unseasonably brutal.

Despite these hazards, in a very short period of time the 22 Special Air Service (SAS) Regiment was successful in totally denying the central corridor of western Iraq to Iraqi Scud units. The result was that the principal areas used by the Iraqis to fire Scuds on Tel Aviv were no longer available to them. They were required to move their Scud missile firing forces to the north-west portion of Iraq and from that location the firing of Scud missiles was essentially militarily ineffective.

4. When it became necessary to introduce United States Special Operations Forces into the area to attempt to close down the northwest Scud areas, the 22 Special Air Service (SAS) Regiment provided invaluable assistance to the US forces. They took every possible measure to ensure that US forces were thoroughly briefed and were able to profit from the valuable lessons that had been learned by earlier SAS deployments into western Iraq.

I am completely convinced that had US forces not received these thorough indoctrinations by SAS personnel, US forces would have suffered a much higher rate of casualties than was ultimately the case. Further, the SAS and US joint forces then immediately merged into a combined fighting force where the synergetic effect of these fine units ultimately caused the enemy to be convinced that they were facing forces in western Iraq that were more than tenfold the size of those they were actually facing. As a result, large numbers of enemy forces that might otherwise have been deployed in the eastern theater were tied down in western Iraq.

5. The performance of the 22 Special Air Service (SAS) Regiment during Operation Desert Storm was in the highest traditions of the professional military service and in keeping with the proud history and tradition that has been established by that regiment. Please ensure that this commendation receives appropriate attention and is passed on to the unit and its members.

H. NORMAN SCHWARZKOPF
General, US Army Commander-in-Chief

DOCUMENT: Fitzroy Maclean,
SAS Raid on Benghazi, 21 May 1943

Prevented from military service by his profession of diplomat, Fitzroy Maclean had obviated the ruling by getting himself elected to Parliament and thus out of the Foreign Office. (Churchill quipped that Maclean had "used the Mother of Parliaments as a public convenience".) Maclean had been on his way to join the 2nd Camerons in the desert when a chance meeting with the persuasive David Stirling in Cairo resulted in him transferring to the SAS.

Maclean accompanied Stirling on the 21 May 1943 Benghazi raid. Also in the raiding party was Prime Minister Winston Churchill's son, Randolph. The intention was to penetrate the harbour, where the team – which also included Cooper, Rose and Lieutenant Gordon Alston – would lay limpet mines on Axis

ships. An earlier SAS venture against Benghazi had come to grief
when the *folbot* collapsible canoe proved impossible to fit together;
for this operation, Stirling had secured inflatable recce craft from
the Royal Engineers.

Escorted by a Long Range Desert Group patrol, the SAS team
set off for Benghazi in the "Blitz Buggy". This was a Ford V8 util-
ity vehicle Stirling had poached in Cairo and had then modified
by removing the roof and windows, and installing a water
condenser, an extra-large fuel tank and a sun compass. It also had
a single Vickers K machine gun at the front and twin Vickers at
the rear. The "Blitz Buggy" was painted in olive grey to look like
a German staff car. Alas, on the long run into Benghazi the Blitz
Buggy developed a distinctly attention-seeking fault. Maclean
recalled:

Once we had left the desert and were on the smooth tarmac
road, we noticed that the car was making an odd noise. It was
more than a squeak; it was a high-pitched screech with two
notes in it. Evidently one of the many jolts which they had
received had damaged the track rods. Now the wheels were
out of alignment and this was the result.

We laid down on our backs in the road and tinkered. It was
no use. When we got back into the car and drove off again,
the screech was louder than ever. We could hardly have made
more noise if we had been in a fire engine with its bell clang-
ing. It was awkward, but there was nothing we could do about
it now. Fortunately, it did not seem to affect the speed of the
car.

Soon we were passing the high wire fence round the
Regina aerodrome. We were not far from Benghazi now. We
were going at a good speed and expected to be there in five or
ten minutes. I hoped that the Intelligence Branch were right
in thinking there was no road block. It was cold in the open
car. Feeling in my greatcoat pocket I found a bar of milk
chocolate that had been forgotten there. I unwrapped it and
ate it. It tasted good.

Then, suddenly, we turned a corner and I saw something
that made me sit up and concentrate. A hundred yards away,

straight ahead of us, a red light was showing right in the middle of the road.

David slammed on the brakes and we slithered to a standstill. There was a heavy bar of wood across the road with a red lantern hanging from the middle of it. On my side of the road stood a sentry who had me covered with his Tommy gun. He was an Italian. I bent down and picked up a heavy spanner from the floor of the car. Then I beckoned to the sentry to come nearer, waving some papers at him with my free hand as if I wanted to show them to him. If only he would come near enough I could knock him on the head and we could drive on.

He did not move but kept me covered with his Tommy gun. Then I saw that beyond him in the shadows were two or three more Italians with Tommy guns and what looked like a guardroom or a machine-gun post. Unless we could bluff our way through there would be nothing for it but to shoot it out, which was the last thing we wanted at this stage of the expedition.

There was a pause and then the sentry asked who we were.

"Staff officers," I told him, and added peremptorily, "in a hurry." I had not spoken a word of Italian for three years and I hoped devoutly that my accent sounded convincing. Also that he would not notice in the dark that we were all wearing British uniforms. He did not reply immediately. It looked as though his suspicions were aroused. In the car behind me I heard a click, as the safety catch of a Tommy gun slid back. Someone had decided not to take any chances.

Then, just as I had made my mind up that there was going to be trouble, the sentry pointed at our headlights. "You ought to get those dimmed," he said, saluting sloppily. He then opened the gate and stood aside to let us pass. Screeching loudly, we drove on towards Benghazi. Soon we were on the outskirts of the town. Coming towards us were the headlights of another car. It passed us. Then, looking back over our shoulders, we saw that it had stopped and turned back after us. This looked suspicious. David slowed down to let it pass. The car slowed down too. He accelerated; the car accelerated.

Then he decided to shake it off. He put his foot down on the accelerator, and, screeching louder than ever, we drove into Benghazi at a good eighty miles an hour with the other car after us.

Once in the town, we turned the first corner we came to and, switching off our headlights, stopped to listen. The other car shot past and went roaring off into the darkness. For the moment our immediate troubles were over. But only for a moment. As we sat listening, a rocket sailed up into the sky, then another, then another. Then all the air-raid sirens in Benghazi started to wail. We had arranged with the RAF before we started that they should leave Benghazi alone that night; so this could not be an air-raid warning. It looked very much as though the alert was being given in our honour . . .

Clearly the battle wagon, with its distinctive screech, was no longer an asset now that the alarm had been given. We decided to get rid of it at once and take a chance escaping on foot. Planting a detonator timed to go off in thirty minutes amongst the explosives in the back, we started off in single file through the darkness.

We were in the Arab quarter of town, which had suffered most heavily from the RAF raids. Every other house was in ruins and, threading our way over the rubble through one bombed-out building after another, we had soon put several blocks between ourselves and the place where we had left the car to explode. Once or twice we stopped to listen. We could hear people walking along the adjacent streets, but no one seemed to be following us.

Then, passing through a breach in a wall, we emerged unexpectedly in a narrow side street, to find ourselves face to face with an Italian Carabiniere.

There was no avoiding him and it seemed better to take the initiative and accost him before he accosted us. The rockets and sirens provided a ready-made subject for conversation.

"What," I asked, "is all this noise about?"

"Oh, just another of those damned English air-raids," he said gloomily.

"Might it be," I inquired anxiously, "that enemy ground forces are raiding the town and that they are the cause of the alert?"

"No," he said, "there's no need to be nervous about that, not with the English almost back on the Egyptian frontier."

I thanked him for his reassuring remarks and wished him goodnight. Although we had been standing under a street light, he did not seem to have noticed that I was in British uniform.

This encounter put a different complexion on the situation. We seemed to have been unduly pessimistic. We might have a go at the harbour yet. And save ourselves a long walk back to the Jebel.

We hurried back to the car. Our watches showed that about twenty-five minutes had elapsed since we had set off the time pencil. If it was an accurate one, there should still be five minutes to go before it detonated and blew up the car . . . Nervously, we extricated it from the back of the car and threw it over the nearest wall. A minute or two later we heard it go off with a sharp crack. We had not been a moment too soon.

The next thing was to make our way to the harbour, which was about a mile off. The screech made it inadvisable to take the car. Accordingly we left Randolph and Corporal Rose to find somewhere to hide it, while David, Corporal Cooper and myself, with Alston as guide, started off for the harbour, armed with Tommy guns and carrying one of the boats and a selection of explosives in a kitbag. Soon we had left the dark alleyways of the Arab quarter behind us and were in the European part of the town. High white buildings loomed up round us, and our footsteps echoed noisily in the broad paved streets. Then, just as we were coming to the barbed-wire fence which surrounded the harbour, I caught sight of a sentry.

Laden as we were, we made a suspicious-looking party, and once again I thought it better to try to set his suspicions at rest by accosting him, rather than attempting to slink on unnoticed. "We have," I said, thinking quickly, "just met with a motor accident. All this is our luggage. Can you direct us to a hotel where we can spend the night?"

The sentry listened politely. Then he said he was afraid that all the hotels had been put out of action by the accursed English bombing, but perhaps, if we went on trying, we would find somewhere to sleep. He seemed well disposed and was an apparently unobservant man. We wished him good night and trudged off.

As soon as we were out of sight, we started to look for a place to get through the wire. Eventually we found one and dragged the boat and explosives through it. Then, dodging between cranes and railway trucks, we made our way down to the water's edge. Looking round at the dim outlines of the jetties and buildings, I realized with a momentary feeling of satisfaction that we were on the identical strip of shingle which we had picked on as a likely starting point on the wooden model at Alexandria. So far, so good.

David, who possesses the gift of moving slowly and invisibly by night, now set off on a tour of the harbour with Alston, leaving Cooper and myself to inflate the boat.

Crouching under a low sea wall, we unpacked the kitbag and set to work with the bellows. There was no moon, but brilliant starlight. The smooth, shining surface of the harbour was like a sheet of quicksilver, and the black hulls of the ships seemed no more than a stone's throw away. They would make good targets, if only we could reach them unobserved. At any rate, we should not have far to paddle, though I could have wished for a better background than this smooth expanse of water. Diligently we plugged away at the bellows, which squeaked louder than I liked, and seemed to be making little or no impression on the boat. Several minutes passed. The boat was still as flat as a pancake. We verified the connection and went on pumping.

Then suddenly we were hailed from one of the ships. It was a sentry. "*Chi va la?*" he challenged. "*Militari!*" I shouted back. There was a pause and we resumed pumping. But still the sentry was suspicious. "What are you up to over there?" he inquired. "Nothing to do with you," I answered, with a show of assurance which I was far from feeling. After that there was silence.

Meanwhile, the boat remained flat. There could only be one explanation: somehow, since we had inspected it in the wadi that morning, it had got punctured. There was nothing for it but to go and fetch another. It was fortunate we had two.

Hiding the first boat as best we could under the shadow of the wall, we crossed the docks, slipping unseen through the hole in the wire, and walked back through the silent streets to where we had left the car. There we found Randolph and Rose in fine fettle, trying with the utmost unconcern to maneuver the car through a hole in the wall of a bombed-out house. Occasionally passers-by, Arabs for the most part, gaped at them with undisguised interest and admiration.

Wishing them luck, we pulled the second boat out of the car and started back to the harbour. Once again we got safely through the wire and down to the water's edge, but only to find that the second boat, like the first, was uninflatable. It was heart-rending. Meanwhile, there was no sign of David. We decided to go and look for him.

As we reached the hole in the wire we saw, to our disgust, someone standing on the other side of it. I was just thinking what to say in Italian, when the unknown figure spoke to me in English. It was David, who had been down to the water to look for us and had been as alarmed at not finding us as we had been at not finding him.

There followed a hurried council of war. All this tramping backwards and forwards had taken time and our watches showed that we had only another half-hour's darkness. Already the sky was beginning to lighten. We debated whether or not to plant our explosives haphazardly in the railway trucks with which the quays were crowded, but decided that, as targets, they were not important enough to justify us in betraying our presence in the harbour and thus prejudicing the success of an eventual large-scale raid. If we were to blow them up, the alarm would be given. We should probably be able to get away in the confusion, but another time we should stand a much poorer chance of raiding the harbour unnoticed. Our present expedition must thus be regarded as reconnaissance.

Stirling's disappointed party were not out of the harbour yet, though. After an altercation with a Somali sentry, the SAS team collected their equipment and were making for the hole in the perimeter wire when two Italian sentries fell in behind them.

Realizing that massive bluffing was now the only option, Maclean led the party to the main gate, where with "as pompous a manner as my ten days' beard and shabby appearance allowed;" he demanded to speak to the guard commander. A sleepy sergeant, pulling on his trousers, appeared. Maclean upbraided the sergeant for not keeping a proper guard. What if he had been leading a band of British saboteurs? Maclean demanded. The guard commander tittered at such an improbability.

With a final warning to the sergeant to improve his security, Maclean dismissed him and they briskly walked out through the main gate. After lying up in a deserted house for the day, Stirling gave the order to leave Benghazi and rendezvous with the LRDG. On the way out of Benghazi a notion to bomb two motor torpedo boats had to be abandoned due to the watchfulness of enemy guards. All that could be said for the Benghazi raid was that it provided useful reconnaissance and taught the SAS a valuable lesson in the virtue of bluffing. In the words of Corporal Johnny Cooper: "If you think of something the enemy would consider an impossible stupidity, and carry it out with determination, you can get away with it by sheer blatant cheek."

CHARLIE WILSON'S REAL WAR

CIA, Afghanistan, 1984–92

Charlie Wilson was a good ol' boy congressman from east Texas, with a line in partying that made J.R. Ewing look like a pauper wallflower. You kinda had to like Charlie, unless you were Amish or Moral Majority. Charlie was once discovered in the hot tub in the Fantasy Suite at Ceasar's Palace with two show-girls and an alpine mountain of coke. The Feds tried to bust him for that, but were never able to prove it was Charlie and not the girls taking it up the nose. "And I ain't telling," added Charlie. When Charlie was appointed – miraculously – to the House Ethics Committee the disgraced Democrat congressman told a reporter, "I'm the only one of the Committee that likes whiskey and women and we need to be represented."

There was more to Charlie than met the eye. From the time he was a boy, sitting listening on the radio to the battles the Allies waged in World War II, Wilson saw himself as a warrior. Graduating from Annapolis (despite a long list of demerits) Wilson spent a while at sea, but never saw any action. So he decided to take up the good fight in the political arena, winning election to Texas Legislature in 1961, then Congress twelve years later. Inspired by John F. Kennedy's inaugural speech, Wilson wanted to do for his country.

In Congress, Wilson became a passionate supporter of Israel. That cause disappointed to the core of the heart in 1982 when he went to Chatila refugee camp outside Beirut, where Ariel Sharon had permitted the slaughter of Palestinians by Christian militias.

But there was always the cause of anti-Communism to fall back on. And it just happened that the mujahedin in Afghanistan were then fighting an occupying army from the Soviet Union. The news coming in every day over the media made for a heart-breaking litany of Russian outrages committed against poor Afghan tribespeople. Helping Charlie feel the Afghans' hurt was socialite Joanne Herring, who had previously persuaded fashion designer friends such as Oscar de la Renta to conjure designs Afghan women could make simply and easily in their remote villages.

Wilson had the will to do something, and was also in the position to do something. He now sat on the House Appropriations Subcommittee on Defense. Wilson called up the staff dealing with off-the-book deals ("black appropriations") and requested a two-fold increase in appropriation for the CIA's funding and training of mujahedin tribesmen in Afghanistan. The CIA saw the tribesmen as freedom fighters . . . and pawns in the shadow war against the Soviet Union. In 1983, Wilson won an additional $40 million for Afghanistan, $17 million of which was detailed for anti-aircraft weapons to allow the mujahedin to shoot down Soviet Mil Mi-24 Hind helicopters. (The US-built Stinger anti-aircraft missile struck a decisive blow to the Soviet war effort as it allowed the lightly armed Afghans to halt Soviet helicopter landings in strategic areas.) Wilson's enthusiasm for getting money for the CIA's proxy war against the Soviets in Afghanistan was noted by the White House. National Security Adviser Robert McFarlane asked a colleague "Walt, Go see Charlie Wilson (D-TX). Seek to bring him into circle as discrete . . . He can be very helpful in getting money. M."

Wilson wanted to do yet more. He just needed the right contacts. Enter here one Gust Avrakatos, a working-class Greek-American from Pennsylvania, roused, like Wilson, by Kennedy's "Ask not what your country can do for you" ideal. Avrakatos was CIA regional head for Afghanistan. Avrakatos's crudeness and political incorrectness was jaw-dropping; he called his black secretary "nigger". He also had the proverbial heart of gold, and was the constant champion of the downtrodden pen-pushers in CIA offices. He was the only white guy to receive the black workers' annual Brown Bomber Award. As the presenter said, "We want to give this award to the blackest motherfucker of us all."

Avrakatos's anti-Communism was of the same crude stripe as Wilson's. In 1984 Avrakatos directly approached Wilson – breaking the CIA's rule against lobbying Congress for money – and asked the Congressman for $50 million more for Afghanistan. Smooth-talking, passionate Charlie boy agreed and convinced Congress, declaring, "The US had nothing whatsoever to do with these people's decision to fight . . . but we'll be damned by history if we let them fight with stones." By the end of the fiscal year, Wilson had also secured the Afghans $300 million of unused Pentagon money. In effect, Wilson had just turned the spigot on for what became known as "Operation Cyclone", the biggest covert operation of all time, with the CIA Special Activities Division able to direct billions of dollars to the mujahedin in Afghanistan. A grateful CIA awarded Wilson its "Honoured Colleague Award", the first time the prize had been given to a "civilian".

But it wasn't only the American tax-payer stumping up funds. Wilson and Avrakatos wooed the Saudis, and persuaded them to "match fund".

Much of the money was channelled into Afghanistan via the Pakistani secret service, the Inter Service Intelligence (ISI). Of the teeming mujahedin bands, the ISI had definite favourites. It liked the hard-core Islamists. Between 1978 and 1992 the ISI armed and trained over 100,000 insurgents, and encouraged the volunteers from the Arab states to join the Afghan resistance.

By 1991 the Soviet Union was careering towards destruction, and the Senate Intelligence Committee, observing that Soviet influence in Afghanistan was waning by the day, approved nothing for Afghanistan. This was not to the liking of the CIA or Charlie Wilson.

Wilson made one of his impassioned appeals to the House Intelligence Committee and carried the day. The committee approved $200 million, which with the Saudi matching funds totalled $400 million. The Afghan tribes also received a bumper load of Iraqi weapons captured by US forces during the Gulf War.

The Afghan pro-Soviet government of Najibulla finally fell in 1992. But its collapse didn't stop the war in Afghanistan, because the factions of the mujahedin now turned on each other. With chaos reigning across Afghanistan, the ISI sent in its own covert army of Islamic extremists drawn from Pashtun refugee camps inside Pakistan. This group, many of them trained by the CIA, was known as the Taliban.

The Taliban seized the capital of Kabul in September 1996, and imposed harsh Islamic law on Afghanistan. The Taliban also granted refuge to Saudi exile Osama bin Laden, who had fought with the Afghan mujahedin against the Soviets in the 1980s. Bin Laden then used Afghanistan as the base of operations for his terrorist organization, al-Qaeda.

Some of the weapons used against American and coalition troops in Afghanistan in the 2001 war were those supplied by the CIA's Operation Cyclone. A principal recipient of the CIA's largesse was Wilson's warlord pal, Gulbuddin Hekmatyar ("goodness personified"), later a senior Taliban leader and a supporter of al-Qaeda.

This was "blow-back" on an epic scale. Hyped on anti-Communism, Wilson and Avrakatos failed to see the true nature of the Afghan warlords they were trading with, though the evidence was all around. Avrakatos himself had to point out to his superiors that their plan to get Soviet troops to defect to the mujahedin was unworkable:

"The muj were supposed to set up loudspeakers in the mountains announcing such things as 'Lay down your arms, there is a passage to the West and to freedom.'" Once news of this programme made its way through the Red Army, it was argued, there would be a flood of defectors . . .

The plan was a non-starter because the "muj" always either murdered Soviet prisoners or turned them into concubines. To make his point he turned up to a briefing armed with five huge photographic blow-ups . . . One of them showed two Russian sergeants being used as concubines. Another had a Russian hanging from the turret of a tank with a vital part of his anatomy removed. "If you were a sane fucking Russian, would you defect to these people?" he had asked.

Wilson himself was not entirely ignorant of the mujahedin's proclivities. When Wilson and Gust arranged for Tennessee mules to be sent in to ferry the arms shipments to the rebels in the mountains, the word came back that the mules had been buggered and eaten by the "muj".

DOCUMENT: CIA: A Study of Assassination

This instructional guide on assassination was part of the training programme for the CIA's covert "Operation PBSUCCESS", the paramilitary overthrow of the Guatemalan regime of President Jacobo Arbenz Guzman in June 1954. With the resignation of Arbenz, the Agency's proposal to assassinate him was dropped; the names of other targeted individuals were redacted when the CIA's files on Guatemala were declassified during the administration of President Clinton, making it impossible to know whether they were killed in the bloody aftermath of the coup.

DEFINITION

Assassination is a term thought to be derived from "Hashish", a drug similar to marijuana, said to have been used by Hasan-Dan-Sabah to induce motivation in his followers, who were assigned to carry out political and other murders, usually at the cost of their lives.

It is here used to describe the planned killing of a person who is not under the legal jurisdiction of the killer, who is not physically in the hands of the killer, who has been selected by a resistance organization for death and whose death provides positive advantages to that organization.

EMPLOYMENT

Assassination is an extreme measure not normally used in clandestine operations. It should be assumed that it will never be ordered or authorized by any U.S. Headquarters, though the latter may in rare instances agree to its execution by members of an associated foreign service. This reticence is partly due to the necessity for committing communications to paper. No assassination instructions should ever be written or recorded. Consequently, the decision to employ this technique must nearly always be reached in the field, at the area where the act will take place. Decision and instructions should be confined to an absolute minimum of persons. Ideally, only one person will be involved. No report may be made, but usually the act will be properly covered by normal news services, whose output is available to all concerned.

JUSTIFICATION

Murder is not morally justifiable. Self-defense may be argued if the victim has knowledge which may destroy the resistance organization if divulged. Assassination of persons responsible for atrocities or reprisals may be regarded as just punishment. Killing a political leader whose burgeoning career is a clear and present danger to the cause of freedom may be held necessary.

But assassination can seldom be employed with a clear conscience. Persons who are morally squeamish should not attempt it.

CLASSIFICATIONS

The techniques employed will vary according to whether the subject is unaware of his danger, aware but unguarded, or guarded. They will also be affected by whether or not the assassin is to be killed with the subject hereafter: assassinations in which the subject is unaware will be termed "simple"; those where the subject is aware but unguarded will be termed "chase"; those where the victim is guarded will be termed "guarded."

If the assassin is to die with the subject, the act will be called "lost." If the assassin is to escape, the adjective will be "safe." It should be noted that no compromises should exist here. The assassin must not fall alive into enemy hands.

A further type division is caused by the need to conceal the fact that the subject was actually the victim of assassination, rather than an accident or natural causes. If such concealment is desirable the operation will be called "secret"; if concealment is immaterial, the act will be called "open";

while if the assassination requires publicity to be effective it will be termed "terroristic."

Following these definitions, the assassination of Julius Caesar was safe, simple, and terroristic, while that of Huey Long was lost, guarded and open. Obviously, successful secret assassinations are not recorded as assassination at all. [Illegible] of Thailand and Augustus Caesar may have been the victims of safe, guarded and secret assassination. Chase assassinations usually involve clandestine agents or members of criminal organizations.

THE ASSASSIN

In safe assassinations, the assassin needs the usual qualities of a clandestine agent. He should be determined, courageous, intelligent, resourceful, and physically active. If special equipment is to be used, such as firearms or drugs, it is clear that he must have outstanding skill with such equipment.

Except in terroristic assassinations, it is desirable that the assassin be transient in the area. He should have an absolute minimum of contact with the rest of the organization and his instructions should be given orally by one person only. His safe evacuation after the act is absolutely essential, but here again contact should be as limited as possible. It is preferable that the person issuing instructions also conduct any withdrawal or covering action which may be necessary.

In lost assassination, the assassin must be a fanatic of some sort. Politics, religion, and revenge are about the only feasible motives. Since a fanatic is unstable psychologically, he must be handled with extreme care. He must not know the identities of the other members of the organization, for although it is intended that he die in the act, something may go wrong. While the Assassin of Trotsky has never revealed any significant information, it was unsound to depend on this when the act was planned.

PLANNING

When the decision to assassinate has been reached, the tactics of the operation must be planned, based upon an estimate of the situation similar to that used in military operations. The preliminary estimate will reveal gaps in information and possibly indicate a need for special equipment which must be procured or constructed. When all necessary data has been collected, an effective tactical plan can be prepared. All planning must be mental; no papers should ever contain evidence of the operation.

In resistance situations, assassination may be used as a counter-reprisal. Since this requires advertising to be effective, the resistance organization must be in a position to warn high officials publicly that their lives will be the price of reprisal action against innocent people. Such a threat is of no value unless it can be carried out, so it may be necessary to plan the assassination of various responsible officers of the oppressive regime and hold such plans in readiness to be used only if provoked by excessive brutality. Such plans must be modified frequently to meet changes in the tactical situation.

TECHNIQUES

The essential point of assassination is the death of the subject. A human being may be killed in many ways but sureness is often overlooked by those who may be emotionally unstrung by the seriousness of this act they intend to commit. The specific technique employed will depend upon a large number of variables, but should be constant in one point: Death must be absolutely certain. The attempt on Hitler's life failed because the conspiracy did not give this matter proper attention.

Techniques may be considered as follows:

1. Manual

It is possible to kill a man with the bare hands, but very few are skillful enough to do it well. Even a highly trained Judo expert will hesitate to risk killing by hand unless he has absolutely no alternative. However, the simplest local tools are often much the most efficient means of assassination. A hammer, axe, wrench, screw driver, fire poker, kitchen knife, lamp stand, or anything hard, heavy and handy will suffice. A length of rope or wire or a belt will do if the assassin is strong and agile. All such improvised weapons have the important advantage of availability and apparent innocence. The obviously lethal machine gun failed to kill Trotsky where an item of sporting goods succeeded.

In all safe cases where the assassin may be subject to search, either before or after the act, specialized weapons should not be used. Even in the lost case, the assassin may accidentally be searched before the act and should not carry an incriminating device if any sort of lethal weapon can be improvised at or near the site. If the assassin normally carries weapons because of the nature of his job, it may still be desirable to improvise and implement at the scene to avoid disclosure of his identity.

2. Accidents

For secret assassination, either simple or chase, the contrived accident is the most effective technique. When successfully executed, it causes little excitement and is only casually investigated.

The most efficient accident, in simple assassination, is a fall of 75 feet or more onto a hard surface. Elevator shafts, stair wells, unscreened windows and bridges will serve. Bridge falls into water are not reliable. In simple cases a private meeting with the subject may be arranged at a properly-cased location. The act may be executed by sudden, vigorous [excised] of the ankles, tipping the subject over the edge. If the assassin immediately sets up an outcry, playing the "horrified witness", no alibi or surreptitious withdrawal is necessary. In chase cases it will usually be necessary to stun or drug the subject before dropping him. Care is required to insure that no wound or condition not attributable to the fall is discernible after death.

Falls into the sea or swiftly flowing rivers may suffice if the subject cannot swim. It will be more reliable if the assassin can arrange to attempt rescue, as he can thus be sure of the subject's death and at the same time establish a workable alibi.

If the subject's personal habits make it feasible, alcohol may be used [2 words excised] to prepare him for a contrived accident of any kind.

Falls before trains or subway cars are usually effective, but require exact timing and can seldom be free from unexpected observation.

Automobile accidents are a less satisfactory means of assassination. If the subject is deliberately run down, very exact timing is necessary and investigation is likely to be thorough. If the subject's car is tampered with, reliability is very low. The subject may be stunned or drugged and then placed in the car, but this is only reliable when the car can be run off a high cliff or into deep water without observation.

Arson can cause accidental death if the subject is drugged and left in a burning building. Reliability is not satisfactory unless the building is isolated and highly combustible.

3. Drugs

In all types of assassination except terroristic, drugs can be very effective. If the assassin is trained as a doctor or nurse and the subject is under medical care, this is an easy and rare method. An overdose of morphine administered as a sedative will cause death without disturbance and is difficult to detect. The size of the dose will depend upon whether the subject has been using narcotics regularly. If not, two grains will suffice.

If the subject drinks heavily, morphine or a similar narcotic can be injected at the passing out stage, and the cause of death will often be held to be acute alcoholism.

Specific poisons, such as arsenic or strychnine, are effective but their possession or procurement is incriminating, and accurate dosage is problematical. Poison was used unsuccessfully in the assassinations of Rasputin and Kolohan, though the latter case is more accurately described as a murder.

4. Edge weapons

Any locally obtained edge device may be successfully employed. A certain minimum of anatomical knowledge is needed for reliability.

Puncture wounds of the body cavity may not be reliable unless the heart is reached. The heart is protected by the rib cage and is not always easy to locate.

Abdominal wounds were once nearly always mortal, but modern medical treatment has made this no longer true.

Absolute reliability is obtained by severing the spinal cord in the cervical region. This can be done with the point of a knife or a light blow of an axe or hatchet.

Another reliable method is the severing of both jugular and carotid blood vessels on both sides of the windpipe.

If the subject has been rendered unconscious by other wounds or drugs, either of the above methods can be used to ensure death.

5. Blunt weapons

As with edge weapons, blunt weapons require some anatomical knowledge for effective use. Their main advantage is their universal availability. A hammer may be picked up almost anywhere in the world. Baseball and [illegible] bats are very widely distributed. Even a rock or a heavy stick will do, and nothing resembling a weapon need be procured, carried or subsequently disposed of.

Blows should be directed to the temple, the area just below and behind the ear, and the lower, rear portion of the skull. Of course, if the blow is very heavy, any portion of the upper skull will do. The lower frontal portion of the head, from the eyes to the throat, can withstand enormous blows without fatal consequences.

6. Firearms

Firearms are often used in assassination, often very ineffectively. The assassin usually has insufficient technical knowledge of the limitations of weapons, and expects more range, accuracy and killing power than can be provided with reliability. Since certainty of death is the major requirement, firearms should be used which can provide destructive power at least 100% in excess of that thought to be necessary, and ranges should be half that considered practical for the weapon.

Firearms have other drawbacks. Their possession is often incriminating. They may be difficult to obtain. They require a degree of experience from the user. They are [illegible]. Their [illegible] is consistently over-rated.

However, there are many cases in which firearms are probably more efficient than any other means. These cases usually involve distance between the assassin and the subject, or comparative physical weakness of the assassin, as with a woman.

(a) The precision rifle
In guarded assassination, a good hunting or target rifle should always be considered as a possibility. Absolute reliability can nearly always be achieved at a distance of one hundred yards. In ideal circumstances, the range may be extended to 250 yards. The rifle should be a well-made bolt or falling-block action type, handling a powerful long-range cartridge. The .300 F.A.B. Magnum is probably the best cartridge readily available. Other excellent calibers are .375 M.[illeg]. Magnum, .270 Winchester, .30–106 p.s., 8 x 60 MM Magnum, 9.3 x 62 kk and others of this type. These are preferable to ordinary military calibers, since ammunition available for them is usually of the expanding bullet type, whereas most ammunition for military rifles is full jacketed and hence not sufficiently lethal. Military ammunition should not be altered by filing or drilling bullets, as this will adversely affect accuracy.

The rifle may be of the "bull gun" variety, with extra heavy barrel and set triggers, but in any case should be capable of maximum precision. Ideally, the weapon should be able to group in one inch at one hundred yards, but 2½″ groups are adequate. The sight should be telescopic, not only for accuracy, but because such a sight is much better in dim light or near darkness. As long as the bare outline of the target is discernable, a telescope sight will work, even if the rifle and shooter are in total darkness.

An expanding, hunting bullet of such calibers as described above will produce extravagant laceration and shock at short or mid-range. If a man is struck just once in the body cavity, his death is almost entirely certain.

Public figures or guarded officials may be killed with great reliability and some safety if a firing point can be established prior to an official occasion. The propaganda value of this system may be very high.

(b) The machine gun

Machine guns may be used in most cases where the precision rifle is applicable. Usually, this will require the subversion of a unit of an official guard at a ceremony, though a skillful and determined team might conceivably dispose of a loyal gun crew without commotion and take over the gun at the critical time.

The area fire capacity of the machine gun should not be used to search out a concealed subject. This was tried with predictable lack of success on Trotsky. The automatic feature of the machine gun should rather be used to increase reliability by placing a 5-second burst on the subject. Even with full jacket ammunition, this will be absolutely lethal if the burst pattern is no larger than a man. This can be accomplished at about 150 yards. In ideal circumstances, a properly padded and targeted machine gun can do it at 850 yards. The major difficulty is placing the first burst exactly on the target, as most machine gunners are trained to spot their fire on target by observation of strike. This will not do in assassination as the subject will not wait.

(c) The sub-machine gun

This weapon, known as the "machine-pistol" by the Russians and Germans and "machine-carbine" by the British, is occasionally useful in assassination. Unlike the rifle and machine gun, this is a short-range weapon and, since it fires pistol ammunition, much less powerful. To be reliable, it should deliver at least 5 rounds into the subject's chest, though the .45 caliber U.S. weapons have a much larger margin of killing efficiency than the 9 mm European arms.

The assassination range of the sub-machine gun is point blank. While accurate single rounds can be delivered by sub-machine gunners at 50 yards or more, this is not certain enough for assassination. Under ordinary circumstances, the 5MG should be used as a fully automatic weapon. In the hands of a capable gunner, a high cyclic rate is a distinct advantage, as speed of execution is most desirable, particularly in the case of multiple subjects.

The sub-machine gun is especially adapted to indoor work when more than one subject is to be assassinated. An effective technique has been devised for the use of a pair of sub-machine gunners, by which a room containing as many as a dozen subjects can be "purifico" in about twenty seconds with little or no risk to the gunners.

While the U.S. sub-machine guns fire the most lethal cartridges, the higher cyclic rate of some foreign weapons enable the gunner to cover a target quicker with acceptable pattern density. The Bergmann Model 1934 is particularly good in this way. The Danish Madman? SMG has a moderately good cyclic rate and is admirably compact and concealable. The Russian SHGs have a good cyclic rate, but are handicapped by a small, light protective which requires more kits for equivalent killing effect.

(d) The shotgun

A large-bore shotgun is a most effective killing instrument as long as the range is kept under ten yards. It should normally be used only on single targets as it cannot sustain fire successfully. The barrel may be "sawed" off for convenience, but this is not a significant factor in its killing performance. Its optimum range is just out of reach of the subject. 00 buckshot is considered the best shot size for a twelve-gauge gun, but anything from single balls to bird shot will do if the range is right. The assassin should aim for the solar plexus as the shot pattern is small at close range and can easily [illegible] the head.

(e) The pistol

While the handgun is quite inefficient as a weapon of assassination, it is often used, partly because it is readily available and can be concealed on the person, and partly because its limitations are not widely appreciated. While many well-known assassinations have been carried out with pistols (Lincoln, Harding, Gandhi), such attempts fail as often as they succeed (Truman, Roosevelt, Churchill).

If a pistol is used, it should be as powerful as possible and fired from just beyond reach. The pistol and the shotgun are used in similar tactical situations, except that the shotgun is much more lethal and the pistol is much more easily concealed.

In the hands of an expert, a powerful pistol is quite deadly, but such experts are rare and not usually available for assassination missions.

.45 Colt, .44 Special, .455 Kly, .45 A.S.[illegible] (U.S. Service) and .357 Magnum are all efficient calibers. Less powerful rounds can suffice but are less reliable. Sub-power cartridges such as the .32s and .25s should be avoided.

In all cases, the subject should be hit solidly at least three times for complete reliability.

(f) Silent firearms

The sound of the explosion of the proponent in a firearm can be effectively silenced by appropriate attachments. However, the sound of the projective passing through the air cannot, since this sound is generated outside the weapon. In cases where the velocity of the bullet greatly exceeds that of sound, the noise so generated is much louder than that of the explosion. Since all powerful rifles have muzzle velocities of over 2000 feet per second, they cannot be silenced.

Pistol bullets, on the other hand, usually travel slower than sound and the sound of their flight is negligible. Therefore, pistols, sub-machine guns and any sort of improvised carbine or rifle which will take a low velocity cartridge can be silenced. The user should not forget that the sound of the operation of a repeating action is considerable, and that the sound of bullet strike, particularly in bone, is quite loud.

Silent firearms are only occasionally useful to the assassin, though they have been widely publicized in this connection. Because permissible velocity is low, effective precision range is held to about 100 yards with rifle or carbine type weapons, while pistols, silent or otherwise, are most efficient just beyond arm's length. The silent feature attempts to provide a degree of safety to the assassin, but mere possession of a silent firearm is likely to create enough hazard to counter the advantage of its silence. The silent pistol combines the disadvantages of any pistol with the added one of its obviously clandestine purpose.

A telescopically sighted, closed-action carbine shooting a low-velocity bullet of great weight, and built for accuracy, could be very useful to an assassin in certain situations. At the time of writing, no such weapon is known to exist.

7. Explosives

Bombs and demolition charges of various sorts have been used frequently in assassination. Such devices, in terroristic and open assassination, can provide safety and overcome guard barriers, but it is curious that bombs have often been the implement of lost assassinations.

The major factor which affects reliability is the use of explosives for assassination. The charge must be very large and the detonation must be controlled exactly as to time by the assassin who can observe the subject. A small or moderate explosive charge is highly unreliable as a cause of death, and time delay or booby-trap devices are extremely prone to kill the wrong man. In addition to the moral aspects of indiscriminate killing, the death of casual bystanders can often produce public reactions unfavorable to the cause for which the assassination is carried out.

Bombs or grenades should never be thrown at a subject. While this will always cause a commotion and may even result in the subject's death, it is sloppy, unreliable, and bad propaganda. The charge must be too small and the assassin is never sure of: (1) reaching his attack position, (2) placing the charge close enough to the target, and (3) firing the charge at the right time.

Placing the charge surreptitiously in advance permits a charge of proper size to be employed, but requires accurate prediction of the subject's movements.

Ten pounds of high explosive should normally be regarded as a minimum, and this is explosive of fragmentation material. The latter can consist of any hard, [illegible] material as long as the fragments are large enough. Metal or rock fragments should be walnut-size rather than pea-size. If solid plates are used, to be ruptured by the explosion, cast iron, 1″ thick, gives excellent fragmentation. Military or commercial high explosives are practical for use in assassination. Homemade or improvised explosives should be avoided. While possibly powerful, they tend to be dangerous and unreliable. Anti-personnel explosive missiles are excellent, provided the assassin has sufficient technical knowledge to fuse them properly. 81 or 82 mm mortar shells, or the 120 mm mortar shell, are particularly good. Anti-personnel shells for 85, 88, 90, 100 and 105 mm guns and howitzers are both large enough to be completely reliable and small enough to be carried by one man.

The charge should be so placed that the subject is not over six feet from it at the moment of detonation.

A large, shaped charge with the [illegible] filled with iron fragments (such as 1" nuts and bolts) will fire a highly lethal shotgun-type [illegible] to 50 yards. This reaction has not been thoroughly tested, however, and an exact replica of the proposed device should be fired in advance to determine exact range, pattern-size, and penetration of fragments. Fragments should penetrate at least 1″ of seasoned pine or equivalent for minimum reliability. Any firing device may be used which permits exact control by the assassin. An ordinary commercial or military explorer is efficient, as long as it is rigged for instantaneous action with no time fuse in the system. The wise [illegible] electric target can serve as the triggering device and provide exact timing from as far away as the assassin can reliably hit the target. This will avoid the disadvantages of stringing wire between the proposed positions of the assassin and the subject, and also permit the assassin to fire the charge from a variety of possible positions.

The radio switch can be [illegible] to fire [illegible], though its reliability is somewhat lower and its procurement may not be easy.

EXAMPLES
[illegible] may be presented brief outlines, with critical evaluations of the following assassinations and attempts:

Marat	Hedrich
Lincoln	Hitler
Harding	Roosevelt
Grand Duke Sergei	Truman
Pirhivie	Mussolini
Archduke Franz Ferdinand	Benes
Rasputin	Aung Sang
Madero	[illeg]
Kirov	Abdullah
Huey Long	Gandhi
Alexander of Yugoslavia	Trotsky

HELL ON EARTH

22 SAS, Oman, 1958

The ancient Sultanate of Muscat and Oman is a small arid country of such extremes of weather that, according to a Persian proverb, a visit there is a foretaste of Hell. Oman, however, has a strategic importance in inverse relation to its size; it lies aside the Hormuz Straits, through which pass 30 per cent of the world's oil tankers.

In 1954 a rebellion against the autocratic (but pro-British) Sultan, led by Ghalib, the Iman of Oman, and his brother, Talib, threatened to destabilize the country and interrupt the oil supply to Great Britain. With understandable *realpolitik*, if with questionable morality, the British government determined to back the Sultan.

An RAF bombing campaign of the rebel stronghold on the Jebel Akhdar failed. An infantry assault on the Jebel failed. A plan to drop the Parachute Regiment was cancelled, because the Prime Minister thought that committing a world-famous regiment to it overemphasized the importance of the situation.

And so in 1958 the shadowy SAS was given the job nobody else could or should do. Lieutenant-Colonel Anthony Deane-Drummond, the commander of 22 SAS, was given fifteen days to round up D Squadron from Malaya and deploy it in Oman. David Smiley, the Sultan's British chief of staff and a former SOE operative, planned and oversaw the SAS's campaign in Oman:

A week later they came – some eighty officers and men comprising D Squadron, under Major John Watts; they were organized in four troops, or patrols, of sixteen men each, together with Squadron Headquarters. Despite their small number they wielded formidable fire-power, with their Browning machine guns, FN rifles and Energa grenades. We had built them a camp at Beit al Falaj, but Watts, a stocky, tough and dedicated professional, sensibly decided to lose no time in making them familiar with their new conditions; for he realized that the steep bare rocks and sharp outlines of the Jebel would require tactics quite different from those they had learned in the swamps and jungles of Malaya. We therefore split the squadron, sending two troops on fighting patrols among the giant slabs above Tamuf and Kamah, and the other two to join Tony Hart [a British contract officer with the Muscat Regiment] at Awabi. Men from the Sultan's Armed Forces accompanied the SAS on all their patrols, an arrangement which greatly improved the morale and fighting skill of my own soldiers, who in their turn provided the SAS with valuable local knowledge.

The need for different tactics struck the SAS forcefully and tragically on one of their first patrols in the Tanuf area. In a skirmish with the rebels one of their best NCOs ["Duke" Swindells MM] incautiously showed himself on a skyline and was shot through the heart by a sniper. This sad incident at least gave them a healthy respect for the enemy, whom they had been inclined to underestimate.

The other two troops, with Hart and some of his men, climbed from Awabi by the Hijar track to the top of the Jebel, which they reached undiscovered. They then pressed on across the plateau until they came under attack from some rebels entrenched among caves in a cliff known as the Aquabat al Dhafar; although held up, they inflicted severe punishment on the enemy without loss to themselves. While a platoon of the Muscat Regiment dug themselves in at the top of the Hijar track to establish a base for further operations, the SAS tried to work their way round the Aquabat al Dhafar. But the rebels had strengthened their positions, and as we were unwilling to commit the SAS to a full-scale frontal assault, a role for which they were not intended, we contented ourselves with strengthening our new base on the plateau, in the hope of demoralizing the enemy and encouraging him to divert troops there from other sections of the Jebel. At least we were firmly on the top.

Action flared again at the end of November around Tanuf, where some forty rebels suddenly launched a determined attack, supported by heavy mortars, on a company of the Northern Frontier Regiment and our troop of 5.5s. At first the defenders wavered, and almost broke, but they rallied under the spirited leadership of the Royal Marine NCOs, until the timely arrival of a troop of Life Guards racing up from Nizwa turned the scales. After a fierce battle, in which the machine guns of the Life Guards' Ferrets took a heavy toll, the enemy withdrew; but the NFR had four men wounded, and we lost two of our gunners when one of their shells failed to clear their sangar and burst on the lip.

On 1 December the SAS troops in that area took the offensive. Eager to avenge their dead NCO and acting on the information they had gleaned on that unlucky patrol, they attacked one of the caves held by the rebels and, supported by a strike of Venoms, killed a number of the occupants; they claimed to have killed eight of them, but subsequent interrogation of prisoners revealed that only two had been killed and three wounded. All the same, it was a useful action, which raised their spirits as much as it must have depressed the enemy.

This morale-boosting action was led by a young troop commander, Captain Peter de la Billière, later, of course, to become the Regiment's commanding officer:

On the night of 30 November we set off at 1930 with two full troops: my own, 18 Troop, was to carry out the assault, and 19 Troop was to give us cover from a higher outcrop. Tanky Smith was carrying the main part of his .30 Browning (his partner Curly Hewitt carried the tripod for it, and hence was known as "Legs"). We were all heavily laden with water bottles, extra ammunition for our SLR rifles and rockets for the 3.5-inch launcher.

It was a dark night, with little moon, but enough ambient light for us to pick out salient features. The ascent was uneventful but tough: to be sure of reaching our assault position in the dark, we had to press on hard, but at the same time make no sound. Even with commando boots this was difficult, for as the rubber soles wore down – which they did at an astonishing rate – the screws securing them grated on rock. After a while the troops separated, each heading for its own objective. Steep escarpments delayed our advance. Several times I feared we had lost our way. The moon went down, leaving us in deeper darkness. But by 0530 we had reached what seemed to me the right place, so I sent a couple of men forward to make sure that the position was the best available. A few minutes later they came back, affirming that all was well. I crept forward and placed every man, spaced out in a line, with a party to guard our rear.

The ground was ideal for our purpose, with plenty of big rocks to give cover. All we had to do was wait. Having sweated pints on the way up, we now began to shudder in the icy pre-dawn air. I pulled on the thin jersey which was all I had in the way of extra clothes, and still kept shivering. The sky started to lighten. We were facing north, so that dawn stole up on our right. I thought about Tanky, somewhere above us, and hoped that the strike by Venom fighter-bombers, which I had laid on with the RAF, would come in on time.

As the light strengthened, I was disconcerted to find that we were farther from the caves than I had hoped. The distance which during our reconnaissance I had reckoned as two hundred yards turned out to be three hundred, the limit of accurate fire for our weapons. Still, we could not move. The sky paled. Light stole on to the mountain. Now at last I could see the black mouth of the main cave, with smaller openings beside it. The air was absolutely still. The cold bit more fiercely than ever. My watch said 0610 . . . 0615 . . . 0620. At last a white-robed figure appeared in the cave-mouth. The Arab looked round, yawned and stretched. When he spat, we heard him as clearly as if we had been in the same room. He moved off to one side to urinate. Another man appeared, then another. I looked to right and left. Everyone was poised for action. The rocket launcher crew, Troopers Goodman and Bennett, were on their feet behind a rock with their weapon levelled. I waited until four or five Arabs were in view together, then at last gave the signal.

Pandemonium erupted. With a *whoosh* the first rocket flew straight into the cave. A flash lit up the entrance, and the boom of a heavy explosion came back at us. The rattle of our small-arms fire echoed harshly round the rock walls. Several Arabs fell, and for a few seconds we had things to ourselves. Then suddenly the whole mountain came to life as shots began to crack out from above us on both sides. What we had not realized was that other caves high in the rock faces were also inhabited. Far from bolting when taken by surprise, the *adoo* counter-attacked with commendable resilience.

The ricochets were prodigious: bullets whanged and whined in every direction, and chips of rock flew. All at once we were in trouble. Where were our Venoms? From high on our left came the comforting, heavy rattle of Tanky's Browning, firing in short bursts. Then I heard the roar of jets, and saw a pair of Venoms high overhead. I put up a Very light to indicate the enemy, and within seconds the aircraft made their first run. Cannon-fire and rockets tore in, helping to keep the enemy's heads down.

With the advantage of surprise gone, the battle degenerated into a long-range sniping match, as both sides took snap shots at fleeting targets. With fire and movement, one group covering another, we pulled back. Still from above came the hammer of the Browning. So great was the noise, and so intense the fire, that when we reached a relatively safe position, over a ridge, I was amazed to find that we did not have a single casualty. Except for cuts caused by flying rock splinters, nobody was any the worse. By then we were short of ammunition, and in no state to run into an ambush. Once on to the big slab, we spread out well and hurried down, reaching base at 0800. After more than twelve hours on the go, everyone was exhausted; even so, we held an immediate wash-up, or debriefing, sitting in the sand, to make sure we recorded everything of importance while events were fresh in people's minds. Then we had some food and went to sleep.

The raid went down as a major success. Early reports indicated that we had killed twenty of the enemy, including the rebels' chief expert on the .5 machine gun. Later it seemed that the number of dead may have been exaggerated; even if it was, the attack gave the enemy's morale a jolt. We had taken them by surprise in one of their strongholds, an area which until then they had thought impregnable, and we had given them an unpleasant glimpse of what we could do.

David Smiley takes up the story of what happened next in the battle of Jebel Akhdar:

In the ensuing weeks we strengthened our positions on the other side of the Jebel. At the end of December the Trucial Oman Scouts put a squadron into the village of Hijar, out of which they maintained two troops at our new base on the top, to reinforce the existing garrison of the Muscat Regiment and SAS. A platoon from the Northern Frontier Regiment joined them, and to provide additional fire-power a dismounted party of twenty Life Guards under a Corporal of Horse carried up eight of their Browning machine guns. We never ceased to bless the authorities for giving us these Life Guards; they really entered into the spirit of our war and, when not engaged in a protective role with their Ferrets, were happy to turn themselves into infantry and carry out arduous and dangerous duties up the mountain.

The SAS now felt they had sufficient support to mount a strong night attack on the Aquabat al Dhafar. They excelled in night operations, and under a protective barrage from the Life Guards' Brownings and the heavy mortars of the Muscat Regiment, they scaled the steep cliffs with ropes and came to close quarters with the rebels in their caves. A wild *mêlée* ensued in the darkness, with bullets, grenades and insults flying between the combatants, but the rebels fought back stubbornly and held their ground until we called off the attack. Although once again they had inflicted casualties without loss to themselves, the SAS emerged from the battle with an even greater respect for the enemy. Although our situation was immeasurably better than in the summer, we were still a long way from victory. John Watts and I agreed that our chances of storming the Jebel with a single squadron of SAS were pretty slim, but that with a second squadron we could be reasonably certain of pulling it off. We therefore sent a signal to Deane-Drummond asking if he was prepared to let us have another squadron; he not only agreed but added that he would come himself with a small headquarters to take over command of both squadrons. Our next problem was to secure the approval of the War Office and the FO. We put our case to the Political Resident on one of his visits to Muscat, and obtained his promise to forward it to the Foreign Office; and in Aden the military authorities agreed to back us with the War Office. With all this support we won our clearance but, needless to say, the FO modified it with a proviso of their own: all British troops must be out of Muscat by the first week in April. The significance of this deadline, apparently, was that the United Nations were to discuss the Middle East situation soon afterwards, with Oman featuring large on the agenda; British diplomacy must not be embarrassed by the presence there of British troops.

Deane-Drummond arrived on New Year's Day, 1959. Our first decision was to set up a joint headquarters to coordinate the operations of the Sultan's Armed Forces, the SAS and the Royal Air Force, and we co-opted a senior RAF officer from Bahrain to serve as our Air Liaison Officer. We installed this "Tac HQ", as we called it, in the Northern Frontier Regiment's Camp near Nizwa, and I moved there from Beit al Falaj on 9 January with John Goddard and a small staff.

My next problem was the chain of command. Officially all British troops serving inside the country came under my orders, and hitherto my second-in-command had been Colin Maxwell. But Deane-Drummond had to be in a position where he could give orders to his own troops, and so, to avoid complications, I appointed him my Deputy Commander. From anyone less generous-hearted and unselfish than

Maxwell this arrangement might have aroused strong resentment, but he accepted my decision with his usual amiability, well understanding the reasons behind it.

On 12 January A Squadron, 22 SAS Regiment, flew in from Malaya under Major John Cooper, one of the longest-serving officers in the SAS. As a corporal, Cooper had been David Stirling's driver in the Western Desert in the earliest days of the regiment, and had taken part in some of its bloodiest actions in Sicily, Italy and France. Dark and thin, with strong, expressive features and a quick though shortlived temper, he was a brilliant soldier whose thirst for adventure and danger was to bring him under my command again in the Yemen.

We sent the new arrivals to relieve D Squadron, who came back to Beit al Falaj for a few days of rest and refit; the special SAS boots had lasted only a few days on the sharp rocks of the Jebel – to the incredulous dismay of the experts in the Quartermaster General's department who had designed them – and so we replaced them with hockey boots, which were much more satisfactory. Fresh from the heat of Malaya, A Squadron needed time to adjust to conditions on the Aquabat al Dhafar, where it had turned very cold, with hail storms and even snow; water bottles froze at night and fires were a necessity, even at the risk of snipers' bullets; although, in fact, both sides took this risk and nobody ever shot at the fires.

Because of the imposition by the Foreign Office of an April deadline we had about three months in which to assault the Jebel. We had agreed that the attack must be launched at night and during a period of full moon – it would be impracticable in total darkness; the full-moon period came at the end of each of the next three months, which meant that the last weeks in January, February and March were the vital ones. We would make our first attempt at the end of January, which would give us two more chances if we failed. We must therefore plan on a very tight schedule, for we had a bare three weeks before our first attempt in which to move all troops to their take-off positions, organize their reinforcement and supply, redeploy our garrisons, find reliable guides and coordinate the support of loyal tribal irregulars – in close consultation, of course, with Sayid Tarik.

At the same time I was faced with a difficult problem in diplomacy. The OC Northern Frontier Regiment, a British Seconded Officer, had an unfortunate habit of quarrelling with everyone with whom he came in contact. Already his Contract Officers had formed up to me, one after the other, to tell me they would "soldier no more" under him; I had to transfer them and replace them with seconded officers, which meant there were no Arabic-speaking officers in the regiment.

Next he alienated the Life Guards at Nizwa, giving them orders which he was not empowered to give them but which, presented with even a minimum of tact, they would almost certainly have accepted; it is only fair to add that, in return, the Life Guards officers baited him unmercifully. The consequence for me was that I had to spend precious time smoothing ruffled feelings as well as preparing for war. The primary object in all our planning was to gain a foothold as quickly as possible on the top of the Jebel, near the rebel headquarters, and hold it for the reception of air supply drops and as a firm base for further operations. Surprise was obviously essential in order to avoid the heavy casualties that we must expect if the assault were opposed.

The Aquabat al Dhafar was too far away from the main rebel strongholds of Habib, Saiq and Sharaijah, and in any case the enemy was already well entrenched on the Aquabat, where he was expecting us to attack; we must encourage him in that expectation and hope he would concentrate the main body of his forces on the northern side of the plateau. On the other hand the shortest approaches to the rebel villages, the tracks leading from Tanuf and Kamah, were known to be guarded. Deane-Drummond and I made several flights over the Jebel, cruising slowly just above the ground and scanning the smooth faces of rock to find a route that men and donkeys could climb. At length Deane-Drummond made his choice, a sloping buttress thrusting out above the Wadi Kamah on its eastern side. We sketched it, mapped it, studied photographs of it, and imprinted every detail of it on our minds; there appeared to be no track, but the slope looked feasible for the pack animals except in one place – a sharp ridge connecting the two main features – where we hoped the Sappers would be able to improve the going.

This approach had two main advantages: first, it was unguarded, so far as we could see, and it was most unlikely the enemy would expect an attack by such a route; secondly, our men could climb it in one night – in about 9½ hours by our reckoning – and so by dawn the leading troops could be in position on the top, where they could receive supplies by air.

Following standard Army practice, we gave a codename to each of the tactical features on the way up. Our principal objective, the top of the Jebel, we christened "Beercan"; the first prominent peak on the approach to it became "Pyramid", while the sharp ridge connecting the two, which we had already noticed from the air, received the name of "Causeway". There was a lesser crest about a third of the way up to Pyramid, which we called "Vincent", and our final objective, a peak beyond Beercan overlooking the village of Habib, went down in our operations plan as "Colin".

The two SAS squadrons would lead the assault, for I had received strict instructions from Aden that all other troops – Life Guards, Trucial Oman Scouts, and Sultan's Armed Forces – were to be used only in support of the SAS. These orders caused some natural disappointment to the Sultan's forces, who had tried for so long to reach the top, and who had in fact been the first to get there – when Tony Hart had taken his platoon of the Muscat Regiment up the Hijar track. However, they accepted the situation philosophically, especially as they themselves had important roles to play: first, they would make diversionary attacks before the main assault; secondly, they would follow closely upon the heels of the SAS and take over successive features as they were captured; and thirdly, they would consolidate the top of the Jebel and hold it against attack while the SAS pressed forward.

"Once we're on the top," I told Deane-Drummond, "and the aircraft have made their supply drops, we'll have to play things off the cuff. It'll depend on a lot of factors we can't foresee at this stage, such as the rebels' reaction and the whereabouts of their leaders. Remember, from our point of view – that is, from the Sultan's – the capture of Talib, Ghalib and Suleiman is very nearly as important as the capture of Beercan."

We agreed that if there was no serious opposition Deane-Drummond would push his patrols on to Habib, Saiq and Sharaijah, while our supporting troops cleared the enemy from the Kamah track and opened it up for the donkey columns.

We planned to launch our attack on the night of 25 January, at the beginning of the full-moon period, which would allow us to postpone the operation if the weather forecasts were unfavourable. It was vital for us to have at least twenty-four hours of good weather following the assault, to allow the RAF to drop their containers accurately; otherwise the leading troops would arrive on the plateau short of food, water and ammunition, for we couldn't expect the donkeys to get there in time. Talib must by now have realized that an attack was imminent, but he had no idea from which direction it would come. In order to confuse him we mounted a series of diversions in the weeks before 25 January in different parts of the Jebel. Between 8 and 22 January D Squadron of the SAS and A Company of the Northern Frontier Regiment carried out offensive patrols from Tanuf, and drove the rebels from some high ground they were using as an observation post. From 18–22 January A Squadron of the SAS, supported by the squadron of Trucial Oman Scouts, made probing attacks against the Aquabat al Dhafar; but on the night of 23 January A Squadron disengaged all but one of its troops and, after a forced march across the mountain, came down to join D Squadron near Tanuf. The following night A Company of the Northern Frontier Regiment engaged the enemy again near Tanuf, while C Company put in an attack from Izki. On every occasion we met strong opposition – C Company had a particularly hard time, losing one soldier killed and several wounded – which showed us the enemy was reacting as we hoped.

But the most brilliant, and one of the most successful of our deceptions involved no fighting at all. "I'm prepared to bet," said Malcolm Dennison, my Intelligence Officer, "that if we call leaders of the donkey men together on the night before the assault, and tell them in strictest confidence and under the most ferocious penalties that the following night they'll be leading their donkeys up the Tanuf track, Talib will have the news within twenty-four hours." In fact, we learned afterwards, Talib received the news in twelve hours. Our plan of attack was necessarily simple, even primitive.

The operation was essentially a straight slog up the mountain face, and everything would depend on whether we achieved surprise; even when we postponed it for twenty-four hours because of a poor weather forecast – a wise decision, as it turned out – there was no need to alter the details. There were to be three phases: in the first, A Squadron of the SAS would capture Vincent, and D Squadron would occupy Pyramid, Beercan and Colin before first light. In the second, C Company of the Northern Frontier Regiment would relieve A Squadron on Vincent, while the dismounted troop of Life Guards took over Pyramid; and lastly, A Squadron would consolidate their position on Beercan and D Squadron on Colin.

Two groups of irregulars would be taking part: on the southern side fifty Beni Ruawha tribesmen under Major John Clarke, a Sultan's Contract Officer, would accompany the SAS squadrons, while a force of 200 Abryeen and a platoon of the Muscat Regiment, under the command of Jasper Coates, would create a diversion in the north and, if unopposed, would climb the Jebel by two tracks leading from Awabi. These two tribes were hereditary enemies of Suleiman and his Beni Riyam, and welcomed a chance to pay off old scores; the Abryeen, in particular, needed to restore their honour after their failure the previous summer to protect the lines of communication with the Muscat and Oman Field Force.

There would be air support the following morning: Venoms from Sharjah would strafe any pockets of resistance, while three Valettas from Bahrain would make a total of nine container drops on Beercan. We also had two helicopters ready at Nizwa to evacuate casualties to our field hospital there. If the weather was still bad we should be absolutely dependent for supplies on the donkey columns; the prospect worried me and my only consolation was that we had a few Omani jebel donkeys to supplement the poor little Somalis.

Such was the preparation for the assault on the Jebel Akhdar. The course of actual events, in all their intricacies, can be seen in the report of Major J. S. Spreule:

D-Day 26 January, 1959. Both squadrons were in camp at Tanuf. Donkeys and handlers brought from the Aqabat under an animal transport officer provided by the Trucial Oman Scouts were at Tanuf. All ranks were briefed by Colonel Deane-Drummond in the morning. The donkeys left at 1000 hours to walk to the donkey assembly area at Kamah Camp.

Both squadrons left Tanuf in transport and arrived at Kamah after last light at 1930 hours. Troops debussed in the assembly area where there was half an hour's wait for the moon to rise. The squadrons then re-embussed and were driven to the start line. The start line was crossed as planned at 2030 hours. Owing to a strike by donkey handlers, the F echelon donkeys, which were to follow A Squadron and precede the Commander's HQ party, failed to arrive at the appointed time. These 25 donkeys, 10 for each squadron and 5 for HQ, were to carry the squadrons' Browning machine guns and ammunition and HQ's wirelesses. The donkeys eventually followed 15 minutes behind the Commander's party. At 2030 hours the diversionary attack by 4 Troop was put in. This could be heard by the assaulting troops. The climb was without incident, but the going was harder than expected. A few unfit or overladen soldiers were left behind to make their own way, while the squadrons pushed on.

27 January. By 0500 hours 27 January, progress had been slower than expected. A Squadron was in position on Vincent, but D Squadron had one troop on Pyramid and three troops bunched round the point where it was thought a track began to lead to Beercan. It was vital to reach the top – Beercan – by first light and so D Squadron commander made two troops leave all their extra loads behind and push on. They reached Beercan at approx 0630 hours. By 0645 hours the first of the Valletas began the resupply drop . . . The troops were too exhausted after 10 hours' almost continuous climbing to do more than collect sufficient ammunition to hold off an expected counter-attack. At 0700 hours they were joined by the Commander's party carrying equipment, with an Air Liaison Officer and ground-to-air radio. The third troop was left to deal with a rebel .5 machine-gun team, which they did by 0630 hours. They then moved up the ridge, arriving at 0800 hours. The .5 machine gun was in a perfect position commanding all approaches. Had it been manned, the outcome might have been very different. During the morning snipers in caves to the east put up desultory fire at troops on the machine-gun position and on troops moving to Beercan. These snipers were attacked by Venoms and were not eventually silenced until about 1430 hours after holding up the leading troop of A Squadron, which reached Beercan by midday. A grenade, exploded by a chance shot, wounded Troopers Carter, Hamer and Bembridge. Carter and Bembridge later died of their wounds. By 1500 hours the last troop of D Squadron on Pyramid was relieved by the Life Guards and rejoined its squadron at 1630 hours. At 2130 D Squadron moved to occupy a feature overlooking the Kamah Wadi, leaving A Squadron to hold Beercan. The Commander went with D Squadron and later returned to Beercan. A Squadron sent a troop reconnaissance patrol out at last light to the village of Habib. In the event it went to an unmarked village on the far side of Nantos because of an inaccuracy of the map. Going was difficult and the village was reported deserted.

28 January. D Squadron took an airdrop and later pushed forward to a feature overlooking Kamah Wadi. A Squadron collected previous airdrops and accepted further drops.

Offensive air support against rebels throughout the day . . . a 62-set was manpacked from Pyramid and with this the Forward Observation Officer was able to range the guns. A request was made to begin psychological warfare. 15 Tribals arrived and spent the night on Beercan. On the night 28/29 January D Squadron with Squadron HQ and two troops occupied a feature which overlooked the village of Habib. The same night, half A Squadron occupied a feature called Nantos, 1,500 yards in front of Beercan.

29 January. D Squadron now had positions overlooking the Kamah Wadi and Habib. They took an airdrop at 1100 hours. Half A Squadron was on Nantos, the other half on Beercan. Colonel Deane-Drummond with his HQ accompanied a patrol of D Squadron which together with 15 Tribals entered Habib at 1200 hours. The village was deserted and had been damaged by bombing. A Squadron troops on Nantos detained 38 Arabs including women and children. They were sent under escort to Beercan for interrogation where a PW compound was set up.

30 January. Colonel Smiley and Said Tariq, Wali of Nazwa, landed at Beercan by helicopter and spoke to prisoners, who were later released. Half of A Squadron joined half of D Squadron, and together they occupied the village of Saiq. Later HQ was helicoptered to Saiq, which was deserted. A number of prisoners were taken and Suleiman's cave was located and searched. Vast quantities of documents and a substantial number of weapons were collected. A further supply drop took place at Saiq. Some prisoners were taken at Sharaijah, and a number of Talib's manacled prisoners released.

31 January. One troop of D Squadron was left at Saiq, two troops of A Squadron, one troop of D Squadron, Squadron HQ and the Commander's Tactical HQ moved to Sharaijah. All resistance on the Djebel had ceased, except for a few minor pockets on the south slopes. These were dealt with by SAS and Sultan's Armed Forces. SAS troops started work on landing strip between Saiq and Sharaijah. A report was received that Talib and Suleiman were in the Wadi Salut area with their families. A party of A and D SAS troops from Sharaijah searched south and a composite patrol from HQ searched north from Mi'aidin. The search was fruitless and was abandoned on 1 February.

The SAS had done what no other military force had done in 1,000 years; it had captured the Jebel Akhdar. More than that, the Jebel Akhdar assault had secured the future of the SAS. As Peter de la Billière wrote, Oman was a turning point in the history of the SAS:

> We had shown that we were a flexible force capable of adapting quickly to new conditions. We had demonstrated that a small number of men could be flown into a trouble spot rapidly and discreetly, and operate in a remote area without publicity – a capability much valued by the Conservative Government of the day. Above all, we had proved that the quality of the people in the SAS was high indeed, and that a few men of such calibre could achieve results out of all proportion to their numbers.

FROM THE ARCHIVES: *TOMBOLA*

SAS, Italy, 1945

The most effective actions of the SAS in the twilight of the Italian campaign in World War II tended to be those jointly undertaken with the partisans, as with 3 Squadron's *Tombola* operation. Newly raised, mainly from volunteers from the 1st and 6th Airborne Divisions, 3 Squadron was commanded by Major Roy Farran. The idea behind *Tombola* was to insert a well-equipped SAS party into the enemy-held province of Emilia-Romagna, where it would cooperate with partisan brigades ("Commando Unico") in operations against the German defensive position to the south known as the Gothic Line. The centrepiece of *Tombola* was an attack on the German corps headquarters at Albinea in the Po Valley. Farran – going under the *nom de guerre* of Major McGinty – was specifically ordered not to accompany 3 Squadron's drop into Emilia-Romagna, but "accidentally" parachuted down with the advance party on 4 March 1945. Meeting the party was Mike Lees, the British SOE liaison officer who subsequently helped Farran birth the "Battaglione Alleata", a mixed partisan and SAS combat group comprising twenty-five SAS, thirty Russian POWs and forty largely Communist partisans under Farran's command. Few of the partisans had any military experience, but two weeks of intensive training by the SAS welded them into a decently effective force. Shrewdly, Farran gave the partisans a distinctive green and yellow feather hackle to wear in their beret, and allowed them to embroider the SAS motto "Who Dares Wins" on their pockets in Italian. (Farran wrote later, "I regret to say that the British often parodied this motto ['*Chi osera ci vincera*'] to read, 'Who cares who wins'.") On the approach to corps headquarters, Farran received a wireless message telling him to call off the attack. He decided to ignore the order, on the basis that the SAS contingent would lose all credibility with the partisans if the attack was cancelled. After lying up at a farm about ten miles from the objective, Farran led the "Battaglione Alleato" towards the corps headquarters, which consisted of the Villa Rossi, the commander's house, and the Villa Calvi, the chief of staff's house, and a number of billets:

The moon glowed palely through the banks of mist. I had not realized we were so close to the limit of the mountains and it was with something of a shock that, at the top of a grassy rise, I suddenly saw the Lombardy plain laid out beneath us. The hills ended so abruptly, and beyond all was dark and flat except for the silver Po that shone in the moon and the pinpoint dots of light that marked farms and villages below. It all seemed so close, and only Albinea, presumably at our very feet, showed no lights. All around us the night was silent.

It seemed so improbable that soon we were to break it with the din of battle. As I slid softly down the hill into the black abyss I looked back once. The long file was silhouetted on the skyline against the background of mist and moon, and their figures were elongated like distant bushes in a desert heat. My Italian guide whispered goodbye and crept off into the night. The main road, he pointed, lay only a few yards ahead. The columns stayed motionless in the wet grass while our scouts went ahead to find it. They tiptoed back, crouching despite the cover of darkness. It was twenty yards in front and there were no signs of the enemy. We moved slowly forward into the ditch and lay still again. I told the columns to fan out on either side of me, but to be careful not to get mixed in their ranks. We would re-form on the other side. Then we scurried across the exposed hardtop and crawled under a thick hedge on the north side, scratching our faces and rattling our weapons alarmingly as we wriggled through. I lay in the grass beside Kirkpatrick, the piper, Morbin and my faithful Bruno, awaiting the message that all our hundred men were safely over the road. In an amazingly short time the word came back. All were with me, even the Russians, ready in their columns to move forward again. A small Italian farmhouse gleamed white in the moon and I recognized it from the air photograph. Now the responsibility for navigation was mine alone and a single mistake might lead us to disaster. I took a north bearing on my compass and began to count my steps. The columns closed up tight behind me, each man less than an arm's length from the next, and we crept stealthily forward. I tested almost every footstep before putting down my weight and paused frequently to listen for danger. A dog barked in the farm and my heart leapt. We made a detour to avoid two more buildings, neither of which I remembered from the photographs. I heard a truck pass along the road we had crossed and I threw myself flat. The others dropped to the ground behind me and we lay still for several minutes before daring to move again.

We came to a ploughed field where the going was heavy and I was terrified the sentries would hear the rattle of our equipment. Twice I stumbled into a wet ditch, stepping into it unawares in the dark. And once I heard a German shout. Then, as my count of paces told me that the time had come to swing east, I caught my parachute jacket in some barbed wire and shook the whole fence as I broke free. Still no sound, and the men were incredibly quiet behind me. It had taken more than an hour to cover a few hundred yards. We were on the objective before I was ready. Suddenly I found myself on the edge of the crescent-shaped wood that lay at the foot of Villa Calvi – the villa which contained the staff-officers and their operations room. I had not expected it so soon, but my navigation was accurate. Our force of a hundred men had penetrated the German headquarters undetected.

The time for action had come, but, since my excitement had been gradually mounting to a crescendo ever since we crossed the road, words seemed to stick in my throat. My mouth was dry and when I did manage to speak the words came in whispered gushes. I sent a runner back to find the Russians, to tell Modena to form his protective screen to the south. Above the half-moon wood I could see the white walls

of Villa Calvi on the top of a small hill. No lights were showing and I vaguely wondered whether we had been misled,
whether the villas were really occupied by Germans. The
British columns stood around me in the dark, but somehow
the Russians had become separated. The air was heavy and
still. Not a single sound disturbed the night – no dogs barked
now, no wind disturbed the trees in the woods, and the men
held themselves tense, ready for my word to advance. The
runner came back. He was so quiet that he was by my side
before I knew he had returned. He had failed to find Modena
and the Russians. I could only assume that without waiting
for orders Modena had already led his men into position. He
must have branched off from the moment I changed direction to the east. We could delay no longer. At any time now
the Russians might alert the sentries and surprise would be
lost.

I called for Riccomini and told him to start. I would allow
him only three minutes before I let Harvey attack Villa Calvi
in front of us, so it was important that he move fast. He was
to remember that the main German strength lay to the south.

That was the direction from which enemy machine guns
would probably fire. After twenty minutes, whether his attack
was successful or not, he was to withdraw back to the mountains. If I fired a red Very light before that, he was to withdraw
anyway.

I watched him go, hoping as I did so that he was not
infected by my obvious fear, by the difficulty I had in speaking. Lees lumbered by his side, a big hulk of a man in the
darkness. Behind him came the ten British and the Goufa
Nera led by Bruno and they disappeared into the darkness
towards Villa Rossi, their weapons carried at the ready.

The black silence was almost forbidding and I shivered
from both cold and excitement as I cocked my carbine. I led
Harvey to the edge of the wood, below the hill that led up to
Villa Calvi. One of the Garibaldini pointed to the wire fence
that surrounded the trees and crossed a narrow path leading
up the bank to the lawns around the villa. Nailed to a tree
behind it was a sign in red letters – "*Achtung – Minen.*" There

was no time to make a detour. The three minutes was up. But Ken Harvey did not falter. He swung through the fence and the British swarmed up the path behind him. Yani and his Garibaldini hesitated, but I pushed them from behind, forcing them to follow the British up the bank to the villa. The minefield was obviously non-existent, a bluff.

I began to move over to my allotted position on the road. The others had lost me somehow in the darkness, but Kirkpatrick, the Highland Light Infantry piper, was still by my side. I walked into a slit-trench and lost my carbine, but Kirkpatrick retrieved it. Then, as I was still recovering from the shock of my fall, the fighting began. The silence was broken by a tremendous burst of fire from Villa Calvi above. It sounded like a whole Bren magazine fired without pause and, as much as if it were a signal for which both Germans and ourselves had been waiting, it triggered automatic fire from every direction – from the enemy billets to the south, from Villa Rossi and from Villa Calvi. The night was shattered by the rattle of machine guns. I heard the harsh rasp of a spandau and knew the Germans were firing back. Bullets whistled over our heads as if the Germans could see us, which was impossible. All along the line to the south Modena's men maintained continuous fire and I saw tracers bouncing off the white walls of the guardhouse. A siren wailed from the direction of Villa Rossi. That was unfortunate because it meant the alarm had been sounded there before Riccomini entered his target. Even mortars added their thuds to the general racket and, between the rattle of small-arms fire at Villa Calvi above, I heard the thump of a bazooka.

Having loosed off the attack, I had no more control and I could only sit with Kirkpatrick and wait. I told him to play "Highland Laddie", just to let the enemy know they had more than a mere partisan attack with which to contend. The British at Calvi cheered when they heard the defiant skirl of the pipes. Our job was to cause panic and confusion and, even if we failed to clinch our attack, this had already been achieved. An enemy spandau singled us out and the bullets whizzed uncomfortably close. I pushed Kirkpatrick into a convenient slit-trench and he continued to play from a sitting position. I wondered whether I should join Harvey at Villa Calvi, but decided against it. Someone had to stay in the middle to fire the signal for withdrawal. So, while Kirkpatrick played his pipes, I sat beside him amidst the bullets, cursing myself for not having restrained Harvey a few minutes longer.

Only later, when we were on our way back to the mountains, did I piece together what had happened. The British at Calvi crept up the bank to the edge of the lawn. Four German sentries were standing on a gravel drive in front of the villa. There was no time for finesse, so Harvey shot them down with his Bren and that initial burst of machine-gun fire which awakened the whole headquarters carried death to these sentries. Then the British charged across the lawns to the house, covered by the Garibaldini who fired into the windows. The front door was locked and several minutes elapsed before the British shot it in with a bazooka. By then Harvey and Sergeant Godwin had entered through ground-floor windows and were fighting Germans in the operations room. Bursting into one ground-floor room, Harvey was confronted by a German with a Schmeisser sub-machine gun. He ducked but forgot to extinguish his flashlight. Fortunately, Sergeant Godwin, who was close on his heels, fired over his shoulder and killed the German in time. Four other Germans, including the staff colonel, were killed on the ground floor, as were two other sentries in the outhouses. But the remainder fought back down a spiral staircase that led to the upper storey. Several unsuccessful attempts were made to climb this stairway but failed in the face of intense enemy fire. The Germans were able to cover the first landing from behind balustrades and could not be seen from below. In one of these attempts Parachutist Mulvey was wounded in the knee. Then the Germans began to roll grenades down the stairs, one of them wounding Corporal Layburn. Harvey decided to raze the villa. It was impossible to take the house in the twenty minutes allowed. Working frantically against time, the British piled maps, papers, files and office furniture into a heap in the middle of the operations room. Then, with the assistance of a little explosive and some petrol found in one of the outhouses, they started the fire. Our men kept the Germans confined to the top floor, shooting up the stairs and through the windows outside, until the flames had taken good hold. After firing the rest of their bazooka bombs and most of their ammunition through the windows, they withdrew from the grounds, carrying their wounded with them. The story at Villa Rossi was similar except that there, because firing broke out at Villa Calvi first, our raiders did not have full advantage of surprise. Riccomini's men were still in the ditch beside the road when the fighting began at Villa Calvi. They had used more caution in their approach than time allowed and were still outside the grounds when sirens sounded from the roof of their villa. Realizing that surprise was lost, the British shot the three sentries in the grounds, firing through iron railings that surrounded the lawn. Then they charged the house, cheering as they heard Kirkpatrick's pipes. Several more Germans were killed in outlying buildings and most of the thirty raiders – British and Goufa Nera – crashed through the windows into the house. In the ground-floor rooms, more Germans were encountered, two of whom surrendered. These two prisoners were locked in an outhouse and presumably lived to tell the tale. As at Villa Calvi, a furious battle took place for the upper floor. The British led attack after attack up the spiral stairway, but were always repulsed when they ran into merciless fire on the landing. Mike Lees led one attack and was severely wounded, as was Bruno, the Goufa Nera leader. Riccomini and Sergeant Guscott tried again and almost reached the top, but, there on the second landing, Riccomini met his death. He was shot through the head and died instantly. Sergeant Guscott dragged his body down. Then, angry at the loss of his leader, Sergeant Guscott led another attempt. While shouting from the landing, urging the others to follow him, he too was mortally wounded and died there on the staircase. Both had volunteered for Operation *Tombola* although entitled to a rest after the operations north of Spezia. Both met their end at Villa Rossi.

Then the Germans, heartened by their success, attempted
to come down the stairs. A hail of fire greeted them at the
bottom and three more Germans died with Riccomini and
Guscott on the staircase. Kershaw, Green and Taylor decided
to light a fire in the kitchen. They poured petrol on the walls,
heaped up curtains and bedding from the other rooms and
started the blaze. Sergeant Hughes and Ramos, one of our
Spaniards, carried the wounded outside. Meanwhile I waited
nervously, wondering whether to fire the signal for withdrawal. The planned twenty minutes had long expired and I
saw flames licking around the roofs of both villas, especially
at Villa Calvi. German return fire was becoming more intense
and mortar bombs crashed into the trees of the half-moon
wood at the foot of Villa Calvi. A few Italian and Russian
stragglers had already joined me, and I knew that soon
trucked reinforcements would be arriving in Albinea from
other German-occupied villages nearby. The time had come
for retreat if we were ever to return safely to our mountain
base. I pointed my Very pistol at the sky and fired three red
signal flares. Immediately the alert spandau to the south
sprayed bullets all around me, sending the Italians scuttling
for cover.

I waited until all the British, at least, had rallied around me.
They came down from Calvi in twos and threes, jubilant at
their success. Corporal Layburn and Mulvey, the two
wounded, hopped between them, supported by a man on
each side. Those from Villa Rossi were less triumphant. They
told me how Riccomini and Guscott had died and that Mike
Lees was being carried on a ladder to safety by Burke and
Ramos. And the Goufa Nera, they said, were also carrying
Bruno, their leader. I waited as long as I dared, but Burke, a
red-headed Irishman, and Ramos never arrived with Lees. In
fact, they carried him on a ladder for four days and, by some
miracle, escaped capture by the hundreds of Germans who
scoured the area after our raid. Considering that Lees, who
was seriously wounded, weighed at least two hundred and
fifty pounds, it was a tremendous feat. Both were awarded the
Military Medal after they carried him to a safe hiding-place

in the mountains. Bruno also evaded capture, and a few days later I arranged for a light aircraft to evacuate him and Lees to Florence. Burke and Ramos later rejoined us at Tapignola. The sky was red from the blazing villas as we straggled west to the River Crostollo. We glanced occasionally over our shoulders at the burning headquarters and at the star shells now being fired over the area by the guns from Pianello. It was a satisfying sight. If only we could regain the safety of the mountain, the raid could be marked up as at least a partial success.

Though our withdrawal was far from organized, by astonishing good fortune most of the scattered parties managed to link together on the banks of the Crostollo. Our progress was slow, since neither Layburn nor Mulvey were capable of walking, and I was desperately anxious to cross the main road before dawn. I led them across the river and then cut south towards the hills. We were extremely tired, but there was no hope of rest for many hours. It was already getting lighter. German trucks drove helter-skelter along the road and once we hid for several minutes when we heard the rumble of tank tracks. Only Green's alertness in spotting a German unit sign saved us from walking into an anti-aircraft battery. Wearily we made yet another detour. Sounds of firing still came from Albinea and I could only guess that either some of the Russians were still in action or the Germans were shooting at themselves.

At last we crossed the road safely and began to climb into the hills. Obviously something had to be done about the wounded. Mulvey was in great pain and could go no farther, even with the help of the others. I took him into a farmhouse and, after laying him on the kitchen table, did my best to bandage up his shattered knee. The peasants promised to hide him until the fuss died down and then to bring him up in an ox-cart to our mountain base. I did not like leaving him, but there was no alternative. And Mulvey himself, well aware that he risked capture, begged me to hurry away while there was still time. I gave the Italians some money and promised more after safe delivery of our comrade. Layburn could limp along with the help of two others and, with some misgivings, I allowed him to accompany us as long as he could. In the event, the Italian peasants were as good as their word and delivered Mulvey safely to the mountains. The farm was searched, but the Germans did not find him.

It was broad daylight by the time we reached Casa Del Lupo. The poor *padrone* was very frightened after the excitement of the night and at last seemed to realize that we were not Germans. He begged us to go away as soon as possible. We did not need urging. After tying Corporal Layburn's wounds with a field dressing, I lashed him to an ancient horse we commandeered from the farmer. The horse was extremely decrepit and blind in both eyes, but it served the purpose. Layburn was much more badly hit than I had imagined. He had multiple grenade wounds in both legs and it was remarkable how he had managed to struggle along so far. I tied him tightly to the saddle with his wounded legs hanging limply by the horse's side. Though those dangling legs, dripping blood most of the way, must have been extremely painful, he never once complained.

There could be no more halts now. According to peasants we met on the track, the countryside buzzed with Germans and we frequently skirted round danger areas. At first the mist was still thick, aiding our escape, but a light rain made the muddy path slippery underfoot. This time I did not doubt peasant rumours. We had to believe all reports of enemy patrols for it was illogical to assume they were not looking for us. We were too short of ammunition and our weapons had fallen too often in the mud for us to look for a fight.

The men were exhausted, but their morale was high. Only the loss of Ricky Riccomini and Guscott marred their good spirits. Incessantly, as we plodded through the mud, they recounted stories of their experiences during the raid. The best anecdote had it that one German officer at Villa Rossi was chased on to the lawn in his pyjamas. But as the day dragged on and I kept them marching without pause, fatigue began to tell and they trudged silently behind me, straggling raggedly down the track. I was probably more tired than most, for the old wounds in my legs ached and I doubt if I was in as good condition as the men. But I was more alive to danger than they were and knew that only a forced march across the Secchia would save us from capture.

The old horse frequently stumbled in the mud, throwing Layburn to the ground. Even on the best of going it was inclined to trip over the slightest obstacle, causing him to slip sideways in the saddle. When it finally collapsed, crushing Layburn beneath, we decided to abandon it. We made a rough stretcher from saplings and parachute blouses and four of us carried Layburn up and down the hills. I took my turn with the rest at this gruelling chore and soon we were all so tired that we could only reel blindly forward. Often, with the poles across our shoulders, we slipped to our knees in the mud.

Layburn volunteered to stay behind, but the men would not hear of it. Actually I thought I made better progress when I took my turn at the stretcher, for then the weight on my shoulders made me forget the aching in my legs. We marched mechanically now, tramping wearily in step with our heads down. If we had encountered any Germans, resistance would have been impossible. Our weapons were caked with mud and we were so tired that we were incapable of anything more than this monotonous trudging along the track. We marched without scouts, for no one had enough energy to climb to higher ground. Soon I even abandoned my earlier practice of skirting around danger points and we crossed the north–south highway without any attempt at concealment. We walked openly through a village, to the amazement of the inhabitants, and were still lucky enough not to meet any Germans.

I remembered that Mark Antony made his soldierly reputation not so much from feats of arms as from his endurance while retreating from Modena through this very country. But our own endurance was close to an end. Without bothering to discover if the German drive was still in process around Baiso, I followed the route by which we had come, up the steep slope to Vallestra. Still we were lucky, although homesteads on the way were strangely silent. I gathered later that the Germans passed through this area and aimed along a Baiso–Carpineti axis, by-passing Vallestra.

We managed to conjure up enough energy to stage a little show for the villagers of Vallestra. Forming columns of threes outside this village from which we had launched our raid, with Layburn leading the way on his stretcher, we marched through the streets to the music of Kirkpatrick's pipes. Women came to doorways and cheered us and little children ran beside the parade, but no men were to be seen. I hoped that the Germans in Baiso would hear the pipes and take them for defiance, for proof that we were safely beyond their reach.

The men tried to pick up their sore feet and to straighten their shoulders as if they, too, realized that more by luck than good judgement we had successfully passed through the German lines without making contact.

After Vallestra, where my immediate fears were at an end, my legs refused to respond to the demands I made on them. I lagged farther and farther behind the rest, even though it was now easy going downhill to the Secchia. Some of the men took mercy on me and found a horse on which I finished the last four miles to Cavola. I was so completely exhausted that I could not appreciate the tumultuous welcome given us by the Green Flames, who carried the men off to celebrate in various houses in the village. I know the mayor made some sort of speech, but I was more grateful for the bed of the local schoolmistress. She, of course, was not there, but even if she had been she would have been safe. I did not awaken for another fourteen hours. We had marched for twenty-two hours without pause and, excluding the eight-hour halt at Casa Del Lupo had been awake for more than two days. When all was reckoned, our raid cost us three British dead and three wounded, three Italian wounded, two Russians wounded and six Russians captured. At first we thought we had killed the German general at Villa Rossi, but apparently this was not so. However, we did kill Colonel Lemelsen, the chief of staff, and many other Germans. We destroyed the two main buildings in the headquarters together with many maps and papers. Above all, we made the enemy realize that he was not safe anywhere, no matter how far behind the front.

A court-martial of Farran, for twice disobeying orders during *Tombola*, failed after an intervention from Colonel Riepe, the US officer in command of clandestine operations in the 15th Army Group's bailiwick. Riepe signalled SAS Brigade: "Farran's gallant actions . . . have completely sold to American . . . the tremendous value of SAS operations." In fact, *Tombola* and the SAS campaign in Italy "sold" the SAS to many, since it proved that the Regiment could operate in any theatre, even the populated confines of Italy. One notable feature of *Tombola* and similar operations in Italy, was that junior non-commissioned officers and private soldiers were put in charge of partisan teams. "It was extraordinary," Farran wrote, "how successful the British common soldiers were as detachment commanders." In this respect *Tombola* and its counterparts anticipated 22 SAS operations in Oman in the 1960s, when the Regiment fought alongside tribal levies.

PRINCE'S GATE

22 SAS, Britain, 1980

Number 16 Prince's Gate, home of the Iranian Embassy, overlooks the peaceful green expanse of London's Kensington Gardens. At 11.25 a.m. on the morning of Wednesday 30 April 1980, this leafy tranquillity was rudely shattered as six men wearing shamags sprayed Number 16 with bullets and stormed through the front doors. The gunmen – Faisal, Hassan, Shai, Makki, Ali and Salim – were members of Mohieddin al Nasser Martyr Group, an Arab group seeking the liberation of Khuzestan from Ayatollah Khomeini's Iran. The siege of Prince's Gate had begun.

The police were on the scene almost immediately, alerted by an emergency signal by Trevor Lock, and were soon followed by Scotland Yard specialist units including C13, the anti-terrorist squad, and D11, the elite blue-beret marksmen. The building was surrounded, and Scotland Yard hastily began putting in motion its siege-negotiation machinery.

While no siege is ever the same as the one before or after it, most follow a definite pattern: in stage one, the authorities try to pacify the gunmen (usually with such provisions as cigarettes and food), and allow the release of ideological statements; in stage two, the hostage-takers drop their original demands and begin negotiating their own escape; stage three is the resolution. The Prince's Gate siege moved very quickly to stage one, with Salim, the head Arab gunman, announcing his demands over the telephone just after 2.35 p.m.: autonomy and human rights for the people of Khuzestan, and the release of ninety-one Arab prisoners held in Iranian jails. If his demands were not met he would blow up the Embassy, hostages and all, at noon the following day. Meanwhile, the SAS had been alerted about the siege within minutes of its start. Dusty Gray, an ex-SAS sergeant and now a Metropolitan Police dog handler, telephoned the Officers' Mess at Bradbury Lines, the SAS's HQ near to the River Wye in Hereford, and said that the SAS would probably be required at the Iranian Embassy, where gunmen had taken over. That night, SAS troopers from B Squadron left for London in Range Rovers, arriving at a holding area in Regent's Park Barracks in the early hours of Thursday morning. The official authority from the Minister of Defence approving the move of the SAS teams to London arrived at Bradbury Lines some hours after they had already left.

Over the next few days the Metropolitan Police continued their "softly, softly" negotiating approach, while trying to determine exactly how many hostages were in the Embassy and where they were located. Scotland Yard's technical squad, C7, installed microphones in the chimney and walls of Number 16, covering the noise by faking Gas Board repairs at neighbouring Ennismore Gardens. Gradually it became clear that there were about twenty-four hostages (as they discovered at the end of the siege, the exact count was twenty-six), most of them Iranian Embassy workers. Also hostage were PC Trevor Lock and two BBC sound engineers, Sim Harris and Chris Cramer. The latter, who became seriously ill with a stomach disorder, was released by the gunmen as an act of good faith. It was a bad mistake by the Arab revolutionaries: a debriefing of Cramer gave the SAS vital information about the situation inside the Embassy as they planned and trained in a new holding area only streets away from Prince's Gate itself. Inside the holding area a scale model of the Embassy had been constructed to familiarize the SAS troopers with the layout of the building they would assault if the police negotiations were to break down.

As the police negotiating team located in a forward base at Number 25 Prince's Gate (of all places, the Royal School of Needlework), the gunmen very quickly dropped their original demands. By late evening on the second day of the siege, the gunmen were requesting mediation of the siege by Arab ambassadors – and a safe passage out of the country. The British Government, under Margaret Thatcher, refused to countenance the request. To the anger of the gunmen, BBC radio news made no mention of their changed demands, the broadcast of which had been a concession agreed earlier in the day. Finally, the demands were transmitted – but the BBC got the details wrong.

For some tense moments on Saturday, the third day of the siege, it seemed as though the furious Salim would start shooting. The crisis was only averted when the police promised that the BBC would put out the demands accurately that evening. The nine o'clock news duly transmitted them as its first item. The gunmen were jubilant. As they congratulated themselves, however, an SAS reconnaissance team on the roof was discovering a way into Number 16 via an improperly locked skylight. Next door, at Number 18, the Ethiopian Embassy, bricks were being removed from the dividing wall, leaving only plaster for an assault team to break through.

On Sunday 4 May, it began to look as though all the SAS preparation would be for nothing. The tension inside the Embassy had palpably slackened, and the negotiations seemed to be getting somewhere. The gunmen's demands were lessening all the time. Arab ambassadors had agreed to attend a meeting of their COBRA committee in order to decide who would mediate in the siege.

And then, on the morning of Bank Holiday Monday, 5 May, the situation suddenly worsened. Just before dawn the gunmen woke the hostages in a frustrated and nervous state. Bizarrely, Salim, who thought he had heard noises in the night, sent PC Lock to scout the building to see whether it had been infiltrated. The hostages in Room 9 heard him report to Salim that there was nobody in the Embassy but themselves. Conversations between the gunmen indicated that they increasingly believed they had little chance of escape. At 11.00 a.m. Salim discovered an enormous bulge in the wall separating the Iranian Embassy from the Ethiopian Embassy.

Extremely agitated, he moved the male hostages into the telex room at the front of the building on the second floor. Forty minutes later, PC Lock and Sim Harris appeared on the first-floor balcony and informed the police negotiator that their captors would start killing hostages if news of the Arab mediators was not forthcoming immediately. The police played for time, saying that there would be an update on the midday BBC news. The bulletin, however, only served to anger Salim, announcing as it did that the meeting between COBRA and the Arab ambassadors had failed to agree on the question of who would mediate. Incensed, Salim grabbed the telephone link to the police and announced: "You have run out of time. There will be no more talking. Bring the ambassadors to the phone or I will kill a hostage in forty-five minutes."

Outside, in the police forward post, the minutes ticked away with no news from the COBRA meeting, the last negotiating chip of the police. Forty-two minutes, forty-three minutes . . . The telephone rang. It was Trevor Lock to say that the gunmen had taken a hostage, the Iranian Press Attaché, and were tying him to the stairs. They were going to kill him. Salim came to the phone shouting that the police had deceived him. At precisely 1.45 p.m. the distinct sound of three shots was heard from inside the Embassy.

The news of the shooting was immediately forwarded to the SAS teams waiting at their holding area. They would be used after all. Operation *Nimrod* – the relief of the Embassy – was on. The men checked and cleaned their weapons – 9mm Browning HP automatic pistols and Heckler & Koch ("Hockler") MP5A3 sub-machine guns. Frank Collins was one of the SAS assault team waiting in the holding area in the Royal School of Needlework. He recalled what happened next:

Instantly the room's full of movement. Not fast, panicky movement. It's quick but it's deliberate. People are grabbing their weapons, putting on their belts, fitting their respirators. Nobody runs out of the room but within seconds we're gone. Outside, the policemen who brought us the food press against the wall as we pass. Now they stare.

Everyone goes in their own direction, some upstairs, some down, some along this floor. I go up. There are twelve of us. As we climb the stairs they get narrower and more secret.

After one flight they aren't grand any more and after two there's no carpet. We reach the top. It's our first position. We're grouped right under the roof now and a sliding wooden ladder will take us up there when the word comes. But the word doesn't come. We wait.

At first I'm tense and my heart is beating fast but as the minutes go by I relax. My weapon feels a little heavier. It's an MP5, a little Rolls-Royce of a machine, smooth with no rough edges. It's my own gun and I know it well. Slowly, quietly, hoping no one's looking, I check the safety catch. I don't want to be the one to screw up. It's the most public operation yet, there are lines of camera crews at the end of the street and, although I have no interest in the politics of this operation and don't even care who the terrorists are or why they're there, I know that mistakes could have reper-cussions, serious repercussions, for the Regiment. If anyone makes mistakes, I don't want it to be me. We wait in silence but it's a noisy silence. The gas masks magnify our breath-ing and there's a slight echo here on the landing so the whole place sounds like one big dirty phone call. The rubber diaphragms on the respirators click each time we breathe and with every breath I take there is a smell of rubber and traces of old gas. It's a peppery, pungent odour. The lenses steam up a little. I start to get that detached, underwater feeling. I think of yesterday's training exercise, when I last wore this mask. Was it only yesterday? I remember that Claire is coming down to Hereford this weekend. She would have arrived by now and found me gone and known better than to ask where. If she switches on the TV she might guess.

Via my earpiece a voice brings me back here to London.

We're being told to stand down.

We return to the long room and wolf La Pierre's pork in cream sauce. Something cold and gooey for pudding. I take off my holster but not my boots and lie down feeling full. Another couple of bobbies have arrived.

"Pizza. From Carlo's around the corner," they say. "The boys thought you'd like it."

I sit up. I can smell the pizza and it smells good. Someone tells him that we've already eaten but the copper shrugs, nearly upsetting the trays, and then puts them down on the floor.

"I was told to bring it in here," he says.

So we eat the pizza too. Garlic, tomato, wedges of gooey cheese. Bottles of cold water. More tea. Overhead the chandeliers are going tinkle, tinkle. Life's pleasant. I almost forget what we're here for. We've just finished when we're told to stand-to again. This time, I grab a pillow as well as my weapon. We're supposed to be alert up there but I like to think I can be alert and asleep at the same time. It's another false alarm. When we return a copper comes in. "The outer police cordon hasn't been fed," he says. "We bought them pizza from a restaurant down the road."

"Oh yeah?" we say pleasantly.

"It's not in here by any chance?"

"Oh no," we say. He looks at us hard and doesn't argue.

Over the next few days we stand-to and stand down again and again. My pillow earns me a reputation and the nickname Forty Winks Frank.

Sometimes my team goes back to the barracks in Regent's Park where we get in a few hours' training and build a model of the next-door building using wood and sack. The abseilers find similar buildings elsewhere in London and go out training in public without anyone realizing why. We get bored. Most of us don't believe we'll be called in next door to do the business and even the TV people are sounding less excited now. Our plan is constantly upgraded. Briefing follows briefing.

Then, suddenly, there's an alert. Television reporters under makeshift lighting start jabbering at the entrance to the street. The terrorists have killed a hostage. There's rustling and readiness. I know the word's going to come soon and when we're told to stand-to again I suspect it's for real. Over the earpiece there are more voices than usual and their pitch is different, more urgent.

I have no idea of the day or the time of day when we take up our first positions under the roof for the umpteenth time but there's something electric in the air which tells me that now, at last, we'll move to deliberate action. It's coded black amber and when I hear black amber, although I'm not surprised, there's a lurching feeling inside my ribs and my heart starts to thud.

Up the sliding ladder, I await my turn and then I'm up so fast that I'm outside before I know it. Out here it's light but not bright. Even through lenses I can tell it's the soft light of an early May evening.

The first thing I see is a London bobby. He's young, fresh-faced and his cheeks look smooth under his helmet. He's been patrolling the roof all day, probably, thinking about what's for dinner, and suddenly here are twelve men in black advancing towards him, dehumanized by gas masks, weapons wrapped around their bodies. Which side are we on? Are we going to kill him? His face goes through an interesting range of emotions from horror to terror. We give him the thumbs up to reassure him but he's already fingering his radio, so nervous he can hardly work it. Er, are there supposed to be a bunch of men up here with sub-machine guns, er, sir? He's trying to control his voice but it's slipping up and down a few octaves. We tell him as kindly as we can in the circumstances that there is going to be a big bang and he should get his head down. He looks at us in disbelief. He's sweating now.

We are to storm the building from a number of different points simultaneously and my team is going down through the roof. My heart is still thumping. I'm not scared, just scared I'll make a mistake. We've trained for this and we're good, the best. The dry spot in my throat is self-doubt. We're on the roof of the adjacent building now and the abseilers are already starting to drop their ropes down the front. My team are lowering the detonator on to the roof.

While I wait I look across the back of the building, down on to a kitchen, a restaurant kitchen. Perhaps it's Carolo's or La Pierre. A couple of elderly women are standing over the sink. One has her sleeves rolled up. Her arms are frozen in the water by the sight of us. The other is pointing and shouting. A few more people come running into the kitchen, flapping their elbows and shaking their heads like chickens. I cannot resist it. I raise my arm, at the end of which there happens to be an MP5, and give them a jaunty oh-I-do-like-to-be-beside-the-seaside wave.

There's no time to see their reaction. Our ball of plastic explosive is in place, so is the detonator. We're waiting for the go, knowing there should be a delay of a few minutes while everyone else gets into position. When the word comes I'm to be first in. A ladder will be lowered for me and I'll go down into the building. I'd like to use these few moments to prepare myself but, before we expect it, things are happening. We're waiting for, "Stand by, stand by . . . go!" but instead we get a voice over our headphones yelling, "Go, go, go!" This is it. Bang. We hit our explosives device. There's a *woomph* of smoke and dust.

I feel misgivings. Everyone can't be in position by now, something must have gone wrong. My heart's hammering. I hear the words, "Go, go, go" again inside my head. Alpha-three is hooking the caving ladder on to the roof rails for me to climb down but there's a problem: it won't hook. I tell him to hurry but he fumbles some more. It's essential to take everyone in the building by surprise by attacking simultaneously so I decide to go down with the ladder only half-stabilized. Alpha-three stands aside for a moment. I lower myself into the dark hole at the heart of the building. I have never felt so alone.

I'm twenty-four and have smelled my own fear on occasions, but this isn't one of them. Once the action starts and I'm climbing down the rope ladder, hand under hand because it's so unstable, I'm no longer aware of my heartbeat, my breathing. I'm working now.

I'm waiting for my feet to touch the ground. When they do, I'm in half-darkness. There is smoke and dust and the smell of explosives. Silence, for a split second. Then the bang and shudder of the building rearranging itself around our bomb. I can't hear the rest of my team behind me or the other lads storming in through the windows at the front. Am I the only one in? Have the terrorists guessed what's happening? I feel vulnerable. I know the others will be inside in a few seconds but I slide a couple of stun grenades out of their holders and chuck them down the stairwell. They're a spectacular light and sound show. Fairly harmless, but guaranteed to terrify the uninformed.

I enter the telex room. The windows have been blown out. I cover the hall, down on one knee. By now the team has sorted out the rope ladder and my partner, alpha-three, is there behind me. The building is smoking. Perhaps my stun grenades have caused a fire.

When alpha-three taps me on the back, I go. We know the layout of the fourth floor. Our job is to comb this area for people, terrorists or hostages. I burst out, sweeping my gun ahead of me. I stop at each door until my partner taps me on the back. I open it, my gun goes in first, then me, then my mate, and it all happens in a split second. I decide on the instant whether to go right or left and he covers me while I search behind curtains, and I cover him while he searches the cupboards and under desks on his side of the room. We've done this back in Hereford a thousand times. It's like clockwork. He yells, "Clear, clear, out, out, out!" We shut the door behind us.

Below us is the sound of gunfire, screams, a cloud of CS gas. In my earpiece voices are shouting. Sixty men, one radio channel. What's happening? a voice is saying. The politicians and top brass are anxious for news but they're blocking the channel with their questions. Shut up, someone tells him, we're trying to carry out an operation here.

My mate and I find no one. One door is locked and alpha-three tells me to shoot the lock. I use my MP5. You'd expect a sub-machine gun to deal with a lock. Guys in detective movies are always shooting them off with 38s, but I feel splinters of brass bouncing off it into my legs and the lock hasn't budged. I use my axe and in a few swings it's off. We open the door. It's empty. It's a loo. I've shot the lock off the Ambassador's toilet.

"Congratulations, alpha-three-bravo," says alpha-three. We've cleared the floor now, our team. The boys upstairs have cleared the fifth. We all go down to the third.

This floor is chaotic. There's a lot of screaming, more gunfire, a strong smell of burning, voices yelling at each other inside my ear.

Someone, I can't tell who, one of the team, runs up to me. My gun is equipped with a streamlight, a powerful torch which is zeroed to my weapon and illuminates the target in the dark. He says, "You've got a torch, come with me." I leave my partner as we run downstairs.

He leads me to a door. "There's a terrorist in here," he says. "Not sure if I killed him or not."

We hit the door. Darkness. Nothing. No noise, no movement. Torches on, I go left, he goes right. I run the beam over the floor and chairs and we advance on the curtains. They're big, heavy velvet curtains and they swish as we rip them down. A yell from the other lad. He's found the terrorist. We both shine our torches on his body. He's dead, fallen back across a sofa, blood on his face, a small sub-machine gun cradled in his arms, grenades strapped to his body. His eyes and mouth are open. Outside, we tell the team leader about the body. We know the next man who goes into that room will be a scenes-of-crime officer.

We join the human chain on the stairwell. The boys have already started grabbing the hostages and passing them from man to man down the stairs. I seize each warm, sobbing body and throw it to my left. Some of them are trying to hug me, but I am not gentle. We're trained to handle hostages and I know that any one of these grateful, sobbing people could be a terrorist acting as a hostage. And then I pause. I'm holding a man by the lapels. He is wearing a green denim jacket. He has bushy hair. Instead of passing him along, something about him stops me. His eyes aren't saying, thank God, I'm rescued. He's afraid. We look at each other but I can't hesitate for longer, the next hostage is being passed to me. I hand him on. A few seconds later a yell comes.

"That's him! That's Salim!" Salim is the leader of the terrorists. I feel sure that this is a man with the fight gone from him, a man whose bravado has been replaced by terror.

But intelligence tells us that he is carrying grenades and he is thrown up against the wall to be searched.

He is shouting, "*Taslim, taslim*." No one understands him.

The firing begins. His body is rapidly riddled with bullets. A question comes into my head: why so many? But, there's no time to ponder further. The embassy is on fire and we are ushering the hostages out through the back door.

The building blazes. There are big flames in the rooms behind us. Outside in the garden we lay all the hostages down, handcuff them and search them. We are still wearing our gas masks. Anyone who takes off their respirator rapidly puts it back on when they see the TV crews. We climb into police vans and are driven away from Prince's Gate.

When we return to the Regent's Park Barracks we're jubilant. We push aside our life-size model of the embassy. We're too busy finding out who was who behind those masks and who did what. We learn that the order to go came early because one of the abseilers put a foot through a window upstairs and alerted the terrorists to the fact that something might be going on. About three people claim to have shot Salim there on the stairs. Eventually the meaning of his last words is revealed to us: he was surrendering. But for all we knew it could have been an Islamic battle cry, particularly since he was believed to be carrying grenades. Most of us speak at least some Arabic but he was speaking Farsi.

Margaret Thatcher arrives with Willie Whitelaw, the home secretary. It's an emotional occasion: Whitelaw is crying openly. When the bangs, flashes and gunfire started they thought it must be carnage in there. To find out that the hostages were alive, we were alive and most of the terrorists were dead was a huge relief for them. The prime minister congratulates us, not in a formal line-up sort of a way but just mingling in amongst us. Then someone shouts, "It's on the telly," and we all of us sit down and watch it, including Mrs Thatcher. There are cheers as we see the boys going in.

Later that night, when we're driving back up to Hereford in the Range Rover, we're stopped on the M4 by a police car. We're still wound up and we just want to get back and we've been driving at 110 m.p.h. We have blue lights which we can use in an emergency but going home doesn't really qualify. The policeman says, "Bit of a hurry, sir?" and we say, "Well, yeah." We tell him we're an army team and give him the special codeword and then watch his face. He says, "You're the boys!" and he and his copper mate shake us by the hand, congratulate us, and radio ahead, "The boys are going through, don't pull them no matter how fast they're going!"

In the weeks following the Iranian Embassy operation, the SAS received 2,000 applications from regular soldiers wishing to join the Regiment. Of these, five passed selection.

SAT CONG: "KILL COMMUNISTS"

US Navy Seals, Vietnam, 1966–71

"I am directing the Secretary of Defense to expand rapidly and substantially ... the orientation of existing forces for the conduct of ... unconventional wars ... In addition, our special forces and unconventional warfare units will be increased and reoriented."

President John F. Kennedy, addressing a joint session of Congress, May 1961.

Taking their name from the elements they are trained to fight under, in, and on – Sea, Air, Land – the US Navy's SEALs have their origins in World War II's Underwater Demolition Teams (UDTs), which cleared the lane through German beach defences for the 1944 Allied invasion of Normandy. During the Korean War UDTs prepared the way for the amphibious landings at Inchon. In 1960 a US Navy working group was formed to study how the Navy UDTs could "assist or participate" in covert operations. A year later, the Navy's Unconventional Activities Committee presented a mission statement for a new special ops "SEAL" unit, and the Chief of Naval Operations declared to his senior commanders, "It is the Navy's intention to provide for the waterborne conduct and support of such guerrilla and counter-guerrilla operations as may be directed in the national interest."

SEALs were also in the Navy's interest; with the administration's favouring of the Army's Green Berets, the Navy needed a role in special forces capability. In January 1962 President Kennedy authorized the creation of US Navy SEAL Teams One and Two, with One based on the East coast of Conus (Continental US) at Coronado, California, and Two at Little Creek, Virginia.

Recruited principally from the UDTs, the SEALs were soon deployed in Vietnam, with SEAL Team One personnel entering theatre in March 1962 to train their South Vietnamese counterparts in covert maritime operations. The following month, a SEAL Team One detachment was sent to Vietnam to train Biet Hai Junk Force commandos.

From 1962 to 1964, the SEALs primarily trained and advised South Vietnamese commandos in guerrilla operations against sites in North Vietnam as part of Operation Plan 34A and under CIA direction. Because Americans were prohibited from entering into North Vietnam, SEAL Team advisers escorted South Vietnamese naval special forces to the 17th parallel, when the South Vietnamese continued northwards on their own.

After the Gulf of Tonkin incident in which North Vietnamese forces allegedly attacked US shipping, America committed directly to the Vietnam War and SEAL Team One activity switched to hands-on covert special ops in the Southeast Asia theatre, beginning at Da Nang, before switching to the Rung Sat Special Zone (RSSZ), a 400-square-mile delta between Saigon and the China Sea. This was a Vietcong stronghold.

The tasks assigned the SEALs in the brown water war ranged from setting up listening posts to the demolition of VC bunkers. More often than not, the SEALs went out in three-man detachments with the simple order, "Sat Cong". Kill communists. In the first operations, insertion was by Mike boat, a heavily armed riverine craft, but later by Boston Whaler, a fibre-glass boat with a shallow draft, or an inflatable boat. Or even by submarine. The SEALs Vietnam arsenal included the 5.56mm M63A1 Stoner light machine gun – a SEAL favourite, because it could be converted to an assault rifle – the M60 GPMG, the M79 grenade launcher, and the ever reliable 9mm "Carl Gustav" sub-machine gun. For clandestine ops, the SEALs carried the 9mm Smith and Wesson Mark 22 Model 0 silenced pistol, nicknamed the "hush puppy" because it was originally developed for silencing enemy guard dogs. Combat knives such as the Randall, the Ka-Bar and Gerber were standard. "Tiger stripe" camouflage fatigues were often worn in preference to the usual combat issue – green-leaf pattern uniform – though many SEALs wore blue denim jeans because these best withstood the mosquitoes. A special combat coat was developed for the use of SEALs, made of camouflaged material – with a built-in flotation chamber – which was designed to carry everything that a SEAL would need on a mission.

They painted their faces green. The Vietcong called them "green faces" and put a price on their heads.

On 19 August 1966 the SEALs suffered their first combat casualty when twenty-eight-year-old Radarman 2nd Class Billy Machen was killed in the RSSZ while on daylight recce. The point man in the patrol, Machen spotted a VC ambush, which he single-handedly engaged; his action allowed his fellow patrol members to take cover and beat off the VC attack. Machen was posthumously awarded the Silver Star.

VC activity in the region was dramatically reduced by SEAL Team One's operations.

So successful was SEAL Team One in the Rung Sat that there was general hollering for SEAL operations. So, platoons were to the Mekong Delta, one of the major rice-growing regions of the world. Like RSSZ the Delta was a hard-core Communist stronghold. It would see some of the toughest fighting of the war. Soon the demand for SEAL missions outstripped SEAL Team One's ability to fulfil them, and elements from SEAL Team Two were deployed to Nam. Yet SEAL "missions" largely continued to be unlike conventional missions, with schedules and objectives. Unlike conventional forces, who were always assigned missions, SEALs did their own thing. As one senior naval commander put it, once SEAL platoons were deployed, "The SEALs made up their own operations." The SEALS called it, "doing SEAL shit." The SEALs liked combat. SEAL Team Two Ensign Ron Yaw said:

> Action was our prime motive in life. Every time we went on patrol we wanted contact. As a platoon commander, it was my responsibility to design a situation where that desire would be fulfilled.

At the war's height, eight SEAL platoons were in Vietnam on a continuing rotational basis. SEALs continued to make forays into

North Vietnam and Laos, and unofficially into Cambodia, controlled by the Studies and Observations Group.

The SEALs were heavily committed to the controversial "Phoenix Program", which, under the auspices of the CIA and South Vietnamese police, formed Provincial Reconnaissance Units (PRUs) of Vietcong defectors. The PRUs were to lead the SEALs into the Delta, so the SEALs could "capture or kill members of the Vietcong shadow government to weaken its capability to support military operations". The American public came to worry that there was no "capture" element in the programme. (See pp 460)

On 18 May 1967, Lieutenant Dick Marcinko of SEAL Team Two led his men in an assault on Ilo Ilo Hon, in what is regarded as the most successful SEAL operation in the Mekong Delta. For leading it, Marcinko was awarded the first of his four Bronze Stars. His citation read:

The President of the United States of America takes pleasure in presenting a Gold Star in lieu of a Second Award of the Bronze Star Medal with Combat "V" to Ensign Richard Marcinko, United States Navy, for meritorious achievement while serving with friendly foreign forces engaged in armed conflict against communist insurgents on Ilo Ilo Island, Republic of Vietnam. In the early morning of 18 May 1967, Ensign Marcinko led a seven-man United States Navy SEAL squad on an eleven and one-half hour reconnaissance mission of Ilo Ilo Island which is covered with dense foliage and muddy terrain. After two hours of laborious movement, a well-concealed, heavily booby-trapped Viet Cong first-aid station was discovered. Ensign Marcinko directed his squad in the removal of these booby traps, fully utilizing safety precautions and quietness to avoid alerting the Viet Cong forces. Deploying his squad for maximum coverage, Ensign Marcinko approached the area where three medical huts, two bunkers and a cooking hut were located. Contact with the Viet Cong was then made resulting in five Viet Cong killed, one Viet Cong wounded and four CHICOM rifles captured. Numerous drugs, medical texts, personal notebooks, and documents were captured and cooking utensils, 20 kilos of rice and two sampans were destroyed. The ensuing ambulation to the extraction point was opposed by sniper fire which was ultimately suppressed by mortar fire from a Mike boat directed by Ensign Marcinko. Ensign Marcinko's initiative, foresight, perseverance and courage under fire contributed significantly to the successful reconnaissance patrol without injury to his own forces and were in keeping with the highest traditions of the United States Naval Service. (Ensign Marcinko is authorized to wear the Combat "V".)

The following year Marcinko was awarded the Silver Star. His citation read:

The President of the United States of America takes pleasure in presenting the Silver Star to Lieutenant, Junior Grade, Richard Marcinko, United States Navy, for conspicuous gallantry and intrepidity in action while serving as Platoon Leader of 8th Platoon, SEAL Team Detachment Alfa, on 14 and 15 May 1968. As patrol leader, he led a squad size patrol to a known Viet Cong infiltration route through 2,000 meters of uncontested enemy terrain and established an ambush site. Three groups of Viet Cong soon approached and set up in the area. With no feasible escape route, the squad was surrounded by 85 armed Viet Cong for over four hours. Lieutenant, Junior Grade, Marcinko ordered artillery to stand by and directed air strikes on the Viet Cong within 300 meters of his own position. When the enemy force started to retreat toward the Cambodian border, he led an attack on a group of 43 Viet Cong and through bold and unselfish tactics quelled the enemy's efforts to outflank and subdue his squad. Enemy fire from a nearby tree line was countered by Lieutenant, Junior Grade, Marcinko's M-60 Machine Gun, his daring companions and the air strikes he directed on the enemy. A reconnaissance, conducted immediately after the enemy broke contact, revealed many heavy blood trails, one Viet Cong killed, and one SKS rifle abandoned and numerous bundles of hot food and clothing within 20 meters of the ambush site. A sweep held at first light brought the total assessment of losses to the enemy force to 24 Viet Cong killed, 41 Viet Cong wounded and six automatic weapons captured. His courage, valor under fire, dedication to duty and accurate prediction of the enemy's tactics were in keeping with the highest traditions of the United States Naval Service.

During the 1968 Tet Offensive, Marcinko ordered his platoon to assist US Army Special Forces at Chau Doc. What began as house-to-house fighting turned into a rescue mission of American nurses and a schoolteacher trapped by the VC in the city's church and hospital. Marcinko's team rescued a nurse called Maggie, bundled her into a jeep, and drove hightail away to safety, with one SEAL having to lie protectively on top of her. "What a great pair of tits", he said after the ride. His citation for his Bronze Star for the Chau Doc action read:

The President of the United States of America takes pleasure in presenting a Third Gold Star in lieu of a Fourth Award of the Bronze Star Medal with Combat "V" to Lieutenant, Junior Grade, Richard Marcinko, United States Navy, for meritorious service in connection with operations against the enemy while serving in the Republic of Vietnam from 30 January to 2 February 1968. As Commander of the 8th Platoon, SEAL Team Detachment ALFA, Lieutenant, Junior Grade, Marcinko, while leading a SEAL reconnaissance patrol near the Cambodian border, located a large Viet Cong unit, and on transmitting this information to the city of Chau Phu, was informed the city was under strong Viet Cong attack. He called PBRs for rendezvous point and led the platoon 3,000 meters through enemy territory for extraction. On arrival at Chau Phu city, the situation was critical. Communications lines were flooded and confusion was rampant. The Viet Cong were throughout the city and friendly forces were tied down defending their remaining positions. Lieutenant, Junior Grade, Marcinko separated his platoon into two units and led them ashore under enemy fire.

Lieutenant, Junior Grade, Marcinko directed his men in actions which resulted in freeing and evacuating six U.S. citizens and four Vietnamese government employees who were trapped in various parts of the city and assisted other friendly units in routing the Viet Cong from their strong points. At one time when a SEAL member was critically wounded, Lieutenant, Junior Grade, Marcinko and two others fought three blocks distance to give assistance to the medical unit by securing a main corridor held by the enemy. Upon arrival of friendly troop reinforcements to the city, Lieutenant, Junior Grade, Marcinko directed an aid station set up where the Platoon Corpsman treated military and civilian wounded alike. His valor under fire, devotion to duty and knowledge of the enemy were in keeping with the highest traditions of the United States Naval Service. (Ensign Marcinko is authorized to wear the Combat "V".)

The Vietcong put a bounty on Marcinko's head. "Award of 50,000 piasters to anyone who can kill First Lieutenant Demo Richard Marcinko, a grey-faced killer who has brought death and trouble to the Chau Doc province during the Lunar New Year".

Marcinko went on to found the SEALs' anti-terrorist unit, Team Six.

The roll call of SEAL casualties mounted. X-Ray Platoon, SEAL Team One, which arrived in the Delta in October 1970, where it spectacularly disrupted Vietcong operations – capturing more than 100 pounds of documents and destroying numerous enemy rice caches and weapons factories – took 100 per cent casualties, with four platoon men killed. On the unit's last mission, 4 March 1971, the platoon's commander, Lieutenant Mike Collins, was KIA. An investigation later revealed that X-Ray Platoon had been compromised; one of its attached South Vietnamese commandos was a Communist agent. By the time of the withdrawal of the last SEAL platoons from Vietnam in 1971 the SEALs were credited with 580 VC killed. Between 1965 and 1972, there were forty-six SEALs killed in Vietnam. The last SEAL killed was Lieutenant Melvin S. Dry, who had stayed on as an adviser, in an abortive operation to retrieve prisoners of war.

PEBBLE ISLAND

22 SAS, South Atlantic, 1982

The Falkland Islands, specks of land almost lost in the vast-ness of the South Atlantic, had been British-owned since 1833. Argentina, however, had long laid claim to the "Malvinas", and on 2 April 1982 the leader of the nation's military junta, General Galtieri, decided to back that claim with a full-scale inva-sion of the islands.

Immediately on hearing the news of the invasion, the Director of the SAS Group, Brigadier Peter de la Billière, and the commander of 22 SAS, Lieutenant-Colonel Mike Rose, put the Regiment on standby and lobbied hard for a role in the military campaign for the islands' recovery, should one be launched. It was.

The Argentinian junta was not minded to give up their new possession; the British prime minister of the day, Margaret Thatcher, was equally determined that the islands should become British once more. War was on. The Special Air Service, de la Billière intended, should share the burden of war and – dare it be said – the limelight, in what might be Britain's last colonial war.

The SAS appeal fell on favourably inclined ears. Three days later, after SAS soldiers had been frantically summonsed back from leave, training courses and patrolling in Armagh's bandit country, an advance party from D Squadron flew south to Ascension Island. A small D Squadron contingent also embarked on the carrier HMS *Hermes*, sailing from Portsmouth Harbour. The remainder of D Squadron, together with all their kit, was airborne for Ascension twenty-four hours later, and so was G Squadron and the regimental headquarters. The swift send-off was a telling tribute to the efficiency of the quartermasters at Stirling Lines.

Although Ascension Island, pinned in the middle of the Atlantic just below the Equator, was 3,885 miles from the Falklands, it was the nearest British territory of serviceable use. Hot and cramped, the island had little to recommend it and D Squadron's ninety troopers were not sorry to find that their sojourn was soon curtailed. Margaret Thatcher was keen that a dramatic and immediate military action was undertaken against the illegal occupiers of Britannia's southern outposts. The chosen target was Grytviken, the former whaling station on the island of South Georgia, 870 miles south-east of the main Falklands group.

The execution of Operation *Paraquet* (soon corrupted to Operation *Paraquat*, after the branded weedkiller) fell to D Squadron, alongside a patrol from M Company, 42 Royal Marine Commando ("The Mighty Munch"), and a section of the SBS – some 235 men in all. On 21 April the small assault force, carried in HMS *Endeavour*, HMS *Antrim* and HMS *Plymouth*, came in sight of South Georgia, an ice-bound mountainous wilderness which formed, before the Argentinian occupation, the base for the British Antarctic Survey. Little was known about deployment of Argentinian forces on the island, so Major Guy Sheridan RM, the commander of the assault force, ordered covert recces. Captain John Hamilton's 19 Troop of D Squadron was inserted by helicopter in near white-out conditions of driving snow. Carrying 77 pounds of kit and hauling heavily laden pulks (sledges), the troops inched down the Fortuna glacier, but after a night of hurricane-force winds Hamilton had no choice but to request extraction.

Three Wessex helicopters successfully landed on the glacier. The weather conditions were so extreme, though, that the take-offs were blighted. Corporal Davey, Squadron SAS, recorded:

> The helicopters lifted off, the Mark 3 Wessex with navigational equipment leading and the two Mark 5s following. I was in the first Mark 5. The flight plan was to follow the glaciers down to a land fall and then out to the ships. The Mark 3 put in a shallow right-hand turn, height probably

about 200–300 feet, the first Mark 5 started the turn but was hit by a sudden white-out in which the pilot lost all his horizons and we crashed into the ice. The pilot managed to pull the nose up before impact so that the tail rotor hit first and the helicopter rolled over on its left-hand side. The main door being uppermost everyone got out quickly, the only injury being Corporal Bunker who had hurt his back. The remaining Mark 5 and Mark 3 then landed and we transferred to them ... the two helicopters lifted off again and exactly the same thing happened, white-out followed by crash. This time the Mark 5 rested on its right-hand side. The Mark 3, unable to return because of extra payload, then flew back to *Antrim*. I and the other passengers were taken to the wardroom where an emergency medical room had been set up.

After refuelling, the Mark 3, with the same crew still aboard, returned to the area of the second crash, but was unable to land because of weather. It returned to the ship, having contacted the troops on the glacier who had no serious injuries. They had in fact managed to erect a survival tent carried by the helicopter and had also retrieved equipment from the first crash.

The Mark 3 then returned again to the second crash, and this time picked everyone up and returned to *Antrim*. It had seventeen passengers, very much overloaded, and the pilot had to fly the helicopter straight on to the flight deck as he was unable to hover and approach normally. It was now 22 April.

The pilot of the returning Mark 3 Wessex was Lieutenant-Commander Ian Stanley RN. For his valour and professionalism, Stanley was awarded the DSO.

With the South Georgia Task Force's helicopter capability reduced by two-thirds, the planners decided to launch D Squadron's boat troop. Although two of their five Gemini inflatables suffered engine failure, three crews got ashore to set up watch on Leith and Stromness on the night of 22 April. Three days later, Ian Stanley successfully inserted an SBS patrol a few clicks below Grytviken.

Choppering back to *Antrim*, Stanley spotted the Argentinian submarine *Santa Fe* on the surface; he immediately attacked,

straddling her with a pair of depth charges. These inflicted sufficient damage to prevent her diving, and she was shortly attacked
by helicopters from *Endurance* and the frigate *Brilliant*. The *Santa
Fe* limped into Grytviken, where her condition, plus the sight of
pursuing British helicopters, caused panic among the 130-strong
enemy garrison. Despite only having seventy-five men immediately available, Major Sheridan and D Squadron's commanding
officer, Major Cedric Delves, decided to exploit the Argentinians'
set-back.

To the roar of supporting gunfire from *Antrim* and *Plymouth*,
an SAS composite troop and two composite RM/SBS troops
landed in the vicinity of Grytviken. Screened from the settlement
by a small mountain, the SAS struck out for the port. Some
elephant seals, mistaken for Argentinian troops, were shot up and
a suspected enemy position was promptly demolished by a Milan
missile; the stronghold, alas, turned out to be a piece of scrap
iron. These hazards negotiated, the SAS team ascended to the top
of Brown Mountain to see the wooden buildings of the port
below festooned with white flags. The garrison surrendered without a shot being fired. With barely a pause to get his breath, SSM
Lawrence Gallagher of D Squadron hauled down the Argentinian
flag and raised the Union Jack. To their incredulity, the SAS
assault party discovered that they had blithely trolled through the
minefield ringing the Argentinian weapons pits. The next morning, 26 April, two troops from D Squadron, together with an SBS
team, took the peaceful surrender of the Leith garrison. South
Georgia was once again in British hands.

While D Squadron had South Georgia on its mind, G
Squadron 22 SAS was sailing towards the war zone on the RFA
Resource. Since there was little in the way of aerial or satellite
pictures of the Argentinian positions on the Falklands, G
Squadron was earmarked for some old-style "eye-ball" reconnaissance. Beginning on 1 May, four-man patrols were inserted
by Sea King, an earlier plan to parachute them in being cancelled
at the last moment. The forward observation posts in the featureless terrain often consisted of a mere shallow depression covered
with ponchos. Life in the hides was unrelentingly grim, with little
or no chance to brew up hot food or drink, and with cold, wet

weather that seeped into the bones. The record for staying in a hide was twenty-eight days, set by Sergeant Mather and his team above Bluff Cove. There was always the danger of discovery. On 10 June an SAS covert "hide" containing Captain John Hamilton – who had rejoined the main task force after the successful taking of South Georgia – and his signaller was uncovered; in the ensuing firefight with the Argentinians, Hamilton was killed as he tried to cover the signaller's escape. For his bravery, Hamilton was awarded a posthumous MC. On more than one occasion SAS and SBS patrols ran into each other and opened fire. One such "blue-on-blue" incident ended tragically, with the death of SBS Sergeant "Kiwi" Hunt.

Despite these set-backs, the recce teams achieved conspicuously successful results. One four-man patrol, led by G Squadron's Captain Aldwin, set up a hide on Beagle Ridge, directly above Port Stanley, in an area heavily patrolled by the enemy. From the hide, the team spotted a night dispersal area for helicopters between Mounts Kent and Estancia; when the intelligence was relayed back to the fleet, two Harrier aircraft attacked the site and destroyed three enemy helicopters. Besides reconnaissance, the regiment was tasked with the carrying out of its quintessential activity: offensive raiding behind the lines. An early target was the Argentinian airstrip on Pebble Island, off the northern coast of West Falkland, the base for 1A-58 Pucara aircraft. Sergeant Peter Ratcliffe was among those slated for the Pebble Island job:

At about eleven o'clock on the morning of 15 May, the Boat Troop commander sent a signal which will go down in the annals of the Regiment. Coded and transmitted in Morse, once deciphered it read, "Eleven aircraft, repeat eleven aircraft. Believed real. Squadron attack tonight." The timescale was very tight – clearly Ted saw the matter as urgent. In the light of this, the squadron commander and the senior planners got together and worked out that any attack launched against the aircraft on the Pebble Island airstrip would have to be completed by 0700 hours the next day to allow sufficient time for the raiding parties to be recovered by helicopter. The reason for this was because the Task Force ships closed up to the islands at night, but steamed away into the South Atlantic so that they should not be vulnerable to air attack when daylight came some time after 1100 hours. As they sailed out of danger, so the distance the helicopters would have to fly back to the ships increased. The plan began to go wrong from the first. Because of bad weather conditions and *Hermes* miscalculating her run in to a position eighty miles offshore, which would bring Pebble Island within heli-copter range of the ships, the operation started running late almost from the start. The South Atlantic lived up to its foul-weather reputation, and the aircraft carrier had to sail in fierce headwinds and mounting seas. Movement on board was risky, which meant that the Sea Kings on the hangar decks could not be safely readied by the technical crews in the time allowed. Once they were ready, there were more delays while the choppers were brought up to the flight deck for lift-off.

The helicopters were carried up from the hold of *Hermes* by huge lifts let into the flight deck, since all the aircraft, Sea Harriers as well as Sea Kings, were kept below deck at all times when they weren't flying. The mood and atmosphere among D Squadron was electric, with everyone raring to go. By then our faces were covered in cam cream and we were all tooled up. Each SAS man tasked for the raid carried an M16 rifle with three spare magazines taped to the butt, and another 200 to 400 rounds of 7.62mm GPMG ammunition in belts. Everybody carried two mortar bombs, one of high explosive and one of white phosphorus, which we were to drop off when we reached the mortar pits that would be established near the airstrip. Several of the guys also carried LAWs – M72 light anti-tank weapons – which are extremely effective against aircraft on the ground.

Adrenalin raged through our systems like rivers of fire, giving us an enormous rush. Armed to the teeth, forty-five of us boarded the Sea Kings; with us also went a naval-gunfire support team from 148 Battery, 29 Commando Regiment, Royal Artillery, whose task was to direct the bombardment from the 4.5-inch guns of the ships lying offshore. We all embarked on the hangar deck, and eventually the Sea King that my troop was to fly in was brought up to the flight deck. The helicopter's engines roared into life. We waited on deck for at least fifteen minutes, only to be told that one of the Sea Kings carrying another troop had developed mechanical problems and would have to be replaced. All in all, this took over an hour, leaving our time on the ground less than adequate, as everything had been planned on the basis of the distance between *Hermes* and Pebble Island and the range of the Sea Kings, making timing absolutely critical.

At last we lifted off, flying low-level over the sea in black-out conditions, occasionally gaining fleeting glimpses of the waves below. I had never experienced surges of adrenalin to the same extent. To be part of the largest SAS raid since the Second World War was something that I would not have missed for anything, especially when I remembered that I should have been back in Birmingham drill hall completing my two-year stint as an instructor.

The navy pilots were terrific, lifting off in the dark and, despite very high winds, flying only forty or fifty feet above the waves to dodge any enemy radar cover. For all their efforts, however, because of the atrocious weather we were already running an hour late when they dropped us off three miles from the airstrip. We estimated that it would take us about two hours to reach the target.

On landing we were met by Captain Ted, the Boat Troop commander, and his men. They had spent the last four days lying up on Pebble Island, watching the enemy without being seen; now it was their job to lead us to the target. The squadron commander and the "head sheds" of each troop were briefed by Ted. Once the briefing had finished, we were told that this was not a night for tactical movement; instead, we had to get our arses in gear and get to the target as quickly as possible, since otherwise we wouldn't have enough time to carry out the mission and rendezvous with the helicopters before the latter had to return to *Hermes*. The plan was for Mobility Troop to attack the eleven aircraft on the ground and destroy them with plastic-explosive (PE) charges. Air

Troop was tasked to mask off the settlement, and Mountain Troop was to be held in reserve at the mortar pit, from where they would be able to go instantly to the aid of any troops that might be in trouble.

My troop, Mobility, was commanded by Captain Paul and his number two was Bob, a staff sergeant; I was number three in the pecking order. Considering the ground and the darkness, we got off pretty quickly. It was not quickly enough, however, for the going was against us. The ground was mainly of peat, spongy stuff that made walking difficult, especially in the dark, and there were lots of fences and walls to cross. Just the kind of thing you'd expect around a sheep settlement. Realizing that precious time had been lost, the squadron commander decided to speed-march in single file, one man behind the other. As a result, rather than observing patrol procedures, which would normally involve a stealthy approach, we often broke into a run. But when we came to a wall or a fence, we adopted "obstacle procedure", which dictated that each man should be covered by others while he crossed, and this slowed us considerably.

When moving in an extended single file, the soldier in front is responsible for the soldier behind. So long as he can see the man ahead of him and the man behind, then everything is fine. That's the theory, anyway, but what we didn't know was that while we were painstakingly crossing obstacles, the squadron OC and the other troops were leaping walls and fences and racing towards the target as though their boots were on fire.

Inevitably, we lost contact with the troop in front. They were travelling much faster than we were, and before long the man at the head of our troop could no longer see the last man of the troop ahead. Going over undulating ground at night, you can simply disappear into the darkness, and once the chain is broken you are as good as lost. In the pitch blackness we couldn't see a thing, even through our night scopes, so our only means of contacting the leading troops was by the radio carried by the troop signaller. When Captain Paul realized our predicament he radioed the OC, who was somewhere up in front of us in the dark, and asked him for a steer. The squadron commander came back on the radio and said he didn't have time to wait for us – if we didn't catch up with him by the time we reached the rendezvous position, we were to stay in reserve by the mortar pit, the task originally given to Mountain Troop.

We didn't catch up. However, a contingency plan had been agreed before we left *Hermes*. Under this, if anything happened to Mobility Troop prior to our reaching the target, then Mountain Troop was to pick up the baton and lead the attack. Its members were carrying enough explosives to complete the mission.

By the time we reached the mortar pit, we knew we had lost our starring role in the attack. Almost beside ourselves with anger and disappointment, we realized that we had been relegated to being just a bunch of extras.

Looking back on that night, the troop sergeant should have detailed someone to be in front as the lead scout. Captain Paul was a good officer and was trying to do things properly, and it was not his fault that a gap had developed, for on this particular night there was drifting mist that continually came and went. To make matters worse, we were the only troop that didn't have a member of Boat Troop attached to us as a guide – a mistake, since by then they knew the way to and from the airstrip better than the backs of their hands. Nevertheless, there can be no excuses. Mobility Troop's delay in arriving at the target was the result of incompetence, and it should not have happened. The important thing to remember, however, is that the Regiment is not infallible. We do sometimes make mistakes. In this respect the SAS is like any other regiment, and its soldiers are not immune from sometimes getting things wrong, especially in the confusion of war.

"David", a soldier with another troop, takes up the story:

At this point it became apparent that we had lost the troop that was supposed to carry out the attack on the actual planes. In all fairness to them, it is sometimes quite hard to locate a

six-figure grid reference in the pitch-dark in the middle of
nowhere in a place where everything looks the same. And
they were one of the troops who did not have a guide. Nobody
knew they were missing until we arrived at the forward RV.
We had assumed they were out in front of us. We had to
change plan immediately. We waited for a bit to see if they
would reappear but they didn't. We now had exactly thirty
minutes to complete the assault.

Mountain Troop, led by John Hamilton, was designated to
do the assault. My troop became the fire-support team for
the assault. Thank God for that. We were so lucky. It meant
we didn't have to do the house-clearing assault on the settlement. We later found out that there were 200 Argentinian
soldiers in the wool shed, which was the starting point for our
operations. There were sixteen of us. That would have been
interesting. The attack opened with a naval bombardment on
to the feature directly overlooking the settlement. Then our
own mortar opened up, lighting the whole place up like it was
bright daylight. The mortar man was having a lot of trouble.
Every time he fired the bloody thing, the whack of the pipe
was kicking the base plate further into the ground. If the
angle of the plate changed, he lost his trajectory and
elevation.

Despite this he kept up continuous fire, eventually giving
the order "check fire" before we withdrew. After a few more
minutes the assault troop went in. As they reached one end of
the airstrip they got into a firefight. An Argentine officer and
an NCO were in a bunker to the side of the strip and opened
up. They were rapidly dealt with. After that there was virtually no enemy fire on us, so the boys got stuck into the planes.
They split into seven two-man teams. It was a bloody big
strip and they had a lot of ground to cover. It's not as if the
planes were all parked in a nice neat row. They were all over
the strip. And all the time the boys were running against the
clock. Five planes were destroyed using the explosive charges
that they had with them. The Pucara was the tallest of the
aircraft. As they approached each plane, one bloke would
give the other a leg up on to the wing. Once up, he then

leaned down and hauled the other one up to join him. The Skyvan was not a problem. The Mentors were very small, and with one great leap the guys got themselves up on to the wings. The other six planes were attacked at close quarters by hand. It's not like in the movies, when you shoot the fuel tank of a plane and it explodes. Planes are built to withstand bullet holes, at least up to a point. Still, the lads used their initiative. They riddled the planes, especially the cockpits, with machine-gun fire and chucked in grenades for good measure. Some of the lads, including Paddy A., got so worked up with adrenalin and enthusiasm that they actually ripped instrument panels out of the cockpits with their bare hands. During the withdrawal there was suddenly this almighty explosion. The Argies had planted command-detonated mines, and as we were leaving someone on their side decided to get brave and initiated one of them. We had no knowledge that they had even been planted. The guys who had done the assault were withdrawing in groups of four. Fire and manoeuvre. One team of two is on the ground providing cover for the other two as they move. One foot on the ground, one moving. Leap-frogging. Two of our guys were caught in the blast of the mine. One had shrapnel wounds and the other was just winded. They were recovered and helped to the original central rendezvous point near the mortar. The base plate had to be dug out, it had sunk so deep. As soon as we could, we set off back to the coastline. There was so little time.

I was in the last chopper to leave. As we were taking off I remember looking back over my shoulder. I'll never forget it. The whole place looked as if it was burning. It was terrific. We all went nuts.

Corporal Davey was one of two SAS men injured in the raid. He wrote of his part in the operation:

Captain Burls led 19 Troop on to the airstrip via the forward RV manned by Captain West and Sergeant Major Gallagher. Once on the edge of the airstrip we began to engage visible aircraft with small arms and 66mm rockets. By this time naval gunfire and illumination were being produced by HMS *Glamorgan* and our mortars also fired some illuminating rounds. We were aware of some incoming enemy small arms fire, but it was totally ineffective.

I was a member of Staff Sergeant Currass's patrol and was the extreme right-hand man. I was hit in the lower left leg by shrapnel at about 0700 hours. Staff Sergeant Currass helped me put a shell dressing on the wound. The troop moved on to the airstrip and started systematically to destroy the aircraft with standard charges and 66mm. Captain Hamilton covered Trooper Armstrong who went forward to destroy the last aircraft. The troop then shook out and started to fall back off the airstrip. We were at this stage silhouetted against the burning aircraft. A land mine was command detonated in the middle of the troop, Corporal Bunker being blown some ten feet backwards.

I was beginning to feel faint from loss of blood and consequently was told to head back towards the forward RV with two others. Just off the airstrip we heard Spanish voices, at least four or five, shouting some fifty yards towards the settlement. I opened fire with M203 and put down some sixty rounds in the direction of the voices. Two very pained screams were the only reply. The troop came down behind us and we moved back through the forward RV at about 0745 hours. During the move back I was helped over various obstacles and so was Corporal Bunker. The helicopter pick-up was on time at 0930, and the flight back to *Hermes* lasted about one hour twenty minutes. Corporal Bunker and I went directly to the sick bay where we were looked after admirably.

It had been a textbook job. It passed through the thoughts of more than one SAS trooper that night that, swap the South Atlantic for the desert, the Argentinians for the Germans, and the RAF helis for the LRDG taxis, 22 SAS was doing exactly what Stirling, Mayne and Lewes had done forty years before.

Presumably, the "Head Shed" at Stirling Lines felt the daring hand of L Detachment's history on their shoulders when they conjured up Operation *Mikado*, in which B Squadron would attack Exocet-carrying Super Etendard fighters on Rio Grande airstrip on the Argentine mainland. In one fell SAS-swoop the war would be shortened. Some members of the squadron thought the operation suicidal – the airstrip was defended by 1,300 Argentinian marines and state-of-the-art AA guns – and the squadron sergeant major even resigned over the issue. When the squadron's commanding officer, John Moss, showed less than requisite enthusiasm, DLB (de la Billière) summarily returned him to unit. Those in B Squadron who did not think the Rio Grande mission suicidal, thought that the Paras would be better equipped to undertake such a *coup de main*. The pessimists grew gloomier when the helicopter inserting the recce team was compromised; the Sea King, at the very maximum of its range, tundra-hopped to plop down just over the Chilean border. At best any attack would henceforth be blind. Tom Read of B Squadron recounts the plan, reparation and frequent postponements of *Mikado*:

Apart from the various troop briefings, we have larger squadron meetings to discuss the full operation. The initial patrol will set up the LZ on the dual carriageway, allowing the RAF pilots to bring in the C-130s. The squadron will then brass-neck it, driving straight along the main road on motorbikes and in right-hand-drive Land Rovers. I like the audacity of that. Our intelligence lads have interviewed a Canadian who used to work at Rio Grande airfield. He's given us details of the layout and the location of the local military base. There are two guards on the security gate and Des has been assigned to take out one of them, while Harry McCallion takes care of the other.

The open-top Land Rovers have mounted machine guns as well as Browning 30s and a handful of M-202s – American-made white phosphorus grenade-launchers that look like something out of a James Bond movie. They're only as long as a shotgun, but they have multi-barrels and when you squeeze the trigger there's a gentle explosion and a wall of flame. It can destroy an aircraft in seconds.

At H-hour we'll pour through the front gate and spread out, splitting into smaller groups and hitting different targets. One patrol will take out the control tower, another will blow the fuel tanks and a third will attack the accommodation bunkers and try to kill the pilots. My Land Rover is to head for the aircraft hangars and use the M-202 to destroy the Super Etendards.

"Okay, you're probably wondering what the enemy will be up to while we're doing all this," says Ian C., the new OC of the squadron. "Our intelligence says the airfield has a limited troop presence. About two miles away there's a military base with about 1,800 Marines. That's why one of the primary targets is the comms centre. Assuming these troops are alerted, hopefully by the time they get their shit together and weapons out of the armoury we'll have finished and gone."

Discussion turns to our escape, but the options are limited. The nearest Task Force ship will be 500 miles away, and the choppers on board have the fuel capacity to reach us but not get home again. This leaves us with a dash towards the Chilean border, forty miles away. Basically we'll have to drive as quickly as possible towards the border on one of two roads until we hit road-blocks or are compromised. After that, it may be a case of tabbing over the tundra.

"Take any vehicles you can get, but try not to kill any civilians," says Ian C. "Once you're across the border, surrender to the Chilean authorities." It's not much of an escape plan, and Rhett, one of the older lads, pipes up, "Boss, I think I should point out that I shouldn't be here, because I cheated on Combat Survival."

Everyone laughs.

Call it youthful enthusiasm, but I don't even contemplate failure. More experienced heads than mine are going to decide what's right. There are no escape maps or cover stories in case of capture. The Argies will doubtless seal off the roads and put up helicopter gunships. Once the element of surprise has gone, we'll be deep in hostile territory and vastly outnumbered.

Until the green light is given, we spend our time going on runs over Green Mountain and doing weapons training. I take the M-202 down to the beach, loading up the barrels and firing it at various rocks. A lot of the lads want to have a go because it's a new weapon. On another day, I go fishing with Charlie and we catch enough red snapper for a squadron barbecue.

A week later, the operation is confirmed. We leave in twelve hours. The compo boxes are opened and we sort out rations and ammunition. I'm jumping with the minimum of kit, just a chainsaw. The rest of my gear is in one of the Land Rovers.

After packing everything away and writing letters home, we get word of a hold-up. Twenty-four hours later it's on again and then off again. This happens all week, and each morning B Squadron goes for a run, trying to work off the frustration. Apparently, there's disquiet in Downing Street about the predicted 60 per cent casualty rate of a mainland operation. Prime Minister Thatcher isn't happy with the odds.

Equally, the RAF isn't thrilled about abandoning a burning aircraft and leaving the crews to tag along with us.

The mainland option seems to be falling apart when, on 8 June, the *Sir Galahad* and *Sir Tristram*, both British transport ships, are hit by Argentinian Skyhawks and Mirages in Bluff Cove. The ships are torched and dozens of soldiers die, most of them Welsh Guards. Some of the injuries are truly horrific. Suddenly, the mainland operation is back on again. We are due to leave on a flight at 0700. I'm in the baggage party, humping all the gear into the cargo hold in the pre-dawn cold. The sky is growing light but I'm sweating. A lot of the younger lads like me are raring to go, but the older blokes are more circumspect. Maybe their instincts for self-preservation are more acute.

A Land Rover arrives beside the aircraft and the news is broken – the operation has been cancelled. Apparently, a British newspaper had published a story saying that an SAS squadron based on Ascension Island was practising for a mainland operation. Within hours the Argentinians had started moving their planes away from the airfields and scattering them about the countryside, parked under camouflage nets. The chance of striking a blow against the Super Etendards had been lost.

Mikado might have been aborted, but there was plenty of "old-style" SAS stuff to come. On the night before the main Task Force landings at San Carlos, the SAS mounted a series of diversionary raids. These included the landing of sixty D Squadron men, who then marched for twenty hours to reach the hills north of Darwin and attack the garrison at Goose Green. To put the wind up the Argentinians they simulated a battalion-sized (600 men) attack, raining down a torrent of LAW rockets, Milan missiles, GMPG rounds and tracers into the Argentinian positions. So ferocious was the barrage that the enemy failed to probe the SAS positions and could only manage desultory return fire. By mid-morning, the main landings accomplished, the SAS disengaged from Goose Green, "tabbing" (only Marines "yomp") north to meet up with 2 Para as they made their way inland. En route, the SAS were intercepted by a Pucara ground-attack aircraft. Fatalities seemed certain, but as the planes winged in an SAS trooper launched a heat-seeking Stinger missile. He scored a direct hit on one plane, which *whumphed* into disintegrating fire, smoke and metal.

Unfortunately, the trooper was a novice with the new American-made Stinger and did not realize that it required recharging with compressed gas; after his next two missiles, worth £50,000 each, flopped after just twenty yards the Commanding Officer ordered him to desist firing. The rest of the patrol had dived for cover. Over the next fortnight SAS patrols continued their recces and probing missions. At the end of May, D Squadron seized Mount Kent, 40 miles behind enemy lines, and held it for several days until reinforced by 42 RM Commando. This was despite aggressive – and courageous – patrolling from Argentine special forces in a sequence of sharp nocturnal firefights. Following their relief, D Squadron was in action again when five teams landed on West Falkland. The considerable enemy garrisons at Fox Bay and Port Howard enjoyed excellent radio-direction-finding equipment and responded vigorously. It was on West Falkland that Captain John Hamilton had lost his life.

Meanwhile, to reinforce SAS numbers in the Falklands, a troop from B Squadron was flown from Ascension in Hercules C130s; the troop was to join the Task Force by parachuting into the Atlantic, from which they would be plucked by Gemini inflatables.

Tom Read wrote later:

We reach the convoy and quickly prepare for a static-line jump from 1,000 feet, directly off the ramp. Whitecaps stretch from horizon to horizon. My dry suit will give me about five minutes in the freezing water before I lose consciousness. It has a hood and feet, but no hands. I stuff my training shoes inside my leggings because the rest of my kit is already bundled and packed into huge boxes to be dropped after us. There are twenty-one of us on board, and seven jump on each pass because there are a limited number of inflatable boats to pick us up and ferry us to the warships. Timing is crucial, because three ships have manoeuvred into a U-shape to act as a landing zone. The C-130 flies up through the middle and the green light flashes on. Another seven blokes go off the ramp. As I hook up my static line, Doomwatch Des is busy looking out the window, with his eyes bigger than portholes. He doesn't want to be here. Reports of enemy action in the area have him totally spooked. On the ramp, I can see lads in the water and inflatable boats moving towards them. The pilot doesn't want to make another pass because he's worried he won't have enough fuel to get back to Ascension. Come on, don't lose your bottle now, I think, as the C-130 does a sharp turn and heads back towards the convoy. Red light . . . Green light . . . Go!

The canopy swirls upwards and opens. Looking up, I make sure none of the lines are twisted and then ditch the serve chute, gone for ever in the sea. The last man is drifting dangerously close to one of the ships and almost bounces off the stern, unable to steer the round parachute. A few feet from the water, I hit the release box on my chest and jettison the chute.

I break the surface and let the water slow me down as my body surges under. The cold slaps me in the face like a punch and I get the worst ice-cream headache imaginable. From a thousand feet, the swells hadn't looked too bad, but now they're huge. One minute I'm in the bottom of a valley and the next I'm on top of a hill. Entire ships are disappearing in the troughs. Full credit to the marine coxswains, banging around in their dinghies – they surf off swells and risk capsizing to get to us within a few minutes. I feel the cold leaking through the suit and see the boat bouncing over the wash. Strong hands reach out and pull me on board. The aircraft makes a final pass and drops the equipment. The boxes, wrapped in cargo nets, burst open on impact and the contents spill out. The seas are now so rough the navy won't risk sending the inflatables back out. Instead, they try using helicopters to winch boxes on board, but only manage to save a few. As I climb the side nets on to the *Andromeda*, someone wraps a blanket around my shoulders. I turn to see my Bergen, rifle and webbing flop through the side of a net and sink to the bottom. Everything I'd personalized, my letters from Chris, a painting that Jason had sent me . . . all of it gone.

Taken down below, I have a shower, a scoff and then head for the Warrant Officers' Mess for a beer. The assault on Port Stanley airport has been overtaken by events. The land forces are within striking distance of the capital, so we are to relieve D Squadron patrols in the West Falklands.

It wasn't to be B Squadron's war. It was then tasked with ambushing the enemy reinforcement of the garrison at Fox Bay, but the enemy failed to turn up. By now it was becoming clear to all that the war was in its last days. There remained one major SAS raid, which was mounted in East Falkland on the night of 13 June. To take the pressure off 2 Para, who were assaulting Wireless Ridge a few miles west of Port Stanley, the SAS volunteered to put in a raid to the enemy rear – from the sea. Two troops from D Squadron, one from G Squadron and six men from the 3 SBS rode into Port Stanley harbour on high-speed Rigid Raiders with the aim of setting fire to the oil storage tanks. As troopers from the Regiment later conceded, the raid was more audacious than wise. Searchlights from an Argentinian ship in the harbour caught them as they approached, and the Argentinians opened up with every available weapon, including triple-barrelled 20mm Rheinmetall anti-aircraft cannon depressed to their lowest trajectory. These spewed out a constant stream of metal, which obliged the raiders to rapidly withdraw if they were not to suffer heavy losses.

The next morning, 14 June, it was all over. Mike Rose received a signal from the headquarters of the Argentine commander, General Menendez, asking to discuss surrender terms. By evening, the instrument of surrender had been signed.

The SAS campaign to liberate the Falklands had its price. A few days after the attack on Pebble Island, a helicopter cross-decking members of D and G Squadron from HMS *Hermes* to HMS *Intrepid* hit some airborne object, probably a giant petrel or albatross, which was then sucked into the air intake. The Sea King plummeted into the icy water with the loss of twenty SAS troopers and attached specialists, plus one of the aircrew. The dead included Squadron Sergeant Major Lawrence Gallagher and Pebble Island raider Paddy Ryan (Paddy "R"). It was the heaviest loss the Regiment had suffered in a single day since World War II. With the end of the Falklands campaign, the SAS returned home to Stirling Lines in Hereford. Although the Regiment had won a DSO, three MCs and two MMs, and chalked up some outstanding actions and important recces, the mood was sombre. The recent history of the Regiment had been in Black Ops; few, if any, of the SAS had fought against a regular army before, and it was obvious that too many mistakes had been made. And the loss of so many men in the Sea King crash touched almost everyone. An address by Peter de la Billière in the Paludrine Club at Stirling Lines served only to lower the mood further. After some preliminary remarks about the Regiment's victories in the Falklands, he began to berate B Squadron for being insufficiently gung-ho for the Rio Grande attack. At first there was stunned silence. Then, despite orders from the regimental sergeant major, the men began laughing derisorily. A clearly angered DLB strode stiffly from the room.

An SAS man through and through, Peter de la Billière wisely passed off the Paludrine Club fracas as evidence of the strong-mindedness of SAS troopers. That he harboured no grudge against his old regiment was amply proved in 1990, when the Iraqi president Saddam Hussein rolled his armour into Kuwait.

DOCUMENT: Johnny Cooper: Attack on German Aircraft at Sidi Haneish, 26 July 1942

The *raison d'être* of David Stirling's wartime SAS was destroying Luftwaffe aircraft. Up to June 1942 the SAS's modus operandi had been – despite its insistence on parachute training – to hitch a ride on moonless nights with the Long Range Desert Group and attack airfields, before scuttling back to base. With Rommel's dramatic offensive during May and June 1942, which rolled up the 8th Army to the outskirts of El Alamein, a new and tempting target presented itself: the Afrika Korps' communication lines, which were at their all-time longest. In order to wreak as much havoc as possible on these over-extended lines of communication as well as the old target of airfields, Stirling determined that the whole of the SAS – some 100 men – should set up a temporary base in the forward area, from which they could raid when they wished, nightly if possible. It followed that the SAS needed its own transport. Employing his customary silver tongue and light fingers, Stirling secured twenty three-ton Ford trucks and fifteen American "Willy's Bantams", as jeeps were initially known. Stirling had each of them fitted with a pair of Vickers K guns, fore and aft, the suspension was strengthened and an extra fuel tank added. He also secured the services of a very human attribute, Corporal Mike Sadler, the LRDG's master navigator. Sadler's old unit would provide an escort to the forward base, as well as wireless communications.

On 3 July an SAS convoy of thirty-five vehicles left Kabrit, and days later slipped unnoticed through the German lines to rendez-vous with Lieutenant Timpson of the LRDG north of Qattara. Timpson penned a memorable portrait of his meeting with the SAS band:

In the afternoon a great cloud of dust could be seen approaching from the east. The country here is full of escarpments and clefts, and one could see the dust and hear the sound of vehicles long before they hove [sic] into view. Robin [Gurdon, LRDG] was in the lead with his patrol. We directed them to a hideout next to our own. Then came truck after truck of SAS, first swarms of jeeps, then three-tonners, and David in his famous staff car, known as his "blitz-wagon", Corporal Cooper, his inseparable gunner, beside him and Corporal Seekings behind. Mayne, Fraser, Jellicoe, Mather and Scratchley were all there; Rawnsley was wearing a virgin-blue veil and azure pyjamas. Here was the counterpart of Glubb's Arab Legion in the west. Trucks raced to and fro churning up the powdery ground, until most of them came to roost after a while in a hollow half a mile away which we had recommended to them. As aircraft had been flying about we did not quite approve of this crowded activity, yet they had gone through the Alamein Line undetected – an ME 110 which now flew over took no notice – and the reckless cheerfulness of our companions was at least stimulating. Having to rely chiefly on LRDG wireless communications – and on our navigators – David kept our operators busy sending and receiving messages for the whole party. We had a conference that evening and again the next morning, in which he revealed his plans and gave his orders.

Stirling's plan was for six raids to take place on the next night, which would support the 8th Army's counter-offensive. Two patrols would head for Sidi Barrani and El Daba, while four patrols would attack airfields in the Bagush-Fuka area.

The Bagush raid, led by Stirling and Paddy Mayne, was conspicuously successful and led to the birth of a new attacking technique. After planting charges on forty aircraft, Mayne was furious when only twenty-two explosions lit up the skyline. The dissatisfaction was caused by damp primers. Waiting nearby at a roadside ambush, Stirling hit upon a solution to the failed cull. They would all drive on to the airfield in their vehicles – a truck, the blitz wagon and a jeep – and shoot up the remaining aircraft with the Vickers machine guns. As with Stirling's best ideas, it combined speed, audacity and simplicity in equal measure. Five minutes later, a further twelve aircraft were destroyed. The only SAS casualty was the blitz wagon, destroyed by an Italian CR42 aircraft when the party was on its way back to the rendezvous.

Impressed by the reliability and manoeuvrability of the jeeps, Stirling wired the deputy director of operations from his desert base on 10 July:

> Experience in present operations shows potentialities of twin-mounted Bantams at night to be so tremendous to justify immediate allocation of minimum fifty Bantams to L, repeat L, Detachment for modification to be effected immediately on my return. Fear owing to miscarriage of plan, only forty aircraft and some transport destroyed to date.

The "miscarriage" Stirling referred to was the almost across-the-board failure of the other parties, frustrated by poor maps, imperfect intelligence and heightened perimeter security at Luftwaffe airfields. Nevertheless, forty aircraft was, Stirling's modesty notwithstanding, a decent "bag", and took the SAS's total so far to 180 enemy aircraft destroyed. Perhaps the greatest proof of Stirling's successes by mid-1942 was that the Germans garlanded him with the accolade "the Phantom Major"; he even became an item in Rommel's diaries, where Stirling's exploits were noted as having "caused considerable havoc and seriously disquieted the Italians."

Stirling's new method of drive-by shootings would also seriously disquiet the Germans. Amassing no fewer than eighteen jeeps, Stirling set off for Landing Ground 126 at Sidi Haneish, with Sadler's navigation getting them all to within a mile of the target in the moonlight of the evening of 26 July. Sergeant Johnny Cooper recalled:

> I walked quietly over to the two column commanders and gave them David's orders, which were to form into their lines as we moved off. The engines roared and we drove on to the perfect surface of the airfield. David took a line straight down

the runway with aircraft parked on either side. The blasting began. It was not long before the whole aerodrome was ablaze. The ground defences had obviously been alerted but they had difficulty as they were using the low-firing Breda, an Italian 15mm machine gun. With the obstruction of so many parked aircraft they were only able to fire at us in fleeting bursts. At the top end of the runway we turned left and right in a complete wheel and came back down again on another track, still firing. We were almost back at the edge of the field when our jeep came to a shuddering halt. David shouted, "What the hell's wrong?" I leapt out and threw open the bonnet, only to discover that a 15mm shell had gone through the cylinder head and had then passed only inches away from David's knee in the driving position. As if by magic, Captain Sandy Scratchley's jeep came alongside and he shouted, "Come along, we'll give you a lift." I jumped into the back, where Sandy's rear gunner was slumped with a bullet through the head. I eased him out of the way and grabbed the machine gun as David piled into the front beside the forward gunner. We roared off the airfield in pursuit of the two columns that were rapidly disappearing in the smoke haze caused by the havoc we had unleashed. The scene of devastation was fantastic. Aircraft exploded all around us, and as we left the perimeter our own jeep went up in a ball of flame – the only vehicle casualty of the raid.

BANDIT COUNTRY

22 SAS, Northern Ireland, 1976–97

On 7 January 1976, Prime Minister Harold Wilson publicly committed the SAS to patrol the "bandit country" of South Armagh.

Northern Ireland would never be a happy hunting ground for the SAS. The orthodox regiments of the Army already deployed to the province were suspicious and resentful – after all, SAS deployment suggested that they themselves had failed – and there was little possibility of implementing the SAS's by now stock "hearts and minds" campaign. Aside from patrolling, the SAS men in Northern Ireland set up covert observation posts and established a new undercover spying squad known as the Army Surveillance Unit (later 14 Intelligence Company).

The Regiment also became involved in a "capture" mission similar to the SEAL Phoenix programme in the USA. This was intended to take out the hierarchy of the nationalist terrorist Provisional Irish Republican Army (PIRA). While IRA commander Sean McKenna was abducted from his home in Eire and neatly bundled across the border into Northern Ireland to be arrested by the RUC in March 1976, a month later PIRA terrorist Peter Cleary was allegedly shot attempting to escape. In April 1977 IRA "lieutenant" Seamus Harvey was killed on the Donegal border; in February 1978 an SAS ambush killed provo "player" Paul Duffy as he neared a weapons cache in County Tyrone; in June 1978 an undercover Regimental team ambushed a three-man IRA "Active Service Unit" as it was attempting to firebomb Ballysillan Post Office depot; in December 1981 two IRA men were killed in an SAS ambush at Coalisland; in July 1984 in

Tyrone an IRA player was killed; in December 1984 two IRA men were killed in Londonderry; in February 1985 three IRA men were killed at their weapons cache near Strabane; in August 1988 three IRA men were killed in Drumnakilly . . .

Perhaps IRA members who lived by the gun could expect to die by it. Unfortunately, SAS soldiers in Northern Ireland – eventually organized in Ulster Troop – took a steady toll of the innocent. By the end of 1978 the SAS had publicly killed ten people in Northern Ireland, of which three were guiltless and one, a PIRA quartermaster called Patrick Duffy, was shot twelve times in the back. The slaughtered innocents included a sixteen-year-old boy, John Boyle, exploring a churchyard where the IRA had cached arms, and a Belfast Protestant pedestrian, William Hanna; Hanna was killed at Ballysillan Post Office purely because he stumbled on the scene and ran away when challenged. This was a clear case of breaching the rules of engagement in Ulster – by which soldiers could only open fire if they believed a person was about to fire, endanger life and if there was no other means of stopping them. Even the SAS's greatest ever blow against PIRA – the killing of eight PIRA terrorists as they attacked the police station at Loughgall in 1987 – was marred by the shooting of two blameless villagers driving by, one of whom died.

Accusations that the SAS were "shooting to kill" amplified in the following year, when three PIRA members, Danny McCann, Sean Savage and Mairead Farrell, were shot dead by an SAS team in Gibraltar. SAS claims that the trio were warned to surrender were challenged by witnesses. When the families of Savage, McCann and Farrell took the case to the European Court of Human Rights, the court found that the British Government – in the shape of the SAS – had violated Article 2 of the Convention, and deprived the trio of their right to life. The court also ruled that, since the three PIRA members had been engaged in an act of terrorism, the applicants' claims for damages and costs be dismissed.

If SAS black ops in Northern Ireland were controversial, they were also deadly dangerous for the Regiment's troopers. In 1974, Captain Robert Nairac, on undercover work, was overpowered by the IRA outside a County Armagh pub while trying to pass himself off as an Irish labourer. Despite fighting back with all the strength and skill he could muster he was bundled into a car, taken away, tortured and shot. His body was left in an alley. Nairac was awarded the George Cross posthumously. His citation read in part:

> On the night of 14/15 May 1977 Captain Nairac was abducted from a village in South Armagh by at least seven men. Despite his fierce resistance he was overpowered and taken across the border into the nearby Republic of Ireland where he was subjected to a succession of exceptionally savage assaults in an attempt to extract information which would have put other lives and future operations at serious risk. These efforts to break Captain Nairac's will failed entirely. Weakened as he was in strength – though not in spirit – by the brutality, he yet made repeated and spirited attempts to escape, but on each occasion was eventually overpowered by the weight of the numbers against him. After several hours in the hands of his captors Captain Nairac was callously murdered by a gunman of the Provisional Irish Republican Army who had been summoned to the scene. His assassin subsequently said "He never told us anything".

Trooper Tom Read recalled a bog-standard undercover SAS operation in Northern Ireland, in which he and his team were tailing a van suspected of carrying PIRA members, when it went "tits up":

> The Escort van has double doors at the back with rear windows covered in what looks like silver paper. I pull away and slip in behind it, putting it between myself and John's car. The dicker sees me leave and gets on his radio – the game is up! Suddenly the van spears off to the left, giving up on the target. As they take the turn, they drop the galvanized tin covering the rear windows and open fire.
> "Contact! Contact!"
>   I can see black masks and the muzzle flashes of an automatic rifle. Within seconds we are hurtling along a narrow

country road at 70 mph. I fight with every corner in the low gears. The van is much faster around the bends and keeps disappearing from view and then reappearing. Beside me, Cyril opens up with the MP-5 and punches a dozen neat holes in the laminated glass. He's trying to aim at the target at the same time as holding on as we swerve around corners. Ernie is leaning over my shoulder, with his elbows braced against the two front seats and the HK-53 pointing directly out through the windscreen. When he opens up with his cannon I think my head has exploded. I half expect to see the van disappear in a ball of flames.

He keeps firing and the red-hot cases spit out of the breach, bouncing off my left ear. Two of them fall down the front of my shirt where I've loosened my tie. Shit, they hurt! The Renault leans heavily on the bends and surges over dips as I try to create a stable platform for the lads to shoot from. Trees and hedges flash past in a blur, but all I care about is not losing sight of the van. At the same time, I'm constantly trying to transmit our location and direction, but part of the windscreen has been shot out and the noise of the rushing air and gun-fire means I can't hear any incoming calls. Each time we swing into view, the terrorists keep firing with what seems to be an Armalite and a shotgun. One round hits the dashboard and severs the electrics for the Renault's windows and sun-roof. Another goes straight through the windscreen and hits the back window, passing between Ernie's head and mine. They're edging ahead . . . thirty yards, then forty. The IRA have selected a good vehicle. I could thrash them on a motorway, but the Renault doesn't like the tight corners and I'm hammering the low gears. The van keeps weaving from side to side; it only needs something to be coming the other way.

"Where's a tractor when you need one?" yells Cyril.

Ernie: "Don't lose them, Tom. Don't lose them."

The windscreen is a mass of holes and cracked glass. I lean back and kick it with my left foot. My side flies out, but the other half blows back into Cyril's lap. A wall of rushing air explodes into the car, lifting debris from the floor.

Suddenly, we emerge back on to Dungannon Road, taking a sharp right. I see uniforms and a bus stop. A half-dozen schoolchildren are crawling out of a ditch where they've thrown themselves to get away from the van.

"Oh, shit!" Wrenching at the wheel, I feel the weight of the Renault shift beneath me. For a split-second, I think I've lost it. I drop a gear and accelerate. Everything happens in slow motion – a young girl with muddy knees looks at me; she's got a red ribbon in her hair and her school books are scattered at her feet.

With every fibre, I will the Renault to turn. The tail-end is sliding. At the last instant, the wheels grip and the Renault responds. We go hurtling past the bus stop and along the old Dungannon Road.

It's a long straight stretch running parallel to the motorway. Now the Renault has the advantage. Flooring the accelerator we begin closing the gap. The van is weaving from side to side as Cyril and Ernie open up. Fifty metres . . . forty metres . . . thirty metres . . . twenty . . . Recognizing where we are, I call in our position. John's car is on the same road, up ahead of us, with the van heading directly towards them.

Fastening his seat belt, John yells at Chris behind the wheel: "Ram it!"

"You must be fucking joking," he says. It doesn't make sense – at a closing speed of 170 mph they'd all die. Chris slams on the brakes and throws the Lancia around, side on, trying to block the road. The van is almost on top of them and swerves up a right bank around them, like a wall-of-death stunt. John tries to get out of the front passenger seat with his seat belt still buckled. It forces him backwards at the precise moment that two PIRA rounds hit the window of his door. If not for the seat belt, he'd certainly have been hit. Chris is out of the driver's side and takes up a firing position, kneeling down near the front right headlight. Jocky scrambles out a back door and also opens fire. I aim the Renault directly at Chris with my foot to the floor and just before I hit him I tweak the wheel and send the car into the ditch and up the bank, riding on the same near-vertical wall as the PIRA van.

Again I close the gap, but the van is zigzagging from side to side. I keep a steady line, giving Ernie and Cyril a platform, even though it makes the Renault an easier target. The van is now on the wrong side of the road, risking a head-on collision with anything coming the other way. I can't understand why. Suddenly, it brakes and spears across in front of me, taking a sharp left turn into Washingbay Road. In a fraction of a second, I realize my mistake – the PIRA driver had been setting himself for the corner. He almost rolls the van but makes the turn. I start pulling the wheel, but at my speed from the left side of the road I have no chance. At the precise moment that I decide not to go for it, Cyril screams, "No way!" I hit the brakes in a controlled skid, overshooting the junction.

"John, it's gone left! John, it's gone left!"

The Lancia makes the turn but we've lost a crucial twenty seconds. Over the road, turn right, then left, where's it gone? The van has simply vanished. There's a Cortina with a single occupant parked opposite a muddy farm track.

"Which way did the yellow van go?" asks Jocky. The driver motions down the road and the Lancia takes off in pursuit. They've been sent the wrong way by a dicker. The van has turned off along a gravel farm track. We scour the area for twenty minutes but all of us know it's too late – the terrorists have gone.

The RUC find the van later, full of empty shell cases, abandoned at the back of a farm. The IRA had taken a hostage, cut the phone lines and made their way on foot across several fields to Derryavena before taking another car. That's how they avoid the police road-blocks.

I'm exhausted and bitterly disappointed, but the news is about to get far worse. An innocent civilian has been killed in the operation. Frederick Jackson had been pulling out of a lumber yard in his car, with his foot propped on the clutch as he looked left and right. One of our rounds had ricocheted off the road and gone through the car door. It hit Mr Jackson in his body and exited through his neck. The car rolled back and re-parked itself.

Three months later, in December 1984, one of Read's team, Al Slater, was shot dead by the IRA after getting out of his car in a lane where an IRA team happened to be hidden behind a hedge. Corporal Slater joined a roll of honour of SAS dead in Northern Ireland, which included Captain Herbert Richard Westmacott, killed by IRA gunfire in May 1980. Westmacott and his team had stormed a house on the Antrim Road in west Belfast – alas the wrong house. An IRA unit engaged them with an M60 machine gun as they made their exit to their unmarked "Q" car.

The cat-and-mouse game between the SAS and IRA continued until 1997 when the IRA announced a ceasefire which has held to this day.

As many in 22 SAS noted, the IRA's willingness to parlay peace did not seem unconnected to the fact that SAS activity had severely depleted the terrorist ranks. There were as few as fifty "shooters and bombers" left in the whole of its stronghold, Belfast.

DOCUMENT: Duncan Falconer, "Eye to Eye with the IRA", 1970s

"The Det" did not only include members of the SAS; operatives from the Special Boat Service also served with Intelligence Detachment 14. Duncan Falconer, an SBS operative manning an Observation Post near Crossmaglen, on the border between Eire and Northern Ireland (Ulster), emerged from his snow-covered hide one morning to place a marker for their pick-up driver to recognize. As he put the marker down, he caught sight of two men climbing through a hedge one hundred yards in front of him.

Falconer was on a two-man patrol. His partner Max was still in the hide:

> They could have been farmers, but there was something about them, the way they were watching me. A ripple of concern passed through me, but ripples of concern were always doing that in this job. You learned to do nothing unless the skin broke and you were drowning in the stuff. I stood to

face them and put both hands in my coat pockets. I did not want to go back for my M16 because it would mean turning my back on them, nor did I want to risk getting stalled by the thicket – if these were boyos they were close enough to run forward and take a shot at me. Anyhow, one of the tricks of undercover work was never to overreact. They might just nod "good day" and pass me by. My left hand went to my hidden radio and my right was through the pocket of my jacket, which I had removed, to grip my 9mm Browning pistol in its holster underneath. I could fire it without having to draw it out of my pocket if I had to, not the most accurate but definitely the quickest method to get off a shot, which was often all that counted. I wondered where Max was.

The two men also had their hands in their coat pockets. I didn't recognize them – if they were boyos they were none I had worked against before. They headed directly for me and stopped a few feet apart at the waist-high border fence, their eyes never leaving me. Their breath, like mine, was a thick steam. The width of the country lane was the distance that separated us – them in the Republic, me in Ulster.

They were older, in their forties I reckoned, their faces craggy and weathered. They scanned around, looking to see if I was alone. Both were cool and cordial but I could sense an arrogance and a malevolence. They were definitely suspicious of me.

"How yer doin'?" one said.

"Fine," I replied.

"What ye doin' out here?" said the other.

"I'm waiting for some mates," I said.

When they heard my London accent any doubts they had as to who or what I was disappeared. There was only one kind of Englishman who hangs around the Irish border in bandit country at dawn wearing civvies and looking as if he'd been out all night. I could not disguise my English accent – it was pointless trying to. A professional actor would have trouble fooling these people with a put-on accent. That's why this job was the most difficult intelligence-gathering of its type in the world. You could not ask anyone questions or strike up an innocent conversation without revealing you were not one of them. I felt certain they were boyos, if not official, then highly prejudiced sympathizers. If they did suspect I was a British undercover man – an SAS man as they called all of us – they would also expect me to be armed. If so, they were too confident not to be armed themselves.

"You're a long way from home, Englishman."

As I answered I triggered my radio, which transmitted everything I said. "My home goes all the way up to that fence you're standing behind."

My voice boomed over the speaker in South Det operations room, some 80 miles away, and jolted out of his reverie the only occupant of the room, the duty bleep (signaller), who had been sitting back reading a book.

As it was early and my operation, which was closing down, was the only one going on that morning, everyone else in the Det was in bed or having breakfast. The duty bleep wheeled his chair over to the operations wall, which was covered with a giant map, and looked at the only operation marker on it, on the border, indicating my location. I never met a signaller assigned to the 14 Int Dets who wasn't as sharp as a razor. They were not trained as operatives, but knew all there was to know about our side of it. He realized I was having a conversation with a local and knew we avoided this type of contact. If I was transmitting the conversation it meant I was trying to tell the Det something.

He punched an intercom which connected him to the rooms of all relevant personnel and said, "I think we've got a standby! I repeat, standby, standby."

Bodies dived out of beds or from the cookhouse or TV room and rushed to the ops room. Within half a minute every member of the operations staff was there. "Standby" was the most serious transmission you could send over the radio. Everyone else on the net automatically went silent to clear the airwaves. It meant an operative was about to unavoidably engage with the enemy. The next thing the ops room expected to hear was shooting. The ops staff always felt helpless in these situations because they could hear and talk to a lone operative in trouble, but could do little else to help. And it was not as if the man on the other end of the radio was a stranger, either. We drank, ate, worked, mourned and celebrated together, and all they could do now was listen and hope that when the shooting stopped, it was the familiar voice that came back over the speaker to say he was OK. This was not always the case.

"Who are you?" I asked.

There was no doubt in my mind now that they were boyos. The aggression was seeping from their pores. One of them was clenching his jaw, holding himself back, waiting. They had either not quite decided if I was alone, or they were carefully choosing their moment.

They had no idea they were being listened to 80 miles away, and they no doubt intended to dust me anyway. They felt in control. As they talked, I kept my radio on "send" and their voices were picked up by the highly sensitive microphone and transmitted to the operations room.

"Michael's the name."

Michael, the one who was clenching his jaw, did not appear to be the leader of the two, but he looked the most eager to have a go. The other quietly stared at me, more intelligent and calculating than Michael. The comms room didn't quite catch the name and I repeated it, at the same time stepping slightly forward so the men's voices could be picked up better. I found myself repeating much of what they said.

"You shy?" I asked the other man, who did not appreciate being talked to like that.

"Cassidy. Jimmy Cassidy," he said confidently.

In the ops room our intelligence officer, still in his pyjamas, jotted down the name and hurried off to check it.

"Where's your mates?" Cassidy asked.

"They'll be along," I said.

"Will they now?" asked Michael.

Our pick-up car was still some 20 miles away and the driver was going like the clappers to get to me, fully aware of what was going on as he listened to the transmissions. I was feeling edgy. Whoever started the shooting would have the advantage. I was daring myself, looking for an excuse to start. My adrenaline was rising. Things were starting to seem like they were taking for ever. I decided to move first and destroy the bastards, but something was holding me back. A doubt, perhaps, that I was all wrong about what was going on. I rehearsed the move in my mind. I would hit Michael first. All I needed was a tiny excuse to start. Then the intelligence officer's voice came through my earpiece and brought me back.

"I've got two possible Jimmy Cassidys of South Armagh. How old is he?" Then, quickly realizing I couldn't talk directly to him, he said, "Is your man in his twenties, would you say?"

I kept silent.

"In his forties?"

I clicked the radio twice.

"That's a yes," said the bleep.

Michael and Jimmy could not hear the transmissions, obviously. They said something to me, but I just stared at them, concentrating on what the intelligence officer was telling me.

"One of the Jimmy Cassidys I have is forty-seven. His hair is thinning – a high forehead."

I clicked twice.

"He's five-ten, stocky, round-faced, about eleven stone."

I clicked twice. Cassidy said something to me during the transmission. I heard myself say, "What?" and continued to listen to the intelligence officer and Cassidy at the same time.

"If it's our Cassidy he runs his own ASU."

"I said, what are you doing out here?" asked Cassidy, repeating his question.

"The other man is more than likely one of his team. Try Michael Doherty."

"Are you deaf?" Cassidy asked.

"I told you. Waiting for some friends."

Michael moved away from Jimmy, stretching the gap between them to a few yards. They were dividing up – getting closer to making their move. I decided if one of them made an attempt to climb over the fence I'd take advantage of his hands being occupied and engage the other first.

"Doherty is thirty-five. Dark curly hair. His eyebrows meet."

I clicked twice and decided to take a different tack.

"You're Michael Doherty, aren't you?" I said.

Michael's reaction confirmed it.

"Yeah, it is Doherty, isn't it?" I was speaking to the intelligence officer in reality.

Michael was staring at me, wondering how I knew him. I'd stalled him.

The intelligence officer started to rattle off information from his file.

"What are you doing here yourself, Jimmy? Bit early for you, isn't it? Don't you live in Armagh? Hall Street, I believe . . . number seventy-seven."

Jimmy's eyes narrowed.

"Two-twenty-four Saggart Road. That's where you live, Michael – when you're this side of the border, that is. Isn't that right? With your sister and her husband."

Michael flashed a look at Jimmy. I talked to the two men as if I were recalling their details from memory, repeating what was said to me over the net.

"How's your brother doing, Jimmy? Another five years and he's out . . . perhaps."

Both men were off balance.

"And how's the bomb-making school doing?" I continued to Jimmy. "I understand you're specializing in mortars these days."

"Who the fuck are you?" Michael asked.

I had nowhere else to go with this. They were no doubt stunned that I knew so much about them. Then I heard a familiar voice break over the radio.

"I'm twenty yards behind you, Duncan, on your left."

It was Max. He had heard everything over his own radio and had run then crawled as close as he could without being detected. He would have his M16 pointed at them.

"If they show armour I'll unzip the fucker on the left," he said.

I now felt in control. My confidence in Max was total. Their lives were in my hands. A desire to goad them into a fight flickered across my mind. Max would take out Michael. I would take out Jimmy. But that's not the way I am. I'm not a murderer, which is what it would have been had I gone for it. We could have got away with it, too. I could have said they had drawn first. We could have upped our score. I could have killed them for Jack and several other friends who had been killed by the IRA over the years. But body counts don't win wars. They are won by convincing the other side they cannot succeed.

"There's a rifle pointed directly at you," I said. "Either one of you takes a hand from his pocket and you'll both lose your heads."

They took this information well and I could see by the subtle changes in their faces that they had no doubt I was telling the truth. Perhaps they read the booming confidence in my threat.

"I'm gonna do you a favour today. Now fuck off the way you came."

They communicated to each other with silent looks. Jimmy nodded to me, then they stepped back and walked away.

OPERATION MONGOOSE

CIA, Cuba, 1959–64

For years Fidel Alejandro Castro Ruz complained about CIA plots to kill him. For years the CIA denied doing anything so improper. As it turned out, the ruler of Cuba was right. The CIA had Castro in its crosshairs for a decade or more.

Born in 1926, Castro led the 1959 Cuban Revolution, which established a socialist state 90 miles off the coast of Florida. As Wayne Smith, former head of US Interests Section in Havana, once memorably put it, socialist Cuba's effect on the capitalist US was that of "a full moon on a werewolf". Neither was Castro's socialist makeover of Cuba exactly popular with the Mafia (which had interests in Havana's casinos), or the supporters of the overthrown Fulgencio Batista. And so the CIA, the Mafia and the Batistas all started hatching schemes to rid Cuba of the hirsute dictator. Initially the CIA's plots centred on merely humiliating Castro; in the psy-op codenamed "Good Times" postcards were to be dropped over Cuba showing a corpulent Castro living the high life ("should put even a Commie dictator in the proper perspective with the underprivileged masses" stated the authorizing memo); another plan called for an LSD-like drug to be sprayed in the air at the radio station Castro used for his speeches so he would start ranting nonsense. No less whacky was an idea to dust the Cuban leader's shoes with a depilatory powder so the hair in his beard would fall out.

When humiliating Castro failed, the CIA tried invading Cuba (the Bay of Pigs debacle) before settling on assassinating him. Most of CIA's assassination plans were apparently drawn from a bad Bond novel, and included:

- Contaminating Castro's cigars with botulin.
- Contaminating Castro's drink with botulin.
- Popping poison pills into Castro's food at his favourite restaurant, with a little help from the Mafia (including Santos Trafficante, Johnny Roselli and Sam Giancana – all incidentally contenders for killing John F. Kennedy).
- Contaminating Castro's scuba-diving gear with tubercle bacilli, and his wetsuit with a skin-disfiguring fungus.
- Placing an eye-catching conch on the seabed off Cuba – Castro was a keen diver – which contained an explosive device, which would detonate on being lifted.

No fewer than eight separate plans were drawn up by the CIA between 1960 and 1965 for the final solution of the Castro problem, only one of which was rooted in reality. Rolando Cubela Seconde, a major in the Cuban army and head of Cuba's International Federation of Students, handily contacted the CIA offering to do their job for them. (Cubela had form as an assassin; as a young student he had murdered Antonio Blanci Rico, head of Batista's secret police.) The CIA gave Cubela the code name AMLASH and a syringe disguised as a Paper Mate pen and told him to inject Black Leaf 40 (an insecticide) into Castro. Eventually, Cubela got the assassin's tool he wanted: a Belgian FAL rifle so he could kill Castro from afar. Before Cubela could pull the trigger, however, he was arrested by Castro's security service. With quite remarkable generosity, Castro asked the court for clemency on Cubela's behalf, and the putative assassin was sentenced to jail instead of a firing squad. Cubela was released in 1979 and went to live in Spain. By then the truth of the CIA's "Get Castro!" campaign had been dragged into the open, following an investigation by US Senator Frank Church.

The Church Committee's "Interim Report" of 1975 detailed the CIA's hapless history of trying to undermine, then kill, Castro, and for good measure delineated CIA involvement in the assassination of Patrice Lumumba of Congo, Rene Schneider of Chile, Rafael Trujillo of the Dominican Republic and Ngo Dinh Diem of Vietnam. The most spectacular proof of the CIA's anti-Castro antics, however, came in 1993, with the declassification of the

"Inspector General's Report on Plots to Assassinate Fidel Castro" (see Document), which had been commissioned by President Johnson in 1967. So controversial, incriminating – and maybe embarrassing – was the report that the CIA refused its declassification for thirty-six years. Even presidents were refused access to the full document.

On the recommendation of the Church Committee, President Gerald Ford issued Executive Order 11905, which ruled that "no employee of the US government shall engage in, or conspire to engage in, political assassination". Jimmy Carter strengthened this proscription with Executive Order 12036, as did Reagan, through Executive Order 12333. Because no subsequent executive order or piece of legislation has repealed the prohibition, it remains in effect.

DOCUMENT: CIA Inspector General's Report on Plots to Assassinate Fidel Castro [Extracts]

The report was drawn up in 1967 at the insistence of President Johnson – who was not allowed by the Agency to see the full version. Neither was President Nixon. Indeed, the CIA regarded their own report as so incriminating that all but one copy was destroyed. The report was only approved for release in 1993.

23 May 1967: MEMORANDUM FOR THE RECORD
SUBJECT: Report on Plots to Assassinate Fidel Castro
This report was prepared at the request of the Director of Central Intelligence. He assigned the task to the Inspector General on 23 March 1967. The report was delivered to the Director, personally, in installments, beginning on 24 April 1967. The Director returned this copy to the Inspector General on 22 May 1967 with instructions that the Inspector General:

Retain it in personal, EYES ONLY safekeeping
[. . .]
This ribbon copy is the only text of the report now in existence, either in whole or in part. Its text has been read only by:

Richard Helms, Director of Central Intelligence J. S. Earman, Inspector General K. E. Greer, Inspector (one of the authors) S. E. Beckinridge (one of the authors)

All typing of drafts and of final text was done by the authors.

[. . .]

It became clear very early in our investigation that the vigor with which schemes were pursued within the Agency to eliminate Castro personally varied with the intensity of the U.S. Government's efforts to overthrow the Castro regime. We can identify five separate phases in Agency assassination planning, although the transitions from one to another are not always sharply defined. Each phase is a reflection of the then prevailing Government attitude toward the Cuban regime.

a. Prior to August 1960: All of the identifiable schemes prior to about August 1960, with one possible exception, were aimed only at discrediting Castro personally by influencing his behavior or by altering his appearance.

b. August 1960 to April 1961: The plots that were hatched in late 1960 and early 1961 were aggressively pursued and were viewed by at least some of the participants as being merely one aspect of the over-all active effort to overthrow the regime that culminated in the Bay of Pigs.

c. April 1961 to late 1961: A major scheme that was begun in August 1960 was called off after the Bay of Pigs and remained dormant for several months, as did most other Agency operational activity related to Cuba.

d. Late 1961 to late 1962: That particular scheme was reactivated in early 1962 and was again pushed vigorously in the era of Project MONGOOSE and in the climate of intense administration pressure on CIA to do something about Castro and his Cuba.

e. Late 1962 until well into 1963: After the Cuban missile crisis of October 1962 and the collapse of Project MONGOOSE, the aggressive scheme that was begun in August 1960 and revived in April 1962 was finally terminated in early 1963. Two other plots were originated in 1963, but both were impracticable and nothing ever came of them. We cannot overemphasize the extent to which responsible Agency officers felt themselves subject to the Kennedy administration's severe pressures to do something about Castro and his regime. The fruitless and, in retrospect, often unrealistic plotting should be viewed in that light. Many of those we interviewed stressed two points that are so obvious that recording them here may be superfluous. We believe, though, that they are pertinent to the story. Elimination of the dominant figure in a government, even when loyalties are held to him personally rather than to the government as a body, will not necessarily cause the downfall of the government. This point was stressed with respect to Castro and Cuba in an internal CIA draft paper of October 1961, which was initiated in response to General Maxwell Taylor's desire for a contingency plan. The paper took the position that the demise of Fidel Castro, from whatever cause, would offer little opportunity for the liberation of Cuba from Communist and Soviet Bloc control. The second point, which is more specifically relevant to our investigation, is that bringing about the downfall of a government necessarily requires the removal of its leaders from positions of power, and there is always the risk that the participants will resort to assassination. Such removals from power as the house arrest of a [redacted] or the flight of a [redacted] could not cause one to overlook the killings of a Diem or of a Trujillo by forces encouraged but not controlled by the U.S. government.

There is a third point, which was not directly made by any of those we interviewed, but which emerges clearly from the interviews and from review of files. The point is that of frequent resort to synecdoche – the mention of a part when the whole is to be understood, or vice versa. Thus, we encounter repeated references to phrases such as "disposing of Castro," which may be read in the narrow, literal sense of assassinating him, when it is intended that it be read in the broader, figurative sense of dislodging the Castro regime. Reversing this coin, we find people speaking vaguely of "doing something about Castro" when it is clear that what they have specifically in mind is killing him. In a situation wherein those speaking may not have actually meant what they seemed to say or may not have said what they actually meant, they should not be surprised if their oral shorthand is interpreted differently than was intended.

The suggestion was made that operations aimed at the assassination of Castro may have been generated in an atmosphere of stress in intelligence publications on the possibility of Castro's demise and on the reordering of the political structure that would follow. We reviewed intelligence publications from 1960 through 1966, including National Intelligence Estimates, Special National Intelligence Estimates, Intelligence Memorandums, and Memorandums for the Director. The NTEs on "The Situation and Prospects in Cuba" for 1960, 1963, and 1964 have brief paragraphs on likely successor governments if Castro were to depart the scene. We also find similar short references in a SNIE of March 1960 and in an Intelligence Memorandum of May 1965. In each case the treatment is no more nor less than one would expect to find in comprehensive round-ups such as these. We conclude that there is no reason to believe that the operators were unduly influenced by the content of intelligence publications.

Drew Pearson's column of 7 March 1967 refers to a reported CIA plan in 1963 to assassinate Cuba's Fidel Castro. Pearson also has information, as yet unpublished, to the effect that there was a meeting at the State Department at which assassination of Castro was discussed and that a team actually landed in Cuba with pills to be used in an assassination attempt. There is basis in fact for each of those three reports.

a. A CIA officer passed an assassination weapon to an Agency Cuban asset at a meeting in Paris on 22 November 1963. The weapon was a ballpoint pen rigged as a hypodermic syringe. The CIA officer suggested that the Cuban asset load the syringe with Black Leaf 40. The evidence indicates that the meeting was under way at the very moment President Kennedy was shot.

b. There was a meeting of the Special Group (Augmented) in Secretary Rusk's conference room on 10 August 1962 at which Secretary McNamara broached the subject of liquidation of Cuban leaders. The discussion resulted in a Project MONGOOSE action memorandum prepared by Edward Lansdale. At another Special Group meeting on 31 July 1964 there was discussion of a recently disseminated Clandestine Services information report on a Cuban exile plot to assassinate Castro. CIA had refused the exile's request for funds and had no involvement in that plot.

c. CIA twice (first in early 1961 and again in early 1962) supplied lethal pills to U.S. gambling syndicate members working in behalf of CIA on a plot to assassinate Fidel Castro. The 1961 plot aborted and the pills were recovered. Those furnished in April 1962 were passed by the gambling syndicate representative to a Cuban exile leader in Florida, who in turn had them sent to Cuba about May 1962. In June 1962 the exile leader reported that a team of three men had been dispatched to Cuba to recruit for the operation. If the opportunity presented itself, the team would make an attempt on Castro's life – perhaps using the pills.

This report describes these and other episodes in detail; puts them into perspective; and reveals that, while the events described by Drew Pearson did occur and are subject to being patched together as though one complete story, the implication of a direct, causative relationship among them is unfounded.

Miscellaneous Schemes Prior to August 1960 [. . .]
We find evidence of at least three, and perhaps four, schemes that were under consideration well before the Bay of Pigs, but we can fix the time frame only speculatively. Those who have some knowledge of the episodes guessed at dates ranging from 1959 through 1961. The March-to-August span we have fixed may be too narrow, but it best fits the limited evidence we have.

a. None of those we interviewed who was first assigned to the Cuba task force after the Bay of Pigs knows of any of these schemes.

b. J. D. (Jake) Esterline, who was head of the Cuba task force in pre-Bay of Pigs days, is probably the most reliable witness on general timing. He may not have been privy to the precise details of any of the plans, but he seems at least to have known of all of them. He is no longer able to keep the details of one plan separate from those of another, but each of the facts he recalls fits somewhere into one of the schemes. Hence, we conclude that all of these schemes were under consideration while Esterline had direct responsibility for Cuba operations.

c. Esterline himself furnishes the best clue as to the possible time span. He thinks it unlikely that any planning of this sort would have progressed to the point of consideration of means until after U.S. policy concerning Cuba was decided upon about March 1960. By about the end of the third quarter of 1960, the total energies of the task force were concentrated on the main-thrust effort, and there would have been no interest in nor time for pursuing such wills-o'-the-wisp as these. We are unable to establish even a tentative sequence among the schemes; they may, in fact, have been under consideration simultaneously. We find no evidence that any of these schemes was approved at any level higher than division, if that. We think it most likely that no higher-level approvals were sought, because none of the schemes progressed to the point where approval to launch would have been needed.

Aerosol Attack on Radio Station:
[deletion] of TSD remembers discussion of a scheme to contaminate the air of the radio station where Castro broadcasts his speeches with an aerosol spray of a chemical that produces reactions similar to those of lysergic acid (LSD). Nothing came of the idea. [deletion] said he had discouraged the scheme, because the chemical could not be relied upon to be effective. [deletion], also of TSD, recalls experimentation with psychic energizers but cannot relate it to Castro as a

target. We found no one else who remembered anything of this plot, with the possible exception of Jake Esterline who may have it confused with other schemes.

Contaminated Cigars:

Jake Esterline claims to have had in his possession in pre-Bay of Pigs days a box of cigars that had been treated with some sort of chemical. In our first interview with him, his recollection was that the chemical was intended to produce temporary personality disorientation. The thought was to somehow contrive to have Castro smoke one before making a speech and then to make a public spectacle of himself. Esterline distinctly recalls having had the cigars in his personal safe until he left WH/4 and that they definitely were intended for Castro. He does not remember how they came into his possession, but he thinks they must have been prepared by [deletion].

In a second interview with Esterline, we mentioned that we had learned since first speaking with him of a scheme to cause Castro's beard to fall out. He then said that his cigars might have been associated with that plan. Esterline finally said that, although it was evident that he no longer remembered the intended effect of the cigars, he was positive they were not lethal. The cigars were never used, according to Esterline, because WH/4 could not figure out how to deliver them without danger of blowback on the Agency. He says he destroyed them before leaving WH/4 in June 1961.

Sidney Gottlieb, of TSD, claims to remember distinctly a plot involving cigars. To emphasize the clarity of his memory, he named the officer, then assigned to WH/CA, who approached him with the scheme. Although there may well have been such a plot, the officer Gottlieb named was then assigned to India and has never worked in WH Division nor had anything to do with Cuba operations. Gottlieb remembers the scheme as being one that was talked about frequently but not widely and as being concerned with killing, not merely influencing behavior. As far as Gottlieb knows, this idea never got beyond the talking stage. TSD may have gone ahead and prepared the cigars just in case, but Gottlieb is certain that he did not get the DD/P's (Richard Bissell) personal approval to release them, as would have been done if the operation had gone that far. We are unable to discover whether Esterline and Gottlieb are speaking of a single cigar episode or of two unrelated schemes. We found no one else with firm recollections of lethal cigars being considered prior to August 1960.

Depilatory:

[deletion] recalls a scheme involving thallium salts, a chemical used by women as a depilatory – the thought being to destroy Castro's image as "The Beard" by causing the beard to fall out. The chemical may be administered either orally or by absorption through the skin. The right dosage causes depilation; too much produces paralysis. [deletion] believes that the idea originated in connection with a trip Castro was to have made outside of Cuba. The idea was to dust thallium powder into Castro's shoes when they were put out at night to be shined. The scheme progressed as far as procuring the chemical and testing it on animals. [deletion] recollection is that Castro did not make the intended trip, and the scheme fell through. [deletion] remembers consideration being given to use the thallium salts (perhaps against Castro) and something having to do with boots or shoes. [deletion] does not remember with whom he dealt on this plot. We found no one else with firm knowledge of it.

Gambling Syndicate:

The first seriously pursued CIA plan to assassinate Castro had its inception in August 1960. It involved the use of members of the criminal underworld with contacts inside Cuba. The operation had two phases: the first ran from August 1960 until late April or early May 1961, when it was called off following the Bay of Pigs; the second ran from April 1962 until February 1963 and was merely a revival of the first phase which had been inactive since about May 1961.

Gambling Syndicate – Phase I
August 1960

Richard Bissell, Deputy Director for Plans, asked Sheffield Edwards, Director of Security, if Edwards could establish contact with the U.S. gambling syndicate that was active in Cuba. The objective clearly was the assassination of Castro although Edwards claims that there was a studied avoidance of the term in his conversation with Bissell. Bissell recalls that the idea originated with J. C. King, then Chief of WH Division, although King now recalls having had only limited knowledge of such a plan and at a much later date – about mid-1962. Edwards consulted Robert A. Maheu, a private investigator who had done sensitive work for the Agency, to see if Maheu had any underworld contacts. Maheu was once a special agent of the FBI. He opened a private office in Washington in 1956. The late Robert Cunningham, of the Office of Security (and also a former Special Agent with the FBI), knew Maheu and knew that his business was having a shaky start financially. Cunningham arranged to subsidize Maheu to the extent of $500 per month. Within six months Maheu was doing so well financially that he suggested that the retainer be discontinued. Over the years he has been intimately involved in providing support for some of the Agency's more sensitive operations. He has since moved his personal headquarters to Los Angeles but retains a Washington office.

A more detailed account of Maheu's background appears in a separate section of this report [. . .] Maheu acknowledged that he had a contact who might furnish access to the criminal underworld, but Maheu was most reluctant to allow himself to be involved in such an assignment. He agreed to participate only after being pressed by Edwards to do so. Maheu identified his contact as one Johnny Roselli, who lived in Los Angeles and had the concession for the ice-making machines on "the strip" in Las Vegas and whom Maheu understood to be a member of the syndicate. Maheu was known to Roselli as a man who had a number of large business organizations as clients. Edwards and Maheu agreed that Maheu would approach Roselli as the representative of businessmen with interests in Cuba who saw the elimination of Castro as the essential first step to the recovery of their investments. Maheu was authorized to tell Roselli that his "clients" were willing to pay $150,000 for Castro's removal.

September 1960
Shef Edwards named as his case officer for the operation James P. O'Connell (a former Special Agent of the FBI), then Chief, Operational Support Division, Office of Security.

O'Connell and Maheu met Roselli in New York City on 14 September 1960 where Maheu made the pitch. Roselli initially was also reluctant to become involved, but finally agreed to introduce Maheu to "Sam Gold" who either had arranged or could arrange contacts with syndicate elements in Cuba who might handle the job. Roselli said he had no interest in being paid for his participation and believed that "Gold" would feel the same way. A memorandum for the record prepared by Sheffield Edwards on 14 May 1962 states: "No monies were ever paid to Roselli and Giancana. Maheu was paid part of his expense money during the periods that he was in Miami." (Giancana is "Gold.")

O'Connell was introduced (in true name) to Roselli as an employee of Maheu, the explanation being that O'Connell would handle the case for Maheu, because Maheu was too busy to work on it full time himself. No one else in the Office of Security was made witting of the operation at this time. Edwards himself did not meet Roselli until the summer of 1962.

At this point, about the second half of September, Shef Edwards told Bissell that he had a friend, a private investigator, who had a contact who in turn had other contacts through whom syndicate elements in Cuba could be reached. These syndicate elements in Cuba would be willing to take on such an operation. As of the latter part of September 1960, Edwards, O'Connell, and Bissell were the only ones in the Agency who knew of a plan against Castro involving U.S. gangster elements. Edwards states that Richard Helms was not informed of the plan, because Cuba was being handled by Bissell at that time. With Bissell present, Edwards briefed the Director (Allen Dulles) and the DDCI (General Cabell) on the existence of a plan involving members of the syndicate. The discussion was circumspect; Edwards deliberately avoided the use of any "bad words." The descriptive term used was "intelligence operation." Edwards is quite sure that the DCI and the DDCI clearly understood the nature of the operation he was discussing. He recalls describing the channel as being "from A to B to C." As he then envisioned it, "A" was Maheu, "B" was Roselli, and "C" was the principal in Cuba. Edwards recalls that Mr. Dulles merely nodded, presumably in understanding and approval. Certainly, there was no opposition. Edwards states that, while there was no formal approval as such, he felt that he clearly had tacit approval to use his own judgment. Bissell committed $150,000 for the support of the operation [. . .] in the Fontainebleau Hotel. "Gold" said he had a man, whom he identified only as "Joe," who would serve as courier to Cuba and make arrangements there. Maheu pointed out "Gold" to O'Connell from a distance, but O'Connell never met with either "Gold" or "Joe." He did, however, learn their true identities. An Office of Security memorandum to the DDCI of 24 June 1966 places the time as "several weeks later." O'Connell is now uncertain as to whether it was on this first visit to Miami or on a subsequent one that he and Maheu learned the true identities of the two men. Maheu and O'Connell were staying at separate hotels. Maheu phoned O'Connell one Sunday morning and called his attention to the Parade supplement in one of that morning's Miami newspapers. It carried an article on the Cosa Nostra, with pictures of prominent members. The man Maheu and O'Connell knew as "Sam Gold" appeared as Mom Salvatore (Sam) Giancana, a Chicago-based gangster. "Joe, the courier" (who was never identified to either Maheu or O'Connell in any other way) turned out to be Santos Trafficante, the Cosa Nostra chieftain in Cuba.

At that time the gambling casinos were still operating in Cuba, and Trafficante was making regular trips between

Miami and Havana on syndicate business. (The casinos were closed and gambling was banned effective 7 January 1959. On 13 January 1959, Castro announced that the casinos would be permitted to reopen for tourists and foreigners but that Cubans would be barred. The cabinet on 17 February 1959 authorized reopening the casinos for the tourist trade. *Time* magazine for 2 March 1959 announced that the casinos had been reopened the previous week. The *New York Times* issue of 30 September 1961 announced that the last of the casinos still running had been closed.) Trafficante was to make the arrangements with one of his contacts inside Cuba on one of his trips to Havana.

Fall and Early Winter 1960

Very early in the operation, well before the first contact with Roselli, the machinery for readying the means of assassination was set in motion. The sequence of events is not clear, but it is apparent that a number of methods were considered. Preparation of some materials went ahead without express approval [. . .] Dr. Edward Gunn, Chief, Operations Division, Office of Medical Services, has a notation that on 16 August 1960 he received a box of Cuban cigars to be treated with lethal material. He understood them to be Fidel's favorite brand, and he thinks they were given to him by Shef Edwards. Edwards does not recall the incident. Gunn has a notation that he contacted [deletion] of TSD, on 6 September 1960. [deletion] remembers experimenting with some cigars and then treating a full box. He cannot now recall whether he was initially given two boxes, experimenting with one and then treating the other; or whether he bought a box for experimentation, after which he treated the box supplied him by Gunn. He does not, in fact, remember Gunn as the supplier of any cigars. He is positive, though, that he did contaminate a full box of fifty cigars with botulinus toxin, a virulent poison that produces a fatal illness some hours after it is ingested. [deletion] distinctly remembers the flaps-and-seals job he had to do on the box and on each of the wrapped cigars, both to get the cigars and to erase evidence of tampering. He kept one of the experimental cigars and still has it. He retested it during our inquiry and found that the toxin still retained 94% of its original effectiveness. The cigars were so heavily contaminated that merely putting one in the mouth would do the job; the intended victim would not actually have to smoke it.

Gunn's notes show that he reported the cigars as being ready for delivery on 7 October 1960. [deletion]'s notes do not show actual delivery until 13 February 1961. They do not indicate to whom delivery was made. Gunn states that he took the cigars, at some unspecified time, and kept them in his personal safe. He remembers destroying them within a month of Shef Edwards' retirement in June 1963 [...] Edwards recalls approaching Roosevelt after Bissell had already spoken to Roosevelt on the subject; Roosevelt recalls speaking to Edwards after Bissell discussed it with Edwards. Bissell does not recall specific conversations with either of them on the technical aspects of the problem, but he believes that he must have "closed the loop" by talks with both Edwards and Roosevelt. Roosevelt recalls his first meeting with Edwards as being in Edwards' office. Edwards remembers asking to be introduced to a chemist. He is sure that he did not name the target to Roosevelt, but Roosevelt says he knew it was Castro. Roosevelt believes that he would have put Edwards in touch with [deletion], then chief of TSD's Chemical Division, but [deletion] has no recollection of such work at that time. [deletion] recalls other operations at other times, but not this one. Roosevelt did say that, if he turned it over to [deletion], [deletion] could have assigned it to [deletion].

Roosevelt remembers that four possible approaches were considered: (1) something highly toxic, such as shellfish poison to be administered with a pin (which Roosevelt said was what was supplied to Gary Powers); (2) bacterial material in liquid form; (3) bacterial treatment of a cigarette or cigar; and (4) a handkerchief treated with bacteria. The decision, to the best of his recollection, was that bacteria in liquid form was the best means. Bissell recalls the same decision, tying it to a recollection that Castro frequently drank tea,

coffee, or bouillon, for which a liquid poison would be particularly well suited.

January–February 1961

Despite the decision that a poison in liquid form would be
most desirable, what was actually prepared and delivered
was a solid in the form of small pills about the size of saccha-
rine tablets. [deletion] remembers meeting with Edwards
and O'Connell in Edwards' office to discuss the requirement. The specifications were that the poison be stable,
soluble, safe to handle, undetectable, not immediately
acting, and with a firmly predictable end result. Botulin
comes nearest to meeting all those requirements, and it may
be put up in either liquid or solid form. [deletion] states that
the pill form was chosen because of ease and safety of
handling[. . .] (Comment: The gangsters may have had
some influence on the choice of a means of assassination.
O'Connell says that in his very early discussions with the
gangsters (or, more precisely, Maheu's discussions with
them) consideration was given to possible ways of accomplishing the mission. Apparently the Agency had first
thought in terms of a typical, gangland-style killing in which
Castro would be gunned down. Giancana was flatly opposed
to the use of firearms. He said that no one could be recruited
to do the job, because the chance of survival and escape
would be negligible. Giancana stated a preference for a
lethal pill that could be put into Castro's food or drink.
Trafficante ("Joe, the courier") was in touch with a disaf-
fected Cuban official with access to Castro and presumably
of a sort that would enable him to surreptitiously poison
Castro. The gangsters named their man inside as Juan Orta
who was then Office Chief and Director General of the
Office of the Prime Minister (Castro). The gangsters said
that Orta had once been in a position to receive kickbacks
from the gambling interests, has since lost that source of
income, and needed the money.) When Edwards received
the pills he dropped one into a glass of water to test it for
solubility and found that it did not even disintegrate, let

alone dissolve. [deletion] took them back and made up a new batch that met the requirement for solubility.

Edwards at that point wanted assurance that the pills were truly lethal. He called on Dr. Gunn to make an independent test of them. Edwards gave Gunn money to buy guinea pigs as test animals. Gunn has a record of a conversation with [deletion] on 6 February 1961. It may have related to the tests, but we cannot be sure. What appears to have happened is that Gunn tested the pills on the guinea pigs and found them ineffective. [deletion] states that tests of botulin on guinea pigs are not valid, because guinea pigs have a high resistance to this particular toxin. [deletion] himself tested the pills on monkeys and found they did the job expected of them. We cannot reconstruct with certainty the sequence of events between readying the pills and putting them into the hands of Roselli. Edwards has the impression that he had a favorable report from Dr. Gunn on the guinea pig test. Gunn probably reported only that the pills were effective, and Edwards assumed the report was based on the results of tests on guinea pigs. Dr. Gunn has a clear recollection, without a date, of being present at a meeting in which Roosevelt demonstrated a pencil designed as a concealment device for delivering the pills. Roosevelt also recalls such a meeting, also without a date. Gunn's notes record that his last action on the operation came on 10 February 1961 when he put Gottlieb in touch with Edwards. Gottlieb has no recollection of being involved, an impression that is supported by Bissell who states that Gottlieb's assignments were of a different nature. O'Connell, who eventually received the pills, recalls that he dealt with [deletion]. [deletion] has no record of delivering the pills at this time, but he does not ordinarily keep detailed records of such things.

In any event, O'Connell did receive the pills, and he believes there were six of them. He recalls giving three to Roselli. Presumably the other three were used in testing for solubility and effectiveness. The dates on which O'Connell received the pills and subsequently passed them to Roselli cannot be established. It would have been sometime after

Gunn's notation of 10 February 1961. Gunn also has a record of being approached about the undertaking by William K. Harvey (former special agent of the FBI) in February in connection with a sensitive project Harvey was working on for Bissell. According to Gunn's notes, he briefed Harvey on the operation, and Harvey instructed him to discuss techniques, but not targets, with Gottlieb. Gunn's notation on this point is not in accord with the recollections of any of the others involved. We are unable to clarify it; the note may have been in another context. O'Connell states that J. C. King was also briefed at this time, although King denies learning of the operation until much later.

Late February–March 1961
Roselli passed the pills to Trafficante. Roselli reported to O'Connell that the pills had been delivered to Orta in Cuba. Orta is understood to have kept the pills for a couple of weeks before returning them. According to the gangsters, Orta got cold feet [. . .] The previously mentioned 24 June 1966 summary of the operation prepared by the Office of Security states that when Orta asked out of the assignment he suggested another candidate who made several attempts without success. Neither Edwards nor O'Connell know the identity of Orta's replacement nor any additional details of the reported further attempts.

March–April 1961
Following the collapse of the Orta channel, Roselli told O'Connell that Trafficante knew of a man high up in the Cuban exile movement who might do the job. He identified him as Tony Varona (Dr. Manuel Antonio de Varona y Loredo). Varona was the head of the Democratic Revolutionary Front, [1/2 line deletion] part of the larger Cuban operation. O'Connell understood that Varona was dissatisfied [. . .] had hired Edward K. Moss, a Washington public relations counselor, as a fund raiser and public relations advisor. The Bureau report alleged that Moss' mistress was one Julia Cellini, whose brothers represented two of the

largest gambling casinos in Cuba. The Cellini brothers were believed to be in touch with Varona through Moss and were reported to have offered Varona large sums of money for his operations against Castro, with the understanding that they would receive privileged treatment "in the Cuba of the future." Attempts to verify these reports were unsuccessful [. . .] Trafficante approached Varona and told him that he had clients who wanted to do away with Castro and that they would pay big money for the job. Varona is reported to have been very receptive, since it would mean that he would be able to buy his own ships, arms, and communications equipment [. . .] dated 24 June 1965, sets the amount as $10,000 in cash and $1,000 worth of communications equipment. Jake Esterline, who signed the vouchers for the funds, recalls the amounts as being those stated in the Office of Security memorandum. (Comment: As a sidelight, Esterline says that, when he learned of the intended use of Varona, steps were taken to cancel the plan. Varona was one of the five key figures in the Revolutionary Front and was heavily involved in support of the approaching Bay of Pigs operation. If steps were in fact taken to end Varona's participation in the syndicate plan, they were ineffective. It is clear that he continued as an integral part of the syndicate scheme.)

When the money was ready, O'Connell took the pills from his safe and delivered them and the money to Roselli. Roselli gave the pills and the money to Varona, whom Roselli dealt with under pseudonym. Little is known of the delivery channels beyond Varona. Varona was believed to have an asset inside Cuba in a position to slip a pill to Castro. Edwards recalls something about a contact who worked in a restaurant frequented by Castro and who was to receive the pills and put them into Castro's food or drink. Edwards believes that the scheme failed because Castro ceased to visit that particular restaurant.

April–May 1961

Soon after the Bay of Pigs, Edwards sent word to Roselli through O'Connell that the operation was off – even if something happened there would be no payoff. Edwards is sure there was a complete stand-down after that; the operation was dead and remained so until April 1962. He clearly relates the origins of the operation to the upcoming Bay of Pigs invasion, and its termination to the Bay of Pigs failure. O'Connell agrees that the operation was called off after the Bay of Pigs but that the termination was not firm and final. He believes that there was something going on between April 1961 and April 1962, but he cannot now recall what. He agrees with Bill Harvey that when the operation was revived in April 1962, Harvey took over a "going operation." (Comment: As distinguished from Edwards and O'Connell, both Bissell and Esterline place the termination date of the assassination operation as being about six months before the Bay of Pigs. Esterline gives as his reason for so believing the fact that the decision had been made to go ahead with a massive, major operation instead of an individually-targeted one such as this. Whatever the intention in this respect, if the decision to terminate was actually made, the decision was not communicated effectively. It is clear that this plan to assassinate Castro continued in train until sometime after the Bay of Pigs.)

O'Connell believes that he must have recovered the pills, but he has no specific recollection of having done so. He thinks that instead of returning them to TSD he probably would have destroyed them, most likely by flushing them down a toilet. [deletion] has no record of the pills having been returned to him, but he says he is quite sure that they were. [. . .]

Schemes in Early 1963

Skin Diving Suit

At about the time of the Donovan–Castro negotiations for the release of the Bay of Pigs prisoners a plan was devised to have Donovan present a contaminated skin-diving suit to Castro as a gift. Castro was known to be a skin-diving enthusiast. We cannot put a precise date on this scheme. Desmond FitzGerald told us of it as if it had originated after he took over the Cuba task force in January 1963. Samuel Halpern said that it began under William Harvey and that he, Halpern, briefed FitzGerald on it. Harvey states positively that he never heard of it.

According to Sidney Gottlieb, this scheme progressed to the point of actually buying a diving suit and readying it for delivery. The technique involved dusting the inside of the suit with a fungus that would produce a disabling and chronic skin disease (Madura foot) and contaminating the breathing apparatus with tubercle bacilli. Gottlieb does not remember what came of the scheme or what happened to the scuba suit. Sam Halpern, who was in on the scheme, at first said the plan was dropped because it was obviously impracticable. He later recalled that the plan was abandoned because it was overtaken by events: Donovan had already given Castro a skin-diving suit on his own initiative. The scheme may have been mentioned to Mike Miskovsky, who worked with Donovan, but FitzGerald has no recollection that it was. [. . .]

Booby-trapped Sea Shell

Some time in 1963, date uncertain but probably early in the year, Desmond FitzGerald, then Chief, SAS, originated a scheme for doing away with Castro by means of an explosives-rigged sea shell. The idea was to take an unusually spectacular sea shell that would be certain to catch Castro's eye, load it with an explosive triggered to blow when the shell was lifted, and submerge it in an area where Castro often went skin diving.

Des bought two books on Caribbean Mollusca. The scheme was soon found to be impracticable. None of the shells that might conceivably be found in the Caribbean area was both spectacular enough to be sure of attracting attention and large enough to hold the needed volume of explosive. The midget submarine that would have had to be used in emplacement of the shell has too short an operating range for such an operation.

FitzGerald states that he, Sam Halpern, and [deletion] had several sessions at which they explored this possibility, but that no one else was ever brought in on the talks. Halpern believes that he had conversations with TSD on feasibility and using a hypothetical case. He does not remember with whom he may have spoken. We are unable to identify any others who knew of the scheme at the time it was being considered.

BAT 21 DOWN

US Navy SEALs/VVN Commando, Vietnam, 1972

30 March 1972. Along the South Vietnamese border, the North Vietnamese Army (NVA) has lined up three divisions of artillery, tank and infantry units for its Easter Offensive. The NVA is ready to rumble, and tauntingly displays its flags for the Army of South Vietnam (AVRN) to see.

It will be a battle of high drama. It will also see acts of extraordinary heroism in what will be the largest and longest combat search and rescue operation of the war in Southeast Asia.

Lieutenant-Colonel Iceal "Gene" Hambleton was a USAF senior navigator and electronic warfare specialist on EB-66C electronic reconnaissance airplanes. The EB-66Cs escorted the less manoeuvrable B-52s, because they could locate NVA surface-to-air missile (SAM) sites and jam their SAM radars. On 2 April an emergency request came through for a pair of EB-66Cs to escort three B-52s on a raid against SAM sites in the southern "panhandle" of North Vietnam. The fifty-three-year-old Hambleton was normally a back officer crew scheduler, but because the unit was under-strength climbed into the navigator's seat of an EB-66C. Its call sign was BAT-21 Bravo.

As the aerial armada approached the border with the North it came under fire from hitherto unknown SAM sites. BAT-21 was hit by an SA-2 Guideline SAM at 30,000 feet. Sitting in the navigator's seat, Hambleton was automatically ejected first. The pilot and the four electronic warfare specialists aboard never made it out.

Hambleton, who was just nine months off retirement, parachuted slowly to the ground, and landed in a rice paddy just east of Cam Lo village in Quang Tri province and slap in the middle of the NVA offensive. Here he waited until it was dark, and then relocated into a wooded area nearby, where he dug himself a hidey-hole. Using his emergency radio Hambleton was able to make radio contact with an O-2 FAC (forward air controller) pilot patrolling in his vicinity. The FAC called in AH-1 Cobra helicopter gunships and F-4 Phantom fighter-bombers to lay down gunfire, bombs and "gravel" (anti-personnel mines) to keep enemy troops away from Hambleton's hideout, while he waited anxiously for rescue.

Hambleton was not the only one worrying about his rescue. Lieutenant-Colonel Hambleton knew more about the US's electronic warfare capability in Vietnam than anyone else. If the NVA got him and made him talk they would have secured an intel mother lode. Hambleton had to be rescued.

For days the downed aviator watched as rescue sortie after sortie was forced to abort because of the intensity of the NVA's ground fire. Exhausted, hungry, bleeding from a shrapnel wound sustained in the SAM attack, Hambleton's blackest moment came at the end of the fifth day; an Air Force Jolly Green Giant rescue helicopter was hit by NVA fire and detonated in an apocalyptic fireball, killing all six men aboard. An OV-10 was also lost, with the pilot captured, but crewman Mark Clark evading NVA searchers. There were now two men on the ground needing rescuing. Five more aircraft were shot down, but their crews were rescued.

At the end of day six, General Creighton Abrams in Saigon ordered that no further helicopters were to be used for CSAR missions to pick up Hambleton and Clark.

The rescue was going to have to come from the ground. Lieutenant-Colonel Andy Anderson, USMC, the commander of the Joint Personnel Recovery Center, believed a team of South Vietnamese commandos he had been working with could undertake the op. But an American was needed as an adviser. Navy SEAL Lieutenant Tom Norris, one of the few SEALs left in theatre, got the call.

Norris knew about covert ops. He even trained Force recon Marines on how to do them. But even he was awed by this particular job: "I was used to running ops where I was penetrating into the opposing forces' territory without much support, but I had never seen anything like this." The ARVN officer in charge of the commandos, General Giai, declared the mission was insane, and refused to allow his team beyond the front line.

The initial plan was to have a team composed of Anderson, Norris, and five Vietnamese commandos, establish a Lying Up Place (LUP) on the Mieu Giang River, and have both Clark and Hambleton float down to the team.

Aware that North Vietnamese radio monitors understood English, the orbiting FAC radioed Clark, an Idaho native: "Get to the Snake, make like Esther Williams and float to Boston" – go to the river and swim east. While Clark was doing this, Norris started leading half of the team through enemy territory towards the Cam Lo; it was slow and dangerous work as the area was heavy with enemy patrols. When they finally reached the river's bank they heard Clark in the water, breathing hard because of the cold.

As Norris was about to step out from cover to grab Clark, an NVA patrol appeared almost directly in front of them. Resisting the impulse to open fire – which would have compromised the mission – Norris waited for them to disappear. By then Clark had floated past. So, Norris entered the river himself to search for Clark (son of World War II general, Mark Clark) and after a few hours found him lying hidden behind a boat on the riverbank. Linking up with the rest of his team, Norris was able to deliver Clark to the safe care of Anderson and his team.

But by now dawn was breaking. The rescue of Hambleton would have to wait.

The FACs in contact with Hambleton reported that his condition was deteriorating. He was now on his eighth day of evasion. He also had to be moved from his hiding position to a place on the river from where he could be rescued.

Knowing Hambleton was a keen golfer, the FAC team gave him radio directions as though he was playing specific holes on courses he knew. Directions any eavesdropping NVA would find impossible to follow. After "playing" nine holes and nearing collapse from hunger and exhaustion, Hambleton had moved to a location where the rescue team could extract him.

Things, however, were not going well at the LUP, which came under mortar and rocket fire. Lietenant-Colonel Anderson and the seniorVietnamese commando chief were both badly wounded and had to be helicoptered out. Norris was now left with just three Vietnamese commandos, two of whom indicated they did not wish to continue with the mission. At this Norris asked for volunteers. One stepped forward: Petty Officer Nguyen Van Kiet.

Leaving the other two men behind, Norris and Kiet headed upriver to rescue Hambleton, now too weak to move. All night long Norris and Kiet cautiously scoured the shoreline looking for BAT-21. At sunrise the two men reluctantly abandoned the search for the night, and returned to their outpost to rest.

Hambleton had now been ten days down.

The next evening, Norris and Kiet once again made their way upriver. Walking through a deserted village, they found some native clothing and dressed themselves as peasants. They then commandeered an abandoned sampan; as they paddled upstream in the dark and fog they could see Vietnamese soldiers and tanks on the shoreline.

The fog was thick and they became disorientated, realizing when they heard tanks crossing the Cam Lo bridge that they had overshot Hambleton's position. Turning around, they edged cautiously downstream, constantly scanning the gloom for a sign of BAT-21 Bravo.

They found him, the needle in the haystack, lying on the south shore, barely alive.

And it was almost daylight. Norris wanted to lie up and proceed downriver the next evening, but with Hambleton rambling on senselessly they had little chance of avoiding discovery. So Norris hurriedly placed Hambleton onto the bottom of the sampan and covered him with bamboo from the riverbank. Then Norris and Kiet started paddling downriver.

They were soon spotted by an NVA patrol, which hailed them but did not fire. The enemy soldiers along the banks were waking up. Seeing the sampan, some NVA soldiers began to loose off bullets at them. Norris and Kiet paddled harder.

But going round a bend in the river an NVA heavy machine gun opened up on them. Norris and Kiet pulled the sampan over to the opposite bank, and took cover in some brush. Norris called in an airstrike, and five A-4 Skyhawks from the carrier *Hancock* arrived within minutes and obliterated the enemy position. Moving Hambleton back into the sampan, Norris and Kiet once more set off downriver.

The three men were not out of danger yet. More Vietnamese opened up on them, and again Norris had to call in airstrikes. Back in the sampan, Norris and Kiet bent to their grim work, and eventually reached their start line, where an ARVN M113 armoured personnel carrier arrived and took the three men to safety. BAT-21 Bravo was home.

A reporter asked Norris if he would undertake such a rescue mission again. He replied: "An American was down in enemy territory. Of course I'd do it again."

For their heroic roles in the rescue of Iceal Hambleton, both Norris and Kiel were decorated for valour. For his role, President Ford awarded Lieutenant Tom Norris the Medal of Honor, America's highest award for courage on the battlefield:

For conspicuous gallantry and intrepidity in action at the risk of his life above and beyond the call of duty while serving as a SEAL Adviser with the Strategic Technical Directorate Assistance Team, Headquarters, U.S. Military Assistance Command, Vietnam. During the period 10 to 13 April 1972, Lieutenant Norris completed an unprecedented ground rescue of two downed pilots deep within heavily controlled enemy territory in Quang Tri Province. Lieutenant Norris, on the night of 10 April, led a five-man patrol through 2,000 meters of heavily controlled enemy territory, located one of the downed pilots at daybreak, and returned to the Forward Operating Base (FOB). On 11 April, after a devastating mortar and rocket attack on the small FOB, Lieutenant Norris led a three-man team on two unsuccessful rescue attempts for the second pilot. On the afternoon of the 12th, a Forward Air Controller located the pilot and notified Lieutenant Norris. Dressed in fishermen disguises and using a sampan, Lieutenant Norris and one Vietnamese traveled throughout that night and found the injured pilot at dawn. Covering the pilot with bamboo and vegetation, they began the return journey, successfully evading a North Vietnamese patrol. Approaching the FOB, they came under heavy machine-gun fire. Lieutenant Norris called in an air strike which provided suppression fire and a smoke screen, allowing the rescue party to reach the FOB. By his outstanding display of decisive leadership, undaunted courage, and selfless dedication in the face of extreme danger, Lieutenant Norris enhanced the finest traditions of the United States Naval Service.

Petty Officer Kiet of the VNN became one of only two Vietnamese in the entire Vietnam War to be awarded the Navy Cross, the highest valour award that can be given by the US to a non-American.

For extraordinary heroism while serving with friendly forces engaged in armed conflict against the North Vietnamese and Viet Cong communist aggressors in the Republic of Vietnam. On 13 April 1972, Petty Officer Kiet participated in an unprecedented recovery operation for a downed United States aviator behind enemy lines in Quang Tri Province, Republic of Vietnam. He courageously volunteered to accompany a United States SEAL Advisor Thomas R. Norris (Medal Of Honor) in an extremely hazardous attempt to reach the aviator, who was physically unable to move toward friendly positions. Using a sampan and traveling throughout the night, they silently made their way deep into enemy territory, past numerous major enemy positions, locating the pilot at dawn. Once, after being spotted by a North Vietnamese patrol, he calmly continued to keep the enemy confused as the small party successfully evaded the patrol. Later, they were suddenly taken under heavy machine-gun fire. Thinking first of the pilot, he quickly pulled the sampan to safety behind a bank and camouflaged it while air strikes were called on the enemy position. Due to Petty

Officer Kiet's coolness under extremely dangerous conditions and his outstanding courage and professionalism, an American aviator was recovered after an eleven-day ordeal behind enemy lines. His self-discipline, personal courage, and dynamic fighting spirit were an inspiration to all; thereby reflecting great credit upon himself and the Naval Service.

Six months later, in October 1972, Tom Norris – who had struggled with SEAL training and almost been washed out – sustained a near-fatal head wound in combat while protecting a withdrawal, and was presumed dead by the ARVN with him. Fellow Navy SEAL Michael E. Thornton, upon hearing the news, went back intending to recover Norris's body, only to discover that Norris was alive. Just. Thornton was recognized with the Medal of Honor for his actions; he was the first person in more than a century to receive the Medal of Honor for saving the life of another Medal of Honor recipient.

MIRBAT

22 SAS, Oman, 1972

The grey dawn of 19 July 1972. In the fishing port of Mirbat, Oman, a nine-man "BATT" (British Army Training Team) slept in a small mud-and-brick building, save for three troopers who were awake talking and keeping guard. The term "BATT" was a ruse; in reality the nine men were from B Squadron 22 SAS. In command of the detachment was twenty-seven-year-old Captain Mike Kealy, known as "baby Rupert" because of his inexperience. As the smear of light on the eastern horizon grew brighter, 250 communist guerrillas, known as *adoo*, stole to within 400 yards of the SAS "BATT house" and opened fire with mortars, machine guns and small arms.

The battle of Mirbat, one of the most storied actions in the history of 22 SAS, had begun.

Despite the success of the SAS attack on the Jebel Akhdar in 1958, Oman had lurched from instability to instability, particularly in the southern province of Dhofar, where a full-scale communist insurrection had blown up, helped by some flame-fanning from the neighbouring state of Yemen. Qaboos, a new, more moderate Sultan of Oman, had wooed over some of the insurgents and begun the training of a loyal militia, the *firqa*. Acting as bodyguards, intelligence-gatherers, "hearts and minds" campaigners and military trainers, the SAS had been committed to Oman since 1970. Such had been their success that the communist adoo had been pushed on to the back foot. To regain the initiative the adoo needed a stunning victory. Hence the attack on Mirbat. Inside the BATT house Captain Kealy tumbled out of his sleeping bag, pulled on some flip-flops, seized his rifle and ran up the stairs to the roof. Kealy had never been in action before, and as he climbed up he was desperately worried about how he would behave under fire, how he would command men technically below him in rank but high above him in experience. Reaching the roof, Kealy was astounded by the sheer intensity of the assault. Previously the adoo had satisfied themselves with desultory mortar and shell attacks, then hastily withdrawn, but now they had descended the nearby escarpment of the Jebel Ali and were on the open ground just outside the perimeter wire, which flanked the north and west of Mirbat. Through the half-light, Kealy could see that a picket manned by the Sultan's Dhofar Gendarmerie (DG) had been overrun, and the adoo were pounding the small stone fort held by twenty-five gendarmes which dominated the town and was about 400 yards away from the BATT house. Like the BATT house, the DG's fort was inside the perimeter wire. Also inside the wire, almost at the water's edge, was Wali's Fort, occupied by a small force of Askari tribesmen loyal to Qaboos. The Askaris were returning accurate but slow fire from bolt-action .303 rifles.

Shells began landing everywhere inside the town, throwing up plumes of dust. The noise was deafening. An 84mm anti-tank round scorched low overhead to explode behind the BATT house. For a moment Kealy thought a blue-on-blue, or "friendly fire", situation had occurred, and that the Gendarmes' picket and a returning firqat patrol were blasting away at each other. However, his radio operator, Trooper "Tak" Takavesi, a Fijian, soon disabused him of this notion; the firqat were still out somewhere in the back country. Assessing the situation in a manner he found almost a reflex, Kealy ordered Trooper Harris to start returning fire with the team's own mortar from the sangar below. Meanwhile, Trooper Pete Wignall opened up with his .5 Browning, mounted on sandbags on the roof, and Corporal Roger Chapman poured out fire from his general-purpose machine gun. Other SAS men calmly picked off the advancing adoo with Armalite automatic rifles. To Kealy's consternation, the adoo continued to move forward, doing so in textbook manner: fire and movement, fire and movement. The discipline and vigour of the enemy advance suggested that they knew the strength of those within Mirbat – a bare fifty men. Next to Kealy, Trooper Takavesi talked urgently over the radio to a gun pit in front of the DG fort manned by another Fijian SAS trooper, Corporal Labalaba. The gun in the pit was a 25-pounder of World War II vintage. Labalaba, with the 25-pounder's barrel almost horizontal, was *whumphing* out round upon round.

Then Labalaba called on the radio to say he had been "chinned". Takavesi asked permission to go and join his friend. Kealy agreed. Picking up his rifle, Takavesi ran to join his fellow Fijian in the gun pit:

I ran up the hill, dodging as much as I could, taking cover when I had to. They were advancing, and the firing was getting heavier all the time, but I had to get there because Laba was on his own with the Omani artillery, and I didn't know how many of them were with him at the time. I got to the top and crawled in to where Laba was and he was alone. Normally it takes three men to fire the gun and he was doing it all by himself. When he said he'd been chinned he meant he'd been grazed by a bullet, either a ricochet or a direct hit.

I started banging on the door of the fort, trying to get the DG to come out. Only one emerged, the gunner Khalid. I got back to the sangar wall but Khalid was hit. From then on it was just the two of us.

By then it was getting light. We could see figures or bodies everywhere, some still a long distance away towards the coast, along Jebel Ali, and some on the plain due north of us. There were people advancing with machine guns, some running, some firing heavy machine guns, mortars and rocket launchers. All Laba and I did was fire close to Jebel Ali. We couldn't fire at the Jebel because the Omani soldiers were protecting one of our high grounds.

At the same time some of the firqas were coming back into Mirbat, and we were worried about firing on them. So we fired towards the plain. That's where most of the guerrillas were coming from, doing a frontal attack.

It was just like watching a movie. It was about 6 a.m. and

it was very, very cloudy and misty too, so they were lucky they had lots of cover and lots of time to make their way in.

When Laba and I were firing, we were really under heavy attack. As soon as you put your head up, you could hear the bullets whistling by. It was so close. We literally had to crawl to be able to do anything. We'd crawl and load the gun, fire it and then crawl down and do it again.

It was ridiculous. They were almost on top of us, shooting from all directions. At least we could hear on the radio that our comrades back in the house were still okay. It was getting very, very fierce, and Laba and I were joking in Fijian. All the fear seemed to go away.

We knew the gun was their main target and we were still firing at point-blank range. We had no time to aim. All we could do was pick up a round, load it in and fire as quickly as we could. But the guerrillas were coming closer and closer towards us, and at the end we had to abandon it. You can't fire a 25-pounder at 50 yards. You'd just get metal fragments in your face. And we had to cover ourselves.

I heard the crack of a gun. Something hit my shoulder and the shock knocked me out for a few seconds. I really didn't know where I was. I totally curled up. The clearest way of describing it is like an elephant charging at you at 120 miles an hour with a sharp, pointed trunk. Laba, still bleeding from the graze on his chin, crawled across to give me a shell dressing to cover the wound which was on my left side. After that I had to fire my rifle singlehanded with my right hand. I still wasn't frightened. It was us or them. I always had a feeling we would survive in the end. So we just fought on.

Then the rebels reached the wire. Kealy and Corporal Bob Bradshaw started potting adoo as they monkey-climbed up the wire. One fell, then another, but others reached the top and jumped down. The adoo were inside the compound. To protect the fort, where the main weight of the adoo attack was falling, Kealy switched the direction of fire of the "Gimpie" and Browning to cover it.

Shinning down the ladder, Kealy went to the communications room. He had already sent a contact report, but it was clear that they needed air support. They also needed a casevac chopper for Labalaba.

Back on the roof, Bradshaw told Kealy that he could not establish contact with the gun pit. Something like an argument broke out when Kealy insisted that he should be the one to make the dangerous dash to the gun pit to find out what was going on. Finally, Kealy agreed to take Tommy Tobin, the medical orderly, with him. Bradshaw pointed to Kealy's feet and said, "You won't get far in those." Kealy was still wearing his flip-flops. He quickly pulled on desert boots. An eerie lull suddenly descended on the battlefield. Having loosed off so many rounds, the adoo were having to wait for new supplies of ammunition. Kealy decided that this was the moment to make the run to the gun pit. As they left the BATT house, so did Roger Chapman, who sprinted towards the helipad 200 yards away.

For the adoo, the appearance of the helicopter was a signal to renew battle. A ferocious barrage of bullets and shells went up from the adoo positions, and Chapman had to warn off the helicopter by detonating a red smoke flare. The unwelcome restart of the fighting found Kealy and Tobin halfway to the gun pit.

Takavesi in the gun pit watched their approach:

> I could hear the radio going but I was too far away to call for help. Then I saw Mike Kealy and Tommy Tobin coming towards me, dodging bullets. As they approached, the adoo were getting nearer the fort, advancing. They were so close you could almost reach out and touch them. Tommy was the first to reach the sangar and as he climbed over, he got shot in the jaw. I heard machine-gun fire and all I could see was his face being totally torn apart. He fell, and Mike Kealy dragged him to a safe area. Then Mike spoke to me. He decided we'd be better off if he got himself into the ammunition pit a few yards away. It was four feet deep. He ran to it and jumped in and landed on the body of a DG soldier, a "powder monkey", one of those who had been detailed to carry the ammo to the gun pit. There was another soldier cowering in the corner. Kealy told him to move the body and checked our situation. Mike and I were now about three or four yards away from

each other. We couldn't see each other but we could talk. I was shouting at him to tell him that I was running out of ammunition. Luckily, he was with one of the local Omani artillery who still had loaded magazines, so he started throwing them to me. At last I could reload my magazine and keep on firing. The battle was really getting heavy. Mike and I could see two or three people on the corner of the fort throwing grenades only about four or five yards away from us. Mike said, "Look, we'll take one each on each corner." When he was firing I was covering; likewise when I was firing he was covering me. We managed to kill a few.

A snap shot by Kealy felled an adoo who had Tak in his sights; adoo light machine-gun fire was now passing so close to Kealy's head that he could feel the vibrations from the spinning bullets.

A grenade landed on the lip of the ammo pit, the explosion almost bursting Kealy's eardrums. The adoo were almost on top of the pits. There was only one hope; Kealy spoke into the short-range radio and told the BATT house to spray either side of the gun pit with machine-gun and mortar fire. To shorten the mortar range, Bradshaw had to hug the huge tube vertical to his chest as Trooper Harris dropped the shells down the barrel.

At the moment when it seemed that Kealy and Takavesi could hold on no longer, when they would surely be overrun, a Strikemaster of the Sultan's airforce appeared on the scene, its pilot steering under a cloud base a mere 150 feet above the ground.

Then another Strikemaster, cannons blazing, screamed over the battlefield. Seizing the ground-to-air radio in the BATT house, Chapman began passing targets to the jets: the shallow wadi near the fort where the adoo were massed for shelter; the adoo's 34mm Carl Gustav; the 7.62mm machine gun near the perimeter wire. Shells and rockets rained from the sky. To identify his friendly status, Kealy broke out a fluorescent marker panel.

The adoo were not finished yet. On the south-east of the town, they began organizing a counter-thrust. By pure coincidence, another SAS detachment was in Dhofar that day. These were twenty-three men of G Squadron waiting to take over from

Kealy's team, who were due to end their tour the very morning of 19 July. At 09.15 a.m. a G Squadron patrol arrived on the beach at Mirbat and surged towards the town; a second wave of G Squadron reinforcements landed and engaged the adoo on the seaward side. Another relay of Strikemaster jets attacked adoo positions on the Jebel Ali.

Perceptibly, the tide of battle turned and the adoo began to slip away through the shallow wadis around the town. Even so, it was 10.30 a.m. before the helicopter evacuation of the wounded could commence. For a while it was hoped that Tobin would survive by emergency first aid, but he died of his wounds shortly after arriving at the Salalah Field Hospital.

Tobin and Corporal Labalaba, who also died of his wounds, were the sole SAS fatalities incurred during the 22 SAS Regiment's hardest test. For this loss the SAS took the lives of more than thirty-nine adoo. They also delivered a telling blow to adoo morale. Proud warriors all, the adoo had been beaten by fighters better than they. The adoo ceased hostilities four years later.

For his bravery and leadership at Mirbat, Kealy was awarded the DSO. Trooper Tobin and Corporal Labalaba were posthumously awarded the DCM and a Mention in Dispatches.

Tragically, Mike Kealy died of hypothermia during an exercise on the Brecon Beacons in 1972.

OPERATION LIGHTWATER

Task Force Knight, Iraq, 2006

On 25 November 2005, peace activists Tom Fox, Norman Kember, James Loney and Harmeet Singh Sooden were kidnapped in the university area of Baghdad. All were members of the Christian Peacemaker Team.

Four days later al-Jazeera, the Qatar-based cable TV channel, received a tape showing the hostages. With it came a communiqué from a previously unknown organization calling itself the Swords of Righteousness Brigade. Their demand was for all prisoners held by the Coalition to be released.

Calls for the release of the hostages came not only from the predictable sources, but from some unusual ones too. Abu-Qatada, al-Qaeda's "emissary to Europe", put his voice to the demand for the hostages' freedom.

All pleas fell on deaf ears. On 7 March 2006 the kidnappers released another video. To the horror of military analysts one of the hostages, the American Tom Fox, was not present.

The worst of fears was confirmed three days later, when Fox's body was found dumped by a railway line in Baghdad. Fox, it was surmised, had been killed because he was both an American and a former Marine.

Fears grew that the remaining hostages would be shot one by one. At this point, the British government stepped up the pressure for a physical rescue of 74-year-old Norman Kember, who was a British subject and Emeritus Professor of Biophysics at Barts hospital in London.

The hostage mission was put in the hands of Task Force Knight, which was B Squadron 22 SAS by another name. Task

Force Knight had previously been known as Task Force Black, but its underemployment had led to 22 SAS's new broom CO, Lieutenant-Colonel Richard Williams, jokingly calling it "Task Force Slack". Williams shared the philosophy of the Coalition Force's head honcho, General McChrystal, that the way to keep the peace in Iraq was to hit the insurgents every day. Williams re-branded Black to Knight.

The search for Kember was codenamed "Operation Lightwater", and because James Loney and Harmeet Sing Sooden were Canadian, a small number of Canadian Special Forces were included in the shiny new Task Force Knight.

Task Force Knight proceeded to kick in doors in Baghdad to snatch and interrogate suspects in the hunt for information. During Lightwater, fifty raids were progressed, forty-four of them by Task Force Knight, the remainder by US Special Forces. Concurrent with the door-kicking-in programme, there was rigorous analysis of all available information from cell-phone traffic to tips from paid informants to electronic eavesdropping. The Joint Communications Headquarters at Cheltenham played its part.

One lead from the Americans led to a house in Mishada, 20 miles north-west of Baghdad. After breaking down the door in the first minutes of the morning of 23 March 2006, the SAS patrol found two suspects; these were subjected to "tactical questioning", or interrogation, on the spot, which had previously been found to be a particularly effective technique as suspects are off-balance. One of the detainees admitted he knew where Kember was held. This was a house in the al-Hurriyah suburb of western Baghdad.

Now Task Force Knight had to act quickly, before the kidnappers realized they had been compromised. The OC Task Force Knight called an ops meeting at 3 a.m., comprising Task Force Knight, along with elements from 1 Para, the Royal Marines, Australian SAS, Canadian Joint Task Force 2, Delta and DEVGRU (US navy SEALs), and assigned roles.

To avoid attracting attention, the assault team approached the target house in a convoy of taxis and pick-ups. Overhead an unmanned Predator and helicopter gunships circled. A security cordon was established around the district to prevent civilians wandering into the middle of potential firefight.

To ensure a minimum of force was necessary, the OC phoned the kidnappers and informed them that an assault force was on its way. He suggested that the kidnappers vamoosed and left the hostages unharmed.

At 8.00 a.m. local time a twenty-five-man rescue element burst into the two-storey building, calling out for "Mr Kember".

The three hostages were found bound but unharmed on the first floor; Kember himself was chained to a door, and needed to be freed by bolt-cutters. There was no sign of the hostage-takers. Less than two minutes after Task Force Knight entered the building the hostages were hustled into a Bradley armoured vehicle and away to safety. No shots were fired.

The irony of peace activists being rescued by the military was obvious to all. Norman Kember himself seemed to be reluctant to thank the men from Task Force Knight.

On 7 November 2006 Iraqi government troops arrested individuals suspected of involvement in the kidnap and imprisonment of Norman Kember. The same day, Kember released a statement in which he refused to testify against them.

Two years later, Task Force Knight was credited with having removed or killed 3,500 insurgents from the streets of the Iraqi capital.

RECON

LRRP, Vietnam, 1967

The first US Long-Range Reconnaissance Patrol (LRRP) platoons were formed in 1965 by 101st Airborne, as a reactive necessity to the US Army's lack of a unit capable of recceing behind North Vietnamese lines. By 1967 formal LRRP companies were organized, most having three platoons; in 1969 the "Lurps" were designated as Rangers. LRRPs usually operated in four- to eight-man patrols, with most personnel being graduates of the MACV-RECONDO (Reconnaissance Commando) School at Nha Trang. During the Vietnam War, the LRRPs conducted around 23,000 long-range patrols, which, aside from recon, also performed hunter-killing missions. According to one estimate the LRRPs accounted for 10,000 NVA and Vietcong killed in action.

Here Frank Camper recounts his first patrol with the 4th Infantry Division LRRP. The patrol was operating out of a firebase near the Cambodian border. The time is February 1967.

The dawn arrived cold and foggy. Mott gave the signal and we came to our feet and entered the ghostly forest, the mist smothering our footfalls.

For an hour there was no noise to disturb the unreal quality of the morning as we trod softly through the dew-soaked bushes. My trouser legs and boots became as chilly and damp as if we'd forded a stream.

You move with care and caution when your life depends on it. We lifted our feet high as we walked, setting them down slowly, toeing twigs and roots out of the way, pausing every few meters to kneel and listen.

When blue sky finally shone through the treetops, and we stopped to rest, we found a trail and made radio contact with the firebase. I had counted a thousand meters we'd traveled, a third of the way to our objective.

No small infantry patrols had been sent into this area, for fear of losing them. Three companies operating out of the firebase were working east from us, in hopes they might drive the NVA this way, west toward Cambodia.

I covered tailgun, Steffens watched the flanks, and Payne and Mott held the center. Mott had a long conversation with the firebase over the radio, his map before him, weapon and hat laid aside.

Mott marked the location of the trail on the map, while the rest of us guarded both approaches. "We'll go north as long as this trail holds out," he said. "You take point."

I resolved to shoot first and ask questions later, switching to full automatic and proceeding up the path. This was baiting the tiger and we all knew it. One of the laws of jungle warfare is that if you want enemy contact, get on a trail.

I began to sweat from nervous tension, finding myself frequently holding my breath rather than risk the noise of inhaling or exhaling.

The team followed me, imitating my every move, watching my reactions, stepping where I stepped. The suspense was numbing.

In many places the overhead was so dense the sunlight couldn't penetrate. The trail was dim, beset by shadows, the rightful province of the ambusher.

The trail had a destination. I spied the first bunker far enough in advance so that I could blend down into the shrubbery gracefully. The team behind me went to earth so quickly it seemed a breeze had blown and, like smoke, they had disappeared.

Something was wrong. We were too close to the bunkers not to be dead already if the NVA were alert. I took a good look around. The bunkers seemed to be deserted. Soil had sunk between the logs and the firing ports were covered with withered camouflage.

I signaled for the team to stay down, and I checked out the nearest hole by creeping over to it. I was right. These were all old fortifications. I gave an all-clear whistle, and the team came out.

"Looks like a company or more dug in here," Mott said, surveying the positions. He took out his notebook and began to make a diagram of the bunkers.

We began to recover from the exertion of the day, muscles unknotting, fatigues drying out, stomachs growling for food. I pulled a chicken-and-rice from my rucksack, boiling a canteen cup of water to reconstitute it, and sat back to wait.

I hadn't eaten all day, and I was starving. The ration slowly absorbed the water, swelling the packet. I had twenty minutes to wait for the dehydrated ration to reconstitute, but it seemed like an hour to my empty stomach.

To top off a hard day, a plague of sweat bees descended on us. They buzzed and lit everywhere, coming right back after being swatted off, trying to crawl into the corners of my eyes and into my mouth. I draped a handkerchief over my face.

I made a mistake then. My attention wandered for just an instant. I heard a slight sound near where I sat, and looked swiftly around to see what it was.

I found myself looking straight into the eyes of an NVA. He had come out of nowhere! I was sitting nearly out of his line of vision as he glanced in my direction. He acted as if he had not seen me. I was too stunned to move. He continued to look around, seemingly oblivious to my presence.

Then he casually turned to my left and walked out of sight. I couldn't function. Had he seen me? We had looked each other in the eye! I snap-rolled into a depression in the earth against some roots, flicking the safety off my CAR. I detected no sound. He had to be still out there. Probably just a short distance away, crouched in the underbrush.

I looked back and saw Payne as he repacked the radio equipment. I waved at him. He didn't look up. I motioned frantically, Payne totally not noticing me for what seemed to be one eternity.

When Payne finally saw me, he reacted by tapping Mott and going down into the thicket. We waited. Disaster on the first day? Maybe not. My heart knocked against my ribs so loudly I wasn't sure I could hear anything else.

Payne inched up to me. I indicated. *One dink, moving that way*, in a sign language. Payne pointed to himself, and to the right flank, then to me and to the left, motioning we should go out and get our visitor.

We tried the impromptu pincers movement, but only found each other and the trail on which the man had made his escape. "This is how he got up on me without making any noise," I whispered to Payne. The trail was well used and wide.

We crawled back to the old bunkers to wait and listen.

I reached over and pulled my ration package to me, still hungry despite the circumstances. I found I was shaking so badly trying to eat, I was spilling half the rice off my spoon. When we had finished trying to eat, Mott told us to prepare to move, pointing to the trail.

The trail passed on through the bunkers and went for higher ground. I walked forward a few meters and found another trail branching off ours.

"We'll go north as long as the trails do," Mott said. "I believe they'll take us right to the Red Warrior LZ. And start looking for a good place to spend the night. I want to find a good one before it gets too late."

I agreed. This place was too damn active for us to be stumbling around in the dark. I searched carefully as we advanced, turning down any place that didn't afford maximum protection. It was easy to stay on our compass course. All I had to do was move from one trail to another. We were in a network.

It was hours before I came across some good high ground, and I led us up into it. It was so steep it was hard for us to climb. That was fine. Anyone trying to do it at night would make a hell of a lot of noise.

I pulled up from tree to tree, resting in places occasionally. I reached the top dripping with sweat and bleeding from thorn pricks and grass slices, but I didn't just barge in. I hugged the hillside below the crest, listening, calculating how fast I could jump backward and get away if the hill was already claimed for the night.

I peeked over a fallen log and scanned the hilltop. Safe so far. Loping in a crouch, I covered the distance across the small knoll and took cover behind a tree, looking down the opposite slope.

It wasn't as steep on the far side, being part of a ridge. I waved the team up, and we secured the hill for the night, spreading out. I chose the lower part of the slope, the team assuming its usual defensive position: team leader and RTO in the center, point and tailgun at the far ends.

A stick thrown by Mott hit me in the back while I waited. I turned and felt my heart sink as he gave me the *Be quiet* sign. Payne had his M-16 ready, his attention on something near us.

I picked up my weapon, moving nothing but my arm, believing we were about to be attacked. Mott and Payne sneaked into the foliage, moving with absolute silence. Then I heard it for myself.

A short distance away people were walking by, the scuffing of sandals on packed dirt very clear, voices in Vietnamese conversing without fear of detection.

They walked away. I had edged downward until I was absolutely flat against the ground. I realized we'd camped right beside another trail. Mott looked up at me, the whites of his eyes showing all around his pupils.

We dared not try to leave the hill – they would catch us for sure – but if we stayed here, all it would take was for one of them to get lucky and step off the trail, and zap, instant catastrophe.

When it became fully dark, we pulled in together. Payne made the last radio report of the day by only keying the handset and saying nothing aloud. We just couldn't afford it. We didn't unpack anything, lying with our rucksacks beside us.

Later, lights began to flash in the sky toward the firebase we had left. No one was asleep, so we raised our heads, hearing the sound of gunfire drift in on the wind. They were getting hit again.

The firebase responded with its artillery, firing out rounds in all directions and ranges. Flares went up, and tracers arced over the jungle, red for ours, green for theirs. A burning parachute flare fell into the treetops near us and took away our night, until it sputtered out.

Several stray artillery shells sailed in and hit our ridgeline, sounding much louder at night, the blasts echoing into the valley. Even a marker-round canister or two came whistling down and smashed into the trees; all too near for us.

And we soon had company again. A North Vietnamese squad rushed by us on the hidden trail, equipment bumping, heading for the action.

The night and the battle progressed. More NVA went past us, all involved in their own problems, none even guessing we were in pissing distance.

Then a roar greater than the fight below us vibrated through the valley. I glanced up and saw what appeared to be a million red tracers plunging out of the night sky.

Puff! The old C-47 cargo plane with the electric Gatling guns! Puff belched another terrific volley, an unbelievable column of pure bullets that soaked the forest below like a deadly rain.

That was the end to the fighting. No army could stand up to Puff. The dragonship's engines droned lazily overhead, occasionally spraying around the firebase with a breath more deadly than anything imagined in King Arthur's day.

Then it started coming our way! We had no arrangement for radioing anybody to get Puff away from us, the mini-guns drowned out everything, and I expected the fire to nail us to the hill. I had heard of men being killed accidentally by Puff, hundreds of meters from the "beaten zone."

All things considered, it was a long night. The NVA retreated on our trail until dawn, trickling by, disorganized, carrying their wounded and dragging heavy loads.

As soon as it was light enough to see, we were ready to leave. Payne made the radio report, having to repeat himself to be understood, he spoke so low into the mike.

We needed speed, and got off the ridge the fast way, via last night's highway. It was a fresh trail, leading into the hills.

Once we were on low ground and headed for the old Red Warrior LZ, we ducked off the trail and took to the woods again. Evidence of enemy movement was everywhere we looked.

The layer of leaves on the ground had been trodden down in many places by men walking in single file. The dampness of the morning dew betrayed them. The untouched leaves glistened damply. The disturbed leaves were dull. It was easy to see the winding routes Vietnamese patrols had taken only hours before.

We covered the distance to the LZ before noon and without incident, being very careful. I had point again, and saw the first of the NVA fortifications that circled the old LZ.

We stealthily slipped into the old bunker line, the clearing visible ahead of us. The team lay back as I advanced to scout the LZ. I parted the high grass and peered into a vast open field. In the center, like a target, was the landing zone itself, the scars of the battle only now being reclaimed by nature. The pitifully shallow fighting holes had begun to vanish under patches of grass and shrubs.

The line of fire from the NVA position to the LZ was absolutely clear. No wonder they got their butts kicked, I thought dismally. It was so easy to imagine the horror out there, exposed from all sides, the helicopters being shot down, no place to run.

It took time, but we walked completely around the LZ, charting the positions and marveling at them. It was very slow work, checking for booby traps, pacing off yardage, guarding and watching.

Every bunker was firmly roofed over, the mortar pits looked like wells, and trenches connected all the heavy weapons positions. Anti-aircraft guns had been set in between the recoil-less rifle and mortar emplacements, so a chopper flying across the LZ would be like a clay pigeon launched before a crowd of skeet shooters.

It was nearly dark when we had finished the reconnaissance job and had eaten. We sent a long radio report back, describing the patrol up to this point. But as Payne signed us off and packed his mike and antenna, Steffens reached down to his feet and pulled up a strand of buried wire.

"Commo wire!" he exclaimed in a loud whisper. It was gray Chinese issue, not the black U.S. Army wire. "Follow it," Mott ordered.

Steffens ripped the line out of the earth until he came to a tree. It joined a terminal there, spliced into another line. Steffens held up the fistful of wire.

The splice was insulated by paper, and the paper was still fresh. We looked it over closely. They had recently wired this place, expecting to use it again. That answered all our questions for this mission.

Mott pointed to the slight rise toward the west. "Let's get into those thickets," he said, "and take cover for the night. Steve, lead out."

Steffens led us to an entanglement of dried bamboo and vines, and we crawled in like rabbits into a warren. After dark, we moved a hundred meters away on our hands and knees before we slept, to confuse any NVA that might have spotted us earlier.

The stars came out brilliantly and we rested, secure in the dense underbrush, wondering what the NVA were doing tonight. My apprehension was subdued, but it did not go away. We had enjoyed incredible luck so far. It could not continue.

We stayed late in our haven, eating our LRRP rations and making coffee, organizing our gear and watching the LZ through a hole in the foliage. The sun was high by the time Mott announced our next move.

"We're taking a straight 270 degrees west," he told me, "right to the border. We have enough rations to stay out two more days."

I was given the point again, and I kept a steady pace, pausing only long enough to examine a bit of evidence here or there that the enemy had also been this way.

It was as hot as two hells by noon. The forest had become lush jungle, enmeshed in swampy lowland and thick, green mossbeds along the streams. We ran out of energy pushing through the mass of it, sweat pouring off us, a direct sun cooking us unmercifully.

We found a slight clearing and fell into it, throwing our gear down and gasping for breath. Payne wiped the sweat from his neck with his flop hat. "Where the fuck are we?" he asked, his voice weak from the exertion.

Mott slipped his map from his thigh pocket. "About right here, I think," he said, indicating a place on the border. So this was Cambodia. It didn't look a bit different from Vietnam.

"We need to get an exact fix on where we are." Payne insisted. Steve looked around. All we could see was swamp and rain forest infested with vines. "Can't tell anything from here," he stated.

"I'll climb that tree," Payne volunteered, gazing at a tall stand of trees about a hundred meters away. Steve picked up his rifle. "I'll pull security for you," he said. Payne stripped off his shirt and boots, and slung a pair of binoculars over his neck.

He came back down skinned up a bit, but loaded with information. "I'd put us right on the border," he said as he dressed. "I could orient my map and get those mountains and these streams lined up just right."

Mott considered that briefly, then stood and pulled on his rucksack. "Okay. We're on our way home now. Camper, take the point. Back azimuth 90 degrees, let's go."

I aimed my compass, the arrow pointing our way back. We slopped through the swamp, trying to keep on the more solid ground as the humidity made the air itself dense and oppressive. Sweat ran in my eyes, and my uniform was chafing and binding, as wet after ten minutes' walking as if I'd dived into the stream.

As I walked through the grass and water, watching where I put my feet, I saw the footprint. It was a tire-tread sandal print, freshly made in the sandy soil alongside the water.

I felt a shock race straight up my spinal cord. They were here, close. Mott looked at the print. "Turn around, go the other way!" he whispered.

I hurried past the team and retraced our steps. The guy who had made that print was only a few minutes ahead of us. I damned the circumstances that had put us here.

I was cautious, measuring my progress in minutes of life and not meters of ground. Mott whistled. I looked around and he motioned for me to hurry, by pumping his fist up and down like a drill instructor ordering double-time.

I signaled an unmistakable refusal. Mott waved me aside and took point himself. I let him go by and fell in behind. He began to move fast, without caring how much noise he made.

We got out of the swamp and climbed a bombed-out hillside, finding ourselves in a morass of dying elephant grass. Mott hadn't slowed down at all. I wondered if he was giving any thought to where he was taking us.

A semi-path through the grass attracted Mott. It had been pushed down before. We tromped on through the grass, chasing Mott, getting more lost by the meter.

Suddenly Mott seemed to fall in a most awkward way, his hat and rifle flying. I thought he'd tripped over a vine. I stopped, and sidestepped off the trail, squatting down, expecting Mott to get back to his feet.

Mott was scrambling to free his rifles from the vines. "Sarge," I whispered, "what's wrong?" Mott looked back at me, his face a mask of terror. Something was very wrong. "Dinks?" I asked. Mott could see something I couldn't. "Shoot!" I said.

He did nothing. "Goddammit, if you're not going to fire, I am!" I threatened, unsure of the situation. I lifted my weapon and was flipping it off safe when a shot exploded from in front of me, blowing the grass back in my face. My ears rang.

I pulled the trigger instinctively, but my CAR fired just once. I almost had heart failure. I glanced down and saw the selector was only on semi.

I didn't take the time to flip it to full auto. I blasted out the whole magazine in a sweeping fan, my trigger finger moving like lightning.

The shit hit the fan for real then. A deafening cascade of small-arms fire erupted from in front of us. I saw Mott twitching, and thought he was being shot. Bullets hit all around him. I changed magazines, though I wouldn't realize I had done so until I found the empty mag in my shirt later.

Leaves flew off their branches around us and dirt hit my face as near misses bracketed me. I cringed, waiting for the impact of the rounds in my body.

I changed to automatic, somehow making my hand obey, as a Vietnamese jumped up surprisingly close, his AK-47 smoking from muzzle to magazine well, trying to see if he had hit Mott.

I was already pressing the trigger again as he exposed himself, and it was only by chance he was in my line of fire. He never saw me. I swung a burst across his chest and he disappeared, arms flung wide, his weapon spinning through the air.

Unhurt, Mott launched himself off the ground and passed me screaming, "*Go! Go! Go!*" I needed no urging. I was right behind Mott, running as I'd never run before.

It sounded like a firing range behind us. What had Mott done, stumbled into a platoon? I raced through the woods, dodging trees, breaking down vines, losing sight of Mott. My hat was knocked off. Where were Payne and Steffens? The NVA were shooting at me with every jump.

I ran into the clearing we'd passed earlier. It was six inches deep in napalm ashes, and I saw Mott ahead of me, leaving a wake of dust behind him like a whirlwind.

I caught up with him when he tried to leap through a forked tree stump and became stuck. I grabbed him by the seat of the pants and lifted as I passed, literally flipping him over the fork; he regained his feet and outran me.

The swamp was straight ahead, and I caught sight of Payne and Steffens waiting there for us. Mott and I dived into the swamp, totally out of breath. The gunfire had ceased.

Mott grabbed for the radio handset from Payne, getting me caught in the middle and tangled in the cord. I accidentally burned myself on my weapon, the short barrel and flash suppressor as hot as a furnace. "I got one, I got one . . ." I heard myself saying.

"My map, I think I lost it," Mott croaked. In my own semi-stupor of exhaustion I heard that statement. A map was gold to the NVA, especially one of ours marked with patrol routes and coordinate codes.

Steffens watched the grass. "We gotta get the hell out of here, I think they're coming after us!" he warned. Mott radioed battalion again. "Three-Three, I am changing to another location, wait out," he said, and began to slog out of the damp. "Let's go," Mott said nervously.

We trotted to higher ground, so tense an insect couldn't have moved without catching our eye. We found a break in the trees and laid out an aircraft marker panel; Payne hastily set up the radio and Steffens and I staked out the security.

Steffens cursed; his weapon was malfunctioning. He discovered it wouldn't change to automatic and had to be pried off safe with his knife. Payne swapped weapons with Steve while Mott called in our position.

We could see two helicopters in the air about five klicks away, and I hoped the firebase would relay our situation to them. But the minutes ticked past and the choppers flew on. "FAC's coming," Mott said excitedly, "get that panel out where he can see it!"

Talk about service. The small green spotter plane was on our radio frequency before Payne could move the panel. Mott keyed the handset and FAC rode the beam in. Payne stood and held the orange panel up like a big bedsheet – what a target.

"He's got us!" Mott said. Payne gratefully dropped the panel. "He says there's a bomb crater six hundred meters west of here, and to get to it!" Mott said.

The two helicopters had caught FAC's call and banked back toward us. Help at last! We ran to the crater, the drumming of the rotor blades getting closer.

I was the first man on the top. It must have been a hell of a bomb that had cleared this hill; it was as bare as a baby's butt. Only one tree was left standing, and it had no bark or limbs.

I saw the crater, the only cover anywhere, and made for it as fast as my rapidly expiring legs would take me. Two helicopters were approaching us in the sky from the east. We'd have transport in a matter of minutes.

But surprise! The NVA had beaten us to the hill. I saw one hiding in a bush, looking the other way. His khaki uniform gave him away.

"Steve, there's one!" I yelled to Steffens, who was close behind me, firing a full magazine at the bush. The man wasn't there anymore when I hit empty. Steffens saw another dink at the far end of the hilltop and blasted him at fifty meters, from the hip.

I saw the man scream and go down. I reached the bomb crater, and the team piled in on me. The NVA ambush was sprung, and its fire was unleashed on us, kicking dirt up all around our hole.

It was a small crater, and the whole team with rucksacks crowded it badly. The first helicopter came in low, trying to find a place to pick us up. Ground fire drove it away.

We threw red smoke toward the trees and Mott called the spotter plane for support. The second Huey was a gunship. He radioed Mott, asking for an azimuth to the enemy from the smoke. Mott quickly supplied that information.

The gunnie made a firing pass, quad M-60s stuttering, hot brass cartridge cases pelting us. The trees in the fire swayed in the onslaught, grass and brush disintegrating in billows of dust.

I crammed another magazine in my weapon and hammered it out in one pull of the trigger, putting out suppressive fire to our left flank. Steve emptied magazines off to the right, and Mott and Payne peppered to the front.

"Get down! Rockets!" Mott shouted in the din, and we pressed into the soft earth of the bomb crater. The Huey barreled in like a fighter plane, rocket pods flaring, streaks of fire roaring over our hole, and the tree line exploded into a deafening storm of roots and flying splinters.

"He's coming back!" Mott said, his voice sounding distant to my numb eardrums. The chopper cleared out his rocket racks, dumping everything. The projectiles went by just a few meters over our heads, but one caught our lone tree.

It was a white-phosphorus missile. It hit the very tip of the only standing obstruction on the hilltop and went off, showering us with a thousand arcing bits of incandescent particles. If there had been somewhere to go, we'd have unassed that crater then.

Incoming fire halted completely after the last rocket run. The gunship chose a new direction to rip up the trees from, and blazed down, machine guns running wild. We added as much of our fire at the tree line as we could, our hole filling with expended cartridge cases.

The smoke from the burning trees covered the hill thickly. We lost our visibility and had to stop shooting as Mott announced, "Slick coming in, cease fire!"

The rotor wash from the Huey blew the smoke down and outward as it hovered in carefully. I stepped on Payne's shoulder as I jumped out of the hole, and Mott scrambled out and outran me again as we dashed for the helicopter.

Mott had so much speed built up, he ran all the way around the ship and came in through the opposite door. Payne made it out of the hole and ran at the helicopter, but something was wrong with his balance. I didn't realize it then, but all during the firefight my CAR-15 muzzle had been inches from his ear, and the firing had temporarily upset his equilibrium. Payne slammed into the door gunner's machine-gun mount, and had to be pulled bodily into the helicopter.

I was third, as I had slowed down to cover Payne, raking the trees with one of my last magazines, and as I ran for the doorway, firing at the enemy with just one hand holding my CAR-15, my last two or three rounds punctured the tail boom of our own helicopter.

Now we were all in but Steve. He had remained in the crater and continued to fire, dutifully covering his team, performing his tailgun job to the last. He rose and made the dash, the strain showing on his face. His Starlight scope fell from under his rucksack flap.

He knew it fell. He stopped, his eyes still on us, and turned, going back after the instrument.

The rotors were spinning at take-off speed, and our skids were off the ground. Payne was lying nearly unconscious on the deck, and the smoke was still obscuring the trees.

Steffens got to us just as the pilot propelled us upward. Mott and I desperately grappled at Steve's pack straps, hoisting him in, his feet dangling out during the fast, high climb.

I took one breath and collapsed against the bulkhead, watching the burning hill get smaller in the distance. My Lord, we were out of it.

In April 1968 the LRRPs of 1st Cavalry Division (Airmobile), Company E, 52nd Infantry undertook one of the most daring long-range patrols of the Vietnam War when they seized "Signal Hill", the peak of the Dong Re Lao Mountain in the A Shau Valley, to enable communications between the various brigades involved in Operation Delaware and the coast. The "Lurps" held the base for three weeks while the operation proceeded.

THE PHOENIX PROGRAM

CIA, Vietnam, 1968–71

The origins of the CIA's involvement in Vietnam predate the establishment of the Agency itself. While the country was still a colony of France, the OSS (Office of Strategic Services), the forerunner of the CIA, was on the ground trying to understand the way the political winds were blowing. They were blowing hard and fast in the direction of the Communists under Ho Chi Minh. With the defeat of French colonial forces in the epic battle of Dien Bien Phu, Vietnam was divided between the communist North, and a French semi-democratic puppet state in the South. But the French were weary and poor, and in 1955 South Vietnam formally requested US military assistance.

The CIA had set up shop in Saigon, the southern capital, the year before under the cover of the "Saigon Military Mission" (SMM). Head of station was USAF Colonel Edward Lansdale, the putative Assistant Air Attaché. The team's task was two-fold: to wage psychological warfare against the North and its supporters in the south; and to wage paramilitary warfare against the same enemies. For the paramilitary war in the North the SMM organized covert action "Binh" and "Hao" teams, which were infiltrated into the north by the CIA's undercover private airline, Civil Air Transport (CAT). The infiltration was hardly demanding; CAT had been officially contracted to evacuate refugees from the North under the Geneva Accords. The Binh and Hao teams were to carry out sabotage attacks on infrastructure and foment the creation of an anti-communist resistance army.

By 1956 the SMM had begun running a military arm. This was the 1st Observation Group, a clandestine special ops unit formed from troops of the South Vietnamese Army, the ARVN. The 1st Observation Group, which was 300 strong, sent fifteen-man teams into the North for aggressive reconnaissance.

But it was not only North Vietnam which posed a threat to the South. In neighbouring Laos communist troops from Northern Vietnam had co-operated with Laos's home-grown red army, Pathet Lao, to seize control of the Laotian "Panhandle". In effect, the communists could now infiltrate the South from the west. In this deteriorating situation, the CIA set up the innocuous-sounding Program Evaluation Office in Laos as a front for covert action against Pathet Lao and the NVA troops illegally operating from Laos. Central to the CIA's shadow war in Laos was the recruitment of the Hmong tribe and their chief, Vang Pao. Eventually, the CIA's Hmong army would number some 40,000 guerrilla soldiers, who were supported and supplied by Air America, as the CIA's private CAT air force had been rebranded. Only the CIA's shadow war in Afghanistan in the 1980s would be a bigger covert operation.

For all the worries on the far-right of US politics that Democratic President John F. Kennedy was "soft" on Communism, he energetically took up the cudgels against the spread of red on the world's map. His personal enthusiasm for undercover war saw a massive increase in the numbers of special forces committed to Vietnam and the wholesale expansion of CIA covert activities in the region, as overseen by the new Agency chief in Saigon, William Colby. Civilian Irregular Defense Groups (CIDG) were established in the Southern Highlands as an anti-communist "home guard" with support from Nung mercenaries. But the CIDGs were essentially a passive measure; the increasing tempo of communist infiltration from the North invited a like response.

Unfortunately for the Agency, the debacle that was the Bay of Pigs invasion of Cuba raised serious questions about its ability to handle covert military and quasi-military operations. A US Commission under General Maxwell Taylor concluded that operations which had expanded beyond intelligence-gathering should be handed over to the Army. In Vietnam this "switch-back" resulted in OPLAN34A, the escalation of covert actions in the North, being handed over to MACV-SOG (Military Assistance Command, Vietnam – Studies and Observations Group) under the command of Colonel Clyde Russell in January 1964.

But the CIA was far from finished in Vietnam. In 1967 the US established the Civil Operations and Revolutionary Development Support (CORDS) office in the South. CORDS, which was run by the CIA's William Colby, streamlined the "pacification" work of MACV-SOG and the CIA under one umbrella. One of CORDS main initiatives was the Intelligence Coordination and Exploitation Program in 1967, which was rechristened Phoenix in the following year. (The South Vietnamese called the programme *Phụng Hoàng*, after a mythical bird that foretold good fortune.) Run by the CIA, Phoenix identified members of the communist Viet Cong Infrastructure (VCI) in the South, and interrogated them. Information on potential VCI members was forwarded to field forces, which included South Vietnamese police, SEALs, US Special Forces and the CIA's own "Provincial Reconnaissance Units" (PRUs). The PRUs were a 4,000-strong paramilitary force directed and escorted by CIA advisers. VCI targets visited by the PRUs (and the other Phoenix field forces) in the villages and hamlets were "neutralized".

The Phoenix programme proved one of the most controversial aspects of US involvement. Critics of the Phoenix programme claimed that, in the hands of the CIA's PRUs, "neutralization" was synonymous with assassination and that 20,000 VCI died from beatings and bullets. The CIA's counter-claim was that if Phoenix targets died only 14 per cent of the 26,369 were killed by PRUs.

The Agency also highlighted the effectiveness of the Phoenix programme. By 1971, when Phoenix ended, the VCI had been neutralized so effectively that it was unable to operate.

The program was terminated because of negative publicity.

DOCUMENT: Testimony of Michael Uhl and Barton K Osborn/MACV-Directive 525-36 Phoenix (Phung Hoang) Operations

U.S. Assistance Programs in Vietnam

Monday, August 2, 1971
House of Representatives, Foreign Operations and
Government Information Subcommittee of the Committee
of Government Operations,
Washington, D.C.

Present: Representatives William S. Moorhead, Ogden R. Reid, and Paul N. McCloskey, Jr.

Mr. Moorhead. Today we will hear from two outside witnesses . . . The witnesses, Mr. Michael Uhl and Mr. Barton K. Osborn, both served in the U.S. Armed Forces in Vietnam during the past several years. Both had command and operational responsibility in the intelligence area, charged with implementing various directives, orders and stated objectives of the Phoenix program.

Both were honorably discharged from the military service and appear here as voluntary witnesses. We will hear their statements and then both will be available for questions from the members of the subcommittee and the staff.

Mr. Uhl and Mr. Osborn, will you come forward to the witness table, please.

This being an investigative hearing, we will swear you both, if you will please rise and raise your right hand.

Do you solemnly swear that the testimony you are about to give this subcommittee will be the truth, the whole truth and nothing but the truth, so help you God?

Mr. Uhl. I do.

Mr. Osborn. I do.

Mr. Moorhead. Mr. Uhl, since you have a prepared statement, why don't you proceed first.

Do you have an initial statement, Mr. Reid?

Mr. Reid. No.

　　Statement of Michael J. Uhl, a Public Witness

Mr. Uhl. Thank you.

My name is Michael J. Uhl. I am currently listed in the Army records as a retired first lieutenant by virtue of my disability.

Upon arrival in the Republic of Vietnam in November of 1968—

Mr. Moorhead. For the record you might give us your address here.

Mr. Uhl. I currently reside in New York City. I am using my parents' address as my address of record: 35 Coppertree Lane, Babylon, New York, Code 11702.

Mr. Moorhead. Thank you.

Mr. Uhl. Upon arrival in the Republic of Vietnam in November of 1968 I was assigned as the team chief of the 1st Military Intelligence Team—1st MIT—11th Brigade, American Division. I remained with the 11th Brigade until late May 1969, at which time I was medically evacuated, having contracted pulmonary tuberculosis.

The 1st MIT consisted of three sections: Counter Intelligence (CI), Order of Battle (OB), and Interrogation of Prisoners of War (IPW). My primary function was to administer the team and coordinate its efforts, in order to fulfill our mission of providing the combat brigade with tactical intelligence for immediate exploitation and security from compromise of its operations. By virtue of my military occupational speciality (MOS) I also had direct supervisory control over the CI section.

Through my testimony today I hope to convey, generally, a perspective shared by many of my veteran comrades. This is a perspective gained from the field, of those charged with the responsibility for implementing ambiguous and often absolutely misleading directives, policies, and standard operating procedures. Most of these I believe to be based on fallacious analysis of the historical and contemporary Vietnamese situation, not to mention a fundamentally misguided concept of what the role of the United States should be in foreign affairs.

I do not make these charges lightly. For those who have strong beliefs in the many revolutionary concepts that first shaped our Nation, disillusionment does not come easily. Our system has evolved away from the best sentiments of Thomas Paine, Sam Adams, Patrick Henry, and thousands like them throughout our history.

William Jennings Bryan, in spite of his failings, summed up many of these sentiments before this very body [Indianapolis, 8 April 1908]. At that time Congress was debating whether or not to withdraw American troops from the Philippines.

And so with the nation. It is of age and it can do what it pleases; it can spurn the traditions of the past; it can repudiate the principles upon which this nation rests; it can employ force instead of reason; it can substitute might for right; it can conquer weaker people; it can exploit their lands; appropriate their property; and kill their people; but it cannot repeal moral law or escape the punishment they decreed for the violation of human rights.

Since this subcommittee is enjoined to hear testimony that bears on the efficiency and funding of governmental operations, I will try to make my comments relevant to these guidelines wherever possible. It is generally fairly obvious that at least with tactical level MI operations, waste and inefficiency are the rule, not exception.

It is not at all unpredictable, given what we have learned from the Pentagon papers, that my operational perspective of MI programs like Phoenix, for example, is diametrically opposed to the administrative perspective of former CORDS chief, Ambassador Colby.

For instance, Ambassador Colby gave the impression that Phoenix targeted specific high level Vietcong infrastructure whose identity had been established by at least three unrelated intelligence sources. In his prepared statement delivered before this committee on July 19, 1971, he cites several interesting statistics. Among these is the number of Vietcong infrastructure (VCI) successfully targeted and "neutralized" during the period 1968–May 1971. 1970 figures show 22,341

VCI "neutralized." Colby thus would have us believe that the vast majority of these people were targeted according to the rules that he outlined.

This capacity on the part of MI groups in Vietnam seems to me greatly exaggerated. A mammoth task such as this would greatly tax even our resourceful FBI, where we have none of the vast cross-cultural problems to contend with.

What types of operations "generate" this supplementary body count then, assuming the figures are accurate? It was my experience that the majority of people classified as VC were "captured" as a result of sweeping tactical operations. In effect, a huge dragnet was cast out in our area of operation (AR) and whatever looked good in the catch, regardless of evidence, was classified as VCI.

MI personnel do not have an "active" combat role. Nevertheless, the 1st MIT had a reputation of being an aggressive unit that did not shy away from initiating and participating in combat patrols. On one occasion, shortly after I had joined the team, I was on the land line, land communication, reporting to my commanding officer (CO) at division. In the course of giving him an account of the week's activities, I mentioned that we had staged several MI patrols. He reprimanded me slightly, saying that he did not want to lose "valuable" MI personnel on routine combat patrols; replacements were hard to come by. He further informed me that the only justification for MI people to be on a patrol was for the purpose of hunting down VCI. From that point on, any "body count" resulting from an MI patrol was automatically listed as VCI. To my knowledge, in fact, all those killed by 1st MIT on such patrols were classified as VCI only after their deaths. There was never any evidence to justify such a classification.

The IPW section, I would estimate—again I stress "estimate"— interrogated an average of 20 people per day.

Mr. Moorhead. Is that your team: 20 per day?

Mr. Uhl. Yes, sir.

These Vietnamese were generally turned over to MI by our various combat units, as VC suspects. There was an extraordinary degree of command pressure placed on the interrogation officer to classify detainees turned over to IPW as civil defendants (CDs). As opposed to innocent civilians (ICs) these are people adjudged to have violated Vietnamese law.

It was a foregone conclusion that the overwhelming majority of detainees could not be classified as prisoners of war (PWs) since the conditions of capture did not meet the rigid criteria set up to make that classification. Therefore, the way that the brigade measured its success was not only by its "body count" and "kill ratio" but by the number of CDs it had captured.

Not only was there no due process, which we as Americans consider to be among man's "natural rights," but fully all the detainees were brutalized and many were literally tortured.

All CDs, because of this command pressure (the majority of our detainees were classified as CDs), were listed as VCI. To my knowledge, not one of these people ever freely admitted being a cadre member.

And again, contrary to Colby's statement, most of our CDs were women and children.

Mr. Colby, in response to a direct question, denied that Americans actually exercised power of arrest over Vietnamese civilians.

In Duc Pho, where the 11th Brigade base camp was located, we could arrest and detain at will any Vietnamese civilians we desired, without so much as a whisper of coordination with ARVN or GVN authorities.

But the impact of this oversight in Ambassador Colby's testimony pales when compared to his general lack of understanding of what is actually going on in the field.

I mentioned above that in order to be listed as VCI at least three different intelligence agencies had to target the same individual. Even if this were true, which it wasn't in my experience, the most crucial omission in this progression is not even addressed.

That is: what steps are taken to assure that information used to denounce any individual is reliable?

The 1st MIT employed 11 coded sources. These were indigenous subagents paid to provide us with "hot intel" on the VC personalities and movement in our AR.

We had no way of determining the background of these sources, nor their motivation for providing American units with information.

No American in the team spoke or understood Vietnamese well enough to independently debrief any "contact." None of us were sufficiently sensitive to nor knowledgeable of the law, the culture, the customs, the history, etc.

Our paid sources could easily have been either provocateurs or opportunists with a score to settle. Every information report (IR) we wrote based on our sources' information was classified as (1) unverifiable and (2) usually reliable source. As to the first, it speaks for itself; the second, in most cases was pure rationale for the existence of the program.

The unverified and in fact unverifiable information, nevertheless, was used regularly as input to artillery strikes, harassment and interdiction fire (H&I), B52 and other air strikes, often on populated areas.

We churned out a dozen IRs per week, not because it was good or reliable information, but it was our mission. Furthermore, it was not possible, given the conditions in Vietnam, for a tactical unit to produce reliable and verified intelligence data.

The intelligence contingency fund (ICF), a classified fund, provides payroll and incentives for these essentially useless subagents. Moral, ideological, and political questions aside, literally millions of dollars must be squandered yearly in operations similar to the one I described extemporaneously, all over Vietnam; all over the world.

If one assumes, as I do, that Phoenix is a hoax—that thousands of Vietnamese are indiscriminately classified as VC—based on no specific targeting procedure—based on no evidence—then this is just one more colossal example of wasted funds and personnel.

So what, a few more millions are wasted among the billions wasted before them.

As the troops return from Southeast Asia, the cost of this war will continue for many years to come. Those addicted to drugs will need extensive rehabilitation.

Those scarred psychologically from having been executioners of brutal policies will not only seek medical and financial relief, but in a real sense, represent a human resource no longer willing or able to believe in the worth of American Institutions.

Mr. Moorhead. Thank you very much, Mr. Uhl.

Before we question you, we will hear from Mr. Osborn.

Mr. Osborn, you may proceed.

Statement of K. Barton Osborn, a Public Witness

Mr. Osborn. Thank you, Mr. Chairman.

My name is K. Barton Osborn. I am a resident of Washington, D.C., 5205 Sherrier Place NW., Washington.

I would like to describe my role as it was peripheral to the Phoenix program and give you an idea of the context in which I was associated with both military intelligence and the Central Intelligence Agency program.

I was in Vietnam from September 1967 until December 1968. At that time I was in the Army on active duty. I had been trained for 6 months at Fort Holabird, Md., in a covert classified program of illegal agent handling, which taught us to find, recruit, train, and manage and later terminate agents for military intelligence.

Mr. Reid. Could you explain what you mean by "terminate"?

Mr. Osborn. Terminate, that is to release agents from their duties as they performed them for the agent handler once they no longer were of use for the agent.

Mr. Reid. Do you imply by that with extreme prejudice?

Mr. Osborn. There are two ways: one is with prejudice and one is without prejudice.

With prejudice means simply—without prejudice first of all, is to tell the man or woman he has done a good job; give them a payoff or whatever and let them go; also to establish a future contact arrangement.

With prejudice is subcategorized into two areas. With prejudice may mean simply that the agent did a bad job; in some way was judged not loyal or whatever, and was not to be hired again and was to be put on a list of undesirable personalities which they call "black list."

With extreme prejudice is to murder the individual right out because he or she constitutes a knowledgeable person who may be compromising to present or future operations. That is a termination process.

There is a whole cycle called "The intelligence cycle," from the point of needing an agent and going to find one through recruiting the person, training them, managing them, sending them out, receiving them back, having them perform missions and then debriefing them and then eventual termination.

Mr. Reid. Were you aware of or did you participate in anything that reflected extreme prejudice?

Mr. Osborn. Yes, I was. Let me explain that.

As I was running agents for 15 months in Vietnam—I arrived there, in 1967—I suppose I became operational after six weeks in Vietnam. The operation was in the I Corps area south of Da Nang City. I lived in the civilian community under a cover name and cover status in Da Nang City. I was under the cover of a GS-9 Department of Defense Civilian who was attached to the civil operations program, specifically: USAID refugee programs and so forth. I made my own covers. I was given no official cover by any headquarters. I was just sent there as a free agent to organize and to provide information to use in combat.

The 1st Marine Division, 3d Marine Division, various Army units were in the area, but all American.

The reason I didn't work with any of the Vietnamese in any capacity is that I performed unilateral operations which are strictly illegal and against the Geneva Convention. I was performing the kind of operation which, if discovered by the South Vietnamese, would constitute a compromise for what we call "a flap to the U.S. Government." I was sent there under cover to perform illegal operations, targeting not only the VC and the NVA, but also the South Vietnamese Government in some operations which I got into, such as illegal green dollar dissemination.

There were no restrictions on any legalities which we used, or illegalities, and military intelligence, for instance, call us "extra-legal activity" which means it is justifiable on the basis of the necessity to collect information. I used whatever I needed to in the way of resourcefulness; defined agents. Specifically I looked through the files of construction companies in the area, American contractors. I found people working on the economy who spoke English and from there I recruited my agents.

I had two nets at the time of, say, the spring of 1968; two nets being two principal agents under whom were subagents running cells of people in a geographical area, each cell constituting perhaps five people at one time. I had 40 to 50 people working under these two nets. Their prime objective was to collect combat information; that is, names, locations, size, plans, supplies of unit which were known to be or learned through my nets to be operating in the area. I reported this information to the combat units which I mentioned, and there I found myself getting an extra product which I hadn't expected and that was political information.

There were people reporting to me names of individuals who were supposedly the Vietcong sympathizers and cooperants. I didn't expect this information and in fact, operationally had no way to deal with it.

I reported this to the 1st Marine Division, G-2, that is the colonel who was the G-2 officer there and he said they had no real capacity to deal with this kind of information, although it seemed worthwhile information.

I disseminated it through them laterally and found I got feedback reports from them in following up the effectiveness of my data that were for the Phoenix coordinator and I didn't know what it was. I investigated this through the G-2 of the 1st Marine Division and found the Phoenix coordinator, in fact, was an Army officer, a major who had a house in Da Nang City which was known in our intelligence community to be the CIA operational headquarters.

I went there to find out if my reporting was being effectively used. He told me: "Yes, they know of the information that came through under my cover name and identified me that way and asked me if I had much of this information." I told him I came by a good bit and had a capacity to collect a good bit more, and asked him how it would be used and he said: "According to the Phoenix program."

The Phoenix description was that it was designed to neutralize the core of the VC, interdiction politically, logistically and so forth. I found myself in possession of this information and in need of funds for my agents, because Military Intelligence, although I had been assigned by them to recruit agents, found themselves short on what Mr. Uhl described as the intelligence contingency funding and in fact had no money to pay the agents once they had been recruited.

I had recruited these people on promises of money to come, but when it came time to pay I didn't have money so I took what incentive gifts—cigarettes and liquor—that were available and had them sold by interpreters on the black market in order to get money for my agents' payment.

The Phoenix coordinator offered me not only the opportunity to utilize the political information I was getting, but also additional money which I may have needed for my agents. From that point on I had no real financial struggle and found myself not only able to pay my agents, but utilize CIA facilities, such as Air America for transportation housing, covert housing in the city areas where I needed it; such things as safe houses which are areas to meet your agent covertly and debrief; money to rent hotel rooms in order to meet them covertly; agent payments, both overt money payments and incentive gifts such as an occasional motorcycle to a principal agent and so forth. From the time of my association with the Phoenix program I no longer had any logistical problems. This is how the information was dealt with; I gave it to them in reciprocity for the money and information I received.

I would report an individual which had been reported to me by one of my net on the assumption that my agent's addressee was combat information which was high, was reflected directly in their VCI information; that is to say they were consistent through all kinds of information which they supplied to me and we had a way of testing the combat information and found it very effective.

I didn't question how they reported or how they selected the individuals whom they reported other than the fact they described them in their activities as Vietcong. I reported this both directly to the Phoenix coordinator in Da Nang and also combat using units and they would use it if they could.

The resulting interrogations are what I would like to describe to you; that is: How the individuals reported were dealt with by American personnel.

The 1st Marine Division was adjacent to the Da Nang Air Base. They had a Marine Division of the 1st Wing, an amphibious force which was adjacent to the air base, and its job was to protect the air base from attack by enemy, either regular or irregular troops.

I at one point was reporting regularly people in that area of Da Nang Air Base who may have constituted a threat to the air base's security. I remember at one time I reported an individual who lived in a local village who was reported to me by the local cell as being a logistical officer for the local farmers' organization, which is the Vietcong structure at the village level, and the counter-intelligence team from that unit went out and picked the individual up and detained him as a suspected VC.

I went back the next day to check out the utilization of my report and whether or not it had been accurately followed through on and so forth. They told me they had the individual detained there and I asked how they were going to deal with him; and they said they were preparing to interrogate him; would I like to attend the interrogation, and I said I would, because I had never seen one. They said it would be an airborne interrogation and I didn't quite conceive that. I went ahead with the marine officer who was a first lieutenant, head of the CI team. We took two Marine enlisted men and two Vietnamese males in their 30s or so and we went out to the air wing and we got on a helicopter and flew northwest of Da Nang over some uninhabited area there of flat terrain.

Mr. Reid. What unit was that?

Mr. Osborn. Counter-intelligence team of the 1st Marine Division.

Mr. Reid. Of the 1st Marine Division?

Mr. Osborn. That is right. They had a facility there on the 3d Marine Amphibious Force's air wing at Da Nang Air Base.

But we flew over some flat terrain, perhaps 20 miles out of Da Nang, and the two Vietnamese were bound with their hands behind their backs and the two Marine enlisted men kept them off in a sling seat inside the helicopter. The interrogation began, not on the individual whom I had reported, but on the extra person, and I didn't know who he was at first and found out that he was a previous detainee who had already been interrogated who had been beaten and who had internal injuries and who was not able to respond to questions. They had brought him along for the purposes of interrogation.

I found out the purpose was this: They antagonized the individual and told him they needed certain information regarding VC activities and he couldn't give it. He hadn't given the information they wanted from him and they demanded it of him and he couldn't respond or wouldn't respond. They antagonized him several times by taking him with his elbows behind his back, hands tied, running him up to the door of the helicopter and saying: If you don't tell us what we need to know we are going to throw you out of the helicopter. They did this two or three times and he refused to say anything. He couldn't respond. He wouldn't respond. Therefore, on the fourth trip to the door they did throw him out from the helicopter to the ground. That had the effect directly of antagonizing the person I had reported, suspected Vietcong logistics officer, into telling them whatever information they wanted to know, regardless of its content, value or truth; he would tell them what they wanted to know simply because his primary objective at that point would be not to follow the first Vietnamese out the door, but rather to return safely to the ground.

Mr. Reid. That was a purposeful, deliberate pushing out the door?

Mr. Osborn. There was no question at all. This was the reason they took this first individual up and the reason that they antagonized him and went through the form of threatening him, and throwing him out three times.

Mr. Reid. Who gave the order that he should be pushed out?

Mr. Osborn. The 1st Marine Division lieutenant.

Mr. Reid. There was a lieutenant on board?

Mr. Osborn. That is right. He was the counter-intelligence team chief.

Mr. Reid. Do you recall his name?

Mr. Moorhead. Because of the rules, we had better not mention names of individuals in such cases in public session.

Mr. Osborn. In all due respect, I do recall his name, but I am not willing to go into that. You can see that that is irrelevant. In fact, the form of the thing is what we are talking about.

So that we returned to the ground and they proceeded with the interrogation on their own. This happened, not once as an aberration, but twice that I attended. The same airborne procedure; the same dummy on the first hand who was antagonized and then thrown from the helicopter; the second person who was then interrogated and gave whatever information they demanded of him.

They certainly did not know how to elicit information from this person without brutality, for there was no real interrogation session short of the brutalization.

I saw other interrogations, to describe them briefly: The use of the insertion of the 6-inch dowel into the 6-inch canal of one of my detainees' ears and the tapping through the brain until he died. The starving to death of a Vietnamese woman who was suspected of being a part of the local political education cadre in one of the local villages. They simply starved her to death in a cage that they kept in one of the hooches at that very counter-intelligence team headquarters.

There were other methods of operation which they used for interrogation, such as the use of electronic gear such as sealed [sic: field] telephones attached to the genitals of both the men and women, the women's vagina and the men's testicles, and wind the mechanism and create an electrical charge and shock them into submission. I had a lot of conversations about the use of that kind of equipment, although I never saw that used firsthand. I did see the equipment sitting around but never saw it used.

Mr. Moorhead. Were these methods that you described conducted by American personnel or—

Mr. Osborn. Americans only. These were unilateral operations not in coordination with or with the knowledge of the South Vietnamese Government.

Mr. Reid. And officers were present as well as enlisted men?

Mr. Osborn. Each time. These were my experiences with reporting names of Vietnamese from my agents to American agencies and the resulting interrogations.

They also used the CSD, combined studies detachment, which is light cover for the CIA in Vietnam, which was part of the Phoenix coordinator—I should say the overall organization under which the Phoenix coordinator existed in Da Nang.

They employed provisional reconnaissance units which were small squads of Vietnamese military who were targeted on villages and which, when military interrogations would not take place, went out to the village to locate the individual who was reported, seized that individual and theoretically they would detain him. But officially they could not condone a murder program overtly.

So, they assigned PRUs to capture these VCI suspects. Naturally the PRUs know unofficially it was preferable to neutralize them rather than go through the administrative problems and procedure of not only detaining this person and keeping him alive to the point of being turned into the interrogation center—

Mr. Moorhead. What was the PRU, again?

Mr. Osborn. Provisional reconnaissance units.

Mr. Moorhead. And they are Vietnamese?

Mr. Osborn. They are Vietnamese.

Mr. Reid. When you say "neutralize," please describe what you mean.

Mr. Osborn. Killed on the spot. I know, for example, of readbacks from this treatment of Vietnamese who I reported through the coordinator although I didn't know the identity of the people in the provisional reconnaissance units, just the fact they had gone and done their jobs: that is: to find the people in their villages and to murder them there.

Mr. Reid. Is the PRU composed of United States or South Vietnamese personnel?

Mr. Osborn. Primarily the provisional reconnaissance units are Vietnamese military personnel. They have American advisers, both military and civilians.

For instance, I know people with the combined studies attachment; that is, the CIA there, who worked with the PRUs and also special forces officers for special forces personnel: usually company grade officers; that is, second lieutenant through captain, who worked with the PRU teams. They encouraged them unofficially on this method of operation. I never saw it codified; that is, I never saw an official directive that said the PRUs will proceed to the village and murder the individual. However, it was implicit that when you got a name and wanted to deal effectively in neutralizing that individual you didn't need to go through interrogation; find out, establish any kind of factual basis leading to the conclusion that this individual was, in fact, Vietcong infrastructure, but rather it was good enough to have him reported as a suspect and that justified neutralization.

After all, it was a big problem that had to be dealt with expediently. This was the mentality. This carries a semi-official or semi-illegal program to the logical conclusion that I described here. It became a sterile depersonalized murder program. I had no way, as I say, of establishing the basis of which my agents reported to me suspected Vietcong infrastructure members. However, I had no reason to feel at that time they were participating in any kind of a personal vendetta, but there was no way to question that. In fact, the description that individuals whom I reported further up by my agents, were either categorical; that is to say: so and so, who is a known Vietcong member, or a known member of the farmers' association, or whatever, is residing at such and such a spot and does such things. There was no cross-check; there was no investigation; there were no second opinions. And certainly not whatever official *modus operandi* had been described as a triple reporting system for verification. There was no verification and there was no discrimination. It was completely indiscriminate and at best the individuals were either able to escape capturing by the people who were to pick them up and neutralize them or interrogated and let go.

I will say this: individually I never knew an individual to be detained as a VC suspect who ever lived through an interrogation in a year and a half, and that included quite a number of individuals. That may be my experience; may be a tremendous exception to the rule, but the experience of my peers there and my own experience firsthand, which I can swear to, and have sworn to, was categorically inhuman and with no rhyme, reason or bureaucratic justification for a murder program which had gone way beyond the level of any competence at that level.

The corruption involved; that is, the reporting of individuals for either the classic protection game or such, any other program would be pure speculation on my part. What are described here are things of my firsthand knowledge which stand as a serious breach of any kind of human orientation or any reflection of an accurate understanding of the Vietnamese as we see our role in Southeast Asia officially.

Thank you.

[. . .]

Mr. Moorhead. Thank you, Mr. Uhl and Mr. Osborn, for this very unpleasant testimony. But I think it is something we have to face up to. So, I think you have rendered a great service to the Congress and to the people of America.

Mr. Osborn, I would like to get a little more detail about the financial operations of your activities. How much money did you handle in setting up your network of agents?

Mr. Osborn. At first I set them up for military intelligence with no money.

I had the mission; the vague mission of operating in the area covertly in alignment with my training at Fort Holabird to establish the agents, but that was an assignment that was understood to be my duty or my job in Vietnam.

I should tell you that out of maybe 10 people who are trained this way and sent to Vietnam perhaps eight of them decide to use that year and their autonomy, which is constituted by their civilian status, and compartmentalization from the military in the inference [sic: interest] of security as the year in which to have a vacation, take off on R.&R.s and so forth.

Of the agent handlers who decide to do anything voluntarily there is very little support from headquarters. [. . .] The lines of communication were almost closed up. They assumed that we would go, be as resourceful as we could, find a way to motivate agents, extract information from them and feed it to combat units.

But on requesting money as a necessary step in motivating agents I found little or no response from the military. That didn't mean I couldn't get money, because I did utilize what things I could get sold on the black market in order to get piasters to convert to new piasters and give them to the agents as payment and say: There is more to come. There is a necessity to maintain the loyalty of the agents.

When I got fully operational and started to get unlimited funds from the Phoenix coordinator, which for a long time was my only source of funds, agent payments amounted to approximately 15,000 piasters per month for the salary of a principal agent and perhaps another 10,000 for what we call agent expenses for the principal agent.

Then under him would be four or five cell leaders who were what they call "option agents" who were out in the field actually helping to collect the information. Under each cell leader there were four or five collecting agents. Their salaries ranged from 2,000 to 10,000 piasters per month, depending on their efficiency, the amount of reporting and the accuracy of the information.

If you would pay an agent on the amount reported obviously you would encourage a papermill. If you, shall I say, if you would pay him in accordance with strictly the accuracy of his information you would make him paranoid about any kind of lack of accuracy.

So, these several factors brought the agent payments in the field to 2,000 to 10,000 piasters a month, and cell leaders maybe one and a half times that for the coordinating duties in addition to the collection.

Support agents, such as couriers and so forth, were paid various amounts of money ranging from nothing, a loyalty factor, all the way up to, say, a thousand piasters per month.

Mr. Moorhead. Was there any bonus feature if a subagent brought in some especially valuable information?

Mr. Osborn. Yes; always an allusion to that, but I never paid a balance.

Mr. Moorhead. Did you have to account to anybody for these expenditures?

Mr. Osborn. To Military Intelligence. There is an intricate accounting mechanism on a standard form which has to be letter perfect and without erasures, and that is the most important, but almost no money.

On the Phoenix program I found no accounting necessary and unlimited funds.

Mr. Moorhead. Is it true that the United States provided funds to enable the Vietnamese informers to buy their way out of the draft?

Mr. Osborn. Very definitely. I can find examples that I know of firsthand. I couldn't get interpreters. I wasn't trained in Vietnamese; I wasn't trained at all to go to Vietnam. I was trained in agent operations in the context of Western Europe, which is the way it is taught in the Army. When I arrived in Vietnam I didn't speak Vietnamese and I needed to communicate to find agents and so forth. I looked around for interpreters and found them in several contexts.

My first principal agent spoke English and that solved that communication problem. After that I needed interpreters in order to contact agents. I can think of one man in Da Nang

City who was my interpreter for several months who was eligible for draft, and I tried to get him out of the draft by getting the Phoenix coordinator to obtain a draft deferment for him through one of the CIA elitist organizations. That has been a while ago, and I don't remember which one it was. It was something like "civilian air regular defense group," but it was one of the elitist organizations where they are authorized a certain amount of draft deferments a year.

I asked if I could get one for him. They said they would try. They didn't succeed, so they simply gave me the money overtly for him to buy his way out of the draft board's review in Da Nang City. That cost us, if I remember, 15,000 piasters every quarter, and he was working for me for several months and so it may be 3 or 4 months I gave him one payment, I remember initially, of 15,000 piasters and then some incentive gifts to give to people involved in the draft selection program. But the 10,000 piasters was the main payment.

So, yes; we definitely had to pay people out of the draft. I can remember two examples in Quang-Ngai Province where I had agents reporting well and who were of a draft age and who were susceptible to that and who reported through channels to me or to the principal agent who they thought they were working for that they thought they were in danger of being drafted and we sent payments of 5,000 piasters apiece and got results inasmuch as the individual kept reporting. Whether he said that or whether he was really threatened or what. But I know the 5,000 piasters which was very inexpensive, kept the agent operating, which was our prime operation. That is the nature of the current system in the draft as I experienced it firsthand.

How it goes beyond that I don't know.

Mr. Moorhead. Mr. Osborn, were you ever ordered to terminate any person? By this I mean to terminate with "extreme prejudice." I mean where you were ordered to murder any Vietnamese citizen?

Mr. Osborn. Ordered. It was suggested by my operations officer, who was a major, American major in the Intelligence

Corps at one point that I neutralize in terminating a principal agent whom I had and who had been found guilty of corruption in the intelligence game.

Let me describe that.

This person was—had been an interpreter for the coordinator of CIA activities in I Corps. He was simply an interpreter. He had no collective function. He was trilingual; he spoke French, English, and Vietnamese.

In the spring of 1967 he had been translating by interpreting for the CIA. They found that he was doing this: when they would have two agents in for debriefing a day he would interview them either on the side, at his house the night before, or somewhere else but not with the knowledge of his boss, the CIA personnel. He would coordinate their material. He would debrief one and take information from that person and give it to the other and cross-inform them of certain facts and tell them to include that in their briefing. That way there was a coordination of information and the agents were assumed to be accurate.

Their payments went up; they increased their own income, and the interpreter took a percentage of that increase. So this was a corruption game he was into.

He was found doing that by the CIA. He was terminated without prejudice by them.

In the fall—this was in the spring of 1967. In the fall of 1967 military intelligence personnel found him in his native context, found he spoke English and went through the whole procedure to rerecruit him. He sent his name for clearance and came back from Saigon marked with all the markings appropriate, saying (a) he was not on the suspected Vietcong list; (b) that he had never worked for American intelligence before; and (c) for all intents and purposes he was okay and could be hired. He was recruited.

He was trained as a principal agent and at that time he was asked if he had ever worked for American intelligence before. He saw obviously there had been a bureaucratic lack of communication and he said, as he knew it was necessary to say: No, I never have: because if he had admitted it, it would have flapped him, compromised him. He was operational as a principal agent until March of 1966, about 6 mouths. He had really gotten his net developed for about 3 months. He was my main principal agent.

Mr. Moorhead. He was one of your main agents?

Mr. Osborn. Yes; he was running the net. That was my main net at that time.

A black list or list of undesirable personalities came out from the CIA on March 25 of 1968, and he was on that list, which surprised me and it was pointed out to me by my operations officer that this person had obviously done something to deserve being included on the black list.

I went to him; I questioned him again as to whether or not he had worked for American intelligence before, and he said: Why did I ask, and I said because I had learned of his previous activities. I learned that, the details of it from his previous employer, the coordinator of CI activities in I Corps. I know him operationally and simply went to him and asked him why and he told me.

At that time the agent admitted yes: that he had worked for intelligence before: that he had been accused of this, but actually he had not done it and that there had been an ulterior motivation by the CIA to let him go and use that as an excuse. I was told by military intelligence to go and to terminate him, to get rid of him and to neutralize him and that was it; to terminate him with prejudice.

I went to him and told him that he had to return all the equipment he had, which were things like a radio which we used for emergency communication; a motorcycle which he used for transportation which I had lent to him, a Yamaha; and some other miscellaneous things, maps and so forth which I had given him for his reports. He returned those things to me; (a) because I needed the things for other operations, and (b) because the maps and so forth were American maps and which compromised him.

We sterilized him of any equipment I had given him and told him what I had been told to do by my superiors.

Mr. Moorhead. What had you been told to do?

Mr. Osborn. I had been told to kill him, to terminate him or neutralize him, which are all the same term. To terminate him, let him go, would be one; then terminate him with extreme prejudice would be to kill him. I was told by this major to go to terminate him, to neutralize him, which is to terminate him with extreme prejudice.

I met him by the Da Nang River and told him what I had been told to do. By the nature of our personal relationship, I was going to do this—I know his wife and several children. I said I would rather not do that but I was going to extract one promise from him and that was that I would not see him in any context, even on the street, for 6 months and he promised me that I would not see him at all and I didn't. I know where he lived. It wasn't far from my house, and his wife worked at an American installation right by my house. There was every reason to see him, but I never did see him for 6 months.

After that I saw him with regularity driving on the streets of Da Nang. It is a very small community.

I didn't terminate him although I was told to. I went back and told my superior that I had been not been able to find him; that at that time he probably suspected—from having got the equipment back and so forth, he suspected my plans for termination and that he had evaporated; that he had gotten loose. That was—that is what I reported on what I was told to do.

An agent handler in the Army is given such autonomy that he can do what he darn well pleases if he produces the information. Military Intelligence knows of its record of production and record of competence, which is low.

Any Military Intelligence personnel who has been with operations, especially in Vietnam, will tell you that the return rate is either inaccurate or insensitive, one of the two. I would tend to think it is inaccurate and insensitive. The terminations were in two forms. The agents were either the one I described in Da Nang, that kind of thing, and the official report went in from the battalion headquarters. But he was taken off the rolls and considered neutral.

The VCI were overt in murder, and that is the experience that I had firsthand.

Mr. Moorhead. Do we have questions from the other members at this time?

Mr. Reid.

Mr. Reid. Thank you, Mr. Chairman. I would like first to thank Mr. Uhl and Mr. Osborn for their testimony. I recognize that it is extremely serious: that it is not easy to testify on these matters. I know that you are doing so out of concern for a principle and hopefully putting an end to practices which most of us think are totally reprehensible.

I would like to ask both of you several questions. Some of them are broad in scope and sensitive. Should you feel that you can better testify in executive session or feel, out of concern for the rights of the individual, that you should, I wish you would feel completely free to so state.

I gather, Mr. Osborn, that you were present when one individual was terminated by being thrown out of a helicopter, and then you referred subsequently to three instances where individuals were tortured; one with a dowel going in the ear to the brain; the second was a woman who died of hunger in a cage. I think you mentioned one other instance.

Were you present on each of those occasions?

Mr. Osborn. Each. Let me describe that.

The first individual, the one with the dowel in his ear, had been reported by my agent and I went back to follow up the report. I was told: Yes, they were in the course of interrogating him then and would I like to see the interrogation.

I went next door to the hooch, the interrogation building with the lieutenant who was the team chief. As we got to the hooch they were carrying out his dead body. They were embarrassed to say that they had punctured his brain and killed him in the course of interrogating him. They had gotten no information from him; they had only tortured him to death and they were embarrassed, because at that time it became obvious, the brutality with which they treated this person.

The main crime in their minds, of course, they made a mistake in not having extracted information before this. They were embarrassed in having gone too far and having been too brutal.

The Vietnamese woman who was starved to death was in a small cage. There were four divisions of that same cage. She was in one of them daily as I would go there. I kept observing her there, along with no furniture, no facilities of any kind, just a bare hooch, bare cage. I would see her daily and finally one day I asked what happened to her. I noticed physical— for one thing she became weaker. She used to stand up and rattle the cage when I first got there. Then she was sitting cross-legged on the floor daily. Then she was in a prostrate position when I last saw her.

If it is to be graphic, that is how I saw her. One day she wasn't there. I asked the lieutenant what happened to her. He said: "She died of malnutrition." I asked had they fed her. "No." Had they provided water. "No."

Mr. Reid. In each of these cases you testified an officer was present. Was that a Marine officer or military officer of the Army?

Mr. Osborn. Marine Intelligence.

Mr. Reid. And this was attached to the 1st Marines of the 3d Amphibious Force?

Mr. Osborn. The 1st Marine Division.

Mr. Reid. Did you, as an individual, in any one of these three cases talk to high authority or a superior officer to express your horror or concern over what had happened; in the case of the woman who was starving to death, did you do anything to raise the question of her health and her conditions with any higher authority?

Mr. Osborn. No; I did not. Let me explain that my status there was illegal and the activity which I performed was illegal. That was by mutual agreement between all agent handlers and the Armed Forces.

Mr. Reid. Let me ask by way of clarification what you are subsequently going to say.

At Fort Holabird or subsequent operations with CIA or with the Marines or Army officers concerned was anyone aware of something called "The Geneva Convention," or the convention concerned with the protection of civilians, of which the United States is a signatory? Were you ever explicitly told to pay no attention to these documents and were you told explicitly you were to do illegal things irrespective of the convention?

Mr. Osborn. The first questions dealing with the Geneva Accords, let me say they were never mentioned during the 6 months training course at Holabird. I believe if they had been raised they naturally would have had to be dealt with. It was impossible to say these are the rules and these aren't; for instance, the rules of humanity involved, and we were going to supersede them without demoralizing some of the trainees. They weren't dealt with at all.

The easier way to deal with them is to avoid them, and that is what they did, in fact.

Mr. Reid. Does Holabird deal with termination by extreme prejudice?

Mr. Osborn. Yes, it does. Termination is described along with all other *modus operandi* of agent operations in a classified manual which advocates the extra-legal, illegal, and covert activities which I described in a manual called "the Defense Collection Intelligence Manual."

Mr. Reid. Mr. Chairman, without objection I would hope that we might direct the committee staff to obtain a copy of that manual.

Mr. Osborn. Yes; that is a classified manual an inch thick and about 8 by 10 and classified, I believe, "Secret."

Let me describe this. The Defense Intelligence Collection Manual acronym is DICOM, and that was my base reference for the course which is given at Holabird to train people in— now it is a course under the cover of Area Intelligence Specialists, and the MOS numbers are for Officers 9668 and enlisted men 9640.

The base reference for that is an illegal manual.

It describes termination, to answer your question, in all respects, as I remember.

Mr. Moorhead. If you want to give us classified information, please tell us and we will go into executive session. But otherwise we will assume what you are giving us is just the names of documents.

Mr. Osborn. I wouldn't say anything in reference to that that hasn't been in print already.

Mr. Moorhead. Thank you.

Mr. Reid. I wanted to ask you next whether this kind of activity, for example, as you mentioned, was known to higher headquarters and to commanding generals, or was this an operation kept so secretly that only those intimately involved were aware of it?

Mr. Osborn. The operations in Vietnam?

Mr. Reid. Of the kind you are talking about.

Mr. Osborn. Yes; those were the official operations and the only kind performed by my battalion of the 525 MI Group. The first battalion in Da Nang City, four battalions, one in each corps, had the function of coordinating covert collection activity. That was its mission.

Yes; it was official. And: yes; it was known by superior officers. They were visited regularly at our operational building, which was on the command post of the 1st Marine Division outside Da Nang and where we operated in a classified manner under the cover of classification programs by colonels who came up from headquarters to review our operations and we briefed them with regularity. So they were quite aware of what was happening and they advocated more of the same.

Mr. Reid. When we talk about the PIC, the Province Intelligence [sic: Interrogation] Center, did this center have liaison with the CIA as well as MI or intelligence officers?

Mr. Osborn. I am sorry, Mr. Reid, I can't answer that because I didn't know the PIC inasmuch as I didn't cooperate at all with Vietnamese operations. As I say, I was there extra-legally and my job was, in part, to keep all that secret from and compartmented from the Vietnamese. So I wasn't into any of their—

Mr. Reid. Did you have access to or see any of the dossiers prepared beforehand?

Mr. Osborn. The dossiers on my agents which worked for and supplied information to Phoenix and for which Phoenix acted without any further need of proof were kept in my files. That was in a large safe in my office. I saw no other agent files from the Phoenix coordinator program because I was—each agent handler, as each agent, is compartmented from one another for security reasons.

Mr. Reid. Mr. Chairman, I think both Mr. McCloskey and I would like permission to have Congressman Jerome Waldie's statement inserted at the appropriate point in the record.

He wanted to be present today, but was unable to do so. But he did ask me to ask one or two questions.

Mr. McCloskey. Will you yield for just a minute?

Mr. Reid. Certainly.

Mr. McCloskey. If I may, Mr. Chairman, I have a copy of Mr. Waldie's statement. I offer it for insertion into the record at this point.

Mr. Moorhead. Without objection, it is so ordered.

(Mr. Waldie's prepared statement follows:)

Prepared Statement of Hon. Jerome R. Waldie, a Representative in Congress from the State of California

Mr. Chairman, during the Easter vacation my colleague from California, Paul McCloskey, and I visited Vietnam and visited Laos, and a series of reports will be forthcoming from that visit. Tonight will be the first report, involving a program that is a part of Vietnamization, as is apparently the case, a program designed, in my view, to suppress political dissent in that country at a time when the war is over, as well as the program that is presently in existence in Vietnam during this war period. It is a program that is called the Phung Hoang program, otherwise known as the Phoenix program.

My first introduction to the program occurred upon the initial briefing that was provided Congressman McCloskey and I in Saigon by the CORDS people.

At that time they were giving what they called "neutralization" figures. They reported that in Military Region 1 in 1971 we had "neutralized" 5,380 members of the Vietcong infra-structure and political dissenters in that country.

The breakdown of the neutralization figures is as follows:

"Kills," 2,000. They are obviously "neutralized," the brief-ing officer said, when they are killed. I suspect that is a fair assessment.

Rallied, 17,000. These are the Chieu Hoi ralliers to the flag of South Vietnam, as they become "neutralized" when they rally.

Sentenced, 1,680. These are people that were sentenced to more than 1 year for their offenses as being identified as part of the Vietcong infrastructure.

Captured, 4,000 people. These are not considered to be "neutralized" because they received sentences of less than 1 year and were not determined to be a part of the Vietcong infrastructure but were people that were determined to have been in opposition to the existing government in South Vietnam.

So of a total of over 9,000 people in Military Region 1 in five northern provinces 5,380 of them were considered to be neutralized whereas 4,000 of them were not considered to be neutralized because they were not given sentences up to 1 year in length.

The figure that startled us who were listening to the brief-ing was the fact that 2,000 people under the Phoenix program were killed and thereby considered to be neutralized.

We sought additional information on precisely what this particular program was, and one document that immedi-ately came to our attention was a MACV—Military Assistance Command Vietnam—directive 525-36 dated 18 May 1970. It was entitled "Military Operations Phoenix—Phung Hoang—Operations" and it was a directive to all U.S. military personnel acting as advisers to the South Vietnamese in that program.

This is part of that statement and, Mr. Chairman, at this point I include this MACV directive in full with my remarks:

U.S. Military Assistance Command, Vietnam
APO San Francisco, Calif. May 18, 1970.
Directive Number 525-36 — Military Operations
PHOENIX (PHUNG HOANG) OPERATIONS

1. *Purpose. This directive establishes policy and responsibilities for all U.S. personnel participating in, or supporting in any way, Phoenix (Phung Hoang) operations.*

2. *Applicability.*—*This directive is applicable to all MACV staff agencies and subordinate commands.*

3. *Policy.*

a. *The Phoenix program is one of advice, support, and assistance to the Government of Vietnam (GVN) Phung Hoang program, aimed at reducing the influence and effectiveness of the Vietcong Infrastructure (VCI) in the Republic of Vietnam (RVN). The VCI is an inherent part of the war effort being waged against the GVN by the Vietcong (VC) and their North Vietnamese allies. The unlawful status of members of the VCI (as defined in the "green book" and in GVN official decrees) is well established in GVN law and is in full accord with the laws of land warfare followed by the U.S. Army.*

b. *Operations against the VCI include: the collection of intelligence identifying these members, inducing them to abandon their allegiance to the VC and rally to the government, capturing or arresting them in order to bring them before province security committees for lawful sentencing, and as a final resort the use of military, or police force against them—if no other way of preventing them from carrying on their unlawful activities is possible. Our training emphasizes the desirability of obtaining these target individuals alive and of using intelligent and lawful methods of interrogation to obtain the truth of what they know about other aspects of the VCI. U.S. personnel are under the same legal and moral constraints with respect to operations of a Phoenix character as they are with respect to regular military operations against enemy units in the field. Thus, they are specifically unauthorized to engage in assassinations or other violations of the rules of land warfare, but they are entitled to use such reasonable military force as is necessary to obtain the goals of rallying, capturing, or eliminating the VCI in the RVN.*

c. If U.S. personnel come in contact with activities conducted by Vietnamese which do not meet the standards of land warfare, they are:

(1) Not to participate further in the activity.

(2) Expected to make their objections to this kind of behavior known to the Vietnamese conducting them.

(3) Expected to report the circumstances to the next higher U.S. authority for decision as to action to be taken with the GVN.

d. There are individuals who find normal police work or even military operations repugnant to them personally, despite the overall legality and morality of these activities. Arrangements exist whereby individuals having this feeling about military affairs can, according to law, receive specialized assignments or even exemption from military service. There is no similar legislation with respect to police type activities of the U.S. military, but if an individual finds the police type activities of the Phoenix program repugnant to him, on his application, he can be reassigned from the program without prejudice.

4. Responsibilities.—Subordinate U.S. commanders are to insure that the policies outlined above are strictly adhered to.

5. Reports.—This directive requires no report.

W. G. Dolvin, Major General, U.S.A., Chief of Staff.

the directive issued by MACV which, frankly, I drafted ...

William E. Colby, July 2 1973.

OPERATION TRENT

22 SAS, Afghanistan, 2001

In late November 2001 the two Squadrons of 22 SAS deployed in Afghanistan received orders to attack an al-Qaeda opium plant 250 miles south-west of Kandahar, and close to the Pakistani border. Intelligence suggested that around 100 al-Qaeda were defending the base, which was heavily fortified by trench lines and bunkers.

For the Americans, the raid, codenamed Trent, was low priority. Their minds were set on finding bin Laden. Neither did they generally seem keen on fighting on the ground, much preferring to bomb targets from the air. The upshot of American disinterest was that the raid would have to go ahead in full daylight, purely because US air force assets would be available then. But only for an hour.

Neither could air assets be made available to infiltrate teams for Close Target Reconnaissance or the setting up of Observation Posts.

A frontal attack on an elevated fortified base in daylight, without full intelligence, is hardly the military optimum. However, CENTCOM gave the British the distinct impression it was this mission or no mission. Probably CENTCOM would have preferred to bomb the facility to atoms; British planners were convinced the plant would yield vital intel.

Operation Trent would also be a landmark in the history of the Regiment. With both A and G Squadrons committed to the action, it would be the largest SAS operation in history. It would also be the first time in wartime that a team was inserted by a HALO (High Altitude, Low Opening) parachute jump.

This was performed by G Squadron's Air Troop who dropped into the desert the night before the main insertion. The eight-man team jumped from a USAF C130 cargo plane at 28,000 feet, only opening their chutes at the last moment, to make their insertion difficult to spot. After landing they tested the ground of the Registan desert to make sure it would bear the weight of the fully laden Hercules which would be bringing in the assault force. The Air Troop then marked out a Temporary Landing Zone 900 feet x 40 feet, and laid up for the day.

Seventeen hours later in the dark desert morning, Air Troop guided in the Hercules of the assault force with infra-red torches. Even before the cargo planes could come to a full-stop the men of A and G squadrons were de-bussing, driving their vehicles down the ramps of the planes as they taxied along. Forty vehicles sped down the ramps, thirty-eight "Pinkies" or Desert Patrol Vehicles (Land Rovers) and two Acmat vehicles. There were also eight Kawasaki dirt bikes, their riders acting as point men and outriders.

On the way to the Forming Up Position (FUP) one of the Pinkies broke down, and its bitterly disappointed crew of three were left behind to wait exfiltration when the main party returned. At the FUP the force split into two: A Squadron was to make the main assault, while G Squadron was to be the Fire Support Base (FSB). About 120 men in all.

Bang on time, the air support arrived. As the US Navy F-18 Hornets and F-14 Tomcats bombed and strafed the plant's depots (containing £50 million worth of opium) A Squadron drove towards the target at high speed, dodging RPG rounds as it went, before de-bussing to cover the last hundreds of yards on foot, with the two-man teams alternatively firing and moving – or, in the parlance, "pepper-potting".

The Pinkies of G Squadron meanwhile had lined up and were pouring suppressive fire into the al-Qaeda positions. Aside from vehicle-mounted General Purpose machine guns, G Squadron was armed with Milan Anti-Tank Guided Missiles, and they lined up and poured suppressive fire onto the al-Qaeda positions.

As A Squadron pressed on, they encountered strong resistance from the trenches and bunkers in front of the fortress, which pinned them down. An air strike was called down to deal with one particularly problematic bunker; the US navy pilot hit it dead on with a Joint Direct Attack Munition-guided bomb. A strafing pass was not so precise, and almost hit an SAS position. Fearing the attack was stalling, the Regimental Sergeant Major, who was in command of the FSB, joined the assault and brought up elements from the CO's HQ party with him to reinforce it.

The RSM was hit in the leg by an AK47 round. Several other SAS men were hit in firefights, their lives only being saved by their body armour.

Eventually, A Squadron cleared the trenches and bunkers, and entered the fortified plant, mopping up the small token resistance that remained. In the al-Qaeda HQ A Squadron troopers discovered an intelligence bounty – two laptops and a mass of information.

After four hours on target, the Squadrons withdrew. At a safe distance from the battlefield, the four wounded troopers were casevaced out by a US Chinook helicopter. The remainder of the men were flown out by Hercules from the TLZ.

Among the awards granted to A and G Squadrons for Operation Trent were two CGCs, a DSO, two MCs and several Mentions in Dispatches.

DOCUMENT: Major Roy Farran: Operation Wallace

Operation Trent was by no means the SAS's first broad daylight mission behind enemy lines against a fortified target. SAS legend Roy Farran had carried out something similar in Occupied France nearly sixty years before.

On 19 August 1944 Farran's squadron of sixty men and twenty-three jeeps was loaded on to Dakotas and flown to Rennes airfield, from where they slipped through the frontline.

So began Farran's remarkable Operation Wallace, which covered more distance behind the lines than any other 2 SAS mission of the war. The party drove the jeeps 350 miles eastwards to join up with Captain Hibbert's Operation Hardy in the Chatillon forest. From there Farran began offensive patrolling.

The local Maquis were active and well organized under the proud Colonel Claude, and Farran realized that they could not be subsumed under his command; "a loose liaison, only combining together for certain joint operations" was the only way to proceed. Not that Colonel Claude was unfriendly; on the contrary, in the pursuance of the *entente cordiale* he invited Hibbert and Farran to dinner. Farran recalled:

> It was a wonderful dinner, and in spite of our beards and dirty clothes the French treated us with as much courtesy as if we had been important plenipotentiaries. Many toasts were drunk and I partly blame the actions of the next day on the quantity of red wine consumed.

Over the wine-fuelled dinner, Farran hatched a wild scheme to attack the German headquarters at Chatillon château with the help of the Maquis.

Thus was the genesis of the Battle of Chatillon. At dawn the next day, 30 August, the combined squadron moved into place. In his war memoir, *Winged Dagger*, Farran wrote:

> My plan was to seize the important junction of the Montbard and Dijon roads. From there we would send a foot party with Brens, carried as far as possible by jeep, to attack the north of the château. The signal for the attack to begin would be the firing of the three-inch mortar on the château from the south. Jim Mackie crossed the aerodrome and occupied the crossroads without incident. I then moved the remaining nine jeeps containing forty men through him into the town. We occupied all the main junctions leading into the market square, while Jaimie Robertson took the foot party round the back. I placed Sergeant Major Mitchell with two jeeps on the Troyes-Chaumont crossroads and Sergeant Young cut all the military telephone wires.
>
> Dayrell began to mortar the château at about seven o'clock. He placed forty-eight bombs on the target in all. Fifteen minutes later a long column of about thirty German trucks, presumably containing the relief, arrived at the river bridge

near Mackie's position on the Montbard-Dijon crossroads. The battle was on. Sergeant Vickers, whose jeep was in the middle of the road, allowed them to approach to within twenty yards before he opened fire. The first five trucks, two of which were loaded with ammunition, were brewed up and we were treated to a glorious display of fireworks. A motorcycle combination skidded off the bridge into the river. I thought I noticed a woman in the cab of the leading vehicle, but it was too late to worry. All the sounds of war echoed in the streets – the rattle of the Brens, the rasp of the Vickers, the whine of bullets bouncing off the walls, and in the background the stonk-stonk of the mortars. I got a Bren myself and, balancing it on a wall, hosepiped the German column with red tracers. The Germans had baled out from the back of the convoy and were firing a lot of mortar bombs. Bullets were whistling everywhere and it was good to see our tracers pumping into them. Parachutist Holland was killed by a bullet in the head and a brave French civilian dragged him into a doorway.

I could hear other shooting from the centre of the town as well as firing from behind the château, so it seemed that Mitchell was also engaged, although by far the greatest weight of fire was around our position on the Montbard-Dijon crossroads.

A pretty girl with long black hair and wearing a bright red frock put her head out of a top window to give me the "V" sign. Her smile ridiculed the bullets.

A runner came up from Mitchell to say that a number of Germans were fighting their way down the street from the château. The situation was so confused that the enemy was mortaring its own side. I sent Dayrell Morris up to reinforce the position in the centre of the town which was now hard pressed. Jaimie Robertson's Brens were firing briskly from the back of the woods to the north.

At nine o'clock, three hours after the action had begun, I felt that since Mitchell was being subjected to such strong pressure from the houses, although only one jeep had been hit, I had better give the signal for a withdrawal. The Montbard column was becoming more organized and there was still no sign of the promised Maquis reinforcements. I walked into the middle of the road, waving to the girl in the red frock, and fired two Very lights into the air. Grant brought out Lieutenant Robertson's troop, while I led the remainder back along the Dijon road for breakfast. On his way back with the foot party, Grant met sixty of the promised five hundred Maquis waiting on the aerodrome. He undertook to lead them into the town with a party of seven men, at the same time sending a message to ask me to cooperate in a second attack. He became involved in a street fight in which he knocked out an armoured car, but was beaten into a tight corner from which the party only narrowly escaped. A bicycle patrol of thirty Germans trapped them in a garden and, while they were fighting their way out, Corporal Brownlee was hit in the most precious part of his body. When I arrived with the main party I posted jeep ambushes on all the main roads leading out of the town, which destroyed eight German vehicles loaded high with troops. Supported by Jim Mackie in a jeep, I led a foot patrol round the east of Chatillon. It was all very quiet except for occasional firing from the direction of Grant Hibbert. With our heads bowed, we stalked round some Germans on a crest among some beech trees, crossed a canal by a lock and walked along the sides of the towpath. There were several Germans around the hospital on the other side, but they did not see us.

After walking for about an hour we found ourselves in a narrow lane leading down to the Troyes road. Looking around the corner, I was astonished to see a German machine-gun post on each side, facing outwards. They were all in greatcoats and had their backs to us. I could not think what to do, so we sat in a garden and waited. Lieutenant Pinci begged a bottle of wine, bread and cheese from a French cottage, so we had lunch.

I tossed up which German we should shoot in the back and it turned out to be the left-hand one. Sergeant Young took careful aim through his carbine, and when I gave the word he pulled the trigger. At the same moment, Pinci, excitable as ever, shot a German on a bicycle to the right. All hell was then let loose. I do not know from where they were coming, but our little lane was soon singing with schmeisser bullets.

It was so high-banked and so open on each side as to make it a death-trap. With angry bullets buzzing round our heads, we burst into the front door of a French house. Running straight through, we scrambled down the bank to the canal.

After we had run along the towpath to the lock, I led the party across country to the east. We had just reached the cover of a thin hedge on a skyline when two machine guns picked us out. I had not realized that we could be seen. We wriggled on our bellies along the furrows in a ploughed field with the bullets kicking up great clots of earth all round. I have never felt so tired. I knew that if we remained on that crest we would be killed and yet I could not force myself to move any faster. Sergeant Robinson, behind me, was hit in the leg and still he moved faster than I. When we had reached a little dead ground I tried to help him, but I was too exhausted. Never have I been so frightened and so incapable of helping myself. Jim Mackie appeared and we loaded Robinson into his jeep. At the friendly farmhouse from which we had telephoned the mayor the day before, I dressed his wounds on the kitchen table, while all the women clucked and fussed around with kettles of hot water. After we had dispatched him to the Maquis hospital at Aigny-le-Duc, we motored back slowly through the forest glades to our base. The Battle of Chatillon was over. They say that we killed a hundred Germans, wounded many more and destroyed nine trucks, four cars and a motorcycle.

Operation *Wallace* ended on 7 September 1944, by which time Farran's squadron claimed 500 Germans killed or seriously wounded, twenty-three cars and thirty-six other vehicles brewed up, one train derailed, and 100,000 gallons of enemy petrol blown up. Many important bombing targets were identified and reported. All this was achieved at a cost of seven men killed, seven wounded, two captured and sixteen jeeps lost. Even so, Farran, one of the most astute of 2 SAS officers, identified weaknesses as well as strengths in *Wallace* in his official post-operation report. The self-same report, incidentally, gives a valuable overview of the operational conditions in occupied France, and is quoted in full below:

It had been proved again that jeeping is not only possible but easy when the front is unstable. As soon as the front becomes firm, however, jeeping becomes difficult. The concentration of enemy troops on the line of the Moselle made penetration by vehicles very dangerous. It might have been possible with strict control of troops by wireless from a squadron HQ and with a firm line of supply. In this operation lack of previous training made it necessary to move the jeeps from one area to another in large parties under experienced officers. If sufficient troop leaders of high quality, reliability and experience had been available, I believe that more damage could have been inflicted on the enemy by widely dispersed troops, only regrouping periodically for resupply. Three jeeps could have penetrated to areas impossible for nine. A firm base is not necessary for jeeps and it is better to maintain mobility by aiming at complete independence, without being tied to dumps. This of course is contrary to our previous ideas when we thought jeeps should always operate from a fixed base where refitting and refuelling could be carried out. When an enemy is withdrawing our type of troops do the most damage when they are placed directly across his axis of withdrawal. In this operation we were faced with two enemy centre lines, one from the west and one up the valley of the Rhône from the south. It was necessary therefore to move our area of operations about fifty miles south-east at least once a week. It was not always easy to find a forest large enough to conceal a base for nine jeeps. On the other hand there were always plenty of small woods adequate for concealing a troop. A troop could move daily with the greatest ease. Movement of a squadron column was always fraught with grave risk. It is possible to equip a troop to be independent of supply for a period of a week and to have a range of 200 miles. I believe that our operations were most effective during the last two weeks in the area of the Vosges, although during this time the enemy was very sensitive to our attacks and made our life very uncomfortable. I take this as proof that he disliked our presence more there than in other regions. During this period we actually knocked out a smaller number of vehicles but our patrols covered a wide area and knocked out important vehicles from large convoys. Another explanation of the enemy's dislike of our activities, apart from the fact that he was thicker on the ground, was that we had reached the point where the axis of the western and southern armies converged.

The best tactical team is two jeeps, but a troop of three jeeps means that there is always one vehicle in reserve in the event of a breakdown. A trailer carrying a 3-inch mortar is valuable to a squadron but the strain on a jeep's clutch over bad country makes more trailers inadvisable. In any case, in view of the tremendous weights carried on DZs, spare clutches must be taken. In ambuscades it is better to sacrifice cover to enable the jeep to take on targets at close range. The twin Vickers gun will cut a truck in half at under fifty yards, but at greater ranges is too inaccurate. The principles of a good ambush are as follows: A position where the jeep cannot be seen until the target is within range but where the jeep is certain of getting a long burst into the bonnet of the truck as soon as it appears. A burst in the front part of the vehicle will set it on fire nine times out of ten. A good covered withdrawal. No banks or undergrowth which enemy troops can use for retaliatory fire.

As soon as sufficient damage has been done, the jeep must disappear. It is not necessary to stay long enough to count the bodies. We were very pleased indeed that we had decided to take a Bren gun on the rear mounting. It was invaluable for accurate fire and foot parties. Fifty per cent of our bags were obtained by the Bren when the Vickers had failed. If the Bren is fired from a dismounted position, it must not be so far away from the jeep as to prejudice a quick withdrawal. Other jeeping principles remain unaltered. Firing on the move again proved to be a waste of time.

Jeep modifications

Although the modifications were quite sound, the workman-ship was so bad that the welding gave way in many places. The following are the chief suggestions. The rear mounting should be on the back of the jeep in the centre. So many airlocks were experienced in the pipes from long-range tanks that it is thought that it would be better to carry three jerri-cans on each side. This would also eliminate the total wastage of petrol if a tank is hit. The clips for Vickers magazines must be secured more firmly. The spigot swivel on the twin Vickers mounting frequently snapped. This was due to the standard mounting being too heavy. A lighter, strong, firm mounting must be designed immediately. The weight of the mounting also hindered accurate firing, being balanced on such a weak small centre point, it was top-heavy and unwieldy. A big iron rack should be fixed on the back of the jeeps for carrying personal kit. The following modifications were unnecessary – spotlights and smoke dischargers.

Personnel

The men and NCOs were all absolutely first class and their standard of discipline was high. Most of the newly arrived officers require training especially in handling men of this type. I suggest that no officers who have not had previous active service experience in a service unit should be recruited. Extremely young officers are usually an embarrassment in operations of this nature, which call for a great understanding of men and unshakeable self-confidence.

Resupply

On the whole was good. The only criticisms are the delay in sending articles demanded. Essential goods should not be put in one plane, i.e. one plane carrying all petrol, all ciga-rettes, etc. Too much ammunition and explosive was dropped when not demanded. There has been practically nothing to blow up in France since D+7. The method of dropping panniers, the irregularity of lever messages.

Wireless

Wireless worked perfectly well. The night emergency frequency seemed hopeless. Many encoded fatuous useless messages were sent on the broadcast which used up signallers' time unnecessarily. More use could be made of the broadcast to ease the strain on control by sending messages when reception on the Jedburgh set is bad. The tendency of No. 22 sets to wander off frequency made them useless for jeep intercommunication. I think a No. 19 set would have been better.

SOURCES AND ACKNOWLEDGEMENTS

The author has made every effort to secure permission to reproduce copyrighted material in this volume. Any queries should be addressed to the author care of the publishers.

Peter Ratcliffe, *Eye of the Storm*, Michael O'Mara, 2001. Copyright © 2000 Peter Ratcliffe

Duncan Falconer, *First Into Action*, Time Warner Books, 2003. Copyright © 2003 Duncan Falconer

Muki Betser (with R. Rosenberg), *Secret Soldier*, Simon & Schuster, 1996. Copyright © 1996 Muki Betser

Cameron Spence, *Sabre Squadron*, Penguin Books Ltd, 1997. Copyright © 1997 Cameron Spence

Chris Ryan, *The One That Got Away*, Century, 1995. Copyright © 1995 Chris Ryan

Fitzroy Maclean, *Eastern Approaches*, Pan Books Ltd, 1956. Copyright © 1949 Fitzroy Maclean

Roy Farran, *Operation Tombola*, Collins, 1960. Copyright © 1960 Roy Farran

Peter de la Billière, *Looking for Trouble*, HarperCollins, 1995. Copyright © 1995 Peter de la Billière

Johnny Cooper, *One of the Originals*, Pan Books Ltd, 1991. Copyright © J. Murdoch Cooper 1991

Frank Collins, *Baptism of Fire*, Corgi Books, 1998. Copyright © 1997 Frank Collins

Tom Read, *Freefall*, Little, Brown & Company, 1998. Copyright © 1998 Livvy Publishing

David Smiley, *Arabian Assignment*, Leo Cooper, 1965. Copyright © 1965 David Smiley

Franklin D. Miller (with E.J.C. Kureth), *Reflections of a Warrior*, Pocket Books/Simon & Schuster, 2003. Copyright © 2003 Franklin D. Miller

M. Eversmann and D. Schilling (ed), *The Battle of Mogadishu*, Ballantine Books, 2004. Copyright © 2004 M. Eversmann and D. Schilling

A. B. Hollis, 'Platoon Under Fire', *Infantry* January–April 1998. Copyright © 1998 A. B. Hollis

Otto Skorzeny, *Skorzeny's Special Missions*, Panther, 1959. Copyright © 1956 Otto Skorzeny

Barry Davies, *Assault on LH181*, Bloomsbury, 1994. Copyright © 1994 Barry Davies

Mark Urban, *Task Force Black*, Little Brown, 2010. Copyright © 2010 Mark Urban

Mark Nicol, *Ultimate Risk*, Macmillan, 2003. Copyright © 2003 Mark Nicol